BRINGING IT HOME

BRINGING IT HOME

Women Talk About
Feminism
In Their Lives

Edited by
BRENDA LEA BROWN

ARSENAL PULP PRESS
Vancouver

BRINGING IT HOME
Copyright © 1996 by Brenda Lea Brown
Essays copyright © 1996 by the contributors

ARSENAL PULP PRESS
103-1014 Homer Street
Vancouver, B.C.
Canada v6b 2w9

The publisher gratefully acknowledges the assistance of the Canada Council and the Cultural Services Branch, B.C. Ministry of Small Business, Tourism and Culture.

Typeset by the Vancouver Desktop Publishing Centre
Printed and bound in Canada by Printcrafters

CANADIAN CATALOGUING IN PUBLICATION DATA
Main entry under title:
Bringing it home

 ISBN 1-55152-034-6
1. Feminism. 2. Feminist theory. I. Brown, Brenda Lea.
HQ1190.B74 1996   305.42   c96-910480-4

Contents

Acknowledgements

I would never have been able to bring feminism home for a chat except with the kindness and encouragement of the following people. Sue Nevill gave me the journal that started me thinking. Caren Holtby gave me Anne Wilson Schaef's book, *Women's Reality*. Stephen Osborne and Brian Lam agreed that a book of women thinking out loud about feminism was a good idea. Susan Crean listened patiently as I made my way towards feminism and asked delicate questions like, "What is it about women like you who think there's some big feminist judge out there?" Linda Field provided editorial insight as each essay came in, then did the precision work of copyediting the final drafts. Mary Anne McEwen worked with me through a mess of autobiographical detail and helped me piece together my own story. And Patty Osborne became my faithful reader, who helped me to shape and polish it. Charlie and Harrison spent a long summer looking at my back and listening to me on the phone with contributors in the final throes of completing their essays. *Bringing It Home* would not exist without the women whose essays it contains; but perhaps not everyone knew the extent to which I was involving her in the raising of my own consciousness. Finally, I must acknowledge the love and forbearance of my mother, Rosamary June Rogers White, and my father, Alan MacLeod White, who brought me up to think for myself and must often have wished they hadn't.

In order to invent strategies that will be big and bold enough for the next millenium, it is crucial that women share our experiences; the chances we have taken and the choices that have kept us alive.

—Mary Daly, "Sin Big"
The New Yorker, Feb. 26-Mar. 4, 1996

Foreword

Rosemary Brown

As I rushed to the hospital to welcome the arrival of my newest grandchild, I grabbed the latest issue of *Ms.* magazine to take with me—not just to read during the anticipated long wait, but to share with his mother during the process of his birth. Regardless of gender, I wanted this new member of the human family to become acquainted with feminism as early as possible. I share with Hubert Marcuse the belief that feminism is the greatest revolution of the twentieth century; every day, it is making the world a different place in which to live, and I wanted my grandchild's preparation for this more enlightened society to begin as soon as possible.

Unlike my grandchild and his mother, I was born into and lived in a world in which women had made some strides toward equality, but nothing on the scale of the movement that has been sweeping the world since the late sixties and early seventies. My generation of women have stories to tell, not only of our witness to this phenomenon, but also of our personal involvement in its evolution. There are days when I envy my grandchildren the world that they are inheriting, with its heightened recognition of human and civil rights, and its attempts, albeit inadequate, to respect and make those rights real. But there are days, too, when I look back on the struggles and I know that I would not have wanted to miss being there and participating in them.

For my generation, the move to feminism was almost the final step in our collective fight for survival. Many of us were survivors of incest, rape, and violence in personal and professional relationships; we were also victims of the abrogation of our right to choice in matters of procreation. We were underpaid, overworked, demeaned, disrespected, and exploited. In short, we were ready for a revolution. By the mid-to-late sixties, feminism was reborn. This time women decided that changes had to be made; our issues were not going to be sidelined and sacrificed to other concerns. This new and more determined approach to the work for women's equality earned feminists criticism for being selfish and anti-family. It also brought women into direct conflict with other movements with which they were involved. And for a time, feminism found itself the target of its allies, members of the civil rights, peace, labour, and environmental movements.

The most severe critics of my feminism were my brothers and sisters in the struggle against racism. To them, my involvement in the women's movement showed a weakening of my total commitment to the anti-racism cause. It took much soul-searching before I was able to justify to myself my right to place my demands for equality as a woman alongside my demands for equality as a black person. It took time to recognize how impossible it would be for me to achieve one without the other, and to appreciate how much the strength I gained from one struggle was transferred to and benefitted the other. Gradually I came to understand that the catalyst that propelled me to feminism was as much political as it was personal. I began to see that attacks on my self-esteem had as much to do with society's messages about my "place" as with my personal achievements and failures. So while r., story is the story of black people living in a world of white people, it is also the story of women living in a world of men, regardless of colour and race; it is the story of the oppression that results from sexism and racism, and my attempts, personal and political, to alleviate it.

The strength of feminism is that it has been able to confront such realities and empower anyone and everyone who seeks to change them. Feminism, too, has given women of colour the strength to confront sexism within our own race, as well as the strength to confront racism among members of our gender. It is the ultimate "eye opener" which reveals that sexism and racism exists in all of us, and gives us the tools necessary to address the personal and confront the political obstacles to our struggles for equality.

Imagine, if you will, my frustration as a black woman, active in black organizations, who saw, time and again, opportunities extended to black men with less qualifications and experience than me—opportunities that were never extended to me because I was a woman. Imagine, if you will, the frustration of young black girls being told that, in their journey through life, black men must come first; racism had so undermined their manhood that their self-esteem, and hence their survival, depended on the charade of black women acting as though their men were smarter, more talented, and more capable than they were themselves. There was a time not so long ago when to challenge that doctrine was to undermine the entire racial struggle, even though the doctrine itself reinforced our status of inferiority. These teachings have receded into myth, thanks to a better understanding of how racism and sexism feed off each other, and how feminism and anti-racism are empowered by the recognition of the common enemies they struggle to overthrow.

I do not think it would be an exaggeration to claim that I was driven to feminism as much by the sexism within the black community as by sexism within the community at large. I am disturbed and disappointed to find racism within the feminist community, and I am determined to fight it as I have in other communities.

Yet I did not turn to feminism so much out of despair as out of excitement. I saw in it a sliver of light indicating that a door I had thought would remain closed was in fact about to open. I turned to feminism because of the promises of equality and freedom it offered. I have remained faithful to it because it has achieved so much more than I ever dreamed possible.

When I look back on the early years and see how timid our demands were, and how little we asked for, I am almost ashamed. The report of the Royal Commission on the Status of Women in Canada, with its 267 recommendations, was considered radical when it was released in 1970, yet it never touched on issues such as the sexual and physical abuse of women and children. Wife beating, incest, and date rape all remained shrouded behind a veil, not to be spoken of publicly, or put on the national agenda. Today, these issues, along with female genital mutilation, bride burning, and other forms of abuse against women and children are on the national agendas of many of the most conservative religious and political regimes in the world. Our allies have returned, too. Trade unionists, environmentalists, and workers for human rights join feminists in their recognition of the struggle for the rights of people regardless of their abilities, sexual orientation, race, gender, and religion.

I still thrill at the memory of the conference of women judges that I attended in Hull, Quebec in 1985. In attendance were more than 100 federal and provincial court judges, as well as one former and two sitting Supreme Court judges. Seeing all of these eminent women together, I thought back to the founding convention of the National Action Committee on the Status of Women, when our dream had been to have a woman judge on the Supreme Court, and a few more at the federal and provincial levels. Today, it is not uncommon to find women in engineering and other non-traditional trades. This fact, and the changing status of women around the world, challenge those who periodically declare that feminism is dead.

All is not won, of course. Poverty remains the scourge of women's lives, but now it is on national agendas because women demanded it be there. The chance of real economic change in the lives of women is likely only to the extent that women have the power and determination to effect these changes. Feminists everywhere know that this is the ultimate challenge. There may be disagreements on how it is to be achieved, but there is no disagreement that the eradication of poverty is a prerequisite to full equality.

The personal lives recorded in this book clearly outline how, with the intertwining of the personal and the political, the struggle continues. We are resurrecting our histories, restoring our ancestors to their rightful places, and preparing our children and grandchildren to ensure that the path to the future continues to be righting the wrongs of the past.

When my children were very small, their father and I used to tell them about the countries in which we were born, where most of the people were black like us—the mail carrier, police officer, firefighter, teacher. The telling was our attempt to assure them that they were not a few of the only black children in the world; that there was a different, not quite so alien, world outside of Vancouver. Years later, my daughter confessed that until they visited Jamaica and found themselves surrounded by black people—including the mail carrier, police officer, firefighter, and teacher—she and her brother had thought we had been telling them "Once upon a time" stories. It is my hope that in the future, when I tell my newest grandson of how it used to be for women in Canada and around the world prior to the 1960s, our lives will have changed so much that he too will expect me to begin each telling with "Once upon a time . . ."

Introduction

Brenda Lea Brown

Three years ago, I set myself the task of writing an essay called "A Feminist Education." I had come of age in the early seventies reading the first issues of *Ms.* magazine, and had dedicated myself then to the project of my own emancipation (I would make my living as a writer and not get married). Twenty years later I was a mother and a spouse trying to make sense of the surprises these roles presented each day. Early in my career I had sidestepped a literary life as playwright and critic to take up the trade of corporate communications. Now, at home with my preschool son, it was time to revisit that old junction and pick up the self who had lost her voice.

But almost as soon as I started writing, it seemed that I hadn't had a feminist education after all, or at least anything that resembled what I thought a feminist education should be. I had never taken a women's studies course, I had not read more than one or two of the feminist classics and almost never read feminist periodicals. I had never rallied on International Women's Day, marched to "take back the night," or volunteered at a rape crisis centre.

I realized that I had no *analysis*. I didn't really know what I thought. The things I knew—my experience as a white heterosexual middle-class married professional woman of almost forty with one son, a strong sense of self and unrepentant optimism—lacked the spit and vinegar I thought I needed to undertake a feminist discourse. Those courses I had never taken and books I had never read might have helped me to build a framework for understanding my biases, loyalties, and concerns in relation to the larger community of women. As it was, I was paralyzed by something I called the "tribunal on my shoulder," a faceless body of censorious women whose judgment focused entirely on all that I was not—not an activist, not a woman of colour, not a lesbian, not a survivor of incest or abuse, not poor or a single parent—and all that I had not done in the name of women's liberation. What could I possibly add?

Though I had adopted Catholicism as an adult, I knew beyond a doubt that a woman's right to carry or abort a fetus belonged to her alone. Also that my conflict about raising our son Catholic was more political than theological (he would be offered ritual privileges, like being an altar server, that would be denied his sisters in the faith). In addition, I had the habit of bowdlerizing his storybooks, omitting words and lines that presented female characters as dumb, manipulative, or glorying in their humble station, and modifying the gender of characters so that as many "she's" as "he"s' joined in his storybook adventures. But vaguely, I also sensed that my world was too narrow and homogeneous for my own and my family's good.

I felt that I needed to read other women's stories before I could write my own—stories by women who were not regular spokespeople for feminism, from different generations, different walks of life, different geographical, ethnic, and religious communities. I especially wanted to know how other women negotiated the sometimes intractable waters between their circumstances and their ideals. In short, I wanted to read *this* book.

When I randomly asked women, "Are you a feminist?" they often rejoined, "That depends what you mean by feminist." A Catholic-school teacher told me that she especially fostered the self-esteem and perform-ance of her girls, but didn't like talking about it. A young artist said she didn't see the need for feminism because her success and her gender were unrelated, then recalled uneasily the professor who had harassed her sexually in graduate school. Many a woman wanted to make it perfectly clear that she didn't hate men. One related how she had once joined an International Women's Day rally but later felt embarrassed when TV clips made the event look exclusively like a gathering of heavy-set, cigar-smoking dykes. Many women distanced themselves from the feminist label, claiming "humanist" instead because "we all have to work together." Others seemed to think that they couldn't call themselves feminists because they weren't dedicated enough to the cause, or because they had focused their attention on other causes.

It was a relief to discover that I wasn't the only woman in the world who felt as though she was living in the shadow of an impenetrable monolith called feminism. It was empowering to learn that individual feminist women do not all think alike; they have not all read the same books or made themselves aware of each others' issues. But it bothered me that I still couldn't write or even talk about my own feminism in a cohesive way. The words male-dominated, patriarchy, and oppression dried in my throat. And when I reached tentatively for words to express my experience of living in a society founded on the prerogatives of white heterosexual men, I could be silenced by a raised eyebrow or sarcastic comment of a male colleague or friend. I despaired of ever being able to design and erect a viable feminist framework from materials I happened to have lying around in my own background and psyche.

Finding contributors involved a serendipitous and highly subjective process. I started by wanting to hear from Ursula Franklin, whose lectures on technology had impressed me: they did not include the word "feminism" and yet they were clearly the result of a different, decidedly feminist, way of thinking. This became my model—the woman whose ideas have progressed to the point where she confidently identifies herself as feminist and expresses her feminist values and beliefs in her work, at home and in the larger community. I found her by asking people who might fit the bill, by introducing myself to strangers, and by happy accident.

When the essays started coming in and I began working with their authors—reading and discussing each story, telling my own, exchanging ideas—I finally began to see how much bringing feminism home, and putting a face on it, still has to do with the telling and retelling and retelling of our experience. Again and again, women told me how much they wanted to read about feminism through the lens of everyday experience. I began to feel confident that there are as many junctions as women on the road to the equitable, safe world that represents the feminist ideal. At some, we find women entering at full speed and driving hard for change. At others, we find women stopped in their tracks, not knowing how to go forward and perhaps a bit afraid of getting caught in the wrong lane. When that happened to me, I put out my hand to see who might help me along. Not everyone I flagged stopped, and not everyone who stopped stayed to be part of the book. But of the twenty-four who did I asked all kinds of questions. How did you get here? Who helped you? Can anyone be a feminist? How do you know you are a feminist? What about family? What about religion? Are you as much a feminist at home as in the world? Where do the personal and the political meet in your life?

This book is the song of their answers. It is exactly the book I wanted, and needed, to read—a composition for women in all their roles, through which we can discover interconnectedness, revel in it, grow from it, flaunt and celebrate it, and even call it feminism. By her willingness to tell who she is, what she values, and how she came to know herself as a feminist, each of the women you are about to meet has helped bring home to me the meaning and importance of feminism. I hope the same will be true for you.

Backing Out of Hell

Fay Blaney

A s the teller of this story, I struggle with my voice and point of view. As an educated woman, I am adept at abstracting and critiquing my situation within the context of the cultural forces that shape me. As a First Nations woman, I also have a very traumatic history to recount. I firmly believe in the feminist principle that "the personal is political," but by experience I know that it can be a double-edged sword: Yes, there is a freedom that comes from disclosing that I am a survivor of sexual abuse and family violence; but in the act of unloading this burden of shame, I contribute to the negative stereotype of my people as inferior.

As an adult student in Vancouver, I always felt uncomfortable with all the talk that my white classmates engaged in. It rattled me then, as it rattles me now, when young Aboriginal people speak so fast I can't understand them. As a child growing up with Homalco traditions I learned to respect quietness, to experience it as part of my spirituality. Adults would be amused by the chatter of children, knowing that with spiritual growth, there would no longer be a need to fill time with outward talk. But, while Homalco people place value upon inner harmony, based upon a comfort with our place in the universe, this trait usually gets interpreted by non-Aboriginals as submissive and mentally sluggish.

First Nations people have been studied and written about extensively by non-Aboriginal academics. At school, according to the course outlines and readings, I was "the other." My propensity for silence seemed to confirm my classmates' view of that stereotype. When I would speak up in class, they would act surprised that "the little Indian girl" was capable of speech and intellectual activity. But they also became interested in the woman behind the stereotype and wanted to know how I was different. It is my hope that this story will reveal many of those differences and bring about understandings that will replace the stereotypes. In telling my story I am neither outsider nor truly insider, but a new voice rising to break the bonds of colonization.

My mother's life was horrendous from beginning to end. When she was born, her father rejected her because her hair and skin were too light. (His grandfather had been Scottish.) I cannot imagine a more violent human being. He beat most of his ten children, and especially his wife, whose pregnancies never stopped him. Some say that she died giving birth to his last child because of a beating she took. Having seen women murdered by their husbands, he knew there would be no consequences for his behaviour. After my grandmother's death, my mother took over the care of her younger siblings. Without her mother there to look out for her, her father viciously and repeatedly raped her. A priest stepped in and sent all but the baby away to Sechelt Indian Residential School. My mother went back to Church House (our reserve, situated on the mainland at the mouth of Bute Inlet, near Campbell River) after leaving the residential school at the age of sixteen. A year later, she married my father, also of Church House. One of the effects of Christianity and colonization was that families were pitted against one another, and mine was no exception.

My mother's family was on the outside because my great-grandmother, being a medicine woman, refused to conform. My father had the same temper as her father and left her with some scars and a permanent bruise above her eye. His family was opposed to their marriage and when he drowned five years later, he left my mother alone with four small children and some very hostile in-laws. Again completely powerless, my mother was repeatedly raped by her brother-in-law and any other man in the village who cared to. The wives, seeing her as competition, hated her and often beat her. In the summers, she used to supplement her income by picking berries in Washington state. A year after my father died, she went to pick berries and just never came home, leaving me—the oldest at age five—a younger brother and two sisters. In escaping with her own life, she abandoned us to violence and sexual abuse at the hands of my father's family. I have always thought it a blessing that my baby sister died in a house fire the year after our mother left, because she was spared what we were not.

After losing my parents I lived with my great-grandparents in Surge Narrows. Granny—Emily Georgison of the Burrard Nation—taught me love, faith, and patience. Her two-room house floated on water in Surge Narrows, and although her original language was a different dialect of the Coast Salish Nation, she spoke my language, Homalco, fluently. In addition to teaching me how to work with fish, gather roots, medicines, berries, and other fruits and vegetables, Granny taught me the importance of communion with the spiritual universe. She would take me on long walks through the forest and the vast clam beds in Surge Narrows where we would sit on the rocks or gather whatever we had come for. In my child's mind, I thought that the Homalco homelands, with all its human and non-human nations, was the extent of the universe. We had no access to television, and due to the cost of batteries, radio time was strictly limited.

On our walks, Granny either talked at length about the stories, traditions, and teachings of our people, or read from the Bible. She spoke English fluently, but never taught me, so I never understood what she read from the Bible. Yet I fully understood the importance of prayer. Granny's faith and beliefs were so strong she was never dragged down with addictions or alcoholism. She too endured the violence and abuse, and often put my safety and well-being ahead of her own. I had only a couple of years with her, but she grounded me in my traditional identity and gave me a sense of personal dignity before she died when I was six.

Papa wanted to leave Surge Narrows after Granny died, so he took me with him to the home of his second daughter and her husband in the B.C. community of Haney. But Aunt Sally's violence was more than Papa could tolerate. After about five months in Haney, he pulled me out of school and we left Sally's home, moving to Vancouver with his youngest daughter, Eva. Some time after that, I was sent to Sechelt Residential School, where I remained for the next two years.

My third set of foster parents were my grand-uncle, Jimmie, and his wife Nora—Granny's youngest son and daughter-in-law. They were still living in Surge Narrows and this is where I went to live for the next five years. I became their slave, working from the moment I woke up until the time I dropped into bed: packing water, chopping and packing wood, scrubbing clothes by hand. When I didn't work fast enough, or if I made a mistake, Jimmie would beat me. His punishments included whippings, punches, kicks, slaps, insults, threats, chokings, and twisting my arms and legs. I went to school, too, but often I wasn't really "present." During the winter, we made our living selling clams, and all night long I'd be out digging clams while the tides were good. During clam season, there was always drinking, and you could be sure that there would be a lengthy party after everyone got paid.

In hindsight, I now see that Nora and Jimmie struggled with the same contradictions that I do. They had many lengthy abstinences from alcohol, periods plagued with anxiety, only to "fall off the wagon." They railed against the severity of alcoholism on the reserve, and chose instead to live in Surge Narrows for most of their lives. They measured their worth by how many white friends they had, and yet when those white people came to our house we hid our smoked fish and bannock, as if it were shameful. And those white people, for their part, clutched their coats and other possessions, for fear that they might get dirty or stolen.

Whenever alcohol was about, I knew that sexual intercourse and beatings would follow. When I could see it coming I used to run to the outhouse and pray, staying there and asking—begging—Jesus or God or whoever to please not let this happen to me again. But it always did. I waited for my mother to come back and save me; my thoughts often turned to suicide. There were times when I wanted to jump into the ocean and die, thinking that I would find my father. Or I thought about walking into the forest and getting eaten by bears.

I took my first drink when I was twelve, under threat by my older cousin who literally forced me to take a drink of wine. I didn't like it at all, so I didn't drink for two more years. When I did, it was to have fun. The alcohol numbed the pain. It made me a different person from the one I usually was. With all my anger and hostility I felt I couldn't be anybody's friend, and I didn't know how to act socially or even to be around people. When I had a few drinks or if I smoked a few joints, I became happy. I had no idea what social drinking was. The moment I started to drink, the goal was to get drunk.

I ran away from Surge Narrows shortly before my fourteenth birthday, after which I attended six different high schools and lived in three boarding homes (similar to foster homes), two residential schools, and the homes of many relatives. Moving away from the isolation of Surge

Narrows proved to be a culture shock that required major readjustments. My exposure to television opened up new ideas and places that had never occurred to me before. While my fellow students chose typing or cooking as electives, my curiosity for more knowledge took me into creative writing and academic courses. I excelled in all types of mathematics and sciences. When I discovered that my intellectual abilities far exceeded the standard "special" programs that Aboriginal children were streamlined into, I saw how I could move a step or two beyond what my parents and grandparents had expected out of life. In fact, I was determined to do so. Through my persistence with the authorities at St. Mary's Residential School in Mission, I got myself transferred to the academic stream where I did just as well as, and often better than, the non-Aboriginal students.

But then my mother died of liver cirrhosis when I was seventeen, in grade eleven. She had come back into my life two years before. I had let her know how angry I was. I hated her for leaving me in an environment where she knew that I would be sexually abused and experience terrible violence. I hated her for breaking up the family, for the fact that I hadn't grown up with my brother and sister. Of course, she had a lot to be angry about too. By then she drank continuously, so when I got mad at her, the alcohol spoke back. She thought I was a selfish brat. Her death was very upsetting for me. I had only just met her again, and now I would never be able to tell her how much I loved her and how much I missed her and how badly I felt about all that had happened to her.

At school I was unable to hide my depression. The supervisors and nuns at the residential school took this as a cue to punish me for setting a bad example for the other girls. They'd send me to bed right after school, or deny me my supper or refuse to give me any time to myself. Not surprisingly, the depression got worse until one morning I got up at five, packed a few things, and went to Vancouver to see my boyfriend. He was from my reserve and had just run away from his boarding home, too. We were both almost eighteen. The main thing we did together was drink.

In Vancouver, despite the drinking, I waitressed and worked in the cannery and finished high school. I thought this would get me into waitressing courses at vocational school. But I was getting As in math and English and biology—in all my courses—which impressed my classmates and my teachers; they were saying that I should go to college. I thought this was a ludicrous idea—me, an Indian, at college! My drinking was alcoholic by this time, but I went to college anyway and started along the road to a B.A. in history and an M.A. in education.

When I wasn't drunk I raged against the wounds and scars that marked me and filled me with a sense of impending doom. I had nightmares in which I was running for my life from Jimmie. Having once controlled every part of my body and spirit, Jimmie continued to taunt and threaten me in my dreams. I held my culture and heritage in complete contempt, equating a better life with being white. Between the ages of sixteen and twenty-five, I attempted suicide eight times. But though I could try to escape my anguish and insecurity by drinking and smoking dope, they returned after each binge.

In 1979, during my second year in college, I got pregnant. I was twenty-two and still drinking heavily. In fact, I was drunk when I learned from the gynecologist that I was pregnant, and I just cried and cried. I had gone without food and other basic necessities because all of my money had gone to alcohol and drugs, and I knew that I could not care for myself, let alone another human being. The decision to have an abortion is one I still struggle with. Homalco tradition teaches generosity, particularly loyalty to family members, and terminating a pregnancy goes against that teaching. Even today, I wonder about that life. I don't know if it was a girl or a boy, but I have dreamed about a little boy. What if he had been born?

My first awakening came early in 1980 when I went to work for the Union of B.C. Indian Chiefs (UBCIC) in Vancouver. This was my first involvement in the First Nations political scene. Aboriginal child welfare was becoming a prominent issue and my job was to co-ordinate a child welfare study. This brought me to the front lines of the struggle to keep Native children in their own communities, and gradually opened my eyes and mind to the view that the word "genocide" is not too strong to describe the practice of removing them.

The three years I worked at UBCIC set my course towards a life committed to social justice. My greatest teacher was George Manuel, then UBCIC President and later first Grand Chief of the Assembly of First Nations. George was an activist from the forties and fifties who had been instrumental in keeping the struggle of Native people alive. I had been raised to hold white people in high regard, without question. But George had no fear of whites. He would challenge non-Indian bureaucrats and politicians for their complicity in destroying Aboriginal heritage, self-sufficiency, and autonomy. And he really paid attention to the well-being of us young employees, making sure we weren't just busy little beavers doing the work that had to be done—that we could make sense and meaning of this work. I was in awe of his radical vision for a traditional, sovereign system of governance and felt empowered by his every statement on child welfare, land claims, Aboriginal rights, and "Indian government." I began to recognize the racism written into legislation that permitted social workers to enter our communities and scoop our children as he taught us about the federal transfer payments to the provinces for each Status Indian child "in care." It had affected me growing up in the sixties and seventies, and it continues in the nineties.

At first I couldn't comprehend why we were fighting for Indian control of child welfare. My experience had told me that Indians were really rotten parents. We didn't deserve to have any children. After all, look what they'd done to me. I hated my Indian identity and wanted it gone. I thought the sooner we learned to pick ourselves up by our bootstraps and merge into mainstream society, the better off we would be.

Working at UBCIC under George Manuel, I too began to think in radical new ways. The source of my own racism towards Aboriginal people, including myself, became abundantly clear and gave personal meaning to the political phrase, "internalized racism." There was no doubt I had it. At the same time, I felt exhilarated by my new-found pride. I lived for those times when I was organizing workshops, writing articles, planning strategies, and travelling to meetings. Just speaking about the value and importance of holding on to my Native heritage was like breaking a taboo. As I learned to give voice to things I had spent a lifetime hiding, I lost some of my anger towards my family and the way they had raised me. I looked at how they had been victimized by a system whose express purpose was to wipe out their identity. Once I grasped the true meaning of colonization, I could not go on hating my family. At that time, I began to choose a course of action that would allow me to challenge the real oppressors.

Although UBCIC was giving meaning and purpose to my being, my personal time away from work was empty. With my new awareness I could see how my drinking and dope smoking played directly into the agenda of the colonizers. But altering my mood and numbing my emotions had become a way of life, and giving this up meant that I would have to face the personal demons I was running from. I knew that in my marriage I was reliving a lot of the humiliation and violence that I had known as a child. I'd wake up some days with black eyes, once with a broken cheekbone. It was hard to sober up on my own, but I did it—I managed for three years to stay away from alcohol. But unfortunately, the nightmares persisted as I continued to smoke drugs in order to feel okay about myself.

The moment I decided to stop drugging was one of utter futility and anguish. With no more money to buy pot, I spent that sad morning taking inventory of my life. I saw myself as a little girl walking around with bruises and black eyes and asked myself why I couldn't put myself into the dreams and aspirations that George Manuel had brought alive in me.

Being sober and straight gave me time to face the cold hard facts of my childhood. Many of my mother's siblings were by then sober, and when I turned to them for help to stay off drugs, they took me out to Alcoholics Anonymous meetings. But the incongruity of being a First Nations woman filled with rage against First Nations people was confounding and more than once stopped me in my tracks. In therapy, I learned how suppressing the secrets of incest and violence was the root of my self-destructive habits. Learning to speak about them made it possible to shed even more of my emotional baggage. As I healed, I read, and the book-learning provided a context not only for this emotional process and the spiritual experiences that followed, but also for what I had learned from George Manuel. I could see how removing my grandfather from his family to residential school in the early 1900s had destroyed his spirit and marked him in unspeakable ways. He in turn abused three generations of his own family, myself included.

But now, instead of focusing my anger on my family and the way they'd raised me, I started to realize how victimized they had been. I began feeling angry in a whole new way and in a different direction. I could see a reason to fight and how, in order to fight, I'd have to be sober. Since 1982 I *have* been sober, and I have studied extensively about hierarchy, patriarchy, oppression, imperialism, colonization, hegemony, cultural genocide, and Native spirituality, with the dual objectives of arming myself in mainstream vernacular and making meaning of my suffering and healing journey. It is so painful to do this, but as we say in A.A., "we get to heaven by backing out of hell."

Which brings me to feminism. My first exposure to the strength of women was during the Concerned Aboriginal Women's occupation of the Department of Indian Affairs' (DIA) regional office in the summer of

1982, a protest that began when five children died in a house fire. Over one hundred of us occupied the floor where the DIA regional director worked. In the eight days we occupied, some feminist groups showed their solidarity with us by holding candlelight vigils outside the building. Then in 1986, a close friend and co-worker introduced me to a group of women who were organizing a women's tour to Nicaragua, a trip and an experience I shall cherish forever. Shortly afterwards, I became involved in organizing a Latin American Women's Conference. Then, when I returned to university in 1987, I took womens' studies and other classes with a feminist focus. Since that time, I have put a lot of energy into voicing an Aboriginal woman's perspective and advancing our issues in both my paid and unpaid work.

My university women's studies classes inspired in me a new understanding of the systems of domination. I found a great deal of merit in the principle that "the personal is political" that was applicable to my situation as an Aboriginal woman. When I arrived in the city, stereotypes about our promiscuity, laziness, drinking behaviour, and intelligence were taken for truth by most of the non-Aboriginal people I encountered. And being able to disclose the bitter legacy of colonization, the other side of the stereotype coin, was very empowering for me and for the Aboriginal people who heard me doing so. Another aspect of the support that I got from my women's studies classes was the compassion and understanding of the professors, usually sessional instructors. They understood and made allowances for the shortcomings of my secondary education and the crises—whether my own or those of my extended family—that kept interfering with my studies. Rather than dismiss me as incapable, they accepted and challenged my intellectual abilities.

My involvement with mainstream feminists is a tough balancing act, due to the racism on one front and sexism on the other. I strongly believe in the need for feminist perspectives and activism in the Aboriginal communities because of DIA-legislated sexism and the misogynist indoctrination of the residential school. But many Aboriginal people disagree with this. Based upon statements made by the leaders of Native organizations in the Charlottetown Accord debates, and the earlier discussions surrounding the elimination of sexist discrimination in the Indian Act, it is clear that they believe that there is no room for debate along gender lines. Other Native people who object to my feminist activities ask, "What are you doing with those white women?"

And feminist groups are not without racism. On numerous occasions, the stereotyped beliefs of my feminist sisters have been borne out in their behaviour—being silenced or passed over or, worse, left out of critical meetings. Of the more blatant expressions of racism, one stands out. It was the time I made a committee report about the objections of Aboriginal women to my involvement. A Chilean woman, taking me for "one of us," commented that the Aboriginal people in her country were just as bad. This is not ancient history; such incidents are occurring today.

I agree with those feminists who say that turbulence is a catalyst for bringing women into the feminist movement. It is certainly true in my case—not only the turbulence of abuse but also the turbulence of domestic life. As a heterosexual woman, I can never help noticing that men enjoy many privileges at the expense of women. Lip service is paid in my community to the importance of the extended family system. In the larger community the ideal of monogamous, life-long commitment persists. As feminists we strive towards another ideal, that of operating on a par with the men in our lives, whether the relationship is professional or domestic. In each of my own relationships (one legal and two common-law marriages) I have been caught in a quandary: Can I remain true to my cultural belief system regarding family *and* maintain an autonomous, dignified identity?

During both my pregnancies, the fathers of my children were sexually active with other women. In the first instance, my husband's affair with my best friend resulted in our divorce and the breakup of that friendship. We were in the process of negotiating our separation when at thirty weeks' gestation I had a set of seizures that put me into a coma for three days. My daughter was rescued by Cesarean after I was given phenobarb to stop the seizures. I was not expected to live, and if I did, I was expected to be a vegetable. When to everyone's surprise I did wake up, I was cross-eyed and saw multiples of everything due to optic nerve damage. Corena herself came into the world at three pounds three ounces. Because she spent her first month in an incubator, we never got to hold her, only to touch her awkwardly through small holes in the covered bassinet. Her father and I separated before her first birthday, leaving me a single working mother—one among the eighty-seven percent of Native mothers in the same situation. I left Corena with my cousin while I went to work each day at the Native Education Centre, knowing for certain that I would never have another child.

But I hadn't taken Glen into account. He was so wonderful in every way that I fell in love with him. Corena immediately liked him as well, and began calling him Daddy of her own accord. When we discussed building a life together, naturally having a baby formed a part of that discussion. Despite my fears of being pregnant, I decided to go ahead with it, knowing that he would be there with me. I cannot adequately express how frightened I felt when he left me in the sixth month of our pregnancy. He went from the perfect caring and considerate husband to an addict out of control. He would persistently call and harass me. At this point my fear of abandonment was at its worst and instead of gaining weight I lost more as the stress took its toll. Much to my relief, he sobered up in the eighth month of my pregnancy and returned home.

I have almost always opted for keeping the family together during my domestic struggles. I wish this was strictly a noble principle adopted to challenge the harsh demographic reality of Native mothers. But I must admit that a large element of my need to remain coupled with abusive men originates with a fear of abandonment that began the day my mother didn't return from picking berries. The panic I have experienced each time a partner has left makes me try even harder to prove my worth. Glen has left me seven times in eight years and each time the panic has been intense and immobilizing. Yet each time, also, I have moved deeper into myself to discover just a little bit more—usually about my mother and the deep wound caused by her leaving me when I was five. With each experience of being abandoned, I have gained in strength, healing, and self-knowledge.

I see myself sitting and crying in a disheveled pile after Glen has once again threatened to leave. He is complaining about how busy I am, how I never apologize or take ownership in our fights and how I never forgive his infidelity and other mistakes he has made while out on binges. He says it is all my fault and that I am to blame for his leaving again. In this state, I am incapable of attending any of my meetings or other responsibilities. I resent this and feel worse. It is all so hopeless. I can't even save myself, let alone the world. I want to get my thesis done, but there is never any time. Every single waking moment is filled. In addition to parenting two children, workings towards a Master of Arts degree, struggling to maintain my cultural identity, dealing with emotional scars, and working as a part-time college instructor, I volunteer my time to the Aboriginal Women's Action Network (AWAN) and represent our women in feminist groups, participate actively in the Native sobriety movement at cultural and political gatherings, and draw attention to the First Nations presence in universities. I am spread too thin. I am drowning. The only thing that saves me is the drive to prevent this suffering from happening to my children. Usually I just brush back the tears and run off to my meeting, but this time I just can't. I have fallen into that dreaded black hole, the site of the worst self-loathing imaginable. I am again that unwanted orphan who has no value and is a burden to those into whose care she has fallen—someone who should never have been born.

As a child I prayed incessantly for intervention to stop the abuse. Yet no amount of prayer seemed to make a difference. As a consequence, I have spent much of my adult life in a kind of spiritual blackout, shunning the spirituality that is an integral part of my Aboriginal identity. I truly believed in a power greater than myself, but I also believed that power had it in for me. I was unlovable, even to the Creator.

My education has changed a lot in my life, yet one of its first effects was to alienate me from my spirituality and my own people, even the activists. I have sat in a talking circle with mounting discomfort as the merits of experience versus formal education are debated and I am openly criticized for being "too intellectual." They say I have forsaken my Aboriginal heritage, that I am a sell-out who has adopted western, bourgeois ideals. I have heard this in group therapy and from my family as well. I have my own nagging doubts about what I have sacrificed to achieve my goals. But I refuse to accept that the expanded vocabulary and perception that have come with my education defines the gap between myself and my own people.

It enrages me that other Native people make assumptions about my identity, especially when they assume that I have no spiritual beliefs. What they do not know is that I speak the traditional form of my language fluently and didn't learn English until I started school. Speaking Homalco taught me my place in the universe and in the Homalco tradition. I was one of the last of my people to go through some very rigorous puberty rites. Although I used my education to escape my Aboriginal identity, the book-learning that I have vested with so much life and energy has returned me to my culture; and the values and beliefs that my great-grandmother gave me now help me to cope with the effects of racism and colonization.

I insist upon presenting my Native spirituality as an important element of my identity. Rather than the one supreme male being of our colonizers, I honour the spiritual value of "all my relations" including the non-human nations of the otter, the eagle, the deer, and the salmon. When Granny or Papa and I used to sit on a log on the beach, we would see an otter poking its head from the rocks. This would remind them of yet another story about the adventures of the otter people during transformation. I was taught that all living things had the power to transform. This is why some individuals possess certain abilities—a deer that transforms into a human would be a fast runner. Some remained in the human form and others preferred to go back to their animal form. With all the birds, fish, and animals that visited us on that beach, the one that consistently remained day after day, through all seasons, was the crane. Granny and Papa told me that the crane was in love with me and was waiting for me to grow up so that he could marry me. He was a dull grey colour with an extremely long neck, and *not* who I wanted to marry.

Ironically, it was Jimmie's death that returned me to my roots. I was able to go home to the reserve in 1995 to teach a life skills and cultural awareness program to young people from my own band. By then, Jimmie had been sober for five years. We spent hours in silence, allowing our spirits to meet, and hours talking and laughing about our ancestors. After the death of his wife, Nora, his drinking had gotten so bad that his health was in grave danger. He made the decision to return to our spiritual practice of cold water bathing, a ritual that I too had practiced during my puberty rites. During our visit, I think he knew it was his time to move to the spirit world. In my sharing about the hardship of my life, he told me that I shouldn't feel that I have to face it alone. He encouraged me to call on him for help, which I do quite regularly now. When the visit was over, he had given me the gift of belonging. Once again, I knew my place in the larger scheme of things, that I could call on the powers of the animal nations and they would work in harmony with me if I was doing what was right.

My relationships with Papa and with Jimmie have many loose ends and irreconcilable facts. How can I be angry with the abuses of my grandfather when he died a respected elder in our community? How can I accuse him when he protected me from the beatings of his son, Jimmie? How can I hate him when he devoted hours to telling me the stories of the families and traditions, transformers, animal nations, and our place in the world? I am able to make peace with Jimmie, a man who stole my childhood, because to remain resentful is to allow the pain to consume me, and to allow the colonizers to shove me into oblivion. While I value my feminist work, I am still an Aboriginal woman to the core and also value my family and community, and more importantly, our survival as a people. If each Aboriginal person who was abused by a relative or friend in our communities went on hating our abusers, our communities would disintegrate. Some are indeed moving in that direction. The spiritual, sexual, emotional, physical, and mental abuse began with the clergy and other workers in residential school. I must constantly remind those who engage in victim-blaming where the dysfunction originates. For myself, I have come to peace with Jimmie and I miss him very terribly. In doing so, I am now open to remembering the positive things he gave me and taught me.

When I returned home in 1995 I began to reclaim my spiritual traditions. I was thirty-eight, and peeling away another layer of internalized racism allowed me to be more open to the spiritual and cultural practices of other Aboriginal peoples. In accepting my spiritual self once again I can pass these teachings on to my children. Although I do not remember all the stories that I heard as a child, I buy children's books about Native legends. Reading these to my children is the vehicle to discuss what happened to me and what I was taught.

I recently became a vice-president of the National Action Committee on the Status of Women (NAC) and was invited to return to Nicaragua as part of an international women's delegation to be an election observer in October 1996. I am still an active member of AWAN and AA. My children have never seen me intoxicated. I have never abandoned them, even in the most trying of times. In contrast to the conspicuous absence of birthday celebrations in my own childhood, their birthdays are always elaborate functions even when money is scarce. And their pleasures form part of my healing process because they get what I never got. When I volunteer during the federal and provincial elections, Corena and her brother Andrew Paull are involved in the foot canvass and know the leaders and candidates. When I went to Ottawa for the NAC annual general meeting, Corena came with me. The Aboriginal women's policy that I will be working on within the NAC will be informed by my desire for a better future for Corena and other Aboriginal girls like her. When I attend A.A. Native groups and walk what we call the "red road," my children join me and fit right in.

In writing this, I wonder how to bring feminism and my Aboriginal world view into my teaching and my work with the NAC. Feminism brings together the private and the public spheres, and my Aboriginal philosophy teaches me to take a holistic rather than compartmentalized approach. To promote the family ties so important to Aboriginal culture and bring an end to family violence, it is essential that we provide healing resources not only for Aboriginal women but also for Aboriginal men.

When I went to my first national NAC conference, I met dozens of strong Native women who are working outside the male-dominated Aboriginal organizations while following the "red road." Just knowing they are there, trying to reconcile their Aboriginal world view and feminist ideals, takes away the feeling that I am working in a vacuum for a cause that no one cares about. But still, every day, I wonder. How can I remain true to my heritage while working within a mainstream feminist framework? How can I remain true to my feminist ideals while working within the Aboriginal community?

On Finding Sisterhood

Photo by John Steeves

Kate Braid

As I write this, there is a concrete truck outside my window. My neighbour is building a house and today the foundation is being poured. All day I have opened and closed, opened and closed my windows. My muscles twitch as if I've had too much caffeine. But it's not caffeine.

I know what those guys (they're all guys) are feeling right now. They're grateful the rain has stopped, grateful there's a pumper truck nestled beside the concrete mixer so they don't have to do it the hard way—filling wheelbarrows one at a time with the wet, heavy mud. The truck has been there for over two hours. They're tired. They're ready for coffee but everyone knows there'll be no coffee until this pour is over.

I hear the hum of a pick-up truck and guess that the concrete finisher has arrived. I leave my desk to peek. Sure enough, a guy in lime-eaten clothes and a handful of finishing tools walks slowly toward the job. So they're almost finished, feeling good by now—and here I feel a pain as clear and strong as a brown bitter nut I can bite down on. I stand up stiffly. Close the window. I can't stand to be reminded.

Ten minutes later, nostalgia overwhelms me and I creep back again, open the window just a little to listen. . . .

So how did a nice girl like me come to yearn for wet concrete like a fading rose for her young lover? What makes a woman forsake her middle-class upbringing to embrace mud and sweat, forgoing all cleaner pursuits? What does feminism have to do with any of this?

I was born in 1947 and raised a dutiful daughter. My mother was delighted that I wanted to become a missionary. As the oldest of six, the neighbours called me "the little mother." Family films from that time show a shockingly righteous and self-possessed ten-year-old, herding four, and later five, docile younger siblings. It was great leadership training but perhaps it was also the beginning of my going off the beaten path because instead of lining up to marry and bear my share of the next generation, I had decided by age twelve I would never marry or have children. I'd already had five, I figured, and I wasn't attracted by the relationship my parents struggled through while my father drank.

I didn't tell anybody my decision. It was simply a fact for all my teen years: I would be a single, childless woman. Full stop.

The only rattle in this otherwise smoothly plotted course was when, around age thirteen, I began a series of battles with my upwardly mobile father that lasted until I was thirty. We fought over everything, but I remember most clearly regular Sunday night fights over the amount of respect working people should get. My soon-to-be-vice-president father mocked anyone, it seemed to me, who wasn't like him: anyone who didn't drive their own car, carry a briefcase, and keep irregular (i.e., long) hours. In fact, most of our neighbours carried brown paper lunch bags to the commuter train each morning at 8:10 and returned home (*sans* bag) each evening at 5:50. According to my junior logic, these people, too, deserved respect.

After the people with lunch bags, Dad and I argued about women. My father, to put it kindly, was liberal with criticism and for no reason I could then articulate, I didn't think this was right. (Thirty-five years later, we have simply agreed not to discuss certain topics and sometimes he reminds me jokingly that I probably have him to thank for the fact that I became both a feminist and a trade union activist.)

These arguments were extremely unpleasant, complicated, I later realized, by the fact that they always took place after my father had had far too many martinis. But they forced me to stand back and see him as a separate person. They also set an early pattern of not being afraid to argue with authority. Later, when I entered into arguments with men in construction or government, I dearly valued the advice he gave me before my first major lobbying speech about being a woman in the trades. "Remember," he said, "no matter what their titles, they're just men like me."

Our arguments were more likely an effect, not the cause, of my growing independence. At any rate, in 1960, when I was thirteen, they brought me to a brief but important conversation with my mother. My mother almost never spoke about my father. If he was late (again) for dinner, or suddenly announced eight people coming for dinner the following night, she never complained. I learned from my mother that a woman suffers in silence.

But this bright afternoon in the middle of winter, she had unexpectedly said something about my father that was mildly disapproving.

"Why," I asked her, "do you always let Dad have his own way?"

"Because," she said, "in every relationship, someone has to give."

I suddenly saw their relationship not as a solid mass of carved marble, something whole and immutable, but as a soft and human thing and therefore subject to change.

"But why," I persevered, "does that always have to be you?"

Even as I asked, I knew the answer as surely as if it had been planted like a weed in the soft dirt of my girlhood, branded on my forehead, tattooed on my still flat little chest. This is the Golden Rule that good mothers pass on to their daughters, the rule that says it's *always* the woman who gives. Who else could it be?

It confirmed my decision never to marry. I accepted the rule. I had nothing with which to oppose it, yet I could not abide by it. This was before I ever heard of Friedan or Greer or any of the other women who articulated opposition and alternatives to how women might be. But I saw my mother's life and the lives of her friends in the neighbourhood and without being able to express it then, I would have agreed with the poet Louise Bogan who wrote in the 1920s, "Women have no wilderness in them,/ They are provident instead,/ Content in the tight hot cell of their hearts, To eat dusty bread." I was sure I would not live my life eating dusty bread, but in 1960 at the age of thirteen to say to my mother, "I refuse to be your kind of wife," was beyond imagination. The only option for me, and this seemed daring enough, was not to be a wife at all.

Later, in university, I became fascinated with the women of the Middle Ages. I wished I could be a nun, not for religious reasons but because it sounded "divine" to live in the company of women, able to read and write, not bothered by a relationship or children. (I never thought about having to keep up a relationship with God.)

More than most of my friends, I had always been a devoted acolyte of the United Church. I attended church eagerly, was in an unholy hurry to win all the gold crosses I could in Sunday School, and at the age of fifteen was the youngest Sunday School teacher they'd ever had. Then I began socializing with a group of teens in the Unitarian Church who did exciting things like hold dances right in the church hall where the chairs swung back and the smooth linoleum was perfect for learning the new rock-and-roll steps.

My minister was horrified. How could I dance in God's holy house? I was shocked that he was horrified. Didn't God like music? Was he opposed to people enjoying themselves in His presence? Wasn't this hypocritical? When the Minister gave a Sunday sermon about "unholy" activities and asked for a private chat with my mother, I stopped going to church. Having been a bully far too long in managing all those brothers and sisters, I knew tyranny when I saw it.

This is easier to say in retrospect than it felt at the time. Then, I simply thought, "It isn't fair." I knew fair—I had fought over it with my father for years—so I quit the Church and continued going to Unitarian social events until I left for university.

In this way, slowly, I became a feminist. There was no single clarion moment, no burning bush, only separate moments that led like footsteps toward a day when I would call myself "feminist." But not yet.

One key step came when, in the summer after my first year of university, I read Betty Friedan's *The Feminine Mystique*. It was a small, thick, blue paperback with a red and white cover. Who knows why I picked it up in the local bookstore? But I remember the exact Saturday afternoon and the cool of our rec room. For some reason everyone was out and the house was uncharacteristically quiet. Drapes were closed to keep out the heat and humidity of a Montréal summer and in the dim cool interior I got part way into the book before I laid it carefully face down beside me. I suddenly felt as if I'd been driving down the same road for years and noticed a street I'd never seen before, one that was well-established, with full-grown oak trees and children running over grassy lawns, a street rich in present as well as past. But how did it get there? Where was I, that I had missed it until now?

Betty Friedan pried open the lid on all the hunches and feelings and nameless urges I had but for which I had no name. She blew into my ear and I discovered new worlds.

You would think everything would be clear after that. After one has seen Truth, why can't one turn to it, like a newly planted flower to the sun so that, by the end of the week or month at most, it's done? But then, I've often been called naive. I spent the next thirty years, and continue still, fighting to integrate the implications of that first book into my life.

Like a little rubber duck in the bathtub of life, I bobbed aimlessly around the late sixties and seventies. As a girl raised in the fifties, especially one who'd decided not to marry, I had three choices on how to support myself: I could be a nurse, a secretary, or a teacher. Since I clearly didn't want to be a nurse (though my next oldest sister was) or a teacher (as the next younger was) or even a social worker (as the youngest was), I became a secretary. I hated being a secretary and was terrible at it. Though I didn't understand it until much later, I couldn't bear sitting all day in one place, being alive (it seemed to me) only from the wrists down.

I dabbled at this and that job until, by the age of thirty, I reached despair, lost in a no-man's land of a Not identity: I was Not married, Not a mother, Not a secretary, nurse or teacher. What was the matter with me, that there were no choices left? Why couldn't I stop being the Maid of Honour and just get married, have a kid and be a housewife like everyone else? I started going to women's consciousness-raising groups, discussion groups for women only, looking for an answer to why I felt so crazy. I didn't fit. There must have been something the matter with me and sure enough, I had what one friend called "a psychic eruption."

Although it was terrifying at the time, I would later learn to read my own "crazy" feelings. I would come to see feeling crazy as a valuable symptom that meant I was onto something—challenging another sexist sacred cow. I learned to handle those feelings by talking to other women. I always thought women's eagerness to talk was our weakness. Slowly, I learned that it is in fact our strength. This world is built neither for us nor by us, nor is it recorded by us or for us. To my vast surprise, I was discovering there is a difference between men's and women's cultures. But the women's culture was not even mapped. What is it to be a woman responding to this world? I had to ask other women: *How was it for you? How did you feel? What did you do next?* When I could confirm my experience with another woman (which, luckily, was never hard), I knew I was on the right track.

But in 1976 I was still figuring this out and dropped out for four months to recover by living in an isolated cabin on the Gulf Islands off the coast of Vancouver. It was there I fell into construction.

Facing the void galvanized me into what then seemed desperate action. Becoming a carpenter was never my dream. After I gave up on being a missionary, I was going to be a private secretary. I never took shop: it was inconceivable; never hung out with my dad in the garage: we had no garage. If anything went wrong with any mechanical thing, Dad ordered Mom to "Call the Man," as if some generic Trades God would/could/did fix all. Only once, using the six-inch paper rule on my knitting pattern and rusty nails found under the house, I had managed to build a flower box.

The way it happened was that, at a party one night, a friend told me he had just quit and suggested I apply for his job as a carpenter at the local community hall being built on the island. It came out as easily as if he were taking off his shirt on a sunny day. He might as well have told me to take off *my* shirt on a sunny day. It was impossible. Everyone knew that girls (as any four-year-old will still tell you) don't build houses.

But why not? I thought, and there it was—lights flashing, terror uprooting ten mighty oaks of tradition—why not? After several beers and an atmosphere heady with marijuana and possibilities, I couldn't actually think of a good reason, and this man's credentials were impeccable: he knew me, he knew carpentry.

I said, "I don't know what to do."

He said, "It's easy. Just do what you're told."

I said, "I don't have any tools."

He said, "No problem. I'll lend you some."

I said, "I've never done this before."

He said, "Lie."

So, after a quick lesson in Bullshit 101 and a sleepless night spent dreaming up "credentials," I applied the next morning at the foreman's small hut. I was shaking with terror, wearing a borrowed hard hat, tool belt and hammer, having no idea I had just taken a step that would dramatically change my life.

That first job was a short-term thing to tide me over. At the end of the first day, the foreman looked at the blisters on my hand and said, "That'll teach her to do men's work," and I knew I was going to be staying in *this* job for as long as it took to prove him wrong. And when he had accepted me as a member of the crew, well, then I stayed because I had fallen in love.

I loved construction with the passion of a drowning person who has by some miracle bumped into a boat full of friends, food and wine. I loved being outdoors all day. I loved getting dirty. I loved wearing big heavy boots and carrying big heavy tools and building great big buildings. I loved having a product that could be measured and judged by just me, at the end of every day, one I could drive by for the rest of my life and say, "I built that." I loved getting paid more money than I'd ever been paid in my life and I loved being on a crew. It is one of the best kept male secrets, I decided, this brotherhood of building, the physicalness of working together in the hot sun and the cool breeze, your body feeling fit and strong, your hammer rich in your hand, the power of making the world happen, the tart humour, the unspoken camaraderie of a crew.

Of course, that was on the good days. My metamorphosis from Nice Girl into Construction Worker was not without pain. I was thirty years old and my life had just taken a major turn in a direction for which I had no preparation whatsoever. I began to keep a careful journal, to write poems and stories, anything to help me spell out what was happening to me. But overall, the joy of finding the thing I loved, my "bliss" as Joseph Campbell would say, was a kind of rebirth. It was important, it turned out, that I be inoculated so strongly at the beginning, because on the very next job, I would be feeling as awful as I first felt good. But by then the drug had taken. I was hooked on building.

Still, I never said, "I am going to be a carpenter." Not after I had been a labourer for two years and could see nothing else to match it for pleasure, not after I had taken pre-apprentice training and several years of apprenticeship with non-union and then union firms. It wasn't until I was a fourth year apprentice, working with another woman in our own construction company, that I dared think, *I, a woman, want to be a ticketed carpenter.* It was one of the unspeakable desires that Betty Friedan had given me permission to speak, years before.

At that time, in 1977, when women were just beginning to break through the trades and technologies barrier, there were various responses to my being a construction worker. Women almost invariably supported it. In fact, they seemed downright turned on by it. Suddenly heterosexual women were flirting with me at parties.

The response from men was more complex. One of the things I had looked forward to on that first job was that my boyfriend also worked there. *How romantic*, I thought. But from the moment I started work, he never spoke to me again. I had offended him in some way, but he wouldn't talk to me to tell me how. What it came down to, I decided, was that I liked construction more than anything. If it was him or it, he would have to go. There was no secret that I was a construction worker first. I had to be. Just to hang on, sometimes, to that bucking horse, demanded all my energy.

But the response of many men left me uneasy. The delivery truck driver watched me one day unloading materials and said, "You must have shoulders like bullets." A male friend told me that the men of the island had been discussing me and agreed they were afraid to sleep with me because I might crush them. He said it seriously.

Certainly, I had noticed the pale purple shadow of biceps appear on my upper arms. As my shoulders grew broader, my blouses no longer fit. After the first few days when I literally staggered home to sleep before finding the energy to cook supper, I had more energy than I'd ever had in my life. But to be told that men who were my friends were afraid of my new strength was shocking and hurtful.

It is something that tradeswomen, especially when we are beginning, talk about among ourselves, this question of femininity. We used to joke about the fact that we met in lingerie departments, fingering silky undergarments. When you wear steel-toed boots and plaid shirts and carry heavy tools all day, how do you reassure yourself that you're still a woman?

The lesbians helped.

Until I started in construction I had only a political sense of lesbians. Since I'd started to hang out around "women only" events, I knew they were the women who had chosen to love women, but I'd never known a lesbian that I was aware of. And suddenly men were afraid of me. Several were intensely interested in whether I was married. Some implied I must be a lesbian, assuming, I guess, that only a "dyke" would want to do construction. Suddenly thrown into the company of lesbians, I became interested in who they were.

This was, it turns out, mutual. After a year of construction I went to a women's conference in Vancouver where, someone later told me, the lesbians assumed I had become a lesbian.

"Why?"

"Because you move differently."

It was true. Even I was aware that my body had changed dramatically in more ways than just taking on muscle. It is hard to describe how, slowly, my body had begun to feel very different. It wasn't just that I had more muscles. I felt different when I walked, as if both feet were now firmly on the ground. I walked consciously, aware of the space around me. Maybe this came from weeks spent on scaffolding, where a wrong step could be my last. Maybe it came from the fact that for the first three weeks on the job I did nothing but trip over every clump of uneven earth, every piece of scrap lumber (and on construction sites, these are everywhere), nails flying, my hammer falling half out of its leather loop, until I finally learned to be aware of where the next step would carry me. My body felt different, too, because now I knew I could trust my life to it. I could hang from scaffolding, walk over roofs, and I wouldn't fall. Suddenly my arms and legs made sense. I knew what they were for, what they could do.

But why, if all this made me move differently and gave me a different body language, did lesbians recognize it as theirs? It is a question for which I still have no answer. What is it about women loving women that makes them more confident in their bodies, while so many hetero-sexual women cower in theirs? Is there something about loving men that makes women hold back in our own bodies? Something about living in a patriarchy that does not approve?

It was this lack of approval for a strong, capable woman's body that so confused me in construction. I could obviously do the work, so what was the problem? Trying to find a name for it, I strove desperately to "fit in," to be "one of the guys," and then suffered because I was not being true to being a woman. I compensated by being more "lady-like" in my off-time. Pink became my favourite colour. As I became increas-ingly confident in my carpentry skills, I began to take chances that seemed wildly daring at work. I sewed rows of brightly coloured embroidery thread around the seams of my coveralls. I wore perfume. A welder friend of mine dared to wear red nail polish to work. My favourite piece of clothing—no, my amulet—became a plaid jacket I found in the Salvation Army store, just like the men's, only mine was pink.

But still I fought a chronic lack of confidence, a sense of never being quite right. This, I knew, was not uncommon among tradeswomen. Every time a nail bent or a piece of wood didn't fit perfectly, every time something took a little longer than it should, I thought, *It's because I'm a woman. Women can't do this.* I would be exhausted after a day of work from fighting the arguments in my own mind. Only when I worked with other women did this sense of being not right, ease.

Apart from the Women in Trades group I helped found, my lesbian friends became my most important support group. They took me in, sometimes with a slight nostalgia that I didn't change my sexual preference, but they took me in. When there was no work in the carpenter's union, they hired me for renovation jobs, fostered me, cheered me, and worked with me. How could I feel bad when some lesbian stood there beaming that I, a woman, was building her a house? And still, I questioned myself constantly.

It was a lesbian, Jacqueline Frewin, who helped clarify it for me. We were renovating a basement together and at coffee break, leaning comfortably against pieces of two-by-ten, Jacqueline grew exasperated with me continuously trying to untangle the inexplicable existence of myself as both woman and construction worker.

"You don't have to keep justifying yourself!" she exclaimed. "This is *your* territory now. You have a right to be here."

It was—it is—a revolutionary statement and it hit the nail, so to speak, on the head. It brought me enormous relief. It also introduced the frightening thought that even after years of actually doing the job, I had unconsciously bought the public assumption that women can't do this. All along, the voice that waited for me to fail was lodged firmly inside my own head. I stared my own internalized sexism in the face and it was not a pretty thing.

I am talking here about power. Women have always been considered less important, less effective in the public sphere than men. After all, we get paid less, don't we? This question of monetary worth is vital to self-respect in a capitalist culture that measures value by how much people are paid. I understood this viscerally when I received my first union paycheque. I was a second-year apprentice, beginning to have some measurable skills. Until then, my non-union bosses had hired me because I would work for lower wages than a man (and I was delighted because I was making more money than I'd ever received for "women's" work).

But in the union, every second-year apprentice was paid the same rate, and my first paycheque was exactly double the rate I had made in the previous non-union job. I was stunned. How could I be worth all this money? The other carpenters laughed at me. They were used to these sums, but I felt guilty, as if I'd gotten away with something. Yet when I looked at the other apprentices, I could clearly see that I worked at least as hard and as well as they did. I *must* be worth it. A single paycheque permanently changed my sense of self.

When women begin to move into what is traditionally men's work, there is no blueprint for how we should behave, how we should be in a world deeply identified as male. Likewise, as the women change, so must the men. Many of the men I worked with went through a parallel process of reclassifying me. First they would assume I was there for the rich array of sexual partners. No? Then I must be there as a mother. One guy came to me once with a mildly bleeding finger, as if I should kiss it better. No again? Then who the hell was I? (I was asking this question myself. There were so few other available roles for me to claim.) One enlightened young man on our crew who had seen me in a union meeting, figured it out one day on the sixth floor of a high-rise under construction. "You're not my girlfriend," he said, thinking out loud. "And you're not my mother. You're like my, my . . . " He groped for words. I couldn't help him. Then his face lit up. "You're like my sister!" That's what we called each other at union meetings, all the brothers and the sister. My union is called the Brotherhood of Carpenters. It was good enough. We were all figuring this out as we went along.

Carolyn Heilbrun puts it differently in her book, *Writing a Woman's Life*. "We must stop reinscribing male words," she says, "and rewrite our ideas about . . . a female impulse to power, as opposed to the erotic impulse which alone is supposed to impel women. We know we are without a text, and must discover one." We are all figuring it out as we go along. As another pioneer, Emily Carr, said in her *Journals*, "One does not always plant one's feet daintily when one is covering rough ground." It's like walking in the dark. It's not always graceful but it has moments of bliss.

I was brushing my hair in front of the mirror when I first noticed my body changing. My immediate response was to be afraid, as if my body was being taken over by forces I did not know, as if I was being possessed by something frightening and it was beginning to show. Along with other tradeswomen, it was the lesbian community who confirmed my changes, the physical as well as the emotional and intellectual. It was okay, they said, to move in the world with competence and confidence. It was okay not to be afraid.

All of this is a long way of saying that the lesbian community helped me to claim construction as my territory. I salute them. There was no one else so consistently unafraid to defy the status quo. I sometimes think that the fear people now show to gays, lesbians, and bisexuals echoes the fear people held for communists in the 1950s. Communists, too, threatened the existing social order by suggesting things could be done differently—that people should be cared for over machines. The gay and bisexual community, by their existence, suggests that the traditionally held order of male authority and the primacy of church-sanctified social convention, is open for question. They are trail-blazers for all of us who wish to live a more balanced, rich, and just existence.

One night, just before I fell asleep, I felt what it must be like to feel like a traditional man. It was a moment of utter confidence that the world was as it should be and that my place in it was splendidly clear. The moment was sublime in stability and security and a chest-expanding pride at being a part of all this perfection. When I slipped, the next moment, back into my woman's consciousness, the space was vast. It would be a long, long time, I knew then, before the two of us reached any equal ground.

Carolyn Heilbrun says that women who transform themselves must have an awakening and that awakening is identifiable only in hindsight. Becoming a construction worker and a carpenter changed me for-ever—physically, emotionally, intellectually, and spiritually. The mo-ment when I was awakened to the power of that transformation occurred near the beginning, when I was still a labourer. I was in a bar at the time, having a beer with two of the guys from work. We were in an intense discussion about the architect's plans for finishing the ceiling of the school gym we were building. It is important that you understand how close I felt to them at that moment. I was an initiate, thrilled to be, for the first time in my life, a member of a team, doing something important. So I was in a happy cocoon when my best woman friend came along and sat down with us.

Instantly, I was plunged into an agony of indecisiveness. Should I abandon this delicious conversation about ceilings and sound-proofing that excluded her, give up the still novel feeling of being "one of the guys" (I had not yet realized that, in fact, it was impossible for me ever to be one of the guys), or should I leave them to discuss more common things like relationships with my woman friend? I felt a physical tearing, as if I had been given an impossible choice and was now splitting down the middle. Looking back, I have probably spent my life since that moment trying to reconstruct myself, make myself whole, not by becoming *either* male- or female-identified, but by creating an amalgam out of both, an androgynous creature rich in double the choices, double the possibilities. This is, in a physical sense, what "equality" means to me—the option of choosing to be, to do, anything.

I have learned invaluable skills in construction, tools that have served me well in the rest of my life. I learned to be practical, to get the work done, to get on with it. I learned to work through minor tiredness or physical pain and to find a balance between being emotional and being effective. When I worked with women and began slowing down on the job because the conversation got too good, we'd tell each other, "Act like a carpenter" and get on with the job, then phone each other that night and "act like women" by talking.

I learned not to take criticism personally. At first, when a foreman yelled at me, I thought it was because I was no good, because I didn't belong. It took me years to realize they were simply saying, "You've just slowed down this job by making a mistake. Other people make them too, but it makes me as a foreman look bad. Don't do it again." I learned to compartmentalize my feelings, to interact with people I didn't like or who were angry with me. What a saving of emotional energy that was! I learned to be direct and say what I meant, to be honest because in the end, your life can depend on another's honest commitment to quality work.

For years, as a tradeswoman, I went out to high schools and elementary schools, urging little girls to consider trades and technologies and sciences as careers. Lately, I work more with men. If some of the pain for women comes not from the work but from men's mistreatment because they misunderstand us, then perhaps I can do some work as a translator.

In the meantime, my mother's dream came true. I *am* a missionary—for women and working people. I also take time out to be a nun, to immerse myself in the company of women because if I did not, I would wither. I set up small centres of safety—a writer's group here, friends there—where I can continue to explore and be renewed. I have also begun to take my writing seriously, writing about being a woman and a carpenter. When I met a man who valued my independence and strength and wasn't threatened by my spending time with women, I finally understood the desire for lifelong commitment and, five years ago, we married.

The poet Adrienne Rich once wrote, "Women have a mission to survive . . . and to be whole people. I believe that this can save the world, but I don't think that women have a mission to clear up after men's messes. I think we have to save the world by doing it for ourselves—for all women." Feminism has brought me to understand that "all women" means just that, and lately I struggle with the enormous implications of race as well as gender and class. To me, feminism is exhilarating because it is so alive. It unfolds and grows daily. It is the juice of my living. After years spent in the Brotherhood, I find there is, after all, sisterhood, and it is very, very good.

Coming Out Feminist

Brenda Lea Brown

Photo by David Dolson

I f I hadn't become a mother, I might never have gotten around to thinking seriously about feminism. The promise of women's liberation had captured my imagination when I was in my late teens and early twenties, provoking in me a kind of reckless independence. But it had never fully possessed my mind. If ever I had been on the way to becoming a feminist in those days, my swan song came in 1977 when I wrote a critical review of Tillie Olsen's *Silences* saying that Olsen was out of date as a feminist and that, furthermore, the plight of women struggling in a patriarchal society was a stale issue.

Fifteen years later, when I turned thirty-eight, I received two birthday gifts from good friends: one, a notebook with a card inside encouraging me to listen and write; the other, a copy of the tenth anniversary edition of Anne Wilson Schaef's *Women's Reality—An Emerging Female System in a White Male Society*. My life had changed radically since the day I had publicly slammed Tillie Olsen. Now I was married, with a toddler son and a partner whose employment enabled him, theoretically, to be home a lot and to look after the baby when I was working. In reality, I was exhausting myself doing most of everything and we were seeing a therapist.

To locate myself each day in my new journal, I set a standard opening, which went: "Harrison [our son] is in his crib, babbling to himself; Charlie [my husband] is at a meeting; I am on the living room couch, wondering . . . ." At first I didn't know what I was wondering and would stop there. But before long I found myself wondering how to break the silence and where I might find myself between freelance writing jobs, housework, mothering and power struggles with my husband.

One day Harrison was at the sitters', Charlie was having the brakes done on the car, and I was at my desk wondering what was keeping me from writing about what was on my mind. It felt like anger—not the craggy and familiar apron of domestic rubble that I was tripping over each day, but a network of deep fissures. All my vital energy seemed to be in those fissures and not with me where I needed it. With me was a self who never quite felt at home; who always knew what she thought and felt until she was challenged; who was over-compensating for her partner's success at holding himself aloof from the daily grind of parent-ing; who always assumed that it was she who didn't "get it" when she found herself in an uncomfortable situation; a self to whom the therapist had said earlier in the year, "You've forgotten that you have rights."

There was a lot in *Women's Reality* to make me think. Ultimately, it gave me a vocabulary and grammar for feelings I knew but had never made myself articulate. I felt at home in Schaef's mild voice and lucid description of the system that makes our laws, runs our economy, sets our salaries, decides when we go to war or remain home, as well as what is knowledge and how it is to be taught. In a few minutes twenty years of concealed shame about aborted writing projects dispersed as I read that the White Male System is just that—a system; that while we all live in it, it is not the way the world has to be.

I read about myself in many of Schaef's descriptions of how women adapt to the system, using the journal to keep my mind on the pulse of my feelings. In the silence of reading and writing, with my child napping, my partner out of the house, and an hour each day to call my own, Schaef's "soft" analysis of the White Male System—her synthesis as a psychotherapist working with women trying to understand what it means to be female in our culture—brought me to see more clearly the place I had made for myself within patriarchy.

I was born into a conventional white middle-class family, the second of two wanted children. My mother was a homemaker who sewed and knitted, made bread every Saturday, and kept a spotless house. Although my father worked long hours as a professional engineer, he was an attentive husband who never stopped courting my mother with flowers, a dad who rough-housed with us kids and listened to what we had to say. My brother and I learned that in our family we asked for nothing, kept to ourselves, and put a good face on things. We were quiet and reasonable and said "I love you" to each other. Our parents tended to be even-handed and non-sexist in their dealings with my older brother and me. At home I was never constrained by uncomfortable clothes, admonished for being a tomboy, or required to be a lady-like. I had no house chores. And Vancouver in the sixties offered girls and boys an array of free programs for improving minds and building bodies, each of which revealed a larger world, and told us implicitly that we had a place in it.

But if the word anorexia existed in the early sixties, it didn't make it into the medical journals read by our family doctor. As a result, we didn't have a name for what was happening in our house when I was between the ages of four and ten. During those years my mother was not absent but not present; my father kept our involvement with relatives and family friends to a minimum. Without a therapist or any friend with whom she was willing to share her troubles, she told them to me. I understood that I was her only friend, that my father didn't know the extent of her pain, and that I was never to tell my brother about it. I developed a nervous tick that made me scrunch my neck and eyes, pronounced enough for the school principal to wonder out loud, "Whatever is the matter with that girl?" When my mother ended up in hospital in 1965 the doctor discovered that she ate almost nothing; by threatening to put tubes down her throat if she didn't eat, he forced her to face herself.

Today, when she talks about having anorexia more than thirty years ago, my mother's voice is firm and definite. She says that as somebody's daughter, somebody's wife, and somebody's mother, the only thing she knew she had control over was her own body. She kept that control by refusing the tubes and making herself eat, becoming in the process a woman who could say "no," "I myself," and "me." It's eerie for me to realize that I started "coming out" as a feminist at the same age, thirty-eight, that my mother started coming into herself as a woman. So much of what she gave me—courage, self-confidence, independence—was what she needed for herself. Ironically, these same qualities, which allowed her to disengage from situations that caused her pain, made it hard for me to make the connections that would relieve my own.

As Mom gained weight, Dad grew sideburns and then a beard. We took up skiing and hiking together as a family. I was no more aware of food once my mother was eating properly than I had been while she was not. There were no diets in our house; I have no pre-teen memories of my mother calling attention to my body or eating habits, or her own. So I don't really know why, at eleven, I would look at my thighs spread naturally on a chairlift seat and see something that should be made smaller. Or why, at thirteen, I refused to allow the home economics teacher to let out a skirt I was making because I was "going to be losing weight." It seems that what I found wrong with my body was something I inhaled with adolescence. When I developed an eating disorder of my own in my late teens, the issue was not body image but control (I needed less of it) as it had been for my mother (who needed more).

My parents were popular with our school friends, their chief appeal being the way they always talked to kids as though we were adults. As we got older, my brother and I were given a great deal of freedom. We were told that our freedom came with great responsibility, which translated into a kind of honour system wherein we were not to use our freedom to override our parents' wishes. So while the sixties revolution stirred our suburban world with change—dope, civil rights, anti-Vietnam War demonstrations, hippies, free love, long hair, brown rice, ecological awareness, and the resurrection of the women's movement—neither of us became directly involved in any of it.

My brother broached his life steadily, tracing a straight and seemingly unconflicted line from high school to university to career to marriage. I did not. Except for a brief idyll in high school when I was perfectly in love with my steady boyfriend and thus perfectly conformed to my parents' quiet, self-sufficient ways, I was restless and uneasy without ever knowing why. I was proud of my mother, especially when she decided to go back to university when I was seventeen. Her unexpected ambition put wind in my sails. When she dropped out, I began losing the thread of what *I* was supposed to be doing. I took a course in Transcendental Meditation, but could never sit myself down behind a closed door for twenty minutes at a stretch. At eighteen, the only way I could imagine being free of my boyfriend was for him to be hit by a car.

None of our relatives lived in Vancouver, and my mother had no women friends, so I had no role models other than her to show me what a woman could be. Nor could I see any way out of the family garden that didn't seem to upset her. When I read Anne Cameron's *Daughters of Copper Woman* a decade later—and learned of a world in which girl children were educated by members of the Women's Society with jokes, songs, and legends; in which girls were taught how to care for, strengthen and enjoy their bodies; how to respect themselves and take their place in society—I could see how not having had a community of women to guide me through my teenage years had made my entry into the world of adults more of a kamikaze mission than a coming of age.

With Women's Liberation in the air, at least there was something to draw me on. From the early issues of *Ms.* magazine, I picked up the notion of emancipation, which I associated first with being unfettered by the conventional expectations for young women of my age and class (marriage and children *after* university) and then with sexual freedom, career, and no marriage at all. Thinking that it was the emotional intensity of my family that I had to escape, I set out to redefine my possibilities by becoming "liberated." I quickly rid myself of the technicality of my virginity and wrote in my journal about food and its perilous position in my life. I suppressed my confusion by overeating. In my efforts to be a free, strong, autonomous and self-supporting woman, I spent a lot of energy exercising what I took to be the male prerogatives of certainty, inflexibility, logic, and bravado. I refused to believe that any outside force could harm me. Underneath that, I was reeling from lack of insight, lack of perspective, and from the ingrained belief that it is better to turn anger inward than to put it out into the world where it might hurt someone else. Though I wanted to see a psychiatrist, I measured my need against the standard set by my mother who had never taken her problems outside the family fold.

During that year, I lost myself completely in the writing of a short story about a once powerful and successful woman who retreats from the world, invites her former lover to visit her one last time in her gothic hilltop house, then commits suicide to escape the barrenness of her lonely life. In the process of pouring all my fears about emancipation into the story, I sensed that liberation could be found by withdrawing completely into a world where one was conscious of nothing but the faithful act of putting one thought down after another in search of truth. I decided to be a writer, then refused to return to university, and let the frustration of being a writer with nothing concrete to show for it goad me into a disciplined routine that resulted in my first play.

At twenty, I wondered if being a lesbian was the only way to achieve autonomy and lusted after my girlfriend, Audrey. We felt at home in the novels of Margaret Atwood, whose heroines' minds tended to be alienated from their bodies. In the evenings, we went drinking at the bar and talked about my writing and her studies, the novels we were reading—Margaret Laurence and John Fowles along with Atwood—and about the men who were perpetually disappointing us. We took it for granted that we were troubled. Her turmoil manifested itself in a bleeding ulcer that landed her in the hospital while I walked everywhere, refusing to be afraid of anything and looking everyone straight in the eye. Audrey and I never called ourselves feminists or looked past the drama of our own lives to find a community of women whose experience mirrored our own. But I have always associated her with my first tastes of freedom and remember her during my feminist friendships today—the ones with women who have learned to sound the fullness of their selves, who can drop into any conversation and share in the spinning of new ways of seeing, who in bringing whole selves to the table always remember what it took to get here and what it will take to move on.

I continued to overeat, bingeing and fasting, my top weight rising maybe twenty-five pounds over ideal to around one-fifty. On a move to Toronto, I started thinking about how my mother had controlled her food intake to gain control over her life. It occurred to me that I could lose control by taking control in the same way. Perhaps if I weren't so physically strong, my mind might loosen up too. I decided to forget everything I had ever been taught, which was mostly a rebellion against regular hours, sensible eating, and thinking everything through before acting. I would look for questions rather than answers.

In Toronto, I continued writing with dedication, often staying up all night, then riding my bike in the early hours of the morning, discovering hot fresh bagels at the back doors of downtown bakeries, eating sparingly, losing weight. I fantasized about going home to Vancouver and lying in bed under my mother's loving care, too weak to get up. One day I was so surprised to find myself eating frantically, I stuck my fingers down my throat to relieve the discomfort by throwing up. This was a revelation. I saw clearly that I could enjoy the energy and sense of power that came from controlling the amount I ate, then lose control by bingeing and finally bring myself back in line by purging. What I couldn't foresee was how much time and vital energy someone with bulimia puts into recovering from the "hangover" that follows each binge.

I binged and purged on and off for seven or eight years, at first not understanding what would set me off and gradually following my fears and feints into their many recesses to confront and make peace with them. In the early days, something as simple as giving myself permission to have as many bakery donuts as I wanted could save me from buying and eating the whole tray. Later on, as I found myself stuck in a one-sided relationship, smoking heavily and drinking more than was good for me, I looked constantly for a pattern that would resolve all my excesses, though in therapy I kept to the surface with talk of writing blocks and "the relationship."

Eventually, my journal writing led me into a kind of extended mental role play, which involved an invalid called Ruth, a majordomo nurse with no name who tried to make Ruth act when she needed to rest, and a girl-woman called Quinella, who went into hysterics whenever the nurse bullied Ruth. Each character embodied a separate piece of my psyche that I needed to either nurture (Ruth), demobilize (the nurse) or listen to carefully (Quinella). By listening to Quinella and protecting Ruth, I gradually overcame the panics that had caused me to binge and purge; after a couple of years, bulimia wasn't a part of my life anymore.

At twenty-one, I quit school for a second time on the strength of the sale of my first play to the CBC. To support myself as I continued writing, I got a job as a waitress at a mediaeval-style restaurant. The French waiters who seemed so attractive to my "liberated" eye, and whom I mistook for ideal lovers because they asked for and gave nothing, were wearing me down. Paul was the perfect antidote. He was my parents' age, but so completely unlike them in his enthusiasms and experiences that our years together were a kind of repatterning of my notions of what life had to offer. I came to see that, far from being self-destructive as my parents had implied, pushing boundaries was absolutely necessary.

The world I encountered on the arm of my lover was so much bigger than anything I had ever imagined that I was sure I was embracing "real" life. Between my writing and waitressing and his work and other (married-with-children) life, our time together happened either after hours over cocktails, or during the days, when other people were at their regular jobs. I fed on this departure from convention, on Paul's stories and laughter, and the way he acted as though he owned the world, all of which I eventually carried with me into friendships outside our relationship with people closer to my own age. Ultimately though, the gap in our ages was a distance that only I could cross by listening, smiling, drinking scotch and making love. When I discovered that I felt embarrassed to be seen as a mistress, I took care to arrange my thoughts about our affair so that I always saw myself as being in it not for his reasons but for my own. But it wasn't long before I was looking for clues about how to comport myself, further away than ever from realizing that the unconventional world I took for real was just another place where I felt ill at ease. I paid close attention to the drivel in a book called *The Mistress Condition*, whose author measured the consummate man of affairs by his foresight and delicacy in carrying a pocket handkerchief to tidy himself up after bedding his mistress in a car.

My notions about what it was to be a woman became more confused as I made my way through the seventies. The only women I knew after Audrey moved away were the lovers of male friends or the slightest of acquaintances. We didn't talk. I learned by attending writing workshops that my own life was not considered viable literary material. Women authors were criticized (by the writing women I was meeting) for putting themselves into their work. My term at the Banff Centre in 1976 was a personal disaster from the moment my assigned mentor, David Fennario, suggested (and I agreed) that we should spend our time talking about politics since he couldn't relate to my lyrical "family" play. It had been good enough to get me into the Playwrights' Colony, but made me invisible among people who thrilled to the fact that Fennario had once actually worked in a factory, and who thought they had found the meaning of life in *The Jones Boy*, a one-act play by Tom Walmsley that brought the sex trade, violence, and heroin to the stage. I couldn't write, and later heard that I had been "difficult." A few years later, Walmsley wrote another powerful play called *Something Red*, which climaxed in a quirky knife-in-the-vagina episode and ended with the death of the woman to whom it had happened. The play rang true for me, whereas a feminist analysis of *Crossings*, a novel by Betty Lambert published the same year, rang false. I didn't see how anyone could find *Crossings* demeaning to women and questioned the demise of Walmsley's character. Wasn't Lambert's heroine—a writer who gets involved with (and finally extricates herself from) an abusive logger—a survivor? What *is* demeaning to women? Admiration for a story in which a woman dies a sordid death in a bid to push her boundaries? Or criticism of a story in which a woman walks willingly into dangerous territory, discovers her limits and lives to tell the tale?

Making a living was always an issue. Writing exhausted me and though I earned money from my plays and reviews, it was never enough; depending on my finances, I moved in and out of my parents' house, using the time to rest and regroup. During one of these sojourns, I spent the winter deliberately not jogging or doing yoga or swimming, trying to get comfortable with the feel of my body and leaving behind the manic need to work off whatever I'd eaten. After my unproductive summer at the Banff Centre, I'd been trying without success to write a full-length play, and jumped at the offer of a copywriting job in an advertising agency when I was twenty-five. With a serious income for the first time in my life, new clothes and widening sense of myself as part of a creative team, I felt confident in new ways. The bulimia was in check. I wanted to get an even better feel for my body and took to walking loosely, swinging my hips to free them, experimenting with the feel of "womanliness." I bought a motorcycle, and became friends with the agency's resident "women's libber," an account executive whose fight for the respect that was her due had earned her a reputation for being more than a little humourless. If the managing director called the office women girls when Sue was in the room, he would laugh nervously and say that he knew he shouldn't talk that way since "women's lib."

After-hours agency life was full of drinking and sexual shenanigans. When the creative director, my boss, turned his attention on me, I put our ridiculous sexual encounters in the light of being on a power trip of my own. I knew (vaguely) that I could say no, but I didn't have a clue about sexual harassment and, in any case, I was still operating under the assumption that liberation was a direct effect of sexual freedom.

During my year at the agency, my brother died in a car accident. No one I knew had ever died before and the abject clarity I experienced in the aftershock gave me a new sense of proportion. Everything I did or saw seem either insignificant or ridiculous. It became clear that suffering was all around me and that mine was particular but not exceptional. Until then, I had been doggedly gathering experience in search of a larger self without acknowledging any boundaries. Suddenly, boundaries appeared like advancing armies: at the outer edge of every thought was the place where my brother wasn't and would never be again.

This made me aware of an inner self who was desperate for structure and integration, even though I continued wasting time and energy on men who wouldn't get in the way of my writing. Occasionally I was attracted to another woman, always someone younger and more vulnerable. I would hold back, on a principle I had adopted after thinking hard about the fundamental imbalance of my relationship with Paul. At thirty, I went to a self-awareness course and discovered that I lied to myself constantly, that somewhere along the continuum of unresolved conflicts I had adopted the habit of acting as though certain things didn't matter, certain pains didn't hurt, when in fact they did. I was lonely, and I was also terrified of being trapped and consumed by someone who loved me. I adopted the words "tell the truth" as my bank identity code to keep me straight. I also made a mantra out of a stanza from Walt Whitman's *Leaves of Grass*: "I think I shall do nothing for a long time but listen, and accrue what I hear unto myself and let the sounds contribute to me."

When a friend told me about a convent where she had gone on retreat after the death of her father, I booked myself in. The Catholic mass enthralled me with its ritual standing, sitting, kneeling, and responses. Somehow, the act of kneeling opened a channel to much long-repressed emotion. I spent most of the first year of my conversion to Catholicism on my knees, in tears. Carol P. Christ claims that a man's spiritual quest involves the giving over of power and embracing humility while a woman's quest involves coming *to* power and shedding false humility. I had identified with a masculine way of thinking and being for so long, and so unsuccessfully, that the letting go I experienced in the Church was a complete catharsis.

I loved the ritual sameness of each mass and saw my becoming a Catholic as a hero's journey—a way to turn my back on the beliefs of my family and peers and the secular timbre of my times. Mary Catherine Bateson hadn't yet published her book *Composing a Life*, so I didn't see that the hero's journey was yet another pattern for being in a system at odds with my own. When I did discover Bateson's notion of life as an improvisatory art, in which women try to make something coherent from conflicting elements, I put my conversion (and subsequent leave-taking) into the larger tapestry that would help reveal me to myself. At the outset, though, I was impressed that so many great names in the western canon (the patriarchal canon) had been formed around Catholic thought. Ultimately, Catholicism let me rest after an exhausting decade and more of freedom. The challenges I received from friends about the Church's sexism and homophobia were something I put aside for another time. That time came when, as a mother, I faced the decision of whether or not to give Catholicism to my son. I discovered that I could not.

By the time I met Charlie in 1987, I was focused and confident. The panic attacks that had once climaxed in bulimia were behind me; I'd quit smoking and drinking in the effort of writing a commissioned book; I'd been celibate for the better part of a year. We married quickly, in a Catholic ceremony, without a single thought about feminism or much of anything other than our perfect compatibility. I had always thought I would keep my family name, White, if I ever married. But when the time came, I found that I was not as attached to my name as I had thought. On superficial grounds, I gave up the name "White" for "Brown" to avoid a life of "beige" jokes. On another level altogether, I approached marriage solemnly. I had been drawn to the contemplative aspect of the Church and tried to live the maxim to be contemplative in action and active in contemplation. I had even flirted with the possibility of entering a contemplative order of Benedictine nuns. The act of kneeling before a compassionate almighty to submit myself to the completely unknown vicissitudes of partnership with a man I barely knew filled me with the sense that I was entering a worldly cloister.

But being married was a big surprise, like being in a three-legged race with someone in a heavy plaster cast. It was not spiritual at all, or even romantic. Since I had never lived with anyone, I was shocked to discover that the person inhabiting my space was not exactly like me. In fact, we are different in every way. He is stubborn, I am tractable. I am high energy, he is low. He is outwardly rebellious and inwardly conventional, I am outwardly conforming, inwardly obstinate. He prefers foods he tasted before the age of six, I like everything I've encountered since the age of eighteen. To live together, we had to make space for each other in my apartment. I found myself going along with his wishes and then railing against my compliance, bouncing between my willingness to bend and the insult of his inflexibility. As a marriage partner, I didn't want control, he did. Even today when I insist that I want joint control, not sole control, he tells me he doesn't believe it. We laugh about this. He can always make me laugh. For the better part of a decade, we've squabbled, made power plays, whined and complained and bullied each other until now, when we both work from home and are equally involved in raising our son. Charlie does most of the shopping, cooking, laundry, and chauffeuring and I do most of the tidying up, filling in, and steady earning.

We both wanted a child, and I had always reserved a place in my habits for one. For years, I had kept my desk in the kitchen (and still do) because I wanted to be in the middle of things. When I became pregnant at the age of thirty-six, the doctor recommended an amniocentesis test for Down's syndrome. I was deeply offended. Having the test would mean committing ourselves to genetic counselling, and I spent weeks railing inwardly against the threat that someone was going to force me to have an abortion if there was something "wrong" with the fetus. Although I was still a practicing Catholic, the Church's inflexibility on abortion played almost no part in my reasoning. I had always held with St. Augustine that I could love God and do as I pleased, and believed firmly in free will and the supremacy of individual conscience over institutional authority. In the end, I refused the test, deciding that our baby would be perfect however it arrived in the world.

My mother had always idealized her lyings in with my brother and me as utterly peaceful times of nursing, sleeping, and just being. I wanted her to help me create that for myself, first by being with us at the birth and then by spending a month with us afterwards. Just having her around helped me prolong the permission I gave myself to simply "be" with our baby in a way that I had never experienced in any other context. That particular closeness between us, impossible except through the connection of mothers, comes back to me sometimes when I catch myself not wanting to be like her, cringing when I hear the similarity in our voices or see how much we look alike. "Not wanting to be like Mom" is quite different from not wanting to possess certain of her habits or views. Nobody taught it to me; it seems to be a reflex I've picked up from a society that in such subtle as well as overt ways seeks to divide women from each other and ourselves. So now, on principle, I try to take my mother as she is, and think of her and be with her as with any other adult woman whom I like and respect. It's a bit like refusing to prefer the company of men to the company of women, and I'm not always able to pull it off. But even the effort of trying to honour my mother changes the way I assert myself in the world.

When Harrison began talking, I was faced with choices about which words to use (would it be fireman and policeman or fire fighter and police officer?). As we spoke to each other more, I would substitute a generic "she" for "he" in an otherwise straight forward conversation. I felt proud that my two-year-old called a girl a girl and a woman a woman. Then one day, as he was beginning to discover words to define and project himself on the world, he tried out the formula "m'n'dad are . . . (bigger, stronger, faster, taller, nicer, etc.) because we're boys." It was funny and perplexing at the same time, especially since he had seen very little television and his father and I didn't make gender-based distinctions in conversation. For a while Harrison took to making his pronouncements several times a day and I decided to challenge his innocent grab for supremacy head on. ("What makes you think you're so strong? Mommy is very strong, too. Here, let me wrestle you to the ground.") I was thinking about feminism, but it was my son who compelled me to clarify my thoughts and find a voice to carry them.

As a mother, I am unable to ignore sexism, whether I see it on a fashion billboard, read it in the otherwise delightful children's stories of E.B. White or hear it from four-year-olds who believe that pink is for girls and tea sets aren't for boys. I see now that I will have to do more than block the habit of gender stereotyping to prepare myself for more complicated challenges to my son's identity and world view as he grows up. Being white, able-bodied, handsome, athletic, strong-willed, and intelligent, he possesses qualities that virtually guarantee his place in the patriarchal system that dominates our culture. I want something more for him, something that begins in the mind and doesn't twist his humanity. As a feminist, I want to engage my son in the emergence of a new system whose essential attribute is equality.

When I first looked at the system of our society as something that could legitimately be examined, clarified, and changed, I felt the thrill of seeing that the Emperor wasn't wearing any clothes. It seemed that nothing could ever confuse me again, and that I would always care more about social change and women's issues than I had in the past. But, as Anne Schaef says, patriarchy is like pollution—easy to forget about once we're in it. It's hard to get perspective on the White Male System because it is everywhere in our culture—*is* our culture; buying into it and surviving can seem like the same thing. I don't think about feminism all the time, and I don't know how I'll use my raised consciousness other than letting it inform the way my partner and I raise our son and relate to each other, the way I read the things I see, and the frequency with which I venture to talk about a different way of seeing, thinking and doing.

I know that I'm not vulnerable any more to what Schaef calls "stoppers." (Anything can be a stopper, she says—a word, a phrase, a hug, a slap, even being told, "You're not a *real* feminist.") At forty-two, I finally get that "been there, done that" certainty not only about my perceptions and ideas but about their legitimacy and my right to make them known. I trust myself, and no longer think maybe I just don't get it.

I am not a feminist because I have a nice career and contribute to the maintenance of my family. I am not a feminist because my husband shares the housework and actively joins in the raising of our son. I am not even a feminist when I challenge sexism. I am a feminist because I care about who has power and who doesn't, and because I believe that recognizing power is the essential first step to changing our society fundamentally. Though I have resisted admitting this for a long time, I am a feminist, finally, because it hurts to deny my own reality. Personal pain keeps my mind off more important things.

I'm not sure where this leads me. But now that I'm out as a feminist, and have my self with me where I need her, everything seems possible.

If We Save Even One Woman

Raminder Dosanjh

I am fifty years old and have been away from India, the land of my birth, for twenty-five years. Although my parents loved me very much, I was an unaccepting, non-conforming, rebellious daughter. They would have liked me to be more pliant. Instead, I was impatient. The morés, values, customs, and traditions of upper-caste Indian culture into which I was born—a culture rich in faiths, languages, and racial diversity—felt more like a prison than the open air university of my dreams. The walls around me seemed insurmountable; I dreamed of visiting an uncle who had once visited us from Canada.

Over the years, I have lulled myself into believing that my uncle's open invitation was what brought me to Canada, but the truth lies somewhere among the limitations I faced—and fled—as an educated young Indian woman. Now as a middle-aged married woman with three grown-up sons, I watch my local Indo-Canadian community growing faster than it is changing, and I still feel harrassed by the cultural and societal pressures I fled half a lifetime ago. I am still battling the Indian as well as the Canadian walls around my being, my womanhood, that I started breaking down in 1973 with the establishment of India Mahila Association (IMA), and the battle continues unabated.

I was born in 1946 in Majitha, a village on the Indian side of the Indo-Pakistani border, created when India was divided after Independence. This division brought about the migration and massacre of hundreds of thousands of Indians—all in the name of religion. Having grown up with stories of the migration—unparalleled in human history—and its religious overtones, organized religion has had almost no significance in my life despite the fact that my mother is a devout Sikh and her village, Majitha, and my father's adopted village, Atari, have played significant roles in the history's only Sikh kingdom, that of Maharaja Ranjit Singh.

My mother was fourteen when she was married—not unusual in the 1930s—and had her first child, a son, when she was fifteen. From age fifteen to her early forties, she had eight children, two of whom died. In my mother's time, most women did not attend school, but she had the remarkable good fortune to have tutors who taught her English, Punjabi, math, and religion, all of which, except the religiosity, have faded from her memory. In India, a girl's marriage might be arranged when she was four or five years old or even when she was born. Families betrothed their children—a *thaka*—and this would move the bond between the families beyond friendship to kinship. It was not uncommon to have a daughter married and then keep her at home until she reached puberty, at which point she would be sent to her husband's family. My mother was ten years younger than my father; when she married him he was already established in his military career and was considered a young man with prospects.

My mother came from a family of *Sardars* who owned land that other people worked. Her family enjoyed a status higher than many others in the village. Her life was relatively rich and there were always servants around to do the cooking, cleaning, and drawing water from the well. Still, my mother is a very kind and humble person who has always believed in self-reliance and the treatment of others with respect. When I was growing up, in spite of the servants, she insisted that my sisters and I take turns at least once a week to cook and clean. I loathed cooking. My mother would ask me, "What are your in-laws going to say? What will you do if guests come to your house?" And I would answer, "I will work and earn enough to take them to a restaurant." Getting out of the house was what I loved most—I would happily volunteer to get on my bike and go to the store for grocery shopping. I learned to trade off jobs I did not like for those I did not mind. Somehow in the back of my mind I always knew that I would work outside the house and earn my living. I never enjoyed housework, and still do it only when I absolutely have to.

My family's gypsy-like existence, hopping from region to region and town to town following my father's movements in the Indian army, was helpful in preparing me for the culture shock of coming to Canada. My father represented change and mobility and my mother provided the stability. And while they played the usual male/female roles in the traditional Indian setting, I grew up almost unconscious of my status as a female. As a child and young woman I instinctively reacted against injustice, but was aware of neither gender nor class. The inequities of the Indian society, especially for the poor and women, were all around me, but I was oblivious to the challenges facing women until I got to college. Ironically, it was in the more egalitarian, more just society of Canada that I became aware of the need for drastic changes in women's conditions globally. Class consciousness was another layer of awareness that came later. In the condition of women in Canada, the inequities were abundantly evident, but so were the opportunities for equality. Women—poor immigrant or non-immigrant and single female parents—did not have an easy life, but change seemed within reach.

My mother taught me from an early age about "one God who is given different names by different religions" and that all people are equal. But she was unyielding about accepting her children marrying outside her religion. When I disclosed at age twenty-one that I was interested in marrying someone not only outside my caste but also outside my religion, she was extremely upset. A lot of pressure was put on me to separate me from my suitor. Our parents met and decided that his family would leave town in the hope that distance would weaken the bond. My studies were interrupted. I was not allowed to register for classes at the college, though I was given permission to register as a private student and study at home. My parents believed in education as a necessary tool for personal growth and prosperity, and wanted their children to have a good one. But they were not particularly keen on their daughter working unless it was a "respectable" job, i.e.: a doctor, teacher, engineer, etc.

One of my father's most precious dreams was to see at least one of his children graduate from medical school, but none of us were able to fulfil it. And while he took great pains to give all of us a good education, I had to do much convincing and arm-twisting before I was permitted to take on my first regular teaching job. Although my father was the only earning member of the family, sending his daughters to work was the last thing on his mind. Becoming too independent wasn't necessarily considered a positive thing because it could reduce the chances of finding a "good" husband. In their eyes educating their daughters was important, as it would enhance their chances of finding a good match and leading a comfortable life. By the time I reached my early twenties there was pressure to get married. They feared that if the marriage was not arranged at the appropriate time, it might be difficult to find a good match later.

After receiving my B.A. and B.Ed. and teaching for a year, I decided to visit Canada. Here again I had to battle with my family. It upset them that I was planning to go alone. They wanted me to marry and arranged several introductions to men who were visiting India from Canada. Since I was determined to go, they wanted to find me someone from Canada with whom I could go abroad as a married woman. A daughter, unmarried and fifteen thousand miles away could easily be the source of "shame" particularly if she were of an independent mind. Fortunately, to their credit, I was not forced into an arranged marriage.

At twenty-four, in October 1970, I left India to fulfill my childhood dream of visiting my uncle in Canada. At first, Canada intrigued me. Everything about it was exciting. I saw all the comforts—cars, central heating, and all the opulent things in life, like a television in every house. These things were luxuries in India at that time, and Canada seemed heavenly.

With the assistance of my uncle and a friend I met on the bus and my uncle, I contacted the local schools and started volunteering. Soon I was in the job market looking for work. The Vancouver School Board rejected my application for a teaching position on the grounds that it did not recognize my Bachelor of Arts degree from an Indian university. They later rejected my application for a teacher's aid position on the grounds that the same degree overqualified me.

Another barrier to my going to school or finding work in Vancouver was that I was not a landed immigrant. I subsequently qualified for the immigrant status as a clerk-typist after having upgraded my typing skills. While I was taking refresher courses at Langara College in order to get my teaching credentials, a UBC professor, whome I had met through my volunteer work, guided me towards a methodology course in teaching English as a second language at the University of British Columbia. Soon I landed a part-time teaching position at Vancouver Community College.

While studying at Langara, I had met Ujjal, who was involved in trying to bring about change in society. Though my background was totally apolitical, I was greatly impressed with his sharp intellectual ability, strong conviction about the importance of fighting against the exploitation of people, and forthright manner of expressing his views. In spite of my ambitious nature, my upbringing had not provided me with the same level of confidence and had left me more passive, polite, and aloof from the political arena. But in spite of our very diverse backgrounds and upbringing, we were attracted to each other. It was like we each had what the other lacked. As we got to know each other better, we spent more and more time discussing issues and doing things together. One day he proposed and I accepted.

Had they been given a choice, Ujjal's family would not have encouraged him to marry me—they thought I was too independent and strong-minded. We got married in 1972 and lived in an extended family household with his brother and wife and his two unmarried sisters. Conflict arose because of very clearly defined roles the family expected me to fit into and my reluctance to do so. Ujjal had taken for granted the attention lavished on him by his sisters, who treated him with a deference that was typical for male members of an extended family. But I had two part-time jobs and he was a full time student when we got married, and I just could not do what his sisters had done. This was fine with Ujjal, who was as accepting of my non-conformance as of his sister's favours.

My in-laws considered my involvement in outside activities not very important and a way of shirking my "real" responsibilities, which were to look after my share of the household chores and to be home with other female members of the family. Tension increased. Ujjal was very attached to his family and did not want to move out, but it became clear that something had to be done. After a lot of soul-searching we all came to the conclusion that our respective visions, approaches, and priorities were too different for us to live under one roof, and we moved out.

A couple of years later, after the birth of our second son, my parents arrived in Canada to live with us. Though we did not experience as great a degree of conflict in this family situation, I found myself at odds with my mother over things like male/female roles and religion. I wanted Ujjal to help with housework; my mother did not think it was appropriate when there were two women in the house. During the six years that my parents lived with us, my mother did most of the housework and provided our children with unconditional love and care while Ujjal and I worked. Living under one roof gave the three generations the opportunity to share and learn from each other. Things generally moved smoothly except when we decided to give Umber, our youngest, a haircut. It became a point of contention: my mother was very upset that we cut his hair, and it took us a long time to convince her to accept the change.

Ujjal and I participated in most community activities together, but I repeatedly noticed a lack of participation by women at various public events and I wondered why. I also experienced a bit of a culture shock each time I was ushered into the kitchen with the women when we visited many of the Indian families. My own upbringing had been much more liberal than that of many who had come to Canada in the forties and fifties. Vancouver culture and traditions seemed frozen in time, about half a century behind those of the modern-day India I had left.

Through volunteer work, I became involved in organizing a series of seminars on understanding the Indo-Canadian culture, organized by UBC's Continuing Education Department in co-operation with the local Sikh temple on Ross Street. As I got more involved in the various community organizations I found myself asking a lot of questions about the state of affairs in my community. I noticed a discrepancy between the involvement and treatment of women and men. Indian women were absent from the socio-political arena, particularly in decision-making positions. All of the volunteer organizations I came in contact with were totally male-dominated, with only one or two token women repre-sentatives, usually in the role of secretary or member-at-large. In the temples, men controlled the administrative affairs while the token woman on the executive was relegated to kitchen responsibilities.

I got to know the men through the community activities, but met their wives only at dinners or receptions. Once, when attending a public meeting on racism, it appalled me to find only seven women in a crowd of close to five hundred. Another time, I went to hear a guest speaker at the Sikh temple; she and I were the only two women in a group of over forty-five.

As I got to know the community more closely, for the first time I became aware of the life of exclusion and suffering many women lived. The hopes, aspirations, and dreams that these women brought to this country, which was supposed to be "full of riches and gold," were destroyed by the isolation, exploitation, and helplessness in a land of strange culture and language. These women either did not know what to do or where to turn for help, or they were afraid to talk to anyone for fear of retribution at home. One day I awoke to a horrible tragedy. In October 1972, Paramjeet and Gurmail Singh Sidhu, a young Indo-Canadian couple, were killed in their basement suite as a result of an explosion which was later determined to have been caused by a bomb concealed in an electric kettle. There were rumours that the couple had married against their parents' wishes. Ultimately, Paramjeet's father and another man were convicted of the murders. A few years later, the bodies of Harjinder Sidhu and her one-year-old child Hardeep were found in the Fraser River. It was believed the woman committed suicide after throwing her baby from the Fraser Street bridge. I did not know either of these women, but I was aware of the circumstances some women live under. Something had to be done. Ujjal agreed, saying, "If you feel strongly about an issue, you have to actively change things. No one is going to give it to you on a platter." I decided to become involved.

I had already been attending meetings in the women's movement and going to conferences. In the early seventies, we saw a growth in the number of organizations, such as women's shelters and rape crisis centres, across the country. But there was a clear lack of participation and representation of non-white women or their issues in the women's movement; therefore immigrant women's issues, such as access to language training, racism, accreditation of foreign degrees, or adequate support services for new immigrants, got very little attention. As I spoke Punjabi, Hindi, and English, I felt I could do more to bring about change in the Indian community.

In 1973, with the help of some friends, we established the India Mahila Association, the first South Asian Women's organization of its kind in Canada. The organization was formed to provide a voice for Canadian women of South Asian origin, to give them the needed support, and to deal with specific issues affecting their lives. There were a variety of issues—discrepancies in the treatment of young men and women, the practice of dowry, imposition of marriages of convenience, isolation and exploitation of immigrant women, training and retraining needs, violence against women—some of which needed to be addressed by the Indian community and others by the larger community. We started with just four women who were known to me. One of them was Ujjal's aunt, Harjit Dhillon, whom I have grown to love and care for more as a mother and political friend than an aunt. Initially we had problems recruiting women. Although many women agreed our work was important, it was hard to get them to take time out and make a solid commitment on top of their already busy workloads. Some who showed interest were quickly discouraged from attending meetings by their husbands and families.

To appear less threatening, we started a weekly folk dance group where women could come together to socialize. This attracted a lot more women and our numbers increased. We spent some of our time discussing women's issues informally, and then initiated more formal meetings. Though there were pockets of support for our cause in the community, it took us a long time to gain any meaningful acceptance. For a long time we were ignored by the mostly all-male establishment and rarely acknowledged or invited to participate in community acivities. Individuals in our organization were labelled "home-wreckers" and "a bunch of single women who have nothing better to do." Our organization was discredited by some as "a bunch of radicals who are spoiling women by misguiding them."

As we became better organized, we established contact with the ethnic media and were able to raise issues affecting Indo-Canadian women on radio and television. Because we did not have an office or a telephone, we gave out our personal numbers for women to contact us. It was a breakthrough. A lot of women started calling, but we also started getting crank calls, abusive messages, and personal threats. A common tactic used by those who disagreed with us was to personally discredit our active members. For instance, when Ujjal set up his law practice, I was accused of trying to split up families so that he could get more work. When another member who was separated from her husband chaired one of our public meetings, detractors commented that our organization "was made up of only separated and divorced women who are here to beat their own drum." While certain elements in the community continued to find ways to discredit both our organization and the women running it, we continued to raise awareness on issues of concern. After hearing and watching our programs, women began calling for help. Many of their stories were sad and depressing, which made us all the more determined to continue. Our work focussed on areas not covered by the organizations in existence at that time, particularly the area of education and prevention. It was not easy because to do any education we had to raise the issues publicly and as soon as we did, we were labelled unfairly, and considered controversial.

One of the first projects of India Mahila was to enroll women in

English-as-a-second-language classes. Our objective was to orient them to the resources and facilitate their integration into their newly chosen home. If the women learned to speak English, they could attend PTA meetings and become involved in their children's activities at school. If they understood banking and the transit system, they could go shopping and get around the city with more ease. We found some women who were really isolated. When our volunteers went to their homes to pick them up, they were sometimes met at the door by the husband who insisted his wife could not go because she had domestic duties to perform.

Our awareness of the realities of Indian women living in Vancouver increased with time and our work continued. Then, one day in 1990, a couple of India Mahila Association members were shopping in the Punjabi-India market and the storekeeper put some flyers in their bags. Written in Punjabi, the flyers advertised the services of a doctor in Blaine, who claimed he could detect the gender of a fetus through ultrasound as early as fourteen weeks. Soon afterwards advertisements appeared in local Punjabi newspapers offering sex selection services along with information on abortion. The doctor was targeting the South Asian community, to profit from some families' desire to have male offspring. These advertisements reminded me of the stories my grandmother had told me about how baby girls used to be killed at birth. I felt compelled to organize against this very dangerous and sexist practice from taking us back to the dark ages.

Historically, people in rural India preferred male children because they could earn money. If a family had four boys, they could all work on the farm and add to the family income. Women were less desirable because one woman in the family was enough to do all of the house-work and cooking. As a product of the patriarchal society, she would leave her family to join her husband's anyway. Because there were a lot of people from rural India residing in the Vancouver area, the doctor was attempting to ply his trade among them.

Were we going to allow this to go unchallenged? The cost of the gender-detection service in 1990 was $500, abortion not included. India Mahila debated what to do and concluded that the best course of action was to educate the community about the impact of sex selection practice on individual families and the community at large. Ultimately, we wanted to stop the doctor from promoting these sexist values and profiting from this ultimate sexist act.

We called the newspapers and asked them to pull the advertisements. We asked the shops and stores to throw away the leaflets and to not accept them any more. We did interviews on radio and television. For a while, we were successful in getting the ads pulled, but in 1993, the doctor's ads began reappearing in the ethnic newspapers. We made requests asking newspaper editors to discontinue the ads as they promoted female foeticide and the devaluation of women, but they countered with the "freedom of the press" argument. Infuriated, we phoned and wrote to the publishers, to no effect. They did not want to relinquish the profits they were making from these advertisements. The doctor was paying them a lot of money for his ads—he could well afford to, as he was by then charging $1,000 for each consultation.

We introduced the issue to the broader women's movement. The politicians were pressured not to advertise in newspapers carrying the objectionable advertisement. We also leafleted the Punjabi Market and got several thousand men and women to sign a petition asking for the ads to be pulled. While a female producer of a multicultural television program refused to run the advertisements, the male editors of four Indo-Canadian newspapers ran them and attacked us in their editorials, saying we were a bunch of radicals with no concept of what women in the community really wanted. A few progressive members of the media presented a more realistic picture and highlighted the moral and ethical issues involved.

During our battle against sex selection some of my colleagues in the women's movement said, "It must be really hard on you to take this stand in your community." Why? Because there is the pervasive and erroneous belief that all Indian people are in favour of sex selection—that it is part of our culture. But certain things—and this is one—are wrong regardless of culture. It was frustrating and infuriating to hear, particularly from those whom you expect more understanding, "We can't do anything about this; we don't know your culture." It should not matter whose rights we are fighting for—women's rights, gay rights, or other minorities' rights. We must understand the issues and not shirk our responsibility by saying, "It's their issue, let them fight it out." We have to look beyond colour, gender, or race and come together to build a caring and just society.

This issue once again showed the lack of attention and initiative taken by the various women's groups on immigrant women's issues. Though I have met and worked with some very hard-working, dedicated feminists who have made genuine attempts to bring immigrant women's issues to the table, during my work at the local and national levels I have been less than satisfied with the recognition and attention given to these issues by the women's movement. In the discussions and deliberations of the women's movement in Canada, immigrant and visible minority issues have continued to be marginalized. This has to change. Women's struggles must reflect the needs of *all* women.

I have also discovered that given the racism that permeates our society, I have to be extra careful about what I say with regard to issues of equality and male domination in the Indo-Canadian community. It is sad that even when I have chosen my words carefully, they have been misconstrued to stereotype the whole community. Having to protect my community from prejudice when I speak to people outside my culture sometimes detracts from the issue at hand.

It is true that some Indian women are forced to marry against their will, and some even die for defying their parent's wishes, like the daughter killed with the tea kettle bomb. I have met young women who have faced a lot of pressure (and sometimes force) to marry a man of their parents' choosing. Boys are not pressured as much because Indian culture, like many others, centres the whole honour of the family on the woman, and family honour is measured by the actions of the women. A man's actions can harm the honour of the family if he behaves badly, but the damage is not considered as serious. A ne'er-do-well young man is treated with a kind of indulgence, but a disobedient female is said to be lacking in virtue, bringing great "shame" on the family. Just about anything a woman does can spoil the family's honour, so women have to be very careful about everything they do, which places incredible pressure on them.

A few years ago, a South Asian baby was abandoned in the woods. Based on the baby's skin colour, sweeping generalizations were made by the authorities that the baby, being of South Asian origin, was possibly abandoned because she was a girl. The implication was that since she was Indian, whoever abandoned her would quite naturally have done so because of her gender. It's absurd to think that all Indians do not like female children. Whoever abandoned the baby could have had any number of other reasons for doing so, including a whole range of explanations for irrational and inhumane acts. The same week, a case was reported of a young Canadian couple travelling through the U.S. who were alleged to have murdered their infant daughter. However, no reference was made in the press regarding the parents' ethnicity or religion. As it happened, they were Roman Catholic Québecois.

The Vernon massacre of a whole extended family of South Asians at the hands of an angry and violent ex-husband was attributed by the media to a failed arranged marriage, while a Marc Lepine mowing down women in Montreal led no one to explore an ethnic explanation for his violence. Child abuse and violence against women are problems in every culture. It is racist to think otherwise.

India Mahila has been a voice for South Asian women and bringing their issues to light. As part of our Project on Violence, we interviewed some fifteen South Asian women, survivors of physical and emotional abuse at the hands of their husbands. We documented their words and feelings directly. Sitting through some of the interviews was a very emotional experience for both the women and myself. It made me realize that our work is not finished. We still have a long way to go.

Trying to bring about change in the lives of individual women is at times as frustrating as it is rewarding. I am infuriated when people argue that, "People talk too much about women's rights. What about men's rights?" In the past twenty years, I have seen many women abused, beaten, and murdered—one of them an IMA member and a personal friend, Nachhatar Dhahan. The other day a man called our television program to claim, "there are lots of men who are being abused by women." One cannot condone the abuse of anyone, but given the power relations between men and women, we cannot escape the fact that women suffer to a far greater extent.

The IMA Youth Committee is conducting a study on date abuse, similar to our program on spousal abuse. I see myself as a link to these daughters of my peers and we have developed a special relationship. These bright young women are outgoing, articulate, interested in community issues, and intent on exploring both their own identities and the issues affecting them as young South Asian women growing up in Canada. It gives me a great deal of hope and satisfaction in that these younger women will continue the struggle.

When we started India Mahila, we sheltered women in our own homes. Soon it became apparent that this was a very dangerous thing to do, so we contacted various transition houses and started referring the women to them. There is still an ongoing debate as to whether there should be a special transition house for South Asian women. In Surrey, where the Indian population is high, a couple of transition houses employ several Indian workers. Personally, I am not in favour of separate transition houses for South Asian women. In the early days through our work with the Rape Relief Sexual Assault Centre, we found that Indian women working at the front desk were easy targets for violent men coming after their wives, whereas if a Caucasian woman was up front, Indian men were more restrained. I think we can all benefit by being more responsive to each other's needs and not breaking off into separate ethnic groups.

It has never been easy to balance full-time work and intense volunteer work with raising a family, particularly when I do not have outside help. I want my family to be able to look after themselves. My husband has never really learned to cook, though he can handle things when the crunch comes. He compensates by helping with preparing food and cleaning the house. I have shown our sons how to cook a few dishes and do the laundry. In their early teenage years, however, they started to rebel at having to do much more than their peers in the extended family. They argued, "Nobody else's kids have to do so much, why should we?" But I notice when I am not home for a day or a week, they feed themselves fairly well.

I feel the pressure to be the ideal mom and wife just as strongly as I desire to pursue other things in life. When my children ask me, "Why do you have to be involved in this volunteer work? Why can't you be a normal mom and be home a lot more?" I reply, "Don't you think I am entitled to a little bit more than just sitting at home and doing things for you? We all live here as a family . . . shouldn't it be your responsibility to do some things while I do others?" They still look at my volunteer community work as "women's things." I have to remind them that this is not just "women's things," that the rights of women and how women are treated in our community or society in general are everyone's issues. I want to instill in them the idea that women have as much right as men to do what they wish. I want them to understand that women are also entitled to freedom and respect. Will I succeed in doing so? Only time will tell.

At times I feel tired and ask myself, "Is it all worth it? Why am I even bothering?" Sometimes I pause to ponder over comments made by my friends and relatives and ask myself, "Would our family life really be a lot easier if I simply went to work, came home, cooked, cleaned, rested, visited friends, had fun and paid more attention to the house?" And then

I tell myself—no, my life has been full of challenges and excitement and that is how I want it to be.

My involvement with India Mahila, for example, has helped me to grow and to meet other like-minded women. Our organization grew out of a strong desire to change the way things were. We have learned from each other's experiences and benefitted from each other's support. We did not come from a position of knowing everything, nor did we have a theoretical framework we wanted to implement. We were just ordinary women concerned about how we and other women around us were being treated. We have made some waves, pleasing some people and antagonizing others in the process. Most importantly, we have spoken our minds and learned to stand up for what we believe in. My job as a teacher of English as a second language has also helped me gain valuable insights. Contact with people from various parts of the world has helped me understand the universality of our issues in spite of our differences.

To break out of the shell that women have been trapped in for generations is a slow process. When I look back at myself twenty-four years ago, I see that I have come a long way. I am more fulfilled, confident, aware, and assertive.

If as feminists we have been able to instill some confidence and pride in ourselves and other women like us, or dissuaded even one woman from ending her life, then we have made a difference. We are gradually redefining the roles assigned to women in our male-dominated society and continuing to work for change. We may not have completely succeeded in bringing about the desired changes, but we have made our community think. Change does not happen overnight.

And while it would be nice to have a cleaner house and not have my children ask me to "be like other moms who do all the cooking, cleaning, and ironing instead of asking their kids to do housework," I just don't worry about a messy house any more. And I don't feel guilty about not cooking.

Dancing With Feminism

Pamela Dos Ramos

Pamela, you get down out of that tree this instant! Good little girls don't climb trees! Pamela, will you stop playing in the gutter! Little girls don't fish or play in gutters, and furthermore, the water is muddy and dirty! As my mind hears these words again, my face feels the warmth of the sun and my body the caress of a gentle, dusty breeze as I am transported back in time to my childhood in Guyana. It is a school holiday in August and I am squatting on the grass beside the gutter with two of my neighbourhood friends, Corinne and Rosemary. We are trying to catch the tiny fish flashing and flitting in the water. I am trailing one hand in the cool murkiness, trying to guide the little fish into the wicker basket I hold in my other hand. *De wata nuh dutty,* I call back to my grandmother, giving her something else to scold me about. *And speak properly. You know you're not supposed to talk like that!* Yes indeed, my mind echoes. It was not socially acceptable to speak Creolese at home or at school, though away from adult ears, my friends and I gleefully indulged in Creolese conversation whenever we could.

During a visit to one of my aunt's closest friends when I was four years old, I said to her grandmother, "You're so old, why haven't they put you in a box and buried you?" There was dead silence in the room. Then all around me splutters and hisses erupted: "Pamela, how could you?" "Pamela, where did you get that from?" "Pamela, little girls should be seen and not heard! You're being rude!" Amidst apologies by my aunt and her friend to the grandmother, the grandmother pulls me near to her, pats me on the head, and gently says, "Let her be. Come here child, let me look at you. My, my, you're growing." She then says to my aunt and her friend, "Why can't she ask questions? How is she going to learn, eh? Let her be!" I beam at her. She is on my side and not at all upset at my question. Her living room is full of knick-knacks and fascinating pictures and she begins to answer my questions and tell me stories about everything that interests me. We become friends, this ninety-year-old grandmother and me.

I grew up in Georgetown, Guyana (formerly British Guiana) in a multi-racial, multi-faith culture comprised of East Indians, Africans, Chinese, Portuguese, other Europeans, and Aboriginals, with East Indians approximately forty-one percent of the population. The Portuguese who had been recruited as immigrant workers between 1835 and 1882 after the abolition of slavery were identified as a separate racial category from European by the British colonial government. The major religious faiths practiced were Christian, Hindu, and Muslim. The customs and culture have been influenced by those ethnic and religious groups. My family was Christian, but I always enjoyed celebrating Christian, Hindu, and Muslim religious festivals. The weather was always hot, whether the seasons were wet or dry.

During my childhood and adolescence, Guyana was coming into its own as a nation state, having first achieved self-government from Britain in 1945, before I was born, then independence and a change of name from British Guiana to Guyana in 1966. I was completely oblivious in my early years, the 1950s, to interracial tensions and prejudices. My birth certificate describes the racial origins of both of my parents as "mixed." Specifically this meant that my father's racial heritage was East Indian, African, and European and my mother's African, Portuguese, and European. My family was middle-class and as I look back now, it appears that issues of skin colour were important, not to my parents or to my father's family, but specifically to my mother's sisters to whom it was also very important to conform to societal expectations of behaviour. As a family, education was much valued and the children—me, my sister, brother, and our cousins—were all encouraged and helped to do well in school. A much loved and protected child and grandchild, it wasn't until my high school years that my view of the world as a loving, welcoming and accepting place began to change.

As I reflect from a distance of more than three decades, it is easy to remember the idyllic times of childhood when the only differences I perceived were of gender and male privilege. How easy it is to forget or dismiss the painful exclusions and inclusions of childhood and youth—exclusions based on skin colour and degrees of darkness and lightness, race, social class, wealth, and intellectual and academic capability; inclusions based on some or all of the above and probably some others that I've forgotten.

There seemed to be so many things I couldn't or shouldn't do as a child if I wanted to be considered, treated, and rewarded as "a good little girl"—a state of being towards which my elders encouraged me to strive. All the fun, spontaneous, adventurous things were for boys to do with impunity. Why not girls too? On those rare occasions when an adult deigned to reply, I would never understand the answer. Boys got to do everything interesting, I thought; they got away with everything and no one ever seemed to tell them, "Behave yourself!" That meant so many different things in so many situations that I couldn't keep track—being seen and not heard, being still, not playing cricket in the street with the neighbourhood kids (mainly boys), speaking "proper" or standard English, not asking "Why" or "Why not," and certainly not continuously complaining, "It's not fair!"

So as a young girl, life sometimes felt unfair. My only brother is nine years younger than I am, and my sister is three years younger. But I had older male cousins who seemed god-like in that no one ever seemed to tell them they couldn't do this or that. And yet, when it came to school work or talent stuff like playing the piano, the message was very different. It was clearly and unmistakably, *You can.*

From my earliest memories, I had many women in my life—grannies in addition to my own natural grandmother, my mother, numerous aunts who were related and unrelated to me by blood, neighbours, and later, teachers. They all had words of wisdom for me. Especially I loved the grannies, my own and adopted. Their words were magical and always made me feel good about myself even though reprimands would sometimes be intertwined with the stories, the musings and teachings. It was a privilege to have had five crones, fifty to seventy years old, as role models until my twenties, to whom I felt "apprenticed." The one to whom I was closest and who influenced me the most was my own grandmother Nennie, the youngest of the lot. She taught me to knit, crochet, sew, bake, cook, and to love roses. The others were my mother's aunt, Alice, fondly referred to by me and my cousins as "Big Auntie," and her three friends, Aunties Trissie, Winnie, and Elsie. Five strong, resourceful, talented, independent, self-supporting spinsters, except for Nennie, who was a widow. Each was a woman who had defied convention and social norms in her own unique way, choosing to live her own life and not one dictated by family and friends. They were women who were deeply respected and appreciated by all who knew them, and feared also because of their strength, independence, and ability to be very direct. They encouraged me to seek my own truth and in their own quiet, unobtrusive, and gently powerful ways taught me about self-esteem, assertiveness, honesty tempered with tact and diplomacy, equality, and pride in my mixed racial heritage. They were women who would be puzzled at being described as "feminist" and who, on hearing the term explained, would laugh heartily and say, "Child, we were just doing what had to be done."

My grandfather worked far away from the city and came home once every two months for a few days at a time, so for all intents and purposes, my grandmother raised her family single-handedly. She led an independent life. Her shrewd business sense (she owned three houses, as well as cows and chickens, and lived off the rents and the sale of milk and eggs), a refusal to take no for an answer, and a sometimes caustic tongue ensured that no one took advantage of her or her family. By the time I was born, the cows were gone and there were only about twenty chickens. I had fun feeding them and collecting the eggs. I also loved going with my grandmother to the grocery store, the butcher, and the market, chatting to her all the while. I believed myself to be an extension of her, that we were somehow equals, and that I was just as capable as she was. I never saw her as old, nor did I think that she was ever going to become infirm. As we both grew older, I always believed that she would continue to be invincible. So you can imagine my shock when at eighty-six years of age, she fell ill and died within a fortnight. By that time, I was married with a two-year-old son. I was numb for several weeks afterwards. As my aunt and I sorted through my grandmother's papers, jewelry, and clothes, I began to realize how much I had learned from her and how many gems of wisdom she had given me over the years. Chuckling with my aunt and father over the memories, I recognized and acknowledged how much like Nennie I had become. Until her death, I had seen myself simply as the eldest grandchild who had a special relationship with her. Several people, including my parents and my aunt, always told me how much like Nennie I was—practical, determined, independent, and assertive. I did not believe them: no one could be like Nennie. Now I could be like her, I *was* like her. It was her legacy to me and I could wear it with pride.

I attended kindergarten when I was three years old and elementary school when I was five. My elementary school was Roman Catholic and mixed gender. Looking back, I recall acceptance, few questions asked or judgments made, and little evidence of the later biases of high school. I was fascinated by the ritual of the Catholic church (I had been baptized in the Presbyterian church) which was taught to us in school, and had many friends who were boys and girls of all racial backgrounds. A bright, carefree child who believed everyone was my friend, I see myself dancing through my elementary school years, leaving with a government scholarship to attend the leading girls' high school in Georgetown.

Attending an Anglican girls' high school opened my eyes to differences I had vaguely heard about, but paid no attention to, and it presented me with painful experiences. Neither my mixed heritage nor my tendency to chubbiness had been a barrier in elementary school, but these two attributes became important as I began high school.

At an age when acceptance is critical to self-esteem, I learned that I could not fit in or be accepted by everyone I liked or wanted to be with unless I gave up something or someone I valued. If I hung out with girls of African descent, then I couldn't hang out with girls of East Indian descent. If I hung out with other girls of mixed race, we were presumed to think ourselves as "better than." My mother pointed out to me that I had to like myself as I was and that if I had friends who wanted me to choose sides, then those friends probably weren't worth having anyway. Through her wisdom, I learned to value everyone regardless of background or viewpoint, and to feel secure in my own opinions and attributes. I was in my early teen years when I began to develop the ability to see all sides of a situation, earning the title of diplomat, because I tended to take a holistic view of most situations, however fraught with conflict.

During this time my fledgling ability was often tested. There was a general strike in British Guiana, followed by riots and civil unrest. Although interracial tensions had their greatest impact in the country districts rather than in the capital city of Georgetown, my high school was a microcosm of the whole country, and there were heated debates and disagreements over events reported in the news. Many classmates of East Indian and African racial backgrounds had relatives who lived in districts severely affected by racial unrest, and it was difficult for me to avoid taking sides.

I enjoyed spending my teenage years in a learning environment consisting of female students and teachers. Looking back, I think that this was when I realized that it was social norms and expectations that imposed the limitations of my earlier years. These restrictions were replaced by newer "can'ts" and "shouldn'ts." Academically anything was possible, but socially there were still expectations over how girls behaved in public and how others, especially adults, might perceive them. I was not expected to have a boyfriend or to go out on a date until I finished high school, although several of my friends had boyfriends before they were sixteen. (I eventually wore my parents down and was allowed to go on a date to a movie matinee when I was sixteen.) High school also taught me to value the differences in my friends—their perspectives, ethno-racial backgrounds, biases, whether they were brilliant or average academically—the things that made them individuals.

And I learned that prejudice and discrimination are divisive and soul destroying. A girl that I knew was high spirited, fun-loving, and often described as a tomboy. She was much darker in colour and had hair much curlier than her older sister. Teachers in high school blatantly favoured her older sister, continually saying how pretty she was and holding her up as a role model to my friend who was much brighter academically and a far superior athlete. I was told that her mother, to whom my friend's sister bore a striking resemblance, also favoured the older sister and often complained that my friend's hair was "hard" and her skin "so dark and she is always in the sun." My friend became more and more defiant, continuously getting into trouble and receiving poor marks in her school work. She eventually dropped out of school. I was quite upset by these events and couldn't understand why the adults could not see this young woman through her friends' eyes, beyond the defiance and their own prejudices to the *joi de vivre* that emanated from her. It appeared that only her friends accepted her for who she was. But at that time, in that place, adults had all the power: it was a power that could dim the brightest light.

I was encouraged to do math and science and indeed many of my friends excelled at those subjects, although I did not. We were encouraged to pursue careers in medicine, the sciences, and law, but I cannot think of any of my contemporaries who are now in what we consider to be non-traditional careers. Many are doctors, accountants, lawyers, economists, teachers, professors; none are engineers, welders or carpenters. When I was sixteen, I wanted to be a psychologist, but was cautioned by my father that I would be limited to working at the mental hospital. That prospect was not enticing. I struggled with wanting to study occupational therapy or drama. Again, the question of where to find paid work after graduation from university was an issue. Occupational therapy was not a growing profession, and I was particularly disappointed to learn that with a drama degree I would probably only be able to teach, unable to turn my talent and love of directing plays into a career which would earn me a salary. There was a thriving and vibrant amateur theatre environment in which I was involved as a volunteer.

Many of my classmates seemed clear about what careers or degree programs they wanted to pursue after graduation. I decided to work, thinking that in a year or so I would know what to do. I was working in a research library, and was being mentored by a woman librarian from the University when I chose to study Library Science. Her encouragement led me to London, England, where I studied for three years, emerging with a professional diploma, the equivalent of an undergraduate degree in Library Science. My studies were assisted by a Government of Guyana Scholarship which required me to return to Guyana to complete a five-year contract.

Returning home, I undertook a work assignment with the government, which provided me with all the flexibility and creativity for which I could hope. I began to train and mentor junior library assistants and, seeing their potential, always encouraged them to continue their education and training. That job in Guyana lasted for seven and a half years, during which time I married and had two boys. After my initial dismay at having two boys and no girls, I realized that I could teach them what I was learning about changing gender roles and relationships, equality, and responsibility, and hope that they would grow to become caring, loving human beings.

During this time, women were coming into their own in Guyana and were being appointed to senior positions in the Public Service, the Judicial Service, and as Ministers of the Government. This was encouraging—my aspirations could be limitless. However, a closer look shows that there were no female Permanent Secretaries (administrative and operational heads of government departments) and that the portfolios that female Ministers held were of Education and Information and not Finance, Foreign Affairs or Economic Development. The reality was that women were still, in the 1970s, an economic, social, and political underclass, although many were highly educated. Nevertheless, the women's movement, if it can be called that, was slowly growing. Women's advancement and development was being nurtured by the President's wife, who had been one of my high school teachers and role models. The focus appeared to be to empower grassroots women to become more economically independent, to help them to develop leadership and business skills, and to have more of a voice and role in politics.

During the mid to late 1970s, it was becoming harder and harder for me to have the quality of life that I wanted for myself and my family. Guyana had become officially a Co-operative Socialist Republic, with political, ideological, and economic ties to Russia, Cuba, and other socialist and communist countries. In order to do well, it seemed that it was necessary to actively support the political party in power. The President of the country often reminded citizens that, "If you're not with me, then you're against me." There was no room for fence-sitters. I was apolitical, having been brought up in a family with no strong political affiliations or interest in politics. Working in a government department, I had to be extremely careful of expressing views contrary to those of the political party in power and maintaining relationships with old colleagues who might be active members of an opposition party. I was actually advised to end a friendship with a protégé who was an active member of an opposition party.

This was very nerve-wracking. A turning point came when my father quietly told me after I complained about having to participate in a political activity, "Pamela, if you won't think of yourself and your own personal safety, then think of that of your husband and children." I had been raised to do and say what I believed to be right and to be assertive about my rights. When it became obvious that I could no longer do so and ensure that I and my family were safe, I realized that it was time for us to seriously consider leaving. Also at this time a very close friend, who had always sworn that nothing could ever persuade her to leave Guyana, left with her family so quickly that I was shocked. She and her family had strongly supported the government and felt very safe and secure, until a close relative had been used as a scapegoat. It seemed to me that freedom of opinion, freedom of speech, and freedom of association had become dreams of the past. It was definitely time for us to leave.

The decision to move to Canada was not easy. It meant sacrificing years of work and dreams to begin again in a world far different from Guyana, in which we might never feel we belonged, however long we stayed. I struggled with the fear that in deciding to leave my homeland,

I was betraying my values and beliefs in working towards its development so that the world could be a better place. Hoping to do this quietly, with no political involvement, I asked myself what risks and sacrifices I was prepared to make to continue to uphold these values and beliefs. I told myself that leaving had become a necessity because of political, economic, and educational oppression, and struggled with the guilt of leaving my parents, brother, sister, and aunt behind. Despite my youth I had somehow replaced my grandmother as the matriarch of the family, and believed that I was letting them down and abandoning them. Quiet discussions assured me that they understood, that the decision was good for my own immediate family. Appearing to be compliant at work became easier after the decision to leave was made.

We expected to find jobs easily. We had received points in the immigration process for our education and work experience. I was a librarian and my husband a business and marketing graduate, both with eight years of work experience at a senior level. I experienced little difficulty. However, my husband hit the invisible barrier that faces many immigrants. It took a Guyanese friend in the Human Resources field to name the obstacle—lack of Canadian work experience and predictable systemic barriers to obtaining it. Our friend advised that my husband should take a job, any job, to get work experience. Having left a very prestigious position where his skills were highly valued, my husband could hardly reconcile himself to the idea of working perhaps as a sales clerk in a convenience store. The reality, and one of the issues of racism that many immigrants face, is that their qualifications, skills, and abilities, and the professional success they may have enjoyed back home, are not valued. One indeed has to start over, often from a position one could not have imagined before coming to Canada.

Living and working in our adopted country was an ongoing learning experience. I had believed that it would be easy to live in an English-speaking western country, that it would be similar to living in England, for example. In fact it was very different. I had left behind a collective approach to community living where the African saying, "It takes a whole village to raise a child," is practiced and where meals are shared with whoever is visiting. I came to a neighbourhood where a parent would give her children a treat and give none to the visiting neighbourhood children. There have been other challenges in raising our boys, none the least of which was teaching our own values while recognizing that our children have to live and learn in a world and environment very different to the one in which my husband and I had grown up. Wherever else we compromised, we have not compromised the value of education and our belief that it provides a foundation for future success.

I became involved in the women's community in Calgary in 1991, ten years after leaving Guyana. During those years, I had been immersed in raising my family, my work in information management and my professional association, the Association of Records Managers and Administrators, and in helping us to become secure. The boys were doing well in school and sports and we were beginning to feel secure when I had an opportunity to participate in a Life Work Planning Course sponsored by the company at which I worked. This was an experience which led me to study for a master's degree in counselling and then to make a career change just when my company was down-sizing. I began my new profession in career and employment counselling for women. That was when I first heard the term "feminist." "What is a feminist?" I wondered.

Through paid and volunteer work, in meetings and on committees, I came into contact with many women who described themselves as feminist. Not one explained what she meant and I must confess that, unusual for me, I was reluctant to ask. It sounded like a profession or even a religious affiliation: "I am Stephanie Jones and I work at XYZ organization and I'm a feminist." When I did ask someone I knew fairly well to explain the meaning of the term as it applied to her, she gave me a puzzled look which I interpreted to mean, "Why do I have to explain myself?" then an explanation which seemed to pertain to me. I believed that we were all working towards women's equality, social justice, the eradication of poverty, and discrimination against those not in the mainstream of society. More specifically, I was also working towards the eradication of the disease and dis-ease of racism through a consultation project with immigrants, immigrant-serving agencies, and other community agencies to identify the major barriers immigrants face in adapting to and integrating into their new society. In addition, I was involved in anti-racism training and education, with my own experience to draw from.

But I thought there had to be more to this feminism stuff and determined to find out what it was. As a forty-three-year old married for seventeen years with sons aged sixteen and thirteen, I began my quest. Though I believed that learning never ceases and each day brings with it new insights and awareness, I had no idea that I was about to embark on one of the most important learning experiences of my life.

Until this time, I had not taken any women's studies courses. Perhaps I should have started at the library. Instead, I wanted to witness "feminist" and "feminism" in practice and to understand what feminism meant to women. I wanted to see it reflected in their work and daily living. Women who described themselves as feminists, I found, were often concerned about similar things, but each seemed to have her own area of interest and commitment. Some white women were very concerned about oppression, equality, patriarchy, and power; others combined these with their actions around the issues of sexual orientation, ableism, and racism. Still others dealt only with specific issues; for example, oppression as it relates to ableism, patriarchy and discrimination as they relate to sexual orientation. Very few women seemed to take what I would consider to be a holistic perspective.

Being a woman of colour, I sought out others like me, some of whom were immigrant women who I thought by their work would have answers for me. Some advised me with a shudder not to get involved with "those aggressive feminists who are all lesbians and do not understand the issues faced by women of colour or immigrant women." This was spoken as if feminism was a medical disease and indicated their own unease and discomfort with lesbianism coupled with a lack of understanding of feminism. Though objects of stereotyping and discrimination themselves, they did not recognize that they were also stereotyping, discriminating, and judging other women. And often they did not recognize that there are women of colour who are lesbians. Yet other women of colour and immigrant women, many of whom were members of the Women of Colour Collective of Calgary, were very articulate about feminism, feminist issues, and their concerns and experiences of racism and marginalization by white feminists in the larger women's movement. They embraced a more holistic point of view that resonated with my emerging ability to articulate and express my own perspective. They became, whether they knew it or not, my mentors and role models.

I realized that I had naïvely and mistakenly believed that I would share similar perspectives with most other women of colour and that there would be some common ground for discussing feminist issues. But I began to recognize that internalized oppressions, including sexism, homophobia and racism, would prevent some women of colour from being my allies. Meanwhile, I met both white women and women of colour who would not have described themselves as feminist, but who were concerned about issues of equality and were doing whatever they could in their communities to address those issues. A picture of what feminism was in practice was beginning to emerge, but I still felt unable to clearly describe it or to put myself into the picture.

I began to understand that there were multiple perspectives, and tried not to be critical of any bias I encountered while becoming aware of where women were at. I took the position that as women we were all in different places in our understanding and commitment, and that many women were mired in issues of day-to-day survival and could not see how feminism could apply to them. Perhaps those women, whom I thought were narrowly focussed, were simply picking their "battles" while still involved in the war. If I had taken a course or two, I may have been better able to relate theory to my own beliefs, values, and experiences and to develop a clear understanding so that I could critically analyze what I heard and witnessed in women's interactions and practice. I might have been better equipped to debate ideas and challenge some narrow viewpoints, including the stereotypes of the "radical" or "aggressive" feminist, and might have been more prepared to effectively question incongruent behaviours of some women. With a grounding in feminist theory I may have been better able to challenge an avowed feminist when she told me that she actively worked to help marginalized women have a voice, yet in reality she did not allow her staff, all women, to speak freely or to have any views contrary to her own.

About eight months after starting my quest, I began to read about feminism. In the book, *Making Face, Making Soul*, edited by Gloria Anzaldua, I found what I needed to focus my ideas in a contribution by Barbara Smith, an African-American women's rights activist and writer, entitled "Racism and Women's Studies." It made perfect sense and resonated with my own emerging theoretical framework. I have adopted her definition that states: "Feminism is the political theory and practice that struggles to free all women: women of color, working-class women, poor women, disabled women, lesbians, old women—as well as white economically privileged, heterosexual women. Anything less than this vision of total freedom is not feminism but merely female self-aggrandizement."

Today, I make choices based on values rather than economics, choosing to work with marginalized and poor women to help them recognize what they need to do to regain their personal power and to become economically self-supporting, including becoming aware of their rights and rediscovering their voice. In my work to educate and facilitate awareness, understanding, and attitudinal change about racism, I have encountered some wonderful women whose lives exemplify their holistic feminist values and beliefs. These are my role models. I have met young women of colour, many of whom are actively involved in the work of the Women of Colour Collective in Calgary, who are passionate about their feminism. They are committed to making change in the women's community, to building bridges of understanding and creating alliances with white feminists while maintaining their own identities and commitments to anti-racism work. These young women have purpose and direction and will ensure that racism continues to be addressed directly by the women's movement. And I have met women who struggle to understand their early internalized oppressive learnings and how they interfere with where they would like to be in terms of holistic feminism. These women I admire for their openness and willingness to take risks and make mistakes, and their continued commitment to learning. I have also encountered women who profess to be holistic feminists but who are, by their actions and others' experiences of them, oppressive.

I do not yet have all the answers I need. I do not claim that I am indeed a true, effective holistic feminist, but I continue to learn and examine my interactions and behaviours in light of my definition of feminist values and beliefs. I struggle to understand my internalized oppression, to develop ways of addressing it, while trying to be open to feedback from colleagues, clients, and friends and to incorporate that feedback. In alliances with white feminists, I try where appropriate to challenge them to examine and address their own internalized oppressions. I believe that being a feminist means continually evolving, learning, changing to meet the social, political, economic, and other demands of the environment in which we live and work, and a total commitment to achieving equality and freedom in their broadest yet most specific senses. Feminism is not about personal gain, acquiring power and control over others, public recognition, or economic rewards. It is about integrity, awareness, and self-knowledge, courage and commitment to change, and about valuing ourselves, our experiences, our varying abilities and capabilities, talents and skills. Feminism demands honesty from self and others about intent and expectations. It is about joining together in support of each other, building allegiances wherever possible, to make our voices and the voices of those who have been silenced, heard.

Confessions

Margaret Dragu

Photo by Renee Rodin

I am a Feminist but I was a Stripper.
I am Everywoman but I am Alternative.
I am an Artist but I am an Entertainer.
I am an Entertainer but I don't make Popular Culture.
I am Social but I am Isolated.
I am Christian but not Right Wing.
I am Big and Tall but I live in a Tiny Place with 2 Others.
I am living Below the Poverty Line but I am Rich.
I am Political but I have Fear of Conflict.

I Confess I am a Socialist with a Cookie Jar

Before the 1993 election that brought the federal Conservative and NDP parties to their knees and brought the Reform Party in to the House of Commons, I was working in a discount bakery outlet. Our Thursday delivery driver was a fellow aging hippie called Les.

"Yup, less is more," Les was fond of saying while pointing to his name embroidered on his shirt, hat, and jacket. "I got it stitched on everything except my jockey shorts." We joked around every Thursday, swapping kid-raising stories, talking music and books and analysis of the world situation. And just before that inauspicious election day, Les asked me how I was going to vote.

"NDP," I said. Immediately. Enthusiastically. As it turned out, there were probably only seven other B.C. citizens who voted NDP in that election. But I didn't know that as I watched Les, holding a tray of twenty-nine-day-old vanilla swiss rolls, looking up at me and shaking his head from side to side. He smiled at me with something close to pity. "You certainly hear another drummer, Margaret."

It's true. I am a socialist and an aging hippie. I reduce, re-use and recycle. I write elected officials about bike paths and Amnesty International. I spend most of my energy on things that don't pay well or at all even though I am surrounded by people who think I am nuts. My hippie ideals still feel right to me. So why switch? Oh, Les! We may be parents and wear polyester uniforms at ho-hum jobs, but . . . voting Reform? Aaargh!

I keep in touch with my inner self through my cookie jar. It is full of platitudes, paradoxes, and recipes. And a few Feminist Moments. I dig in and pull out a pink index card. It says, "The personal is political." A feminist axiom from the seventies.

I Confess My Personal Purple History

I spent the early seventies insisting that I was not a feminist. I felt too different from those I was meeting who were older, more educated, and richer—not to mention our different backgrounds, class, experience, opinions, and beliefs.

I was a lonely only-child stubblejumper of the vast Canadian prairies, born in 1953. My mother was one child of thirteen (eleven survived). She wanted a small family. "Two would be nice," she often said; but the other one never came. Our milk was delivered by horse. We walked on wooden sidewalks, played hide and seek in the culverts. We battled grasshoppers and cutworms, watched black clouds of summer electric storms bear down upon us. The winds pushed tumbleweeds ahead like scouts announcing enemy attack. We suffered in air so dry in the summer it gave me nosebleeds. At school, the wicked witches strapped and beat the boys. Halfway through kindergarten we moved to the suburbs which dropped off right back into the endless horizon of the bald prairie. At five years old, I would stand in the wheatfields beside the railway tracks of Saskatchewan against big sky, big field, big grain elevator—knowing there had to be Something More Than This and wishing myself away away away on any train out of there.

When I was twelve, we moved suddenly to Calgary, which was like entering America. What was New Math? Who were these kids from Houston and Corpus Christi? I felt lonely, anxious, and depressed. Finally, I was fifteen, and it was still the sixties. Time for sex and drugs and rock'n'roll. I found older teenagers and young adults in their twenties who were at community centres, church basements, drop-in centres, art groups, film groups, theatre companies, underground presses, coffeehouses. I started taking dance classes. I started performing. And I still wanted *out!* I balanced part-time jobs, high school, the dance company, and a lifestyle dedicated to experimentation while living mostly away from a degenerating home life. Before my eighteenth birthday, I escaped to New York City.

There, I was an idealistic teenaged hippie artist under the wing of older New York and European beatnik artists. But as ecstatic as I was to be studying and performing in New York City, I wanted even more, so I moved to Montréal. I performed in art galleries, taught dance classes, and began a long career as a stripper. I was trained by Québecois transvestites and transsexuals and toured the province of Québec. I re-invented myself as a Jungian archetype—the Stripper as metaphysical "Nun/Whore" wanting to create an artistic and spiritual lexicon for myself and the world around me. I had to provide parameters for my experiments and I wanted the world to validate my experience. I wanted to cross-pollinate popular culture and fine art by inverting the sacred art gallery and the profane striptease club. After a summer of landlord-created insurance fires, I returned from a week stripping in Québec City to find my entire street had burned to the ground. I moved to Toronto. I was quoted in the newspaper as saying, "Toronto is like stripping in a bank." It certainly was a culture shock. But I had great opportunities to work in film, TV, theatre, galleries, nightclubs, cabarets, and in the Toronto institution called "The After Hours Bar." There had been no "after" hours in Montréal because Montréal never closed. I became part of the art-making community of Toronto, both "legit" and "underground."

In the mid-seventies, it was very hard and very lonely being the only stripper at feminist meetings or media-organized panel discussions. Feminists were getting in touch with their Feminist Rage about Violence Against Women and All Forms of Abuse while exploring many of these issues through investigating Pornography. It was a time of passionate and lengthy discourse about Sexuality, Morality, Power, Violence, and Pleasure.

Being a well-known stripper, artist, and (briefly) media personality meant I would find myself discussing these issues under media-invented titles like "Yonge Street Spokeswoman" or "Libertine Intellectual" or "Wild and Crazy Free Speech Artist." I had some really unpleasant and gruelling battles with feminists on live television. Phone-in callers screamed at me on radio shows and even at home, on my answering machine, accusing me of supporting the patriarchial power play that objectified women and led to violence against them. Some wanted me to look at snuff films and admit I was responsible for the death of other women and to see myself as a traitor. One woman invited me to her apartment for a gourmet lunch (cold stuffed fish, gado–gado sauce and salad, I recall) then whipped out her hidden agenda for dessert: a non-stop harangue that my stripping at a Toronto club was the direct cause of her receiving sexual comments from construction workers, her sister the secretary being pawed by her boss, and children being lured into cars by pedophiles with candy. Some feminists merely pitied me and wanted to save me. They were willing to hire me as their cleaning lady so I wouldn't have to work as a stripper any more.

Although I was a famous cleaning lady as well as a renowned stripper, I wanted these feminists to see that I was an independent artist and working in a sexual and working-class world that they knew nothing about. I wanted working conditions in strip clubs to improve and I wanted their support towards that goal. I didn't want to be censored or judged. I was twenty-five years old and full of ideals and absolutes. I felt more solidarity around class lines than gender lines.

Even though my experiences weren't something the feminists I was meeting could relate to, I enjoyed the grassroots contact in conscious-ness-raising groups, gatherings on snowy Ontario nights outside Mor-genthaler's abortion clinic, and the sharing of pots of Earl Grey tea during folding/stuffing/mailing sessions for various causes.

The concept that "the personal is political"—that pink card I peri-odically pluck from my cookie jar—helped me make sense of the world and my life in it. The idea gave me a sense of self-esteem by demonstrat-ing that I and women like me counted. It gave credibility to my personal, domestic, and community problems. Instead of thinking I was "crazy" or "a complainer," I began to feel my problems and concerns were actually important issues for everyone. Accepting "the personal is political" gave me the conviction that I could help change things for the better if I acted with other women; it also gave me the commitment to do so.

Eventually, with the help of the Canadian Labour Congress (CLC) and the Association of Canadian Television and Radio Artists (ACTRA), the short-lived strippers' union was formed. We called it the Canadian Association for Burlesque Entertainers (CABE) and eventually got support from the some of the feminists I had worked with in demos, meetings, and pamphlet-stuffing sessions. There was a rise in the voice of bisexual women who felt ostracized by both straight and lesbian feminists. There were articulate spokeswomen for sex workers in the United States and Europe during important Women's Conferences on Sexuality. There was a lot of excellent writing by Feminists Against Censorship. There was a parallel anti-censorship movement in the art community. All these voices felt welcoming and inclusive. Women who called themselves "Feminist" and accepted me naming myself as one, too, reached out to me and I was ready to reach back. I closed the seventies saying: "I am a feminist."

I Confess that "Feminist" is Not an Easy Thing to Call Yourself
Have you ever noticed how many women say, "I am a feminist, but . . . " then add qualifiers like "I don't hate men," "I am a woman of colour," or "I am an eco-feminist"? I used to do it, too, but now I plant my feet on the ground (like John Wayne suggested) and Just Tell the Truth.

My unease is because the word has been chewed to smithereens by the media and, like anything that gets so much media attention, the word "feminist" has been damaged. The right used to ridicule feminism by painting images of angry overweight women burning bras and narrowing the debate to the morality of males opening doors for females. Now the right is more sinister; their intelligentsia declares equality has been achieved and we are now in a "post-feminist" era while their extreme end employs hit men to shoot doctors who perform abortions. Yet feminism keeps growing and becoming more inclusive. More women from more classes, races, and countries are calling themselves feminists and entering women's organizations.

I have a love-hate thing with groups: a desire to belong attended by an equal revulsion of crowds. (Scan your memory bank to the Hitler Youth singing "The World Belongs to Me" in *The Sound of Music* or the sweater set conformity of the laquer-lipped girls in *Rebel Without a Cause*). Ironically, since most of my art is live performance, I need crowds. I want them to enjoy my performance. But I can't allow my need for crowds and my love of applause to pressure me to change the art work itself.

I Confess that "Artist" is Not an Easy Thing to Call Yourself
When asked what I do, I say, "I teach aerobics," or "I work at home on
the computer." If I feel confident, I say, "*I am an artist.*" To some
people, an artist is a painter so calling myself an artist can be confusing.
Or it can lead to a nasty fight because some people hate art, believe art
can only be the ballet and symphony, or say artists are "sucking off the
public tit." But art is central to my life. Let me dig in my cookie jar and
ta-da—here is my Art Manifesto:

Art transforms the artist and those who see the art.
Art reveals the ugly as being beautiful through compassion and
     really seeing.
Art reveals the lies we had agreed to accept as gospel.
Art is getting down/getting dirty/getting obsessive and compulsive.
Art illuminates without pinning down its literal hems.
Art eschews the vaudevillian punchline and sweetened laugh track of TV.
Shit. Hey Artist Asshole! If you're so smart, why aren't you rich?
Art is not technique, training or schooling although some artists
     have these things.
Art can make you laugh and cry until you beg for mercy but it is
     not entertainment.
Art lives.
Art is what I do with my life.

On the other hand, I read art magazines at the library and events listings
in the local newsweekly and feel alienated from both art *and* popular
culture. I rarely go out, only partly because living in a fishing village puts
me so far from the city and its urban culture. My girlfriend Susan says
that even though she lives right downtown, she, too, often cocoons at
home. Maybe my geography is only a metaphor for a larger sense of
isolation and a shared experience of the breakdown of community.
Going out is more expensive than it used to be; transportation is hard,
and finding and affording babysitters is even harder. Twenty years ago, I
used to go out all the time. I used to get crazy from going out too
much—I knew no personal boundaries and was often paranoid and
hysterical. My social life was so vast, and so completely wrapped up in
my work, that I couldn't tell the difference. A quarter of a century later,
I am not vegging out watching TV—I am doing interesting stuff at

home. Like writing, making art, and making bread. My partner plays the violin and helps our daughter with her homework. We are not couch potatoes. But it is hard to get motivated to go out even for fun. I feel I must fight the urge to cocoon like Dorothy, Scarecrow, Tinman, and the Cowardly Lion resisted the lure of the poppyfield en route to Oz City.

I Confess My Politics and Art Come from the Kitchen

I think of myself as Everywoman. Despite what to some might appear an unconventional life (stripper, artist, activist, leftie) I am also a member of the Baby Boomer Bell Curve and a Mother. I sense that somewhere a target marketing squad has my number. This is proven by the fact that every time I decide to line up at the bank there is a huge crowd ahead of me who decided to do precisely what I wanted to do at exactly the same time. When I have finished my transaction, the rush is over and the bank is again filled with echoing emptiness. I find a classic angora sweater at the second-hand store for $1.75 and later that same day decide to start roasting vegetables before adding them to my pasta sauce. Bingo! The entire world is wearing my sweater and eating my pasta. Worse, they are discussing it in *Vanity Fair, Chatelaine*, and *Australian Women's Weekly*. I am forced to realize I only follow cultural cues and do not really make discoveries at all.

For the last ten years, I have lived on the south arm of the Fraser River with my partner and our daughter. Our closest shopping/school/working and services community is a suburb of Vancouver. After ten years, I have a place in this community. When I go to the mall, which I think of in its more cosmopolitan guise of zocolo or town square, I am greeted and chatted up by people who recognize me from my job at the bakery, from the fitness classes I teach at the community centres and from volunteer work at my daughter's school. When I bicycle through the farms to go home to the river, the farmworkers, fishermen, truckers, and municipal workers all wave and acknowledge me. I am known and accepted. I love this sense of belonging.

But, belonging is an illusion. I am not Everywoman. I am actually an aging hippie who could be called Marginal Madge. My politics, beliefs, values, aesthetics and income are completely different from those of the community within which I function. Clashes with the other side are frequent. I have learned to choose carefully when and how I challenge or contradict the other side. I try to advocate and be positive, but sometimes I just remove myself from the conflict. When my customers and co-workers persistently made racist comments about Asian immigrants I could have said, "Now listen here—my husband is Chinese," but I preferred to just quit and find another job.

Then there is Linda, who covers for me for patrol duty at my daughter's school. While synchronizing our calendars, Linda offered up this infobyte. She has recently banned "Sesame Street" from her kids' television list after seeing an episode that introduced same-sex parenting in a positive light. Linda said her kids would never meet "people like that" (her face scrunched in distaste like a Pillsbury Doughboy who has bitten into a slice of lemon). I stood frozen for what felt like two and a half hours. I considered telling her that Jim and I were a same-sex couple and that I had recently undergone a sex change operation, or that Jim was a lesbian with a five o'clock shadow. But I knew this would only personalize our conflict and would not change her tolerance of gays and lesbians. I let the room temperature drop to thirty below celsius and excused myself, leaving Linda with a confused and alarmed expression on her face. The Pillsbury Doughboy wondering what went wrong.

This ain't *radikal aktion*. But sometimes it's all I can do.

I am less of an activist in the nineties than I was in the seventies. I have been around the block with lawyers, letters, and fundraising. I have marched for affordable housing and daycare, Morgenthaler, Amnesty, the Disappeared of Central America, Rainforests and Their Tribes, the Massacred, the Penalized, and the Damned. But what about recently? My values haven't changed. My life has, and I feel completely overwhelmed. Having a partner and a child means that my decisions affect people other than myself. It takes two and a half hours to bike and bus into town and the same back. This is a factor when I am dovetailing mommy-duty, babysitters (none), my partner's schedule, and biking off to teach that eight a.m. special needs aerobic class.

As a mother, I am among the lowest paid (and unpaid) workers in our society. Domestic work is invisible. That is why illegal immigrants are nannies for the middle and upper classes. No one is watching. And this is why it is so common for women just past their childbearing years to be divorced by their mates and find themselves suddenly in comparative poverty while their ex-husbands are at their financial peak and taking younger wives to begin their second family. This is the story of my girlfriends. It is wrong. I know I must try and change this. When I was a stripper, I used to think the world was a strip club: I mean, the politics and powerplays I discovered in strip clubs were replicated elsewhere. If the cops come into a strip club to bust someone, you know it's going to be the Jamaican stripper with no working papers because she is the most vulnerable. When CABE was formed, the CLC tried to encourage us to develop a liaison with the truckers' union who delivered the beer from the brewers (picture the solidarity over striking suds workers) or the taxi drivers' union (because both strippers and taxi drivers are maverick), but the only neophyte union I could relate to was the domestic workers' union from Ottawa, which was busy exposing members of parliament who hired illegal aliens to be their nannies and cleaning ladies. After all, I was a stripper, a cleaning lady, and a woman. I liked the domestic workers' union's understanding of class and race issues. There are a lot of similarities between strippers and cleaning ladies. And mothers. Perhaps this is because my politics and art come from the kitchen.

On my kitchen radio, I hear anti-choice hysteria and the complaints about French immersion in the schools. I hear intolerance towards immigrants, artists, intellectuals, gays and lesbians, the poor. I get so angry and sad that I am moved to silence. Or, I feel like punching the nose of someone from the other side, which is disturbing. If I feel this way about people expressing right-wing views, they must feel the same towards me, too. I don't want this conflict in my life. But it is everywhere and in suprisingly intimate places: at work, at school, on the street where you live.

I Confess My Love-Hate Towards My Extended Family

When I criticize the platform of the Reform Party, my Aunt Rose always asks me, "If you're so smart why aren't you rich?" This is her barometer. She feels the government has a holy duty to cut back on social spending to schools, prisons, welfare programmes, medical plans, and hospitals. To make the rich richer and the poor poorer. Aunt Sophia always explains, "But sweetie, we aren't meant to all be the same—we can't all be bosses—some of us have to do the work!" She is telling me I should know my place and stay there. My Aunt Rose listens to my indignant rebuttals while handrolling her always boomerang-shaped cigarette and puffs her complete agreement even though she worked her whole life in the hospital laundry.

The right-wing is growing. My polarization with it is growing as well as my anger towards members of my extended family who are Christian fundamentalists and card-carrying members of the Reform Party. I feel divided and alienated from them. And sad. It is a loss to be so other from "my own." If I am an alienated daughter, will my daughter feel alienated from me? It is depressing and crazy-making to live in a world that doesn't reflect my values. I see the right using fear and intolerance to manipulate the world at large and the microcosm of my extended family.

I remember as a young child being cautioned by well-meaning women relatives never to marry a Catholic because Catholics forced you to convert, and if you were in a life and death situation while giving birth in a Catholic hospital, they would save the child and let you die. I was also taught that the United Church had rewritten the Bible proving them to be blasphemous while the Unitarians were a bunch of fruitcakes. This misinformation and fear was dumped on all "other" Christian sects. You can imagine their feelings towards Muslims, Buddhists, Shintoists, etc. Even as a young child, I could tell there was something wrong about judging and hating others' religions and beliefs, not because I was particularly smart or sensitive but because there are many stories of compassion and tolerance between all the war stories in the Judeo-Christian canon.

I feel my family's religious beliefs are being manipulated by the right's agenda of fear. My relatives are given stock characters and dramas in the right-wing media which reinforce a sense of moral outrage and the conclusion that punitive justice and economic systems will reward people who are good and punish those who are bad. The right vilifies Single-Mothers-On-Welfare who, they claim, destroy the family unit, are responsible for crime and violence, and are the cause of the national debt. The right wants my family to feel they are hard-working working class stiffs who have been "used" to support undeserving and lazy individuals (indeed, whole countries of undeserving and lazy individuals) who are poor and evil and not like them in any way. I see my family members feeling angry and therefore justified in not sharing. They aren't rich but they have a lot—they are plugged into the consumer culture. In this swell of the right, it is both a crime and a sin to be poor.

I once told my relatives about a radio panel discussion concerning the appeal for ordination of gays and lesbians in the United Church. As Christian fundamentalists, they would not entertain the question because their answer would instantly be "no." The radio programme was an interesting debate but I know God never spends any time wondering about this issue. God hears all religions and creeds. All languages and voices. All sexual orientations. God does not label, classify, or discriminate. Questions about who to allow in or who to keep out are immaterial. God is love, goodness, harmony, justice, and balance in nature. God can be called He, She, Creator, Higher Sentient Being, Life, or The Force, or whatever. It is of no consequence to God.

I Confess I am a Feminist . . . But a Christian
Believe me. I would rather be a Buddhist. I have Japanese friends who were raised as Buddhists, and WASP friends who have chosen Buddhism. It looks so good. It is non-judgmental, basically non-violent, and Buddhist missionaries are never on your doorstep trying to tell you what to think. I love the laughing Buddhist monks who live at the temple at the edge of the farms where I live. I love their bald heads, flowing robes, and jolly laughter when the bus is forty-five minutes late. I love the calm they radiate which comes from meditating and letting go—getting rid of the busy busy busy mind—and paying attention rather than fighting. I like the shrines of incense, bowls of rice and water, candles, and fabric. The smells and bells. The gongs. But it just isn't me. It would feel like putting on a costume. I know the Christian stories. I can sing the songs.

I say "I am a feminist . . . but I am a Christian" as a response to complex feelings I have towards my Christian fundamentalist family. They are of me and yet I am not of them. I long to belong. Yet some of their values revolt me. However, since the Church has long been a source of oppression, "God Talk" can clear a room of lefties, beatniks, and freedom fighters pretty damn quick. I have a jazz musician friend who is willing to play Christmas songs at parties "until the Christians start to puff themselves up like Cock Robin when they get to the big Jesus repertoire—it means time to go." Nor will the pentecostal/fundamentalists have any truck with any goll-durn "feminist talk" either. So I rarely stand up and make this kind of pronouncement unless I am asked.

A lot of friends have died over the past five years from various AIDS-related causes or from cancer. Of course, I wonder how God can allow this to happen. I get overwhelmed by my busy life and snap at my daughter and partner and feel guilty and spend oodles of time analyzing all of my day-to-day concerns. I often feel like a rotten mother, a terrible daughter, and an awful spouse. I obsess about myself and all my problems. I know that meditating or talking with God would help but I put it off along with the community college courses I mean to take and all the letters I should be writing. I stagger under bags of procrastination and guilt. Pointless to carry that bag around because God doesn't hold a grudge and never dumps guilt. God reaches out (just like Bell Canada) to touch me.

And God sends me messages through angels. Not every day. Usually when I least expect it—at the grocery store, on subways, even airplanes.

Once, while I was on tour as a stripper in Quebec, I got this *feeling* that I should change my ice queen policy of *never* talking to customers. The next night I implemented my new policy of being open to any and everyone who wanted to talk with me for at least fifteen minutes. Amazing people sat at my table. To confess, discuss, compare, insult, challenge, beg, share, complain, laugh, and cry. Some were psychic; some came with drugs; and some came with messages from God.

God also sends the spirits of dead friends to talk with me. Richard died under mysterious circumstances in Japan. Although he had lived in Toronto for years, his family was in New York and Haiti. The funeral was held in one of those places where I never saw the body or had that closing funeral rite. I didn't have a chance to say goodbye. A month after his death, I was trapped in bed with a broken foot wrapped in ice, unable to sleep. Finally, I napped. I dreamed that Richard was sitting at my kitchen table saying that he was okay, very comfortable, and living in a place that felt a lot like Gaspé, Québec. Richard said he was working in a kind of children's theatre company with very good people and that I mustn't worry about him any more. When I woke up, I felt a cool and damp presence swirling above the bed. It was visible but just barely. The dampness and chill were real, though. It was Richard. He swirled a few times over the bed, flew around the room, and zipped up the chimney. Bye-bye, Richard. Thank-you. I needed that.

Then there was the kind man who sat beside me on the flight to my father's funeral. I suspected he was chatting me up and buying me a drink in the hope of getting a date. But he switched gears and became a good samaritan listener (all night, it was the red-eye flight) with a patience that is the special grace of angels.

I am reaching into my cookie jar and oh—hmmmm—voila—I find purple praying hands from Sunday school with these words printed by my five-year-old fingers:

Jesus Loves the Little Children, All the Little Children of the World
Red and Yellow Black and White, All are Precious in His Sight
Jesus Loves the Little Children of the World

The quality I most loved in my father was his belief that we are all equal. This allowed him to challenge our relatives on their one-adjective-per-group view of the world as in clean Germans, drunken Indians, inscrutable Japanese, or one that affected him personally, thieving Gypsies.

I Confess My Faith in the Currency and Power of Beans

My parents were raised in Saskatchewan during what they called the Dirty Thirties and what historians call the Great Depression. They baked in the summer heat and froze in the winter blizzards. They starved. They were plagued by grasshoppers and never escaped the deadly dust of those depressed dry times. They walked miles to one-room school houses with rags tied on their feet because their families could not afford shoes. It left them with two deep feelings: faith in frugality, and the fear of the return of hard times, both of which I absorbed. Just thinking about this gives me "a feminist moment."

I am about ten. Around 1963. I am arguing with my father about my mother voting in an upcoming federal election. My father is exasperated and screaming. My frightened mother is nodding her head after his every sentence and wringing her hands. She looks like the terrified mother hen in an apron from hundreds of children's books. My father is chain-smoking the cigarettes my mother rolls and cuts by the tin every Sunday.

"A husband and a wife must vote the same," he says. "If the wife votes differently than her husband, his vote is cancelled out. Any idiot can see that. How can you be so stupid? If your mother votes NDP and I vote Conservative, I end up losing my vote. She must vote the same as me!"

I am outraged that he feels justified in possessing my mother's vote. I feel he is stealing her vote through intimidation, crooked logic, and he isn't even sorry when this is pointed out to him. Even at ten years of age, I know enough of the struggle for votes to feel totally betrayed. Betrayed by someone I love.

For many years I was angry with my mother for not defending me (and ultimately herself) during my arguments with my father about politics, values, and my campaign to be what I wanted to be (an artist) and not what he wanted me to be (a journalist). But I have come to understand and sympathize with the necessary silence of her place. I am discovering a lot about my mother (and all mothers) as motherhood and partnership reveal me to myself. I am beginning to see how her status as wife and mother was economically entrenched through her alliance with my father who ultimately could come and go in economic freedom but that she could not. Neither can I. Neither can most women.

Women earn less money than men. Divorce is wrenching, depressing, and scary. It almost always plunges a mother with children way down the economic ladder. So there is a lot of silence in that place of women where my mother lived. She was silenced by that place. It is frightening to try and move from there, but remaining in that place is also painful and scary. And unhealthy. Even for the people who try and keep us there.

Parents want their children's lives to be better than their own. I am not the patient and nurturing mom I want to be. But I have faith that if I keep trying, I will get better. Sandy, an Aboriginal mom buddy, told me that her people say healing takes seven generations. Remembering this always makes me feel better. Neither of my parents beat me, although they both came from families of terrible physical abuse. It was common in immigrant rural families during the Dirty Thirties. Through their mutual determination not to continue the cycle of beating, my parents managed to make a huge leap forward in terms of the seven generations of healing because they didn't do the easy thing (the natural thing?) of giving out what they got.

I complain about their lack of support, understanding, tolerance, and nurturing of self-esteem—but they weren't ready to do those things. It was a badge of maturity and evolution that they rose above physical abuse as the common family language. Considering where they came from and where they got to, they are much better parents than I am.

Mothering is like plumbing: if it isn't perfect you end up wading through a pile of shit. My kitchen faucet isn't quite perfect so it sprays and leaks. When I am impatient and judgmental I get a whining, defensive, and unhappy child. I need a witness here. Praise the Lord!

Kitchen Scene 7:30 a.m.

Child: I don't want to bike to school with you—I want Papa to drive me in the car!

Me: Papa has gone to work with the car. There are no buses.

Child: I want to go by car!

Me: I just explained. We cannot go by car. We can walk or bike.

Child: I want to stay home.

Me: You can't stay home. You must go to school. Mama is teaching the blind people today and you cannot come with me.

Child: I don't want to eat breakfast and I don't want to go to school.

Me (losing it while packing two backpacks, aerobics gear, audio cassettes, and lunchkits, while accidentally pulling two bike helmets onto my head from the overstuffed front closet): When I was your age, I walked three miles to school in blizzards at forty degrees below zero! Now, eat your breakfast, get dressed, and get on that bike by eight a.m. sharp or you will lose all privileges and treats for two weeks. No McDonald's either!

Child (crying): I want to go by car! Why don't you drive like other mothers? I want a new mom! I hate school! I have a stomach ache!

Me: (gritting my teeth): BE QUIET!

Child: I want to go by car!

Me: I AM GOING TO COUNT TO TEN AND I WANT TO SEE YOU EATING THAT BREAKFAST OR I WILL GIVE YOU A SMACK ON YOUR HAND!

Child: Aaaaaaaaaaaaaaaahhhhhhhhh!

Me: I am counting! One! Two! Three!

You can see where this scene is leading, right? The toilet, eh? Do I need a witness or do I need a plumber? I need to work on myself (my inner life) to become a better mother. But being poor (my usual outer life) is an obstacle to good parenting as well.

In the mid-eighties, I visited New York after an absence of ten years. I needed to see my former dance teacher whose husband had just died. She took me to a poetry nightclub. There were tons of poets dropping by all day to sign up for five-minute slots to perform/read their work that night. In the daytime, the nightclub was a neighbourhood restaurant. All the waitresses were punk gals with micro black leather minis and tattooed spiders on partially shaved heads (the other part of their heads hosted hyper-peroxided spears). Despite the death makeup and fangs, they were young and friendly. The clientele included skinny alienated white beatnik poets with ragged blue jeans and torn turtlenecks, and middle-aged black truckers from the garment district having a great time on their lunch break. The restaurant served a one-choice lunch of chicken, beans, and rice. I listened to the droning poetry/muzak and nursed a beer and felt I could see the future. Economic downturn. Existential poetry. Blue collar jobs alternating with gaps of unemployment. Beer. And beans and beans and beans and beans and beans.

Beans are power (methane gas), currency (they're cheap) and solidarity (most of the world eats beans and rice). It has been more than ten years since my New York trip and during that time I have become Queen of the Beans. I have carried my bean skills into my new life as partner and mother. And since most of us appear to be funded by the Department of Dwindling Resources, I would like to share a bean recipe with you.

Alabama Blackeyed Peas

Sauté chopped green pepper, onion, celery, and garlic in oil. Stir in 1 cup chicken stock. Add 1¹/₂ cups cooked blackeyed peas, allspice, cayenne, thyme, freshly ground black pepper. Bring to a boil and simmer. Add 1 more cup of chicken stock and ¹/₂ cup cooked brown rice. Cover. Simmer for 20 minutes. Serve with cornbread and salsa.

I Confess that I Eat My Words
It is 5:15 a.m. The beans are soaking. The bread is rising. I am writing these last snippets knowing that you, too, may be up at this time. I am making quiet little clicking sounds on my computer in the dark. I revel and despair in this domesticity and privacy. I get up early to have time for myself and yet I feel quite lonely. I feel young but the woman in the mirror is middle-aged. I want to be popular and loved but I also want to be subversive and underground. I want money but I hate the rich. These raging polarities are in me, in my body, and in the world. I want to make peace with my inner opposites and also my external opposite which I call the Right. My hope is that if I can do it, then the world can, too. I gaze at my computer screen. I type these words:
Wise Crone/Virgin Bride
Everywoman/Alternative
Warrior/Hausfrau
I print them. I eat them. The computer screen flashes to fuschia and lime green.
Something is happening. I remember reading that laughter comes of

feeling simultaneously OH YES OH NO. My screen flashes to pumpkin and cerise, then teal and red. There are whirling toasters and stars with a symphony of jungle sounds and chanting monks. Slowly, some words appear on the screen. Is this a message for my cookie jar from the constellating forces? It says:

Enter Laughing. This is the Feminist 5:15 a.m. Shift.

Balancing Rights and Responsibilities

Rachel Farahbakhsh

My name is Rachel Farahbakhsh; Rachel, known as "the mother of Israel," means "ewe" in Hebrew, and Farahbakhsh, the Persian name I adopted from my beloved husband, means "someone who brings joy." I feel my name reflects who I am trying to be. My given name draws upon my Jewish roots, and my adopted name celebrates the marriage between two cultures and two religious traditions. Khosrow and I have two small children ages one and three-and-a-half. It is our greatest wish to bring joy to their hearts and to all with whom we meet. My three-year-old daughter Carmel reminds me of this purpose daily when we share prayers together and she recites from the Bahá'í Writings: "Let your heart burn with loving kindness for all who may cross your path."

I was born in Michigan in 1963, the "caboose" of four children. My eldest brother, David, died of cancer at the age of eight before I was born, and my two remaining brothers, Jona and Windy, showered me with their love and tenderness throughout my childhood. When I was three the family moved to Toronto to further my father Irv's career as a biochemist. My mother, Helen, died three years later at forty-four of breast cancer. Sadly, I remember the Indian and Philippine housekeepers who looked after me better than I do my own mother. That lack of memory is my greatest sorrow. As I understand from the stories about her, my mother was an exceptional woman who had managed to thrive while balancing home, academic, and community life. I wish I knew her secrets. I deeply miss the experience of sharing my joys and frustrations of motherhood with my mother.

My father quickly remarried after my mother died, in spite of my best efforts to interfere with the plans and ongoing efforts to make my stepmother leave the marriage. Angela was a twenty-six-year-old who had little experience with children, especially angry seven-year-olds suffering with unexpressed grief and loss. Instead of making a long-term commitment with Angela, I suggested my father could hire another housekeeper and simply ask the employee to leave if things didn't work out. I collected cousins and friends to go and speak to my father to give him their "opinion" (which was what I had told them to say) about why the marriage with Angela was not a good idea. I was flabbergasted once I realized that their opinions, and mine, had no effect on my father's decision. Since Helen's death, my father had tended to spoil me so I couldn't believe that he was refusing to grant me this small request. To me, my reasoning was very logical. I realized my tactics had to change.

One afternoon after Angela had lightly slapped me on the leg for being rude or cheeky, I ran to my room crying, and spent the next hour pinching my leg until six o'clock when my father returned home from the lab. By the time he opened the door, anticipating the usual greeting I was known for, I had developed quite a bruise on my leg. When I greeted him with tears at the top of the stairs sobbing, "Look what she did to me!" he looked horrified and asked Angela to come talk with him in the living room. However, I wasn't able to convince my father that Angela was abusing me, so being the determined girl I was, I tried another approach. I began to try to weaken Angela's spirit. I wrote her hate letters, gave away presents she had given to me, aligned with my teenage brothers to try and eat all the food in the house. It must have been pretty unbearable for her, but to her credit she withstood our ploys. Within a year after marrying, Angela started working full-time outside the house as a CBC producer, first for television, and then for radio. I began to feel proud to have a "mom," as I began calling her so as to avoid questions, who was so articulate and accomplished. Angela devoted a tremendous amount of love and time to me, but she really won me over when she gave birth to her first child when I was eleven. I fell madly in love with little Zoë as I immersed myself in her care. It seemed as though I emptied pools of unrestrained emotion on this beautiful baby; nurturing Zoë soothed my own loss of Helen's nurturing.

From the time Zoë was born, I realized how intensely I enjoyed playing with children. I remember being told that I was "gifted" in this area and took pride in this since Helen's mother Charlotte had devoted her adult life to studying child development. I was always proud of her achievements, but I puzzled over the irony that her academic and community involvement prevented her from raising her own children. I knew to satisfy my own needs, my husband and I would raise our own.

A distinct childhood memory of my father was his love for world news. I still catch myself at times humming the march which leads into the BBC news report. I heard it every morning blaring from the bathroom as he prepared for work. Stacks of *The Globe and Mail* lined our back porch, and he would watch the evening news habitually. My father was acutely aware of world politics, but he rarely ventured into the political area himself. "The world is a crazy place!" I would hear him mutter as he walked down the stairs from the TV room. I remember telling him that I was not going to watch world events unfold from the sidelines. He offered his best wishes, never doubting that whatever I wanted to accomplish would become my future.

After the age of thirteen, I was perpetually involved with global-minded work. I saw myself as a relatively rich and well-educated person whose good fortune was attended by great responsibility for the welfare of my many impoverished cousins, especially in the developing world. I was determined to integrate the concept of a great global family into my own identity. I always remember feeling completely at ease familiarizing myself with various cultures; perhaps that was the greatest gift all the housekeepers gave me. My search for a worldwide community certainly stemmed from the fact that as a family, we did not belong to any defined groups or spiritual organizations. My father always said he was not a "joiner," and his childhood experience attending his neighbourhood synagogue proved to him that organized religion countered reason and often was hypocritical, ignoring the spirit of the sacred teachings. His need for belonging was satisfied by the international scientific community; my need to be part of a vibrant, diverse group committed to the welfare of humanity was not. Consequently, I became increasingly committed to raising my own global awareness. I spent my high school and university years performing services for many international organizations, as well as organizing public speakers series. My focus was to provide students with speakers who could present personal accounts of international events. Inevitably the discussions would question what role a student could play to assist in any situation. I felt this work was my education, and ultimately it allowed me to reach the goal of my desire: an international spiritual community.

The feeling of being a citizen of the world jelled for me during a summer seminar after my third year at Mount Allison University. I was in Thailand with World University Services of Canada (WUSC). This wasn't the first time I had the opportunity to travel; in fact that was all I did with the money I would save from summer jobs, *et cetera*. This trip, however, was unique; I had never before travelled to the Far East, never been in a place so far removed from my own Judeo-Christian-North American experience.

One early morning I was alone in a market in northeast Thailand watching women and their children set up their wares on wicker mats and tables in the village square. Babies were strapped to their mothers' backs while the women displayed woven crafts, began cooking delicacies on simple hibachis, and set out produce. I sat under a flight of stairs and watched as mothers fed children with one hand while serving a customer with another. Although I understood very little of what was said around me and my mind rebelled at the thought of eating the steamed grasshoppers I noticed in one pot, I felt very connected with these women, and knew that we shared much in common. They were nurturing families while farming, vending, socializing, being artisans. I don't think I fully understood what I witnessed until I became a mother years later—internationally, women act to hold families, communities, and economies together.

When I returned from Thailand, I continued my work in the student council at Mount Allison University. Nineteen eighty-five had been declared "International Year of Peace" by the United Nations. As part of the "external affairs department," we asked students to submit material for an evening to commemorate the anniversary of the United Nations and to celebrate the theme of that year. In honour of the occasion, the local Bahá'í community approached me to see if a new student who had recently escaped from Iran would be able to read excerpts from, "A Bahá'í Statement on Peace" addressed to "The Peoples of the World." I had been in contact with the Bahá'í community the year before when one member had presented an update on the persecution of Bahá'ís in Iran in the public speakers series I organized. At the time, I had been struck by the graciousness of the individuals I had met, although as my father had taught, I still carried with me a healthy suspicion of any organized religion and its possible hidden agendas.

I agreed to meet with the student with the unpronounceable name and go over the excerpts he chose to read. During that meeting my heart melted as we read together: "Whether peace is to be reached only after unimaginable horrors precipitated by humanity's stubborn clinging to old patterns of behaviour, or is to be embraced now by an act of consultative will, is the choice before all who inhabit the earth." The "Bahá'í Statement on Peace" discussed true human nature not as aggressive but noble. It described the evolution of humanity analogous to the passing stages of infancy and childhood in the lives of the individual members. Reassuringly, our present age is described as "turbulent adolescence approaching its long awaited coming of age." The statement discussed various prerequisites to peace including recognition of the oneness of humankind, the establishment of equality between men and women, and the elimination of prejudice. It outlined the barriers to peace such as the dangers of unbridled nationalism, the inordinate disparity between rich and poor, prejudice, and religious strife. The material was empowering, uplifting, and it made sense. Near the end of the statement we read: "We hold firmly the conviction that all human beings have been created to carry forward an ever-advancing civilization . . . and that the virtues that befit human dignity are trustworthiness, forbearance, mercy, compassion and loving kindness towards all peoples."

I came home to talk with my roommate after that meeting a little stunned. I had been raised to think that religious teachings suffocated individual thought, that they held little relevance for the needs of today, that logic and spirituality could not co-exist, and that faith was for weak-minded individuals. In fact, this had been confirmed to me the previous summer when I had worked on a kibbutz and visited orthodox Jewish communities in Israel. As much as I had been drawn to the melodious prayers and the disciplined rigorous study, the rigidity and the isolation of the religious communities took me back to the Middle Ages; it contained little relevance for me. Now, in a small town in New Brunswick, my understanding of faith was widening. As much as I tried to resist, I began to feel that my inner spiritual thirst was being quenched. Since there is no clergy in the Bahá'í Faith, and one of the tenets of the Faith is "individual investigation of truth," I started reading. To my delight, I found principles I had always known to be true. In the same way Christianity emerged from Judaism, the Bahá'í Faith emerged from Islam. Though the Bahá'í Faith is an independent religion in the sense that its founder defined new laws and renewed spiritual teachings, one of the basic tenets is that all faiths originate from the same source, from one God, and form a spiritual continuum, leading humanity to its destiny: a peaceful world.

The poetry of the Bahá'í Writings, intertwined with the spiritual teachings, warmly embraced me, especially the Writings about women and equality. They described humanity as a bird with two wings: one male, the other female. When one wing is less developed than the other, the bird cannot fly (or alternatively travels in endless circles). Humanity will never reach its potential as a peaceful and prosperous global society until equality is firmly established.

As I began to ask Khosrow (the Persian student whose name I finally learned to pronounce) more about the teachings of the Faith and how he applied them to his own personal and community life, I became intrigued with the challenge of striving for those high ideals on a daily level as a personal commitment to developing world peace. I was struck to find out that backbiting was considered the "most great sin" since it was divisive, and the negative effect lasted "well near a century." I was overjoyed to find out that the principle of equality was an integral part of the Bahá'í Faith. The Writings specify that if a family is forced to choose between the education of a son or a daughter, the daughter would always take precedence. Since mothers are the first educators of children, educating women is a priority. Khosrow's grandfather had followed this principle and consequently, Khosrow's mother in Iran was the first woman in her village to attend high school.

Before I knew it, after many moonlit walks down the country roads in Sackville discussing religion and science, the existence and nature of God, philosophy and religion, I surprised myself and started asking my new friend about the Bahá'í approach to marriage. I hadn't thought about marriage seriously before, and certainly never imagined I would entertain the idea with someone I had not even known for a month. Within the next two weeks we both knew that, parents willing, we would eventually marry. One of the Bahá'í laws is that parents must give their consent for marriage. The purpose of this is to maintain unity within the family, as well as provide the parents with the opportunity to assist in one of their children's most important life decisions. Irv was understandably shocked when I called about my sudden plan to marry an Iranian Bahá'í whom he knew nothing about. He asked us to wait for at least a year until he was more comfortable with Khosrow: his aspirations, his background, and his faith.

At the time I was upset that he didn't trust my choice and thought he was being over-protective, but in retrospect he clearly made a wise choice. By the time of our wedding, Angela and Irv were rejoicing as much as we were. In the spring, I graduated from university with a degree in international development and Khosrow graduated with his certificate in engineering. Soon after, we married in Irv and Angela's garden in Ontario. In the fall, we moved to Halifax. Khosrow was working towards a degree in chemical/environmental engineering, and I felt I needed more practical skills, so I pursued a diploma in nursing.

As a young newly-married couple, we were energetic and had time to do everything. We tutored at the Native Friendship Centre, organized regional Bahá'í youth camps, and had endless youth gatherings at our house which we shaped in and around our studying schedules. Becoming consumed with the needs of others, we learned that we also needed privacy to devote time to nurturing our new union. I talked too much and didn't allow Khosrow the chance to verbalize his thoughts in his second tongue. Khosrow had to learn to express his feelings before they boiled over. I had to stop rationalizing his emotions and recognize when his feelings were hurt. Most importantly, however, we had to learn how to consult and make personal choices together as a unit. For me, that was the greatest challenge. It took a long time to realize that decisions I made about allocating my time affected both of us as a family. I had, and still do in a sense, a tendency to devote myself to whatever I am doing at the expense of my other responsibilities. We are maturing as a couple as we think less about satisfying our own needs in isolation. No choice is made in a vacuum. Inherent in our struggles, I felt incredibly blessed and thankful that Khosrow and I were companions, that there was great energy in our union.

The first big project we embarked upon started very small. In early summer the next year, we were picking strawberries with a group of five close friends and in the car ride home I remember feeling that as a group of Bahá'í youth (we were still fairly young then) we had a tremendous amount to offer humanity. We talked about it and decided that night to organize a youth conference in which participants would be empowered to realize their potential as peacemakers within their own community. We decided to call ourselves "Metro Youth for Global Unity" (MYGU) and the conference "Building World Peace by Piece." We decided that we would focus upon two prerequisites for peace outlined in the Bahá'í peace statement: equality of men and women, and the recognition of the oneness of humanity. As youth, we embodied that wonderful capacity to become excited with a vision without letting material barriers interfere. The conference was held at Dalhousie University on a weekend in September. We had no idea how many would attend, and were pleasantly surprised with the turnout from a variety of religious, cultural, and educational backgrounds.

Following the conference, with a swelling MYGU membership, we brainstormed about possible local projects we could initiate to carry forth the spirit of the weekend. We had been inspired by a Brazilian peace project that had collected soil from various countries and layered the samples in a glass tower with the inscription, "The world is one country and mankind its citizens." We decided to write to every country in the world, via their embassies, inviting them to contribute to the construction of a peace pavilion. We requested that every country send us a rock and a brick from a place of significance; the rock was to symbolize the earth we all share and the brick was to symbolize the ability to shape our collective future. The first letters were sent in March 1990, and by July the first rock arrived, turning our dream into a reality.

Turkey sent an engraved brick and rock from Gallipoli, the site of the devastating World War I battle, but now a place where the former adversaries meet annually to celebrate increased economic and cultural ties. The same day the piece from Turkey arrived the Mayor of Dartmouth called us to offer an exquisite waterfront site upon which to build the pavilion. By the time of the opening ceremonies of the G-7 Economic Summit in June 1995, seventy countries had contributed collectively thousands of years of history to a shared vision of the need for world peace.

In many ways the peace pavilion was our first baby; we were completely absorbed with the project and would offer anything of ourselves to assist its development. Our home held the meetings and the precious rocks as they arrived. My nursing salary and Khosrow's scholarships covered the costs of postage, phone calls, et cetera. I spent hours on my days off writing individual letters to various embassies which requested more information, and publicizing and promoting the group and the project among the various youth groups in the city. I came home one day elated and exhausted. Khosrow asked me what I planned to do when I became a mother: would I become so absorbed in other projects that I would neglect our childrens' needs? I remember reflecting on the question and realizing, no, the children would absorb me. But

Khosrow had brought up an ongoing issue; we needed to ensure our family time remained sacred and was not divvied up for other people or causes. In the midst of our community work, we needed to assist each other to reach our full potential as well as helping our marriage to grow.

As two of the founding members of MYGU, our intense involvement in the project fell in both different and overlapping spheres of work; ultimately the division of labour taught us both a great deal about the interconnectedness of all efforts focussed upon accomplishing a shared goal. Being the most easily accessible with my nursing schedule, I became the co-ordinator and spokesperson for the group while Khosrow spent hours on behind-the-scenes work for the project. Because I was in the public eye, I tasted the uncomfortable feeling of receiving excessive credit for the project while Khosrow received little. Ironically, this reversal of traditional roles heightened for us the need to honour all the valuable efforts offered to help the success of any project; the final performance as well as the unnoticed drudgery behind the scenes.

After working as a caseroom nurse in the maternity hospital for four years, I had no interest in returning to work in a hospital setting once I had given birth to our daughter Carmel. My intense love for her began at conception and grew daily. As much as I enjoyed assisting women give birth, I knew I could easily be replaced as a nurse, but no one could replace me as mother to my child. I knew the profound amount of nurturing I wanted to offer Carmel would be for the both of us. My sense of deprivation over the loss of my own mother filled me with a deep need to give my children my time. For me this is an inherent part of mothering: helping our children bring out the best in their potential. I honestly cannot think of a better way to channel my energy. The Bahá'í Writings confirm that conviction: "O ye loving mothers, know that in God's sight the best of all ways to worship is to educate the children and train them in all the perfections of humankind, and no nobler deed than this can be imagined."

I used to cry for joy nursing Carmel, thanking God for such a beautiful, healthy child and the opportunity to cherish such a miracle. Carmel's rhythm became my rhythm, her needs became my needs. My purpose as an individual had become to nurture this little newborn whom I loved with a kind of intensity that I didn't know I was capable of expressing. I wanted to envelop her with love, security, support, and trust; to share every step of growth with her, each one a cause for celebration. I wanted to carry her all the time, to sing or pray to her every waking moment. I remember feeling that I didn't want to miss the feel of her warm head under my chin and the perfect fit of her foot in the palm of my hand. For at least two months my sense of joy and responsibility overwhelmed me. Thankfully, during this daze, Khosrow was not yet employed, having just finished his Masters. Together we muddled through housework and meals while being captivated by our daughter.

After two months of this family retreat, former responsibilities began to regain importance—namely, the pressing work for the pavilion. I finally could begin to digest the significance of the most recent contributions. The Czech Republic had sent a piece from Lidice, a village destroyed by Nazi Germany. The Slovak Republic had sent a plaque especially designed for the pavilion made out of melted down ammunition, remnants of the Slovak national uprising. By October 1992, the project began to feel increasingly urgent, as powerful reminders of history were collecting around our coffee table.

Rocks and responsibilities associated with the project presented themselves sporadically over the first two years of Carmel's life. I made a conscious effort to incorporate her into the peace pavilion work, and luckily it wasn't very demanding or time-consuming. She would help me open the parcels of rocks as they arrived, come with me when I gave school presentations about the project, and sit on my back during radio interviews. As she grew too large for the backpack, she would even assist me with school presentations, passing around the smaller rocks and telling people about her favourite one, "the pink one!" (Despite Carmel's love for camping, snakes, climbing, and swimming she would do anything to have a Barbie wrapped in pink satin. We differ. I am repulsed by the "girl" section of the toy department and Carmel is drawn to it like a magnet. Consequently, we stick to second-hand stores.)

We sustained the project by continuing to write letters to the various countries (we had done six mass mail-outs to embassies) and began to develop the design for the pavilion with a volunteer architect. However, the pace of the project had slowed down considerably. I was immersed in the challenges of raising an active toddler and Khosrow's job demanded that he travel extensively in the Maritimes. After becoming pregnant with our second child, we realized that if we didn't consider the project pressing then, it would never be completed. MYGU started meeting more regularly again during the summer of 1994 to discuss fundraising, recruiting more members, and a schedule for completion of the pavilion. As my due date approached I became more anxious, realizing that post-partum I probably wouldn't have the energy to organize the enormous amount of work that had to be done. I had no idea under what circumstances that work would be completed.

Just weeks before the delivery of our second child, we were approached by a local architectural firm that was developing a plan for the Dartmouth Waterfront. For us, the exciting part of the project was that they wanted to incorporate the peace pavilion into the plan and try to complete it by the G-7 Economic Summit—only six months away. The architects had received city council's approval in principle and the firm quickly began to develop conceptual drawings. Funding was tentative, but the pavilion was closer than ever to completion.

Days before the delivery of our second child, I went through a different kind of "nesting syndrome." I had finished washing all of the diapers and sleepers, baby toys, snugli and mobiles, and found myself making appointments with the Mayor, our Member of Parliament, and the Premier to confirm the funding that would ensure the completion of the pavilion. I felt a tremendous sense of urgency, and as I stood in the Mayor's office on my due date, I think she did too—she knew the history of my precipitous labour and wanted me out of there before my membranes ruptured! From my experience with Carmel I knew that I wouldn't have energy for the project for at least six weeks post-partum. I wanted reassurance that I had done all I could to ensure the growing momentum of the project before I retreated into the joys of becoming a new mother again. But at this point the project had a momentum of its own, well beyond the power of individual intervention.

Thankfully Isaiah was not born in the Mayor's office, but decided to wait until early morning when Khosrow was home to drive us to the hospital. I didn't make it to the bed, but delivered him in a room where he could receive the immediate assistance he required after such a precipitous delivery. My labour was so fast that I didn't have time to receive pain medication. I'll never forget the sensations associated with his birth. The intensity of the labour was like being carried away by the force of a raging ocean that I was powerless to resist. I remember thinking that the force which was propelling Isaiah out of me was the same force that centuries of women had experienced; this reassured and comforted me. Even though poor Isaiah looked swollen and bruised after his abrupt entrance, he of course was the most beautiful boy I had ever set eyes on.

At home again, assuring Carmel that she was still deeply loved while caring for Isaiah, myself, and my husband was a great juggling act. I didn't have the same family support after Isaiah's birth as we had enjoyed with the birth of Carmel. For Carmel's birth, my family had come from England, and my husband was conveniently unemployed. For Isaiah's birth in the middle of winter, no family could attend and Khosrow had to return to work after a week. I remember feeling so fragile and raw; I missed my mother intensely and truly mourned her for the first time. My tears were for both joy and grief—the blessedness of life and the pain of loss.

About six weeks following Isaiah's birth, we received a phone call from City Hall. The proposal to develop the waterfront had been officially accepted and the City had held a competition for the tendering of the project. We met the architect, Robert Parker, in the second week of March, and from then the project sped like lightning. Since he had never heard of the project, we wanted to clarify for him the fundamental purpose and spirit of the pavilion. We wanted to ensure that he understood that the pavilion was to be a symbol of the unity of the human family. The rocks and bricks had to be displayed in a way which demonstrated their interconnectedness yet also accentuated their exquisite diversity. The pavilion needed to be a reflective, quiet space as well as a place groups could meet for events inspired by the testimony of global co-operation displayed in front of them. We wanted visitors to feel the power of a shared vision for peace echoed by over seventy countries around the world. A quotation from the Bahá'í Writings was to be inscribed over the rocks and bricks: "Let Your Vision Be World Embracing."

To meet the G-7 deadline, Robert Parker, the architect, had to design the pavilion in five days. He asked to have time alone with the rocks and bricks which when lined up spread sixty feet. This meant that the collection had to be moved from our basement to a City Hall storage room. Khosrow spent hours preparing the rocks to leave their adopted "home" in their best condition. That night we laughed about the Great Wall of China arriving in B.C. and how after numerous phone calls on our end, Air Canada graciously agreed to send it to us without charge. This led to another recollection of the 220 pounds of the Berlin Wall which arrived via military attaché in Labrador and was generously transported to Halifax by Air Nova. Another 220-pound contribution, from Brunei-Darussalam, had been seized for two weeks by Canadian customs to verify that the pieces were pure sandstone. We caressed some of the smaller pieces: the head of the pre-Colombian gavel from Mexico which like a baby's foot, fit perfectly in the palm of my hand; the sea shells from Antigua; the vial of sand from Singapore; volcanic rock from Mount Kilimanjaro; and a bottle of volcanic ash from Mount Pinatubo.

For the next three weeks I spent weekday mornings at the City Hall offices with other MYGU members faxing every embassy information about the G-7 ceremonies, and to the countries that had not yet sent anything, a final invitation. The G-7 office wanted to ensure the participation of those seven countries whose Ministers would be dedicating the pavilion. Three days before the event, the goal was finally accomplished. Isaiah was with me during this faxing frenzy; being in the snugli, he accompanied me to all of the meetings. Less than six months old, he was easy to care for.

Carmel and Khosrow bore the brunt of these efforts. Carmel would spend each morning visiting friends young and old who offered to take care of her while I was busy. For the first time in her life she was being shuttled from place to place. I knew she was feeling neglected when I heard her say to her dolls one morning after lining them all up, "I'm going out to work on the peace pavilion. We just got a rock from Zambia and it's very important. See you later!" Besides not being available for her, I was usually tense while shuttling her around trying to meet appointments on time, and certainly less patient overall as I tried to cope with all the demands. Under the pressure, my expectations of this three-year-old became outrageous: I had no tolerance for unco-opera- tive behaviour; I expected a child who would listen to my requests once and follow them. If she didn't, I would grab her arm, something I had never done before, glare into her eyes and hiss, "Listen to me!" I remember her saying to me one morning during our morning prayers, "This is a prayer for you, Maman," and she recited: "O God guide me, protect me, illumine the lamp of my heart, and make me a brilliant star, Thou art the Mighty and Powerful." Tears swelled in my eyes. In my heart, I implored God to forgive my impatience and to give me the ability to mother her with more wisdom. I thanked Carmel and apologized. I told her I would try more diligently to live that prayer.

In early April my mother-in-law arrived. She was like an angel. She cooked and cleaned and took care of Carmel three mornings a week as

MYGU colleagues and I worked. Even with the help of City Planning staff, the load was overwhelming for all of us. I knew that with the exciting pace and fast developments of the project, I was becoming very neglectful of my duties as a mother and a wife. It hit home like a dagger when Khosrow reminded me that his mother was not a cleaning lady and he was not able to be unconditionally supportive while I seemed consumed with the project.

I felt sick. On the one hand I felt that I was the only one who could do the bulk of this high-pressured work during this short, intense period. On the other hand, Khosrow was right; I had become consumed with being in the limelight, while at the same time I was distancing myself from other priorities. It was a call for my ego to deflate. To add insult to injury, a close friend mentioned that Carmel was not as courteous as she once was. I remember feeling the painful irony of working on a peace pavilion while my family relationships which I valued so highly were disintegrating. The next month I decided to work from home, but for poor Carmel this was probably a mixed blessing.

All day the phone would ring as embassies, news reporters, G-7 organizers, and politicians called for their hundred different reasons. I never knew who was on the other end or if Carmel would beat me to the phone. And there was always the threat that Isaiah would decide to start screaming at an inappropriate time. This happened one morning when the Premier called to ask about the progress of the project, and just as I picked up the phone, Isaiah began howling. I was grateful that the Premier graciously agreed to call me back in a few minutes and wondered if his good humour came partly from having seven children of his own. When the same thing happened again while speaking to the High Commissioner of the Jamaican embassy, I was sure that we had lost our credibility as an organization. We were pleasantly surprised when a wonderful piece from Jamaica arrived a month later. The High Commissioner must have been a mother as well.

My favourite question asked was, "Is your office still open?" as the callers would be subjected to the sound of the washing machine, or dishwasher, or supper cooking. When the Mayor's office called one day, I picked up the phone just in time to hear, "Hi! What's your name? My name is Carmel." Trapped, I put on my professional voice and asked Carmel to please go and stick her glow-in-the dark stickers inside her closet as any responsible assistant would do. Luckily, she seemed happy enough with the request to leave me alone on the phone.

When the opening ceremonies finally took place in the middle of June, the celebration felt like a royal garden wedding. The grounds were packed with expectant school children and citizens waiting to catch a glimpse of the leaders. Khosrow had written a speech to be read for the Foreign Ministers, but at the eleventh hour decided I should read it, since all the Ministers were men. By the end of the week I was overloaded; all I wanted to do was hide.

For at least two weeks after the project was over, I felt numb. I didn't want to talk to anybody or discuss anything but be with my children and husband. Leading up to the dedication, Khosrow's engineering work had been very demanding, so he too was exhausted. We needed healing time together, time to reconnect, to be private, to feed the needs of the family unit, to nurture our union. Immediately after the project was finished, I wanted nothing more than to create a quiet, slow-paced family life. I didn't want to take on any responsibilities which would take me away from that refuge; I was basking in the joys of being with the children again. Later that summer my brothers and their families visited Nova Scotia, so thankfully our children were doted on even more than usual.

The fall and winter was devastating for all the family. My father's stomach pains led to a diagnosis of cancer. Within two months he died. I travelled with the children three times to England during that time period. It was draining for everybody. Again we retreated from the larger world around us. The winter allowed for intense mourning, reflection, and finally, preparation for resurgence.

With the onset of spring, I began to feel I was gaining some of my energy back. I was ready to start giving beyond the family again, but at a slower pace and in a more balanced fashion. My youthful energy had been replaced by a need to know my limits. I began to give weekly school presentations, often at the pavilion itself, often accompanied by Carmel. I started developing educational material to complement the display in the pavilion and in the evenings at home I began writing a children's story, as well as offering to serve on the board of "Peacemakers," the Bahá'í children's classes.

The beauty of my involvement now is that I both enjoy it and can manage the pace. I can maintain a balance without becoming impatient, can make sure that the children and I spend stimulating time together, learn new prayers, that we eat relatively well, and the house is . . . at least welcoming. Khosrow and I have time to consult together in the evenings about the children's needs (as we pick up all the dumped toys) and how we plan to meet them. We have time to discuss other family plans for the future. We are learning how to live up to our name—to bring joy to each other's hearts.

As I have grown, so has my understanding of feminism. I feel feminism is a dynamic, multi-faceted concept that evolves and develops as humanity evolves and develops; ultimately feminism has as many different meanings as individual women express. For me, feminism means striving to reach one's potential within the context of one's family, local and ultimately global community while encouraging others, including children, to do likewise. My faith teaches that we will not achieve world peace until "women participate fully and equally in the affairs of the world." Intertwined with this mandate is the common thread that connects women around the world: the life-giving gift of bearing and educating humanity. I have always felt that amongst all the individuals we encounter, the people who we will influence most in our lifetime will be our own children; they will be the next generation of peacemakers. For me, balancing the two responsibilities is the greatest challenge women face.

Letter to a Graduate Student

Ursula Franklin

Dear Marcia,

A few months ago, you came to me to talk about your future. Should you, a feminist and a graduate student in science, embark on a doctoral program in a physics–related field? Is not the gulf between the goals of a scientist and the goals of a feminist too great to be bridged, within one person who wants to live in peace with herself?

We talked for a long time and I spoke a lot about my friend Maggie Benston and how her life and work illuminates your questions and helps to answer them. Yet, after you had left, I felt uneasy. Did my argument for not giving up on science make sense to you? Was I able to give you an idea of the nature of Maggie's pioneering contribution and of her, a vibrant woman and an original thinker and doer?

Now I want to return to our conversation and pick up on three strands that ran through our talk. You asked about Maggie as a person—what made her tick? Why did she have such a strong influence on people's understanding of the technological world around us? What does her life's contribution mean for young women like yourself?

For me, the uniqueness of Maggie lies largely in the unity of her life. She wasn't a scholar or an academic on Monday, Wednesday, and Friday, a unionist on Tuesday and Thursday, a member of the Women's Movement on the weekend and an environmentalist when on vacation. She was all of these—and more—at the same time. Each of her activities was rooted in the same soil, each aspect of her life was linked to and informed by all other aspects of her being. The pattern-setting force in her life was her belief in the possibility and practicality of a feminist, egalitarian, and non-oppressive society. Whatever Maggie did, as well as what she did not do, must be understood as a direct consequence of that belief.

People have often commented on how few hang-ups Maggie seemed to have. As I recall, she did not spend much time agonizing about joining a particular demonstration or supporting a struggling solidarity group—her response was quickly derived from her general standpoint, the place where her life was anchored. Once her basic position, that *patriarchy or hierarchy is not an option*, had been taken, daily hang-ups faded into the background. Much strength flows from a fundamental decision not to accept the rules of an alien convention. There is the liberating effect of declared non-conformity, the joy of sharing and following one's own conviction, the lack of inner contradiction. A lot of creative energy becomes available when the internal conflicts have been eliminated. Indeed, I feel that the great influence that Maggie asserted on so many people sprung directly from the qualities of her own life—its inner consistency, its openness and rootedness in a feminist vision.

By the way, Marcia, don't overlook the trap here. In dress and lifestyle, demeanor and politics, Maggie stressed her ordinariness—she was just like everybody else. Don't let this fool you. Maggie was in many ways quite extraordinary and exceptional, not the least for her ability to integrate the ordinary and the extraordinary into one seamless life. Maggie's theory and practice were inextricably linked and she would joyfully deny the existence of a tactical boundary between them.

Her two major theoretical papers were the fruits of considerable search and research. *The Political Economy of Women's Liberation*, published in 1969, had an instantaneous impact on feminist debate. When *Feminism and the Critique of the Scientific Method* appeared in 1982, Maggie had been at Simon Fraser University in Vancouver for fifteen years and held a cross-appointment in the Departments of Chemistry and Computer Science. Although the latter paper did not have the same immediate impact as the earlier work, it became a central contribution in the debate on the nature of science and on the intrinsic limitations of the scientific method. You will be familiar with this rich discourse on the social and political structuring of knowledge, to which feminists have added so many fresh insights.

For me, the importance of Maggie's work was two-fold. In the first place she explored, explained, and illuminated the notion of science in all its aspects. Secondly, she drew practical consequences from what she and others found, and acted upon them in her own work.

In her critique of the scientific method Maggie dissected, like a good anatomist, the concepts and practices of science using feminist and socialist analysis as her instruments. Looking at science as a social and political structure, she found it wanting, as she had found economic systems wanting when she critiqued the political economy of women's liberation. She then laid bare for all to see the postulates and assumptions, the methods of work and the internal reasoning within the enterprise of science.

This pedagogy of understanding is embedded in all of Maggie's work. It challenges the core assumptions of scientific practices—that there exists an orderly, objective material reality separate from and independent of an observer; that the material world is knowable through rational inquiry, which is independent of the individual characteristics of the observer; that knowledge of the material world is gained through measurement of natural phenomena and can be reduced to some form of mathematical description; and, finally, that the goal of scientific understanding is the ability to predict and control natural phenomena, a postulate that tends to equate science with power.

By interweaving her analysis with the insights of other feminist scholars, notably Ruth Hubbard and Marian Lowe, Maggie exposed the double myth of the objectivity and neutrality of the scientific method, pointing out the inherent limitations that the methods of science place on the scope of any scientific inquiry. The impact of reductionism, this pre-ordaining of certain variables as being more important or indicative than others, is an important focus of the pedagogy of understanding. Maggie agreed with Ruth Hubbard, who challenged the role of scientists as socially-sanctioned "fact-makers" in *The Politics of Women's Biology*.

And Maggie had definite thoughts on the impact of reductionism and bias in scientific practices, which will be of special interest to you, Marcia. On the notion of side effects, for example, she believed that there are no "side effects," only effects. She found a good example in the birth control pill, pointing out that suppression of ovulation is one of its effects, while another is a change in blood chemistry that may make blood clotting more likely. A less distorted methodology would not dismiss this second effect as lightly as does present medical science.

In speaking of *present science* and *present technology*, Maggie referred to the methodology and practice of science and technology as it is practiced *now*. She believed "that ultimately feminist and other critiques would lead to a quite different conception of what science can be." Maggie never gave up on science; she advocated a different science, one in which women and feminists "must begin to deal with the science and technology that shape our lives and even our bodies." She believed that women have long been the objects of a bad science and must become the makers of a new one. Quoting Ruth Hubbard, she wrote:

> What is needed in such a new science is, first of all, a sense of the limits of the appropriateness of reductionism and the development of a methodology which can deal with complex systems "that flow so smoothly and gradually or are so profoundly interwoven in their complexities that they can not be broken up into measurable units without losing or changing their fundamental nature." Difficult as this may be in practice, its very adoption as a goal must mean a major change in scientific methodology.

And this is precisely what she did in all her own projects and studies. She conducted scientific or technical studies using new and different methodologies reflecting her own different values. The fact that these studies had realistic goals and practical results—be they new designs of computer networks or a novel way of automating clerical work—should not camouflage the emergence of radically different methodologies. Please, Marcia, don't let the down-to-earth attributes of Maggie's projects blind you to their *theoretical* importance; each one is an experiment, testing the methodologies of a new contextual science.

Vividly imagining the new and cultivating constructive dreaming were important to Maggie. Did you know that she had a great deal of interest in science fiction and in utopias, particularly in the feminist ones? She taught several courses on utopias, emphasizing their different sciences and knowledge structures as well as their novel social relationships. Her 1988 paper on "Feminism and System Design: Questions of Control" begins with reflections on Marge Piercy's utopian novel *Women on the Edge of Time*. For Maggie, science fiction and utopian writing provided a space where the social and the scientific imagination could meet and play. Had she lived longer, she might well have written in this genre, too.

But now I must return to your initial question, whether there is a place for a young feminist in science. My answer is clearly, "yes," although you and other women should understand the political and social structure of present science and technology and try to become equipped to deal with this reality. However, this need for an understanding of the political and social structure of the enterprise in which one invests one's labour is not required only from those who prepare for work in science and technology. If you were to go into law or medicine, social work or architecture, the same questions about assumptions and paradigms would exist, although some disciplines might be more prepared to face such queries than is present science and its practitioners. Maggie certainly was not prepared to give up her participation in the practice of science or technology. In "Marxism, Science and Workers' Control," she said quite explicitly: "In general, I don't want to be understood as being "anti-rational" or "anti-science." What I argue is that it is necessary to recognize the problems inherent in the present practice of science." And, she could have added, do something about it.

Let me assure you, Marcia, that I know how constrained the choices for graduate students in terms of research subjects and supervision have become in these tough times. Yet there are choices and they have to be made with care. Choose your supervisors, if you can, for their human qualities; you must be able to respect them, even when you have to disagree with them. To me, considerations of human substance are of greater importance than the selection of a sub-discipline.

Among the research areas open to you, choose, if at all possible, one that has been neglected because of the very biases Maggie discussed. The field of solid state physics presents a good example. We have seen how fifty years of concentrated research has yielded a very complex and complete body of knowledge related to the interaction of solid inorganic materials, radiation and currents of any kind. Without this body of knowledge there would be no semiconductors, no microchips, no fibre optics—you name it. Now compare this situation with the very small body of uncertain information regarding the interaction between living organic solids—blood, tissue, cells or bone—and the same currents and radiation. Isn't it amazing how little research effort and attention the organic materials have attracted?

Unquestionably, the experimental context is more complicated and "messy" for organic materials, i.e., less amiable to reductionist simplification. But most problems look complicated and messy until one has a conceptual handle on them. You may want to ask yourself whether the neglect of this research area could have a political component. The beneficiaries of the neglected sub-field would likely be, in the main, "mere" people, while the present solid state knowledge has yielded enormous industrial and military benefits. Here is clearly an area of inquiry that is crying out for the new methodologies, for new forms of collaboration and data gathering. Try to associate yourself with those who worry about such neglected fields, as Maggie always did.

Let me also urge you not to forget how much joy the study of science can give. The world in which we live is rich and full of wonder and beauty, as Rachel Carson so often said. Can you recall the feeling of sheer joy when you grasped for the first time the underlying reasons for the regularity of the periodic table of elements or the nature of crystallographic transformations? I certainly can, and even now, almost fifty years after my Ph.D., I still find microscopic examinations of samples a joyful and wonderful activity.

There is the joy of mastery and understanding (not at all unique to scientific studies), the pleasure of seeing patterns emerging where none were seen before, the elegance of a fresh mathematical approach. All these treasures are there, and should not become invisible because of the shadows cast by the over-reach and over-application of *present* science and technology.

Yes, you may say, all this is fine and good, but what about the "chilly climate"? Good question! I do acknowledge that the structurally and—at times—personally unfriendly environment deters young women from planning research careers in a scientific or technical field. Yet, as a feminist, you are less vulnerable than young women who have no understanding of the social and political structures of science and technology, and who might still fall for the myth of the objectivity and neutrality of science and technology.

You may think that I am joking, but let me give you my argument: first and foremost, don't check your feminism at the laboratory door; it is an important layer of the coat of inner security that will protect you from the chilly climate. As your values will be questioned constantly—implicitly and explicitly—you will depend for your sanity on an ongoing rootedness in the women's community.

Take the time to keep involved in women's issues and don't ever believe that you are "the only woman in. . . . " Likely you are not, just as I have never been. Wherever men work, there are women working, usually for much lower pay. You may well be the only female doctoral student in a particular group, but what about the secretaries, the cleaning staff, the librarians or the technicians? You may link up with them and gain their support and friendship. As you watch over the safety and well-being of others, your own will take care of itself and the chilly climate will warm up a bit.

Don't become petrified by rank. Only hierarchy pulls rank; as feminists, we see rank as the institutional equivalent of a postal code, not as a figure of merit. In other words, rank or title tells of people's sphere of work and responsibility, not that—by definition—they know more or know better than those of lower rank or title.

Remember also that what is morally wrong and unjust is, in the end, also dysfunctional—a point Maggie made often. All the advanced science and technology for war has not brought peace to anyone. All the advanced systems of oppression have not brought security to their owners. As a motto for her paper on technology as language, Maggie used a line from a postcard of the International Women's Tribune Centre: "If it's not appropriate for women, it's not appropriate"—a good phrase to remember.

And finally, when the going is tough and you feel yourself surrounded by jerks, take an anthropological approach. Take field notes (and I mean this in real and practical terms) and regard yourself as an explorer, having come across a strange tribe. Observe and describe the tribe's customs and attitudes with keen detachment and consider publishing your field observations. It may help you and be of use to future travelers. I know from experience that the exercise works.

Please keep in touch and remember, you are not alone.

Your friend,
Ursula Franklin

Passing on the Torch

Lyndsay Green

Several months after Lauren, my first child, was born and my maternity leave from the National Film Board (NFB) of Canada was coming to an end, I wrote in despair to a friend. *This is a no-win situation. I can go back to my job, work sixty hours a week and never see my baby. Or I can give up my work and become a bitter woman who at some point will turn on my daughter and scream, "Look at what I sacrificed for you."*

I was thirty-five, looking through a new lens at my job with Studio D, the NFB women's studio, which had satisfied both my personal and political ambitions for three years. Although we had planned to have Lauren, I had not planned on falling head over heels in love with her. I was besotted with her. I couldn't bear the thought of being separated from her. Yet giving up my career was equally unthinkable.

I had been hand-picked by the NFB to set up and manage the Federal Women's Film Program. Over a five-year period that began with my hiring, the program produced and distributed fourteen films for, by, and about women. We made films about services to battered women, films that looked at the lives of Native women and physically disabled women, films that encouraged young women to work in non-traditional jobs, and films provoking discussion about the impact of technology. One of our contributions was training women in all aspects of filmmaking, from cinematographer to sound editor to producer.

One of the innovations of this $2.5 million program was its collaborative organizational structure. I chaired the advisory committee which was comprised of representatives from twenty government departments. Some of the people around the table had contributed money to the program through their departments and others were there because of their expertise. An extraordinary accomplishment of the program, given traditional government line management, was the way the committee operated on a consensus basis, with contributions judged on their merit, regardless of the financial clout of the committee member. Our objective was to run a program that was grounded in feminist principles of women's equality, right from organizational structure through to film content.

I had been in the workforce for over ten years at this point and loved to manage large complicated projects with socially worthwhile goals. My ambitions were being realized completely in this job. Yet here I was, faced with the dilemma of knowing that I could not simultaneously do the job and spend the kind of time I wanted with my daughter. How I made my personal peace with this impasse is a story shared by many of us who grew up feminists in the sixties and seventies and became mothers in the eighties and nineties.

I was born the eldest of three children, the other two being boys. My parents treated me as their "eldest son," with every assumption that I would achieve great things. Indeed, I have made the Freudian slip, "I am the eldest of three boys." My parents' expectations that I would excel were echoed by the changing social times. I was fourteen in 1963 when Betty Friedan published *The Feminine Mystique* and the stories of the women's liberation movement were the fabric of my teenage years in the sixties.

Looking back, I must have been aware of the fragility of my emerging emancipation. My top marks all through high school and university were not just the effortless result of someone who naturally excelled. I was obsessed with doing well. I remember being conscious of trying to reduce any factors that would prevent me from getting ahead, and marks were one factor within my control. Even though I had no idea what I wanted to do, I had a nagging fear that someone would try to stop me. As it turned out, I was right, but that someone turned out to be me. And I did not so much stop as redirect myself. I didn't give up my personal ambitions, I just learned to fulfill them in ways that were not exclusive to the world of work. I'm not sure whether the person of my youth would have appreciated the distinction.

One of the most significant factors in living my feminism has been my choice of mate. And I use the term "my choice" advisedly because initially I was the suitor in our relationship. I had a chance to explain this to Andrea, our second-born, one glorious spring day. She and I were sitting at the kitchen table watching Mother Nature at work in the backyard. The squirrels were chasing each other and the birds were flying back and forth with nest-building scraps in their beaks. You could almost feel the sap running though the trees. At five years of age Andrea was firmly wired into her biology. And I'm afraid to admit she'd already been influenced by the fairy tale images of the knight in shining armour pursuing the beautiful princess. She put her chin in her hands and sighed, "Mommy, how did you attract Daddy?" I replied, "I didn't attract Daddy. He attracted me." She smiled with relief and I could see lifting from her little shoulders the burden of having to make herself an object of desire in hopes the prince would notice her.

I can trace my decision to reverse roles and become the prince to advice I received from one of my mother's friends when I was nineteen. Throughout high school I had many dates. A boy would phone and invite me to go with him to a party or a dance or a movie. The invitation was strictly a one-way process. One evening, after returning home from one of these dates, Phyllis took me aside in the kitchen and said, "It's time you figured out who *you* want to be with. I've seen the boys who ask you out and it's not going to work. Men aren't necessarily attracted to what suits them. We're better judges of the kind of man we need." Although I didn't necessarily agree with the stereotype, I took her advice to heart. I decided it was time to look around for the kind of person I wanted for a partner.

I found the man for me in my first year of university. I heard Hank Intven speak on a panel with John Howard Griffiths, the white man who wrote the book *Black Like Me*. Griffiths had stained his skin black and traveled through the United States to experience discrimination firsthand. His book had made real for me the issues underlying black people's legitimate demands for equality. Hank was on the panel with two other university students who debated the issues raised by Griffiths' talk. I was impressed both by what Hank said and the way he said it. Plus, he was pretty cute. I pursued him for several years and by my third year of university he decided I might be right.

Our partnership has lasted over twenty-five years and is still going strong. I have never felt that my relationship with Hank threatened my feminism. He has been an unqualified supporter of my professional and personal ambitions right from the beginning. When we got married, I kept my own name. Hank explained to his parents, who were a bit taken aback, that this made perfect sense given that I had already established a professional name for myself and a change of name could set my career back. This was perfectly true, but I hadn't thought of it in those terms. I just liked my name and didn't want to go by any other. Hank has been consistent in recognizing how important it is for me to retain the totality of my identity—both personal and professional.

Hank and I did not get married until we'd been together for five years. By that point we had lived together for two years and had bought a house with our joint resources. To reduce the social pressures we chose to get married by a justice of the peace with only our two sets of parents present. I was terrified of marriage. I wasn't secure enough in my own liberation to feel confident in my ability to fight the powerful, custom-laden role of wife. "The wife" was a composite of those anxious women in the TV commercials, worried about "ring around the collar" and getting the yellow off the bathtub. For me, living together before marriage was an essential step in making sure "the wife" did not move in along with me. Without marriage, I could work out my alternative to the roles of husband and wife. I was aiming for a partnership where we shared both an involvement in the world outside the home as well as the work within the home.

I had a powerful ally in my mother. By caring little for housework herself, she effectively innoculated me against "the wife." She would have filled out "housewife" under "occupation" in any household survey, but this had little impact on her self-image. She was a good cook and kept a tidy house, but took limited satisfaction in these accomplishments. She measured her self-worth by her relationships with her family and her friends, and her volunteer work with groups like the Cancer Society. My mother taught me to measure the success of a dinner party by whether people had a good time, and showed me how unrelated that was to what food you served or how splendidly the table was laid. She taught me that time is better spent in contributing to your community than colour co-ordinating your bathroom accessories. Thanks to her I felt quite liberated from measuring myself against the demanding task-master of "wife."

While Hank and I were simply roommates, not husband and wife, we worked out our living arrangement without the heavy hand of gender-based roles. At the outset, I proposed that we share the housework, just like any roommates. Considering himself a liberated man, Hank agreed, but proposed that we concentrate on what we did best. Since he wasn't a great cook, this meant he would be the handyman, and I would be the cook. "Unfortunately," I replied, "I can't cook." In truth, I might have had slightly more cooking experience than Hank, but an equal lack of interest. We adopted my counter proposal to cook on alternate nights, and we instituted a rigid schedule of alternating culinary duties. Hank's practical approach to the assignment was to whip up a monstrous batch of chili on his night to cook, and what we couldn't eat in one night he would freeze, to be retrieved on his next turn. This unrelenting diet of chili on alternating nights lasted for weeks. A person of less stamina or weaker bowels might have given up, but I was determined to break down the traditional assignment of job by gender. I wanted to bring out the champagne the night Hank said, "I think I better find some new recipes. I'm getting pretty sick of chili."

We took the same rigid approach to the division of other household tasks including washing, ironing, and cleaning. Our inflexible approach as to who did what was the source of much amusement among our friends who would watch us negotiate and swap chores back and forth: "You were away so I did the laundry, so you owe me two toilet cleanings." Gradually, as we could afford it, we took clothes to the cleaners, bought takeout food, hired a cleaning woman. For me, however, the critical point had been made. These were not *my* chores, these were *our* chores. And both of us wanted to spend as little time on them as possible.

Relentlessly focused on self-realization, I doubt that I would have had children if I had not had the extraordinary good fortune to work for the Inuit Tapirisat of Canada (ITC) for six years. ITC is the organization representing the Inuit of Canada whose Board of Directors is comprised of elected representatives from Inuit communities across Canada. I was hired by ITC, at the age of twenty-six, to tackle the daunting task of improving communications among Inuit communities. Twenty-two Inuit communities stretch from Nain, Labrador to Aklavik in the Northwest Territories. For telephone service, many had only unreliable HF radio. As their highest priority, Inuit leaders wanted to establish dependable satellite telephone service in every community. Their second priority was to mitigate the negative impact of television. With CBC TV importing a foreign language (English) and an unfamiliar and often undesirable way of life into the largely Inuktitut-speaking culture, the

Arctic was becoming a place where, as one Northerner said, "We can watch Woody Woodpecker but we can't call a doctor."

My six years with ITC was a time of constant work, continual travel and relentless efforts to improve both telephone and television service in the Arctic. We raised millions of dollars to improve Inuit communications, and our work culminated with two historic achievements: the establishment of satellite telephone service in every community, and the licensing of the Inuit Broadcasting Corporation (IBC) to provide Inuktitut-language television service for, by, and about Inuit.

During my time in the North I was strongly affected by the Inuit sense of community, by the values of this non-materialistic culture, and by their powerful love of children. My teacher was my project partner, Aani Palliser, an Inuk from Inoudjouac, Quebec. Aani and I were born on the same day, five years apart. She was the younger one but when I was in her territory I was the one lacking experience. As we worked together, often day and night, we seemed to swap back and forth our lens for viewing the world. I began to understand why an Inuk woman, even one well past child-bearing age, did not feel complete unless she was carrying a baby on her back. I understood why many Inuit, when visiting the South, find the separation from family and community unbearable. I understood why the call of an Arctic spring was irresistible and people dropped important commitments to head out on the land with their families.

Our work immersed Aani ever more deeply into a southern world view as we agonized over political strategies and prepared Ministers' briefing books and submissions to regulatory bodies. I despaired that I was dragging Aani into a cultural no-man's land. She was at the age when she should have had several babies, and here she was with neither time nor opportunity to even find a suitable man. To wield power at the Inuit community level, she would need the kind of social integration and acceptance that comes with having a husband and children. As for the southern world, I knew that although the trappings of this culture held a definite allure for her, she would always find them ill-fitting. I spent some sleepless nights worrying that one day she would feel comfortable in neither her world nor mine.

The irony of my misplaced anxiety plays itself out today as Aani lives a life of immense satisfaction with her husband and four children in an Inuit community where she has earned the respect of her peers and participates as a powerful spokeswoman. On the other hand, I would spend weeks on end in Inuit communities where children were welcome participants at every activity, from late night community meetings to square dances. Then I would return to southern Canada and rarely see a child. I began to miss their presence deeply and decided that I very much wanted children in my life. Aani and the values of her culture opened me up for the first time to the potential joys of motherhood, and I was, in the final analysis, much more profoundly affected by her than she was by me.

When I told Hank that I wanted to have a child, we had been together for thirteen years, and his response shows how dramatic a life turn this was for me. He joked, referring to our sharing of other household tasks, "You mean they've found a way for men to breast feed?"

After several years of trying, I was finally successful in becoming pregnant, which leads me back to where this story began and my anxiety over how to resolve my personal and professional life after the birth of Lauren. One of my preoccupations in my professional and volunteer activities had been working for support systems such as maternity leave, daycare centres, and flexible working hours in order to allow women to combine their child-rearing and working roles better. I was employed by one of the most progressive employers in Canada in terms of support for working mothers, and my immediate boss was willing to restructure my job in whatever way I wanted to make it work for me. But I realized that the nature of the job itself, which required extensive travelling and adherence to film production's long and unpredictable schedules, was fundamentally incompatible with my needs as a mother.

As I extended my maternity leave and struggled with this dilemma, I became increasingly anxious about what was best for Lauren. After several months of giving her my undivided and dogged attention I began to have recurrent nightmares in which I appeared as a monstrous spider queen with Lauren trapped in my web. I would wake up in a cold sweat. I recognized this psychic warning bell and remembered that I had quit cold turkey a career in which I managed multi-million dollar projects and worked ten- to twelve-hour days. I was in the process of re-focussing all this energy, like a laser beam, on this little child. My subconscious, at least, had the good sense to realize that this was dangerously unhealthy. I needed to get back to some kind of fulfilling and challenging professional work.

One day I heard about another woman's solution to a similar dilemma. Susan was a senior federal civil servant. She had taken a leave of absence after her child was born because the job was too demanding to lend itself to part-time work. She wanted to "keep her hand in," however, and had negotiated a contract to do another more flexible government job, until she was ready to return to her permanent position. The idea of taking a leave of absence from a permanent position and negotiating contract work with the same employer seemed an extraordinary stroke of genius in 1984. Organizations now offer myriad family-friendly policies and it is difficult to convey, a decade or so later, how Susan's solution hit me like a revelation from the heavens. Susan went a step further. She told me how to improve upon her position. Her payment under the contract was based on her full-time salary and she urged me to avoid this approach and negotiate a higher rate to reflect the lack of benefits as a contract employee.

Armed with this sage advice I went to my employer, the National Film Board, when Lauren was three months old, with a proposal to do contract work for them during my unpaid leave of absence. The contract I negotiated involved co-ordinating public support for a television application to establish a non-profit children's channel. Although the work was demanding and time consuming, I could do most of it on my own schedule. The flexibility of this arrangement meant that I could share child care with an *au pair* from Denmark who lived with us. Usually I only asked her to take care of Lauren several hours per day, but she could work longer hours if need be.

As it turned out, I was never to return to full-time work for the NFB, nor for any other organization. I bought the newly-released Macintosh computer in 1984, set up my home office with answering machine, fax, and modem, and used the power of computing and telecommunications to give me the flexibility I needed to combine work and family.

When I first set up my consulting practice my friends were anxious that I not commit professional suicide. They urged me to disguise the fact that I worked from home. They cautioned that I would never be taken seriously as a professional if it became known that I had chosen to work as a consultant in order to spend more time with my children. Instead, I should present this decision as a strategic career move. Their advice, which I tried to follow, was to set up my practice in such a manner that people would assume I worked from a real office. To maintain this image, I should arrange to meet clients in their offices, not in mine.

I must confess to mixed feelings when I read a recent laudatory profile in *The Globe and Mail* of a male professional engineer who has set up a home office and proudly displayed his ingenuity, a decade after I was hiding mine. By working from home, he explained, he saves time and money and is better able to focus on the task at hand, without distracting interferences. He gave details of his finances and I noted with some satisfaction that he earns less than I did, even when I first started out. No one questioned his commitment to his profession. However, if he is working this way in order to spend more time with his children, he didn't mention it. This much hasn't changed, at least not in *The Report on Business.*

For the past decade I have been doing consulting, primarily for social and cultural agencies, focussing on the use of communications technologies for development, education, and training. Four years ago I started a new business venture that publishes information and provides consulting about the use of new technologies in adult learning. My work has been enormously rewarding and even prosperous, but certainly does not fit with my father's alma mater Harvard Business School (HBS) criteria for career advancement. I think the HBS credo went something like, "Your c.v. should show a chronological progression of positions of increasing responsibility with commensurate compensation."

Women have often found themselves unable to fit into this profile, as Mary Catherine Bateson describes so eloquently in *Composing a Life.* Now, the ravages of the recession have meant that more and more men are being abruptly pulled off the corporate ladder, forcing them to revise their thinking as to what constitutes success. Maybe even HBS is buying more into my approach. I just opened a solicitation letter from the *Harvard Business Review* that starts off, "Dear Lyndsay Green, Your career isn't about money, is it? I didn't think so. It's about something deeper. Something so central to your core, to what makes you tick, that you can't imagine living without it. It's about leadership. Having your say. Making things happen. Putting your stamp on the future." This description does come pretty close to the way I view my career. Fortunately you do not have to be in the traditional corporate world to pursue or attain these goals.

I am able, more or less, to have a career, raise two children, keep my marriage intact, and maintain some connections with family and friends only by forming partnerships with others. My two most significant partners, apart from my husband, are my business partner, Anna Stahmer, and our housekeeper/nanny, Ofelia Whitely.

Anna and I are joint owners of *The Training Technology Monitor,* a consulting and publishing business that looks at the way technologies like CD-ROM, teleconferencing, and the Internet are used for workplace learning. She and I substitute for each other in all aspects of our partnership—doing the work, participating in meetings, giving speeches at conferences. We are each other's back-up as we juggle the demands of our personal and professional lives.

Ofelia has been with our family since before the birth of my second child. She is a skilled professional and manages our entire household including the cooking, washing, and shopping. Most importantly, she is a third parent to our children. She makes impeccable decisions about their well-being and loves them to pieces. The presence of these two women in my life means that I am able to survive, even enjoy, a day such as I had last week. Here's how the day went.

My major *professional* commitments for the day were as follows: complete the layout of our newsletter for delivery to the publisher's the next day; attend a meeting to present the final report on a consulting contract; and, prepare overheads for a presentation to be delivered the next day in Ottawa.

The more pressing *family* commitments were as follows: spend time with my sister-in-law and three-year old niece who had flown in from Vancouver to spend two days with us so that my children could get to know their cousin; find or buy missing items that had to be packed in Lauren's camp trunk ready for her departure the next morning; and, purchase and deliver a dinner to a sick friend, (a commitment that had been made some time ago).

I start my day at 6:00 a.m. to get in some work on the newsletter layout. From 7:30 to 9:00 a.m. I help the children get off to school and feed the house guests. I continue working on the newsletter layout until 11:30 AM. Anna offers to replace me at the noon hour meeting so that I can pick up the children from school and we can have lunch with their aunt and cousin at the Swiss Chalet. From 1:00 to 3:00 p.m. I search for and finally track down the outstanding camp items. I spend the balance of the afternoon completing my work on the newsletter layout. We have dinner and say goodbye to the cousins who are going on to visit my parents in Ottawa. After dinner we pack the camp trunk, the children have baths and stories and are put to bed. From 9:30 to 11:45 p.m. I work on my presentation and produce the overheads for the next day's presentation in Ottawa.

Not every day is as long or as complicated as this, but many are.

Here's how I was able to pull it off. Ofelia worked behind the scene the entire day doing all the household management chores, including preparing the meals. My sick friend told me she would give me a rain check on the meal offer. Anna covered for me at the meeting. And I figured out, just in time, how to move text from Microsoft Word into Power-Point and produced professional-looking overheads at record speed.

Where was Hank through all this? He worked late at the office, arrived home in time to kiss the girls goodnight, and then continued working at home. He is a lawyer who works the killer hours associated with his profession. His international specialization requires him to travel extensively. Last year he spent a third of the year out of the country. He and I occasionally talk about switching roles, with me taking on the tough, demanding job again, and he assuming more of the family responsibilities. On certain days I'm sure I could get him to make this switch, but I am the one who is not prepared to do that. I don't want to miss sitting in the Swiss Chalet with the kids as they colour their place mats, bat their balloons, slurp their Shirley Temple drinks. I want to watch them as they pack their camp trunks, checking off the packing list item by item, and excitedly putting everything into place.

I got a real rush at midnight as my terrific looking overheads came off the printer. Days like these happen to me because I'm not willing to give up any of it, and because I think it is fun. Even though trying to keep all the balls in the air can be frustrating, my life would be impoverished without the juggling act.

My partnership with our nanny has been the glue that holds the crazy patchwork of our household together. She works thirty-five hours a week, from 10:30 am until 5:30 p.m. She is also there in case of school emergencies—skinned knees and the like. I try to end my working day at 5:30 p.m. because I find the evening hours both important and fun times to be with the children. We sit down to dinner and talk about the day. When the children were younger I had to jump-start the conversation with the game of everyone telling the best and worst things that happened to them that day. Now that they are twelve and eight years old, they happily chat away without prompting. After dinner they work on their homework and practice their musical instruments. I like to be around just to make sure these things are happening. When my working day is unavoidably extended or I have to go out of town, Ofelia stays for the extra hours required and I pay her for anything beyond her thirty-five hour week.

Even with this totally dependable and flexible support system, the arrangement only works because I have an extraordinary amount of control over when, where, and how I do my work. Some jobs, like my former one with the NFB, would never lend itself to this kind of balancing act. Recently, I went out to lunch with a friend who is about ten years my junior. She is a tremendously talented lawyer; a partner in her firm, with two small children. That day, she told me, in tears, that she was a failure—as a lawyer, as a mother, and as a wife. Thinking that I had somehow managed to be successful at everything, she wanted to know my secret. I felt a tremendous amount of personal guilt at hearing her plea because I realized the lies the women of our generation have been telling. Our lies have been mainly sins of omission. We have hidden the personal costs we have incurred to pull off the juggling act that I describe above. We have also exaggerated our accomplishments. The truth is, I have never tried to do what Marion is doing, let alone been successful at it. She is working within a very rigid professional structure, with extremely high expectations, competing with colleagues with enormous support mechanisms like Hank's. I, on the other hand, have circumscribed my career to make it doable in a forty to fifty hour week and, usually, can carry out my work when and where I wish. I have to meet deadlines within specific contracts but, as for my overall productivity, I am mainly accountable only to myself.

I set up a lunch with Marion and Peggy. Like me, Peggy is ten years older and, unlike me, she *does* lead Marion's life, raising two children while working as a partner in her law firm. Peggy feels that the unremitting demands of juggling her professional and personal life have exacted a heavy toll. Her marriage has broken down. She has migraine headaches that have become so disabling she has been required to take disability leave from her firm for months at a time. Peggy is one of only two partners in her law firm who are mothers. The other woman has a stay-at-home husband.

A story that appeared in the local newspaper profiled me as a "Woman on the Move." The photo accompanying the article shows me sitting in front of my computer, holding Andrea. The caption reads, "Lyndsay Green, with daughter Andrea, 2, believes in taking kids along on business trips." Anyone who has a two-year-old knows the insanity of this supposed belief. The person who wrote this caption has either never encountered a two-year-old, or she is a mother getting in her own sly dig on this whole idea of superwomen. The article follows the formula for these profiles and lists my accomplishments, paragraph after paragraph. This unremitting litany of success depresses me even as I read it six years later. It takes a conscious act of will to remember that the reason I cannot keep up with this former self is that she never existed. The accomplishments were mine, but the wrinkles acquired in getting there were airbrushed away.

Let us face the facts. We cannot have it all, at least not all at once. By *all* I mean a highly demanding heart-and-soul professional career *and* the joys of motherhood *and* the happiness of family and friends. I know this seems obvious, but we continue to put these expectations on ourselves. Since my children were born I have turned down several exciting opportunities to run large social change projects that, pre-motherhood, I would have snapped up in an instant. Last year I removed myself from the boards of several women's organizations because I was starting to get very run-down and my doctor told me something had to give. Marion decided to refocus her professional life to retain her sanity. She now works from home and is developing a niche specialty that allows her to use her legal training but gives her more control over when and where she works.

I think my mother summed it up best. She patted me on the shoulder one day and said, "I don't think it's working out." "What part?" I laughed. "The whole thing," she replied. "I thought you young women were really going to work it out. You were going to have your career and your family, too. But you're working all the time. You don't have any fun." But she also admitted that, given the way I was raised and the tenor of the times, I wouldn't be happy living the life she led, even though she had more fun. She gave up her nursing career when I was born and only after her children were grown did she complain about missing the satisfaction, and the paycheque, of a job.

I look at my daughters and I am excited for them about their futures. I like to think I am passing on the torch. Our house has been the gathering point for formal and informal meetings of women working for change ever since they were born, and they have absorbed discussions of feminism along with their breast milk. Lauren subscribes to *New Moon*, the magazine "for young girls and their dreams," an adolescent version of *Ms.* magazine. At age twelve, her ideas about the role of women in society are articulate and well-developed, and she sees no barriers in front of her. She is as quick to call people on gender stereotyping of boys as she is of girls. Unlike me at her age, she wants it all. She talks about four children and a career. As for Andrea, right now it looks like she might even follow in my footsteps. I was absolutely thrilled when she chose my job as the occupation she wanted to explore for her grade three project. She made a big poster with a copy of our newsletter, photos of people using computers, and an interview with me about what my job was like and how I got into it.

I have just a few words of advice for my daughters. Make sure you are financially independent. Unless you win the lottery, this means that you need skills that will allow you to earn a living. Try to acquire these skills and get work experience before you have children. The only way I was able to set up a consulting business, post-children, is that I had acquired a strong professional reputation, pre-children. Try to marry your best friend, as I did.

Most importantly, don't be too hard on yourself. The old me would not have been very impressed with the way my career has been given short shrift when compared to my original ambitions. But that old me is gone.

And take your grandmother's advice. Have a little fun!

Raise My Hand, Raise My Voice: Speaking of Myself

Photo by Suzie Ungerleider

Joelle Hann

The titles of the Feminist Literature 201 syllabus were posted on a professor's bulletin board at Queen's University. It was the end of my first year and I knew I should leave the hall and return to my room to finish packing for my flight home to British Columbia. Instead I dawdled, reading the names Virginia Woolf, Sylvia Plath, Margaret Atwood. In my hand was my final paper on Rousseau and the perfect state from History of Western Thought, the most difficult course I'd ever taken. But the list of women authors before me challenged my eighteen-year-old self more than anything I'd ever seen. What if someone saw me? I looked up and down the hall. I opened my bag, grabbed a pen, and copied the titles onto the back of my term paper, then I ran away and burst out into the glare of spring, nervous sweat dampening my face and a giddy triumph easing into me. Back in B.C., I would spend my summer reading the books on the list.

The only other memory I have of being drawn to women's issues is my curiosity about the purple house between my residence and the student health centre, which housed the birth control clinic. I had wondered about the women who went in and out its doors and imagined the clinic as a refuge from campus harassment, connecting in my mind the politics of birth control with the unformed—but felt—question of women's, and my own, autonomy. I picked up a registration form for clinic volunteers but hid it from my curious roommate, telling myself I'd fill it out later. Eventually it got tucked under some books and disappeared altogether, my interest stifled by the thought of what the girls on my floor would say if I volunteered and, worse, what the boys would do to humiliate me if they saw me going into the clinic.

Harassment at Queen's was a given. In the little details of campus life, the superiority of the male student was evident. At one party a student demanded to make a handprint on my shirt and I gave in, not wanting to be a prude. He put a hand up my shirt, palm out, and pressed it into the other painted hand to make the print. He took his hand away and just as I began to relax, he pinched my nipple and pulled hard. He and his friends laughed themselves onto the ground. The student ghetto housed many of these men, and for the rest of the year I would walk forty-five minutes out of my way into Kingston rather than through the rows of run-down houses. I was never angry until they were long gone. Their comments and touchings shocked speech right out of me. The university seemed to sanction harassment by ignoring it.

At the time I didn't make the connection between the threatening young men around me and my low confidence. I just found university difficult and felt much less smart than I had before, and much more alone. I had never been afraid to walk anywhere by myself, day or night, and I had always valued my mind as a means of gaining acceptability and respect. It was as if I'd been knocked down and no one had the time to examine me. I did not speak up in classes, I argued feebly at parties. In the large lecture halls, I sat right at the back, not to be cool, but to be invisible.

My first encounter with feminism happened during the 1970s when I was growing up on Saltspring Island. My father had landed a job with BC Ferries, my mother had just had a baby, and we were newly resettled from Toronto. Saltspring was teeming with hippies, artisans, lesbian farmers, and movie stars trying out new lifestyles. Our white and green house had once been a garage. Our next-door neighbours were a family of two men, a woman, a goat, some chickens, ducks, and sheep all living under the same roof.

In my mother I saw a woman who could turn a sheep and jam a vaccination needle in its shoulder or throw bales of hay up into the barn. She hauled the wheelbarrow, drove the tractor, and built garden sheds. I, too, never liked to say I couldn't learn to do something, or that I was too weak. I was responsible for carrying heavy buckets of water to refill the animals' troughs every evening. My mother never stopped working.

After a day outside on the farm, she took off her stained overalls, showered, and made dinner, then washed up and spent the last of her waking hours writing letters to people she'd known in England, or reading. From her I learned industry. As I watched, she made the farm she'd always wanted.

My mother was very able, but she wasn't sympathetic to the feminist movement. During debate over whether women should be "Ms" instead of Mrs. or Miss I remember her snapping off the radio and saying, "What are they making such a fuss about?" Taking on my family's attitude, I lumped feminists and hippies together—not only the ones across the lane but the pot-smokers at the farmer's market and the nude bathers at Stoal Lake, our summer watering hole, who named their children Rainbow and Tree. My mother didn't like me playing with the hippie kids and, far from seeing their parents as liberated, she thought them weird.

Our home had been moved from the Burgoyne Valley to the top of Lee's Hill and converted into a house. Skunk cabbage grew in the wall between the kitchen and the living room and in the summer gave off a putrid smell. My room was on the second floor and looked out over the valley and across to Mount Bruce, where we'd watch the brightly coloured hang gliders sailing down into the valley. Its thin carpet smelled of dust, and the steep chute that was a stairwell had no handrail, just a string of yellow nylon rope. My father bought a small trailer, the kind you hook up to your car and take camping, and locked himself inside to study for BC Ferries' nautical exams. He was going to be a captain. My mother hushed me and kept me away from the trailer. She worked days with a machete, clearing back the blackberries and thistles that overran the few arable acres before the forest.

My father and I had been buddies. We sang "My Lariat," "Sunshine," and "Alouette" on the way to nursery school in the Austin mini. When he picked me up, he'd ask, "What did you learn today?" He coached me to stand tall, ask questions, and think for myself. We'd come home laughing and singing to Mom who would be home from her job.

My father and I were also the renegades. After a tense meal at my grandmother's, he'd give me a special look and I'd know to get my coat and shoes. Within half an hour we'd be driving to our favourite place to eat fish and chips prepared by a burly man in a white apron. The fish came in huge bouquets of newspaper, soaked with hot fat. Then there was the delicious sting of vinegar and salt on our lips. We drove to a lot near the water, where we ate listening to the BBC.

But trouble began when we moved to Saltspring. My father started to come in from work only to fall asleep in the La-Z-Boy with a paperback open in his lap, the TV on. His frustration spread over us at the dinner table. When we sat down to eat, my once inquisitive father sat with one fist tight against his face, eyes lowered. One time, after a few mouthfuls, he pushed away his plate, collected his cutlery, and stormed from the kitchen. "You know I hate chicken," he hissed as he passed behind my mother's chair. My brother and I had stopped eating. "Bob, you like this dish, you've always liked it," Mom cried, reaching for him. The La-Z-Boy creaked as he raised the footrest. My father lit a cigarette and glared at the TV. This continued through the evening.

Yet on Saturday nights, special nights in our family, when we ate informally in the living room and watched the hockey game on TV, I remember my father putting his arms around my mother as she cooked our hamburgers. After my brother and I set up the portable trays we were allowed soft drinks, a Saturday-only treat. I would eat potato chips from a tupperware box and watch as my father reached around my mother and took her breast in hand. I wondered, impatiently, how he could do this vaguely disgusting thing; I wanted my hamburger and I wanted to watch the hockey. It puzzled me that my mother just laughed.

We all felt responsible for my father's unhappiness, but none of us really knew what it was about. My mother did not protest because she was fulfilling her duties as wife and mother. Perhaps my father wanted her to fight him, to force her to be a more challenging partner. His rages came more and more frequently, more unexpectedly. We tried to appease him. I followed my mother's example and accepted all blame.

Unlike families in which physical violence controls women and children, we could point to no bruises, no broken bones. My father's need to control and his strange need for revenge made us ashamed of ourselves and fearful of the effect we might unknowingly have on others. Consistent humiliation over money eventually became humiliation over desire: what I or my mother wanted, we often just gave up.

Unless I changed, I feared my life would always be controlled by men like my father. When my mother began to confide in me, at age eleven, the year Mount St. Helen's erupted, I resolved to become independent however I could and to rescue my mother. The role-reversal presented a strange question: how would I save her if I had no guidance or protection? As my mother and father had few friends who might act as new examples of womanhood, I looked to characters in books, at first the historical romances my mother read, and then vaguely, because I was too young to understand the nuances of social affairs, Jane Austin and the Brontës. Approaching this "new mother" was slow, impeded by my uncertainty of what was right and wrong. But by eighteen, the year I read the Feminist Literature syllabus, I had discovered my direction and began also to understand that I could not save my mother. She had chosen her role, and would not leave it. She liked her life and loved her husband. Seeing this, I had to come to terms with the mother who actually existed, not with who I wanted to exist. My summer reading the Feminist Literature 201 syllabus was as much a search for "literary mothers," who would help me break with my own mother's model, as it was to discover a new genre of writing. In the company of Virginia Woolf, Margaret Laurence, Sylvia Plath, and Anne Sexton, I gave up my quest to save my mother and began to listen to and act for myself.

On a bright Sunday morning in October six weeks after I arrived at Queen's University, Kevin called to invite me for a walk. I turned him down. He insisted. I hung up. We had been in the same orientation group, and I remembered him as the one who got boisterously drunk, turned his back on the game being played, and yelled, "You cock-suck-ers!" Even though I agreed to meet him against my better judgment that night, we started walking regularly together in the evenings from then on. Lake Ontario stretched out to the horizon, an enormous expanse of water that suggested marooning and shipwreck, trapped as I was in Queen's unwelcoming environment. I was afraid to trust Kevin, despite the hours we talked about high school and family. We sat on park benches and he would say, "Wow, you're so bold. So frank." I softened towards him. I showed him my poetry and met him more frequently.

My mother's letters came every week with news of the weather at home and the farm, of my brother and my father, the cats, the garden. There was no sign that the family knew how much I hated Kingston and Queen's. On Hallowe'en, when Kevin's girlfriend stood him up, I agreed to join him at his house.

Writers included in English Literature survey courses frequently allude to and extemporate on women's virginity, its loss, its value, and their own rapacious desire. I read these undertones and overtones of rape in Donne, Pope, Swift, and explicitly in Marvell's *To His Coy Mistress*,

Browning's *My Last Duchess*, and *The Rape of Lucrece*. Rape happened to women and women accepted it as a part of their role in the poem. Men felt desire and women did not, and desire was almost always fulfilled against someone's wishes. Until the fall of 1986, when I was walking with Kevin, I had been naïve about boys, romance, and sex, probably taking my cue from the historical romances I had read at home.

That Halloween night, we drank rum-and-cokes until I saw two Kevins, two desks, two doorframes. I was unable to speak; words became like lumps of mud, fell out of my mouth in gloops and made a mess around me. I crawled to Kevin's bed and lay down to cry. I saw Saltspring, the maple tree I used to climb, the cedars, smelled the brine of low tide. I wistfully recalled high school peers. But how could I miss home, where I had been ashamed of myself? How could I miss peers who had ignored me? Kevin came over to the bed. I hoped he would tell me it was all right. Instead, he lay on top of me and undressed me. The image of Yeats' swan beating its huge wings over Leda reminds me of the weight of Kevin's body on me as I struggled in and out of consciousness.

Unlike others who have been sexually assaulted, I had no feeling of danger during the assault. The violation was no more than a routine disregard of one person's wishes for another's. Just like my father's disregard for the hurt he exacted from us as payment for his own sense of worthlessness. Just like the boys who harassed me in the student ghetto. But thereafter, in classes I felt drugged, constricted by my need to have nothing terrible happen to me, whether it be slipping on ice, being mocked in conversation, or being alone with bullies. Kevin's betrayal and my loneliness consumed me. During exams, I took my pregnancy kit into the white-brick basement of my residence and locked the door. I cried all through the Christmas vacation. Because sex was taboo in my parents' home, I said nothing about Kevin. Assault was not real to me, so I did not name what had happened. More devastating was that Kevin extinguished the flicker of hope he had given me about relationships and friendship and trust.

I requested to transfer out of Queen's. Everything in me said retreat, go somewhere else, somewhere untainted. After visiting a friend in Montréal I decided to enroll at McGill. The summer between was filled with books by women. I took their novels and poetry on long visits to Beddis Beach, Stoal Lake, Walker Hook where I read and wrote until I could see where I was again.

For my second year of university I was happy to simply not feel threatened and to enjoy my classes. I remember one day in my third year, sitting on the edge of my bed and reading about a gang-rape at a frat party in the university paper. I felt angry and the lime-green walls seemed to close in on me. In the next *McGill Daily*, a group of women condemned the lack of response to the rape. I wondered. Wasn't it normal for women to accept violation? Who would help this woman? Of course rape is a crime, at least morally. But everyone knows that it can be overlooked if used to form solidarity between men. I thought protest would be useless as it had been at Queen's. But at McGill in 1988 protest flourished; the women did not accept apathy and I discovered feminist activism.

I had not yet acknowledged Kevin's assault for what it was, but I joined the fledgling McGill Coalition Against Sexual Assault. My anger was enormous, volcanic, confused.

I argued with everyone, I shouted at male gawkers and I openly despised men who dismissed women's protests. At the McGill Coalition Against Sexual Assault, which supported the woman and fought to get her case heard, I met women who felt the same way I did. We asked, how is violation going to end? What about our rights to walk freely and talk freely? What I found were not a bunch of strident, highly sexualized loud-mouths (my childhood idea of feminists), but smart women my own age, saying things that I, too, had thought. We all had been affected by the gang-rape, and it seemed that next time, at some other party, it could be one of us.

The coalition attracted so many volunteers that there were soon enough people to organize a Sexual Assault Awareness Week. In March of 1989, we flooded McGill with seminars, discussion groups, films, demonstrations, speakers, petitions, and performances on sexual assault. A group of actors staged a mock rape in a busy lunch-time cafeteria. The speaker's bureau spoke to student and faculty groups. Films and discussion panels drew crowds. From within the coalition I felt justifiably angry, emotionally and intellectually viable, and for the first time, like I had the right to protest. Somewhere during the furor of this first Sexual Assault Awareness Week, a university psychiatrist asked me, "Why do you think you feel so passionately about this group? Do you think you've ever been sexually assaulted?" I had no response for him, but the question rattled me.

While I organized more and more feminist events, I began to take more women's studies courses and to write with an awareness of women's history and needs. This culminated in a graduate course in Feminist Methodology and Consciousness, dubbed by my boyfriend "your group therapy session," which connected the philosophy of literature courses with my life and experiences. I learned to speak by first identifying my background (white, lower–middle class, female) which at the time made me feel aware of who I was and where I'd come from. The class did not attempt a traditionally academic objectivity that would wipe away the influence of my experiences on my analysis of course materials. What had happened in my life up to my participation in the seminar was meaningful. I felt seen and heard; I realized how my other courses constricted me.

The feminist seminar also brought together my tendency to read, write, and analyze. I discovered, from the hidden voice that emerged in my words, what I valued and what I felt. After studying literature for several years I discovered that feminism and poetry had common ground: new languages are forged in both, new rhythms in which we can hear that our experience is valid and the rhythm we make in it, hear in it, is real. Feminism and poetry construct spaces in which we reparent ourselves through hurt and injustice. Feminism directly said it is okay to have a different opinion or to cry, shout, march, talk. It made room for my experience and held me steady while I fell around finding my feet. Power, love, the knowledge of being valued, and the space to act, to speak: these are the recreative powers of feminist thinking, seeing and doing. Poetry, too, affirms the existence of a private self which fights fear and shame.

Before I graduated from McGill, I had another lesson to learn about being female: I discovered I was pregnant. I was twenty years old, in my fourth year of university, and rallying and petitioning to support Chantelle Daigle's right to an abortion. Her boyfriend was applying for an injunction that would force her to carry the unwanted pregnancy to term. When the nurse told me the test was positive, I burst into tears. This could not be happening to me.

Part of the reason for my pregnancy, aside from my feeling physically invincible, stemmed from faulty birth control. I hated the Pill, which controlled my hormones; my boyfriend hated latex. My body had never let me down before. I had decided to chart my ovulation, take my body temperature, monitor my vaginal mucus and when I was sure of my infertility I would have sex. I did not think I was crazy. It worked. I could not imagine the unforgiving reality of failure.

The preliminary physical exam was done in a medical building off campus where I was surrounded by pregnant women waiting to see their doctors, and magazines covered with pictures of smiling parents. When at last the doctor examined me, he conducted the physical in cold silence. He answered my questions impatiently. And, when frustrated by his unhelpfulness and not comforted by the news that the operation would take only five minutes, I asked still more questions and continued to look upset, the doctor said, "You'll be fine. Or else—this!" and shook his fist in my face.

My experience of abortion was as much an education in reproductive politics as it was a personal trial. I had known nothing about the physical procedure of abortion, about emotional fallout, or the frequency at which women aborted (more than live births). What I knew had been garnered from pro-choice rallies: I knew about coat-hanger deaths, back-alley botch-jobs, shame, anti-choice equals anti-woman. I knew nothing of what to expect, where to go, who to talk to. I grieved for the lost child, and this shocked me. I was enraged by the surgical explanations of the operation that were liberally dosed with words that shamed me. As the needles punctured my cervix, I grabbed for the nurses hand and she withdrew sharply. I felt pressure to overcome my confusion quickly or else be disqualified as a sexually liberated woman, as if abortion were just a physical inconvenience. Clearly the experience and the philosophy behind abortion were completely separate worlds.

Several weeks after the abortion, once I was clear enough to think, I realized that within feminist activism at McGill, intellect still held authority over emotion. There was a lot of co-operation and intellectual risk-taking when it came to challenging assumptions, but by some unwritten rule, emotions were to be confined to privacy. The transformative ideas of feminist practice were subject to the limits of each individual who carried them out. When I had an abortion, my experience embarrassed women who fought for me to be able to have an abortion. My peers' faces wore blank expressions when I complained that no pre- or post-abortion support was available in Student Health Services or in the Women's Union. Nor was abortion—the actual operation—ever discussed openly among otherwise vocal and intelligent women. I felt a block when I wanted to talk about it. I felt suddenly like an outsider.

When the professor of my feminist theory course granted me permission to write my final paper on the abortion she gave me a public forum to speak and an important validation of my experience. The paper marked a beginning of owning my emotional history in general. In myself I made room for the emotions which otherwise would have been swept away with that from Kevin's sexual assault and my family history.

Writing the paper on abortion consumed most of my time in December 1989. One night while I was working in my draughty apartment on deBullion Street, my boyfriend called. He'd just returned from the McGill pool. "I heard on the radio . . . it's terrible . . . fourteen women have been killed at the École Polytechnique." I felt so palpably female, subject to purposeless attack. Just five weeks after my abortion I was struck by how directly the violence was connected to my gender. Here again, feminist theory, which helped me to think and enjoy my mind and to feel like an active agent in the world, could not protect me. My mind, which was my best defence, was useless against violence. December sixth marks a time of fear and grieving for me, as I remember each year those who were, for a few moments, me, had Marc LePin targeted a feminist seminar instead of an engineering class.

Two years after graduating from McGill I was still very aware of my abortion and the implications of the Montreal Massacre and I decided to enter a sexual assault survivor's group. I was teaching a course in women's literature and working full-time at a magazine, which limited the space I could give the group-process. As well, I appointed myself intellectual in the group, the one who knew the theoretical and historical basis of the arguments against violence against women and I used this position to stay on the outer edges of pain. I was unwilling to fall apart. I could not abandon my mind which had got me out of my father's house, out of Queen's and into feminism. But even though I resisted emotional processing, by the end of the ten-week group session, a change had begun. The catch-words "patriarchy" and "sexism" no longer satisfied me. I could no longer ignore the question, "What does it mean to be a woman?" I realized that I could not embody the woman I was because the "Woman" of my imagination was a weak creature, someone other than me.

Since 1993 therapy has been the means by which I have continued feminism; I have taken it inside to address my own history. By feeling the rage of the wrongly accused child, and the devastation of the betrayed adolescent, I know more about where I come from and what is mine. I like to think that my pusuit of independence is akin to the suffragists' pursuit of the vote and the second-wave feminists' pursuit of access to abortion. Once I have charted some painful emotional territories I will be stronger, a better writer, and once again an advocate for women's rights. And while I still don't know the limits or limitlessness of power, sexuality, emotion or intellect, I do know that feminism set me on the path to discovering them and gave me the permission and gumption to begin.

Duet

Suzanne Hénaut
& Dorothy Todd Hénaut

When I slowly came out of the ether, the first words I heard were, *"C'est une fille!"*—"It's a girl!" I remember my heart swelling with the most ineffable joy that my first child was a girl. Can feminist education start from the minute one pops out? I think my daughter's did, at that moment in 1956 when I became a mother.

My own birth in 1935 suffered from mixed messages, because on the one hand, my father had wanted a daughter first, but on the other, my mother took a while to realize that she hadn't "failed" when her firstborn was not a son, according to the prevailing attitude of the time.

After waiting five long weeks for the amnio results, hoping that the baby wouldn't have any major problems, I found out that I was expecting a girl. I was delighted. I would be able to imagine her as her own being, not just "the baby." I named her Belkis, which means Goddess of the Sea. I was also rather relieved, since I was going to be a single mother, not to have the challenge of bringing up a boy in these troubled times for men and their self-identity. The path for women, although still full of hurdles, has been somewhat opened up by our feminist mothers and sisters. Men seem to be in more of a quandary than we are at the moment. It is not easy to find examples one would like one's son to follow.

Perhaps my aim has been to encourage Belkis to have a solid sense of self, and to believe that she has a right to have all her needs met. At any rate, she is four-and-a-half at the time of this writing, and she is an articulate little companion who fills my life with delight. And she definitely has a mind of her own, thank goodness.

I was brought up believing that I could choose my own path in life. Both of my parents encouraged me to be strong and independent, and they somehow managed to ignore the extremes of stereotyping that were typical of the era. A baby photo shows me, at eleven months, sitting on the lawn, clutching a truck in my little round fists. At the age of two, I not only had pretty smocked dresses, I had an electric train (in 1937!). At five, Dad taught me how to sail a nine-foot dinghy he had built—not just sail in it, but skipper it myself.

Of course I was also taught to be a little lady; when I was thirteen I attended dancing class, and Mom made me a beautiful ball gown. But that summer, Dad took my ten-year-old brother and me on a hundred-mile canoe trip in the Adirondacks, which ended with a climb to the top of the two tallest mountains in the range. We cooked pies and cakes and still love to talk about that trip. It would never have occurred to him to exclude me from such a trip because I was a girl. He simply calculated that at five-foot-six I could carry a twenty-five pound pack on my back. He was just as matter-of-fact when he taught me to drive at fifteen, and threw in a crash course in car mechanics for my mother and me, because he believed we should know our tools.

When I stayed for three months with Grandmère and Grandad when I was twelve, he taught me woodworking. I remember building stairs, and I still have the pencil holder I made myself. It seemed a natural thing for us to do, and even suited my structural type of mind. I didn't realize at the time that it was considered unusual for girls to learn woodworking.

Dorothy also instilled in me a great sense of self-confidence by her conviction that I could learn to do anything I wanted. In my mind there were no limits and in my upbringing the thought was never formulated that girls didn't do certain things. In my early teens I wanted to be a motorcycle-driving drummer and a marine biologist.

My parents' confidence in me, and their encouragement, helped me learn to value myself, even to value that I wasn't necessarily like everybody else. Dad, in particular, taught me to go as far as I could in any endeavour, to become as skilled as I was capable, without comparison to others and without competition. Even when I participated in junior swimming or ski racing, he didn't mind where I placed, as long as I tried to do my best. I remember he was so proud of me when I lost a ski after the third gate in a slalom race and completed the course on one ski.

I don't know if it was because we didn't have much money, or because we lived in the city, but our family didn't really engage in any sports, let alone competitive ones. Dorothy certainly never encouraged competitiveness in our household. As a matter of fact, I played chess for many years, and one of my weaknesses was the final attack. I hated eliminating the other person. Sometimes now I wonder if we shouldn't have learned to be a bit more competitive, because it occasionally seems to be a handicap in the real world to feel uncomfortable competing with our colleagues. Yet, I still feel happier and more satisfied if everyone comes out of a negotiation feeling like a winner.

I couldn't teach my children to compete because I loathed competition and loved collaboration. I just figured it should give a woman a real head-start in life to believe in herself and her ability to do whatever she sets out to do, and to do it in her own way. Then when she walks headlong into the walls of patriarchy and finds herself bruised or broken, she won't waste time blaming herself; she will have confidence that she can survive the setbacks, and will then look around for allies with whom she can understand the patterns, devise new strategies, and then struggle to change the system.

My parents continued to encourage my self-reliance. At the age of eighteen, I went off to the Sorbonne for a year and somehow managed to elope to Scotland with a charming Frenchman. We moved to Montréal, where we struggled not only with poverty and the challenges of immigration, but also the tensions between a Canadian wife who wanted a fifty-fifty marriage (in 1954) and a young French patriarch who frankly thought that ninety-ten was about right. Just as I began to lose hope for the marriage, I learned I was pregnant, so I decided to plunge wholeheartedly into motherhood, determined to fit myself into the mold of the woman my husband wanted.

My mother had set an example of cheerful motherhood. While my father travelled as an industrial salesman all week, my mother ran the household. She loved to rearrange the furniture and push the piano around. She whistled as she worked, ran a tight ship, and had lots of energy to write poetry, work on a radio show with a group of friends, and run a Girl Guide troop. She was an artist whose palette was her home and garden. Later on I could never share the contempt for housewives that became prevalent among some feminists, because I knew my mother had been profoundly happy.

When my time came, Mom's support and advice were indispensable, and our friendship blossomed. In spite of my oppressive marriage, I loved being a mother. Suzanne was the girl I had unconsciously wanted, and when Marc came along two years later, I was delighted to have one of each. I vividly remember watching their two young lives unfold and thinking how wrong it was that society had stacked the deck against them, in different ways. Suzanne supposedly had two options: to learn to earn her own living, or to find a man who would earn it for her. Marc, on the other hand, had no options: he not only had to earn his own living, he probably had to support a wife and family as well. It was a trap for each of them in different ways. I decided to encourage them both to earn their own livings, with the idea they could negotiate a deal with a partner in the event one of them wanted to stay home for a while with their babies. They were both given dolls to play with as well as trucks and trains and art materials.

The first things that surface when I think of my childhood are the allergies that plagued my life since I was born, first in the form of eczema, later with asthma. I was allergic to cow's milk, but Dorothy only learned that when I was two, and by then I was covered with cracked and bleeding skin, from my eyelids to my ankles. At school, the girls wouldn't let me play ring-around-the-rosy or touch the skipping rope because they thought I might infect them. I was always set apart because I was allergic to wool and had to wear a cotton tunic Dorothy made for me which stood out from the school's uniform. I was often ostracized. At nineteen, I wore a turtleneck all summer to keep myself from scratching and because I was tired of being asked what was on my neck, not to mention the other unexposed parts of my body. And I abandoned my desire to be a drummer or dancer because the eczema made it impossible to hold the drumsticks, and open cracks in my knees meant I couldn't bend my legs. Mostly I swallowed all this and didn't let it bring me down, but I became too mature for my age. I swore I would never be as cruel as those girls in grade school. I don't ever remember being carefree. Yet, though I always looked hopelessly different, Dorothy taught me to have pride in my individuality and difference.

Suzanne's allergies were a nightmare for us. Very little was known about them in the fifties and sixties, which was also the era before health-care insurance. I spent much of my time and a substantial part of our meagre resources looking for a doctor who could help. My relationship with Suzanne was strained because I was her "torturer" who put on creams that made her scream, and put her in baths that stung. I would try to hug her and she would be all elbows and knees. How could this poor little thing realize that the hands that hurt her were really trying to make her better? For a mother, there can't be anything worse than to feel absolutely helpless and unable to protect her child from suffering.

Over time we learned to discover and eliminate many of the allergens that caused my eczema and asthma. My skin got somewhat better, but was subject to setbacks far too often. Medication kept my asthma in check. I'm afraid we didn't realize that asthma could be fatal. When I was twenty-one, I visited a friend's farm where there were lots of animals. After a couple of bad nights, we went out to the maple grove with a horse and wagon. Barely able to breathe, I lost consciousness and went into a coma. When they got me to the hospital I was considered clinically dead, but with oxygen, adrenalin, and luck (the hospital wasn't too far from the farm; my friends' car was willing to start), it was my fate to survive. The near-death experience profoundly affected my character and how I would live from then on as a survivor.

Some people might back off and live as sheltered a life as they could, but it didn't affect me that way. I didn't stop myself from embarking on special adventures. I went to the desert in Algeria to live with the Touaregs as I had planned prior to the attack. But I wasn't foolhardy; I travelled with a bag full of medication and syringes. I refused to distress myself physically any more and became adamant about not being around animals. At that point, I rejected the notion that you can control your allergies with a mind-over-matter approach. This had brought me close to death, because it was an era when allergies were thought to be emotional in origin, and the power of animal dander was dangerously underrated.

Most importantly, though, the experience taught me that you can't count on tomorrow so you have to live your fullest today. To me this means some form of daily pleasure, enjoying the process as well as the goal. It means being mostly content every day, having as few regrets as possible, and embracing life with all its risks as wholeheartedly as I can.

Suzanne reminded me of the St. Lawrence River: she appeared as calm as a broad lake, but you knew that underneath powerful currents were running. I did a lot of thinking about what it means to be a mother. When the kids were born, I had a strong feeling that they were separate, free individuals and that my job was to guide them to autonomy. There was no question that as a parent I could ever own my children; I was just a temporary custodian, with a lot of loving and guiding to do. It was only later that I was able to voice the connection between "ownership," dependency, and patriarchy. In fact, *pater familias* means "the male owner of a group of domestic slaves."

When husbands think they own their wives and families, they sometimes think they also have the right to batter and murder them. Every time I read of another "family tragedy," I see the same pattern and it enrages me. Here in Montreal recently, a father knifed his wife and two daughters to death, leaving two other daughters in intensive care. The wife had separated from him and then allowed him back. He seemed to believe he owned his family and they had no right to an autonomous life. What kind of society permits men to believe that they can interfere with the rights of their wives and daughters? Remember that old seductive song, "You Belong to Me"? I never see newspapers or television explain such incidents in terms of patterns, only in very individualistic terms. As feminists we have so much work to do to make these shameful patterns visible and recognizable to all, and then to get rid of them.

My marriage, though absolutely non-violent, limped along, ninety-ten, as long as I tried to play the little French wife. After a few years, I had a revelation: marriage is simply legalized prostitution. That's what it felt like. My husband kept power over me by criticizing me constantly, chipping away at my self-confidence, and keeping a tight hold on the purse strings. My psychic freedom was evaporating. Without the head-start my parents had given me, I might have been done in.

After eight years, I realized that I did not like my husband, and I did not like myself. Although I couldn't do anything about him, I could do something about me. It was 1962, Suzanne and Marc were six and four, and since I didn't have a specialized education, I didn't have many options. I decided to take a secretarial course, so I could earn my own living and not be trapped in that damned dependency.

While I was taking the course, a momentous thing happened—I joined the Voice of Women (vow), a peace group campaigning against nuclear testing, and was invited to join the Quebec executive. This was perhaps the most important single event in my life. Here were powerful women, who included Thérèse Casgrain and Simonne Monet-Chartrand in Quebec, as well as Muriel Duckworth and Ursula Franklin in other parts of Canada, bringing great competence, energy, and gusto to the task of changing the world. Here was solidarity among women, and a calm assurance that we could accomplish what we set out to do. Here were women with great confidence in my abilities. We used to joke that this was the only women's group we would consider joining. Most women's groups seemed so trivial, so auxiliary.

My first jobs were offered through Voice of Women friends, including my job at the National Film Board (NFB), and I learned many skills that served to advance my career. Very early on, then, I learned the value of solidarity among women, of mutual support, of the importance of other women in my life, and of the impact women can have on society. My children's tooth fairy was Dr. Ursula Franklin, who organized a nation-wide scientific study of Strontium 90 in baby teeth, gathering the teeth through Voice of Women members, about 20,000 strong across Canada, who blanketed their local schools. The strength of her report factored in the American government's decision to cease testing nuclear weapons in the atmosphere.

The personal growth I went through with my Voice of Women activities helped me find the strength to leave my husband. When I did so, he kidnapped my son and returned to France. That was the worst moment in my life. With financial support from my parents and moral support from my vow friends, I struggled through divorce and custody proceedings in France, with the small comfort that at least the dice are weighted on the side of the mothers in custody battles. In the meantime, Suzanne and I were drawing closer, and overcoming some of the tensions we had gone through with her allergies. A year later Marc came home, and we were a one-parent family of three. My children were seven and nine years old.

I wish that, at the time, someone had told me, "Of course you can parent these children well by yourself. Yes, it will be hard, and exhausting, both physically and emotionally, but you are perfectly capable of managing quite well." It took me several years to realize it myself, during which I often felt inadequate, and even occasionally looked for a replacement father—a fool-hardy project.

I wonder if it is easier to bring children up with a feminist viewpoint when the father is not around? It was possible for Dorothy to do this with my brother and me because our father was on the other side of the Atlantic. If he had been here, she would not have had the freedom to bring me up the way she wanted. On the other hand, Dorothy's father was a strong pillar in her egalitarian education, and one of her boyfriends, who lived with us for three years, gave her crucial support as she started to build her career. He was a Spanish anarchist who profoundly believed in an egalitarian society, and lived up to his beliefs.

All this time, as I was working and educating myself and was occasionally lucky with boyfriends, my children were growing up. Marc leafleted against war toys with me, and he also helped us learn about video cameras when we first started experimenting with video at the National Film Board. Suzanne used the video once in a class project. But I was careful not to drag my kids willy-nilly into my enthusiasms, and I tried very hard not to brainwash them. I just hoped that my example would encourage them to get actively involved when some political issue struck them as being worth fighting for.

The problem was that Dorothy was so passionate about her politics, her work and in fact, her life that there was little room for our own passions to blossom. Our house was so full of political posters that when I moved into my own place I didn't want anything on the walls and I wanted them all white.

As I look back on those years, the thing I most regret is that my friends had no time for my children. Just remembering that, the old anxiety floods back. I was no longer active in Voice of Women because I couldn't spare the time between mothering, homemaking, and carrying a full-time job. Ironically, one branch of vow evolved into the first feminist consciousness-raising group in Montréal, but as much as I needed it, I couldn't participate.

While my mother was juggling her various roles and teaching us to cook and do the housework, I was growing towards adolescence. I had been brought up a feminist, and didn't have much to rebel against. Kids used to talk about having an idol, like rock stars, and I would say, "I don't have any idols, but I rather admire my mother." Then the year I turned twelve I was sick all fall, and when I returned to school I just couldn't catch up, so I started to skip school and lie to my mother. Of course she caught me, and decided to send me off to my grandparents from Easter to summer, and then, as usual, to my father in France for the holidays. When I got back, I decided that home with my mother was the best place to be after all. Somehow those five months away had given me a new perspective. One day I announced to my mother, "Dorothy, I don't idolize you any more!" From then on our mother-daughter relationship evolved on non-traditional terms, based on free communication, without the usual patterns of authority or manipulation, without lying, and without trying to please in order to obtain something. We began a dialogue of equals, which was totally honest. My friends kept getting trapped in their lies to their parents, and I thought it was too much trouble to remember fictitious stories.

When Suzanne told me she didn't idolize me any more, my heart burst with joy. I had been struggling to find that delicate line between being a strong parent my children could count on, without attempting to live up to the myth of the supermom. I wanted my children to know that if you want to live fully, you can be strong and vulnerable simultaneously, that you can cry and rage and laugh and be sad and make mistakes and still be strong. I didn't abdicate my parental role, but I trusted Suzanne, and she knew her confidences would be treated with respect. She was willing to take responsibilities. We proceeded along that slow transition from a child–parent relationship to a friendship between equals.

I had a lot of freedom for a girl my age and people were often surprised, but I also had responsibilities. Dorothy believed that the amount of freedom you could have was in direct relation to the amount of responsibility you carried for yourself and for the household. You couldn't live on a free ticket.

Establishing these principles did not come easily. We did not manage to get through her adolescence without serious conflict. It centred around housework.

During my teen years, Dorothy travelled a fair amount, and she demanded that the house be clean and tidy when she got back. As the eldest, it was my responsibility to make certain that this occurred, although Marc certainly helped. When Dorothy was home, I figured housekeeping was her responsibility. She thought I should at least participate, but I was sick and tired of it. Not only that, we often had friends of Marc's or mine seeking haven with us for months at a time, as well as friends of Dorothy's visiting from all over the country. It got hopelessly hectic, and we started some serious squabbling. By the time I was eighteen, it became clear to me that we needed to live in separate homes, if our growing friendship was to survive. Only then would it be possible for me to develop my own passions, whatever they might be. I would decide when to do my own dishes. I would no longer just be an observer in life. I realized that Dorothy did not leave us much space, because she took up so much space herself. I was discovering my own sense of self, my own strength.

I didn't realize I took up so much space, although even if I had, I wouldn't have censored or put a damper on myself. I had no intention of sacrificing myself on the altar of motherhood, as I had when I tried to become the perfect housewife. After Suzanne left home, we sometimes saw each other once a week, sometimes once a month. When we did see each other, it was because we wanted to. We enjoyed each other.

In the mid-sixties, Mom sent me a copy of *The Feminine Mystique,* which started me on the path to looking at the patterns that were taking shape from my experiences. Almost in the same breath I landed a job at the Expo '67 Youth Pavilion, where women held prominent positions, and seemed to be getting a head-start in building a feminist power base, and making real changes in their world.

In 1968 I was hired by the National Film Board of Canada to work in "Challenge for Change," an experimental program designed to improved communications and provoke social change. At the time the film world was almost an all-male domain, and here, unexpectedly, was a job that would allow me to channel my passionate involvement in the peace movement and in the struggle for civil liberties and social justice. Our first experiment was to "give a voice to the voiceless" by putting video in the hands of a citizens' committee. This was the beginning of my discovery, made again and again as I travelled in Canada, Great Britain, Denmark, and Australia, that hard-working women were the heart and muscle of welfare rights groups, neighbourhood groups, ecology groups, and co-operatives of all kinds. Women were moving beyond auxiliary roles to positions of leadership and influence. It wasn't utopia—there were always struggles—but I was heartened by what I saw.

I was learning a great deal about grassroots activism. By the time I attended a Women and Ecology conference ten years later, I felt I had come home to a feminism that said what I wanted to say. Eight hundred women came together to talk about changing the world. The overwhelming message was that feminism was not merely a fight to obtain half of the old, polluted, competitive, unjust pie; it was a fight for a whole new recipe, based on ecological sustainability, peace, and social justice.

Dorothy and I both worked on our first films the same year. I was at the New School at Dawson College during its first year, and management was threatening to close it down. A group of the students decided to make a Super-8 film about the school to show to management and the board of directors, to prove to them how important it was to keep the school open. It worked. The following year we made another film to show at an educational conference. By then I was hooked.

After that, while I guaranteed my rent by working as a barmaid, I helped a friend in the editing room, then got a few more apprenticeship contracts, and finally work as a production assistant on commercials. My next jobs were as location manager, then unit manager, then production manager, on commercials or large productions in private industry where conditions were very cut-throat. There was no room for mistakes. Fortunately, I happen to be a perfectionist, which fit in well with that world, even though I challenged some of its power games with my non-confrontational style. After sixteen years in the industry, I became a producer.

I have found that in the film world in Québec, because of the long history of women's roles in mothering/bossing/organizing large families, it has not particularly been a struggle to be a woman in a strong position in the industry. There is a good history of female production managers and producers, and their authority is not often questioned. There was no particular support for women, but little discrimination, either. One worked one's way up the ladder, period. It took me years to encounter the consequences of the "boy's club" mentality, which is particularly exclusionary towards women directors, whose films are diminishing in number every year, even in Québec.

That is not to say there haven't been some hurdles. In one incident, I was hired to be a production manager on a beer commercial, but the client didn't think that, as a woman, I could know enough about beer to have that kind of position on the production—after all, women had not traditionally been seen as beer drinkers. Another time I was to be hired as production manager for an action film to be co-produced with France. The French producer did not believe that a young woman could be right for the position—an action film in the wilderness of Canada needed a man for the job. Subsequently, I occasionally encountered surprise when, in my position as producer, I would meet possible co-producers in France. My relative youth, regardless of my experience, put them a bit off kilter. It has become clear to me that we still have battles left for equality, that so many of the old structures and mentalities are still in place.

A mother's comment: Sometimes it would be like an I.Q. test, to see how long it took these men to realize Suzanne was serious, efficient, and knew her job well.

Working in the commercial film world resembled working in a factory that happened to make images; it lacked the human touch. I didn't mind doing a lot of hard work, but I wanted a more people-oriented context, so I started working on much smaller projects that were closer to my heart. I love producing small, unique feature films by creative authors, the "film d'auteur," and I have produced seven first features for up-and-coming filmmakers. Unfortunately, Canada's funding agencies are supporting commercial, "international" work (i.e., imitation American) at the expense of cultural, creative films that are still produced by experienced professionals, but don't have millions in pre-sales. Fewer and fewer "auteur" films are being produced. I'm afraid we are turning into a nation with no cultural vision, and no awareness that our future depends on one.

No matter where women work, there are both setbacks and leaps ahead. In 1976 the women were squeezed out of "Challenge for Change," and by 1978 the program was dead. Meanwhile, in 1977 I was invited to join Studio D, the fresh, young women's studio in English Production at the NFB. Here was a chance to work collaboratively, in solidarity with other creative women. It was us against the world, against the bureaucracy, us against all those men who were out to "git us." It was also a chance to work in all-women crews (after the Studio fought to obtain training for women in camera, sound, and lighting). I loved the atmosphere of an all-women milieu; the gentle voices, the absence of grandstanding and other macho games. We had the freedom to aim our films at the women in the audience, who responded enthusiastically. We knew we were doing useful work.

Then Bonnie Klein directed and I produced *Not a Love Story: a Film About Pornography*, which was finished in 1982. Making the film was a long and arduous process, because the hate-filled nature of our subject matter affected us deeply and ground us down emotionally. We were very close to man-hating at that time, but I could never quite write men off when I had such good men in my father, my brother, and my son; Bonnie's husband and son were also steadfast in their support. When it was finished we took our film on the road, working with audiences, a simultaneously draining and invigorating process. Women were moved and distraught and angry, and then they thanked us for making it. Male film critics were furious with the film, and men in the audience were shaken. The film took off in world-wide distribution. The studio, which had also produced two Academy Award-winning films, *I'll Find a Way* by Beverly Shaffer and *If You Love This Planet* by Terre Nash, became a success. We were called "the jewel in the crown corporation."

How do you take a feminist stance when you are successful? Personally I thought we deserved to be successful, that we should celebrate our success and use it to leverage more money for films that would help women change their lives. By nature, I had always been upbeat, optimistic, self-confident, and prone to speaking up for our talents and accomplishments. Unfortunately, I was considered unrealistic by a few studio women who fueled their feminism with anger at the plight of women as victims. It is true that the NFB bureaucracy was uncomfortable with our success, and persisted in giving us only ten percent of the budget. There were constant battles to be fought. But we rarely celebrated our own achievements, and always focussed on the blocks and barriers in our path.

Ironically, the Studio D films about women were strong, hopeful, and powerful, and attracted huge audiences. Yet many of the women making them were suffering a process of disempowerment. For example, I had been the person who dealt with young freelancers or students who wanted some sort of aid from the studio. I helped films like *A Wives' Tale*, by Sophie Bissonnette, Joyce Rock, and Martin Duckworth, and a number of others, something I loved doing, but the task was taken away from me. I wanted to make a film about mother and daughter friendship—a decade ago, before any of the films that have since come out about mothers and daughters—but the idea was refused, with the suggestion that there was no such thing as mother-daughter friendship. By the end of my twelve years in Studio D, I felt much less powerful, and had far less support for accomplishing my goals than I had had in "Challenge for Change." I had myself collaborated in the process by attempting to fit in. What we don't do to try to belong to our chosen group! I sincerely admired the intelligence, erudition and clear analysis of my chief and was often in agreement with her ideas, which made me vulnerable to her put-downs. She mouthed the words of egalitarianism and non-hierarchical collaboration, but she held the reins of power with an iron hand.

By 1984, I was finding Studio D's rhetoric tiresome and misguided. It was like living with a psychiatrist who is constantly psychoanalyzing you. I watched Dorothy suffer because she was not allowed to hire the best person to help her on a very difficult shoot, and had incompetent people imposed on her film just because they were card-carrying feminists. Yes, affirmative action for women is necessary, and yes, you want women to acquire experience, but not at the expense of the film. It was difficult for me to see my mother pay such a high price for the rhetoric. But Dorothy was also mired in the ideology. Our friendship was becoming strained, and seeing the professional incompetence drove me batty.

In 1989 all the staff film directors in Studio D were summarily turfed into the "men's" studios in English Production, ostensibly to make room for younger women, who would be freelancers and therefore would not be in a position to question management decisions. I can't describe how much pain I went through. We had invested our hearts and guts in Studio D; I felt totally betrayed. I took a year's sabbatical in order to heal. My shining vision of a feminist way of working, collaborative and non-hierarchical, was dead as the proverbial door-nail.

I don't know if I would have permanently joined the ranks of those bitter ex-feminists still licking their wounds from the in-fighting if I hadn't had the regenerating experience of working with the women of *Regards de femmes*, the women's studio in French Production. Their refreshingly frank acknowledgement that we lived in the hierarchical world of film, and their respect and encouragement, allowed me to experience again what I had lived long ago with Bonnie Klein: the pleasure of teamwork with other women, along with the men who supported us.

My healing continued through a course at Concordia University on Women and the Fine Arts. My creativity blossomed as I threw myself into painting, and my classmates, as well as the professors, Corinne Corey and Nell Tenhaaf, created a dynamic atmosphere of positive, tough but useful criticism. In this atmosphere, I could see that at Studio D we had never really perfected a method of positive criticism. We had been perhaps too polite, or too repressed. Perhaps we feared being unpopular, or hurting others. Whatever the reason, it was a lesson we could have learned, and didn't.

As I write this in the summer of 1996, seven years after the staff directors were ejected from Studio D, we have just received the news that Studio D is being shut down. There has been barely a whimper.

Yes, there had been some wonderful films made by freelancers in the meantime, but the heart had gone out of the studio itself. It had become a producer with a telephone. Now the National Film Board is getting rid of most of its staff directors, including me, "in order to hire young, up-and-coming freelancers." Although I'm angry at having my career cut short at sixty years old when I'm just hitting my stride, I am relieved to be leaving this place I have always loved, because it has been decimated and feels like a morgue. The technocrats have taken over, and they believe that human beings are merely interchangeable parts, like gears in a machine. They don't understand that films come from passionate, gutsy, vulnerable people who need support and encouragement and tough challenges, and a milieu that helps them blossom. They think the corporate-commercial model is suitable for the National Film Board. I am deeply sad to watch the Film Board being dismantled, and horrified that the technocrats carrying out the pillage are women. Margaret Thatcher was always an embarrassment, but when carbon copies of the Iron Maiden take over your own institution, it's devastating. Who knows if the Film Board will survive another seven years? Yet the old NFB that knew how to raise tough questions and seek humane answers is needed more than ever.

For my last film, *You won't need running shoes, darling,* I could not get support from the "men's" studio. I had to go out and buy my own Hi-8 camera and learn to do the camera work myself. I finally got support from English Production late in the shooting, and was able to have a wonderful editor and musician. It's a film about growing old, about living fully and loving life no matter how much your body is going to hell in a handcart. I shot it with my parents, and there are perhaps little echoes in it of that long-cherished mother-and-daughter friendship, as well as my father-and-daughter friendship too.

I've had more than one reason to be grateful for my friendship with my mother and our close family ties. I had not set out deliberately to have a baby on my own. Deep down, though, I had always known that there were no guarantees for the length of a relationship. When I met a wonderful, charismatic African filmmaker, our mutual attraction deepened into love. He lived in France and Africa, and was separating from his wife. Our commitment to one another was strong enough that we set about the project of conceiving a baby, not an easy task when you have to cross the Atlantic at the right time. Just as I called him to tell him we had succeeded, he told me his family council had determined he should return to his wife. I felt like a tornado of joy and pain. I was thirty-six years old. At that time my mother told me that if I decided to keep the baby, conceived in love, she would help me in any way she could. When I decided I would, our close-knit family came through for me, offering co-parenting support. My brother Marc and my mother attended prenatal classes with me and we were all together for the birth. Marc since then has started a family of his own, and Dorothy is committed to remaining a vital component of our life.

Being a single mother would have been very difficult without the support and involvement of my mother. It has been a blessing that we decided to buy a triplex together when I was in my early twenties. Up until Belkis' birth we saw each other whenever our professional lives permitted, sometimes not for months at a time, sometimes fairly often. But when Belkis was born Dorothy just had to come up the stairs from her apartment to mine to help and be around. We slipped into a routine of eating our meals and doing all our activities together. Apart from sleeping in different apartments, we were a family unit. There are some very positive repercussions to this situation, such as Belkis having a grandmother as a co-parent. I think that whether you are a single parent or not it is important to expand the notion of family to include many generations.

I am also surrounded by friends who have started their own families, including several single mothers, so we can share our problems and our joys. Although Belkis is an only child, these friends and their children are an important part of her life. I saw us as living the new/ancient notion of extended family. We may be evolving one of the solutions to the challenges of being a mother with a profession, although I have to say that a really good daycare centre is an important part of the mix.

There are practical benefits to having another adult sharing your life—like one taking the daycare run and the other cooking—but it isn't ideal to share your day-to-day life with your mother. There are definitely some down sides to it: as our co-parenting routine evolved, we came to do all the cooking and living in my place. This meant that Dorothy gave up her kitchen which had always been the heart of her home, while I felt mine was invaded because she wanted to change things around. Because I worked out of my home, I wound up doing the cooking all the time while she picked Belkis up at daycare. We both suffered from the loss of privacy.

By the time Belkis was about two, it dawned on me that Dorothy's and my situation gave us all the stresses of a couple without the perks of sex. We were about to start giving each other more space when my brother's partner had to be hospitalized for the last three months of her pregnancy so she wouldn't lose the baby. Suddenly we had my toddler nephew, Louka, living with us for four months, and then staying with us every weekend after that. We had to continue our tight rhythm for another year. Things are never easy.

Some things that are easy are the simple elements of tending a home together. I have shared an apartment with several men and women, and it always seemed to be the men who needed to be nudged, while women see what there is to be done and just do it. But in the end, I don't want to be a couple with my mother. After all, I still hope to share my life with a man some day.

Luckily, fate came and saved us. I was offered a job at TFO, the French network of TV Ontario, and have been living in Toronto for the last year. Belkis misses Dorothy and so do I, but we have lots of friends here, and we have also managed to see Dorothy at least once a month, if not more, since we left. My grandfather lives half-way between Montreal and Toronto, so we plan to meet there as often as we can. I have to admit, it sure is nice to have my privacy back. I'm still doing all my own cooking, though.

After having plunged wholeheartedly into co-parenting, I have enjoyed getting my adult life back, now that Suzi and Belkis have left. I love watching the babies grow, love watching them affirm themselves, love being with them. I have more patience than I used to, I think, although Suzi isn't sure about that—she doesn't think I have enough. I don't begrudge giving them my full attention for long periods of time. I have fun with them. I also loved hanging out with Suzanne, although she can be pretty prickly sometimes. She is the only person I know who can intimidate me. But I missed my freedom, I missed the time to paint and sew and write and go to the movies after work. Slowly we had eliminated most other activities from our lives except work and kids. Both of us wanted more space, but we stuck to each other like glue. We always agreed to spend more time separately, but then just drifted into the everyday activities together. It's a bit of a mystery to me why we couldn't find a better balance in our co-parenting and our private lives. We did, however, become less communicative, and I think it had to do with at least wanting to keep our thoughts private, even if we were busy tidying the house together. It was really a gift of fate that she went to Toronto. We now take renewed pleasure in seeing each other, although the communication is only returning slowly. Underneath the surface tensions, however, we have absolute faith in each other, and we know that each can count on the other when needed. We know we are linked for life.

That indissoluble bond may be what differentiates a mother-daughter or a sibling friendship from a love relationship. There are fewer highs and lows, although no fewer tensions, and we know we're in it for the long haul. I must say that my relationship with my mother went through several falling-out periods when we wouldn't phone each other for months. Luckily we were blessed with bad memories, and soon we could not remember why we were mad. We missed each other. So we struggled through the hard parts and knit our friendship back together. Suzi and I do the same.

I had waited a long time to have a baby, essentially for two reasons. One, I had few illusions about the amount of work involved in parenting, although I have discovered its true extent "on-the-job"; and two, I had spent too much time nurturing others in my work to envisage the additional job of parenting. I had always wanted to have children, but I didn't feel the pressures of a biological clock.

As the mother of little Belkis I have distanced myself from the demands of the film industry in order to be with my daughter as much as I can while earning my living, because I can't count on the future to live with her. This approach has been neither professionally nor financially rewarding. To keep up in the film industry, women have to work the same hours as the men, who rarely appear to have family lives or responsibilities. You can't call the daycare at six p.m. and ask them to hold on to your daughter until you finish negotiating a contract. What does society intend to do with single mothers: keep them on welfare or work them into the ground? There has got to be a better way to organize work so we can survive—even flourish.

When Belkis was born, I had to cut down the amount of work I attempted to accomplish in a day, because my other job as mother required my attention. Kids need to eat properly, to play, and go to bed at a decent hour. Mothers need to sleep. I realized that I didn't have the energy to put together a major project. This insight came to me only after I came out of that phase, although I had consciously decided to do smaller projects that I thought wouldn't eat me up. In fact they may have taken fewer hours of my day, but they took several years of my life.

I had always likened my role as producer to that of a parent, but I didn't fully realize how accurate I was. As a producer I have to be fully aware of what the screenwriter and director are doing, I have to encourage them, I have to discipline them, I have to go into minute detail with them and I have to be able to keep a broad perspective at all times. All the problems land in my lap and I have to keep the hope going. It feels like mothering all right. Pushing or pulling a project along takes a lot of energy.

As I struggled to balance my work time and my mothering time, I had to begin dealing with Belkis's education in the face of racism. Dorothy had always taught my brother and me to have pride in our individuality, in our differences, in our multiple roots. I am bicultural, and it was not easy to fit into Québec as the product of the two colonizers. You face conflict when you don't want to choose between Georges Brassens, Joan Baez, and Robert Charlebois, when there are words that express your thoughts perfectly in the language other than the one you're speaking, when you refuse to take cultural sides. I was and still am deeply committed to Québec, but not to the exclusion of Canada, or France for that matter. I decided I would try to take the best of all worlds and look outward. I still try.

My bicultural experience has given me a tiny insight into what my daughter's life will be: the sense of never wholly belonging to one camp or the other, the ostracization and racism that may follow, but also the possible strength that can arise from a multiple vision of the world.

One has to resist the pressure to compartmentalize life into small holes. Luckily Canada might have a head start in this for two reasons. One, we don't have to identify ourselves officially by our race. This is important, not only because people do not know your race without seeing you, but also because the powerful culture bombarding us from the United States forces "half-black" people to divest themselves of the half that doesn't show, and encourages self-hatred of at least part of the self. Two, in Canada we identify ourselves as a mosaic and not a melting pot. Although this can sound like a contradiction, I believe that to be as happy as you can with your multiplicity, you must know its various components. Through knowledge we gain a healthy perspective on our humanity.

This view led to my concern that my daughter get to know her African heritage. I have only asked one thing of her father—to provide her with knowledge of her African roots. He is willing but inconsistent, since he lives on the other side of the Atlantic, mostly in Europe and sometimes in Africa. He is an artist with strong political and social positions, which I greatly respect, but these notions cannot be infused without contact. She has been with him four times, at the ages of two months, a year and some, at two-and-a-half, and at four. I have videotaped them together so that she has a permanent record of him and their activities. He phones fairly frequently, if erratically. On her last trip, she stayed with his family for a few days, and finally met her older brothers. I hope this is the beginning of a solid connection with them.

I haven't developed an African network, although I do have some African friends. The complexities of francophone West African cultures are somewhat daunting to sift through and one doesn't want to do the wrong thing. I had just joined an interracial family alliance that could offer a certain level of support before I moved to Toronto. It's not easy for a white mother to know how best to bring her multiracial daughter up, except to make sure she is open to people of different backgrounds.

When Belkis encounters the English-speaking North-American world, she will be perceived as a black North American (or Afro-Canadian, as they are now saying, and although this is not the place to discuss this, it is a term that is questioned by Africans), but her specific racial and cultural backgrounds bring up different issues from the many other groups that have followed a vast diversity of paths to be in Canada. There is maybe one thing that is comforting: that she might have somewhat less of a struggle to be multiracial than the previous generation by the sheer fact that she won't be as isolated in numbers. Then again it might bring on new hurdles to overcome. All I can do is try to infuse her with as much self-confidence, joy, knowledge, and strength as I can so that she may have some of the tools to deal with life.

I have been grateful to my parents for their total acceptance of their little caramel-coloured great-granddaughter. They were brought up in a fiercely racist world, but racism never had a hold on them. My father believes it is lucky that Belkis has all that melanin in her skin to protect her from the sun's rays as the ozone layer diminishes. He also worries, not without reason, that she will suffer discrimination and cruelty. In daycare, she has already been told that brown skin is ugly, and white skin is best. I am very conscious that the white world is profoundly racist, even though attitudes have been changing. The National Action Committee on the Status of Women has been doing some good work in challenging racism. I'm still educating myself on the issues, but I try to move people forward on racism wherever I happen to be active. I have learned to understand the patterns and power structures, and I know I'm not alone in the struggle, so being connected to feminism makes it easier.

Being brought up a feminist has not made it easier to find a partner. I have not given up the hope that one day I will find an independent man who wants to share my life as an equal partner, but I have not had much luck up to now. When I was much younger, my looks were ethereal and delicate, with tumbling hair and romantically pale features, and I loved to wear velvet and lace. I can understand why my Québecois boyfriends were confused. They seemed to be looking for someone they could take care of and boss around. And when I wore sweatsuits, I attracted those who were looking for a mother figure, someone who would do the bossing. I didn't seem to meet anybody in between who might have been struggling towards equality.

Some of my male friends would say, "I admire you, I love exchanging ideas with you, but I can't see you as a sexual being." Perhaps I didn't know how to flirt, or play seduction games. I don't think I wanted to know. Some of my boyfriends saw my vulnerability without perceiving my strength, and then later, when the strength began to dawn on them, they took it as a personal insult. They couldn't see that I had struggled all my life, and that makes you strong. Most of the men whom I encountered, who didn't fear me or perceive my strength as threatening, came from an entirely different culture, including my daughter's father.

I think one of the reasons for our present quandary comes from the confusion that men in our North American society are going though in terms of their sexual identity. Feminism has provoked serious questioning about the forms of sexual interaction. Most of these questions are crucial to the well-being of an egalitarian society, but I think that one of its temporary consequences is that men are struggling to develop their sensitivities without desexualizing themselves. Women who have defined what they don't want, have not quite defined what they do want in men. I think we are in an era of confusion and constant questioning. What is feminine, what is masculine, and how much of each should we all have?

It is a dilemma. I would like to share my life but it is not easy to create a couple when I don't need someone else in order to function. Couples are often described as "two halves of a whole"; maybe it's time it became "two wholes who fit together well" and want to share the path their lives take.

My life's path has taken many twists and turns, and yet its evolution has not deviated from the commitment to family, and to the struggle for a better world, as I see it. Looking back, I think feminism has contributed to my life on several levels. One is the real changes that have come about in our society with regards to women's legal status and the options open to women, which need to be celebrated. Yet we must continue to roar like lions over the injustices that are growing as our governments jump in the lifeboat and leave us stranded on a sinking ship. The feminists' fight to create a society of social justice is becoming even more difficult as the corporate forces array themselves against us to consolidate their power. I plan to spend my energies in retirement in fighting injustices, whether it is racism or the economic juggernaut that is removing the social safety net so essential for our society's survival. I want to try to make the world a safe and good place for my grandchildren.

Another level of change has been that increasingly we value women working together. We are no longer women's auxiliaries to men's associations; we have achieved a great deal in our own organizations, and have learned to value our collective strength.

We also value the small groups of women who gather together in friendship and treat each other with respect. When I grew up, one always accepted a date, even if it meant letting down the group of girls you were to go out with. Friends understood that dating a man was *more important*, but not any more. Women are no longer willing to play second fiddle in their own lives. We have also come to understand that mother-and-daughter friendship, that relationship it was said we couldn't have, is possible, and well worth the effort.

We're also speaking up for friendships through several generations. Belkis was born on the very day of Grandmère's eightieth birthday, and their bond was strong and immediate. For a year and a half, we were four generations of women, woven together by history and love.

When my mother died, I felt the profound loss of a beloved friend, and the mantle of the matriarch in the family passed to me. How do we keep memories alive? I was so grateful to have hours of video of my mother to show to my grandchildren, to keep the ephemeral nature of life at bay. When it is my turn to go, how long will I be remembered? Eventually we all leave with barely a trace.

I always wanted to hear stories from my grandmothers. Knowing about my family helps me know more about myself. By sharing our life experiences, maybe we can encourage others to feel less alone, even as we recognize our uniqueness. Somehow it feels good to share what it is to be a woman with the next generation. We keep people alive, in our memories, when we talk about them.

Our daughters reflect us, and we reflect our mothers to them, so that traces of ourselves pass on down the line. From one generation to the next weaves the thread of women loving, supporting and struggling with each other, as it must be if we wish to live as fully as we possibly can.

I Will Not Be Silent

Meg Hickling

Growing up, I cannot ever remember thinking that as a girl I was not equal to anyone. Nor do I remember noticing that the females in my extended farm family were not equal partners with their menfolk. It seemed to me that they were all agents of their own lives, although each was also a victim of external circumstances such as the Depression of the 1930s or World War II. The very real dangers of farming were shared equally by all.

Of all my family, my grandmother seemed to me to be the most intelligent and broad-minded. She had had only a few years of primary school, but she read voraciously to educate herself and to satisfy an insatiable curiosity about the world beyond her experience. She had raised two sons (including my father) and three daughters who all chose their own lives. For the boys, the war intervened, but the girls were educated beyond high school for the careers of their choice. Each of the five siblings chose their own marriage partners and no one ever seemed to judge or malign the one sister who chose not to have children. All of the women, as well as my mother, seemed to have marriages based on mutual respect—they did what they wanted to do with their lives and never seemed oppressed. I remember them taking afternoons off from the daily farm chores to hold enormous tea parties, bridal showers and shopping trips to neighbouring towns. Although these women worked hard everyday, they also took holidays with and without their husbands. They took their duties to their children and to aged relatives very

176

seriously but none was welded to her husband's side. At the same time, in the 1950s, there was a great deal of sexism in society, especially for girls and the careers they could choose. Some of this was also classist. Working-class girls who didn't marry straight from high school were expected to go to business school to train as typists and clerks. Middle class girls went to normal schools for teacher training or to hospitals to train as nurses.

My parents and grandmother had survived two World Wars and the Depression. Although no young woman in my family had been widowed, we were all aware of women who had been, and my family did not want me to be unable to support myself. Interestingly, my brothers were also taught to look after themselves, in case they were widowed or had invalid wives—a not uncommon condition among our farming neighbours. My brothers were taught to cook, to do sewing repairs and to clean house. My father and uncle often cooked meals and kept house when their wives were pregnant or ill. Divorce was never considered, but premature death or chronic illness was always present in our community and careful planning was necessary to deal with it. Marriage was ideal, but perhaps because my parents and their siblings all married late, I felt no pressure to get married.

The childhood life I led unfolded on a small, thirty-acre mixed farm, which my dad had inherited from his father, an Okanagan pioneer. Perhaps it was being raised a triplet (my mother said) with younger twin brothers that reinforced the idea that I could do anything a boy could do. I had indoor responsibilities, my brothers had outdoor chores, but I was encouraged to belong to the 4-H Club and to raise a steer each year just as my brothers were taught to cook and to help with dishes, etc. My dad sold livestock and my mother had a separate income from egg and milk sales. I refused to learn to milk the cows. My father and brothers loved to fish and often went to mountain lakes on Sundays. I loved the solitude of those days, reading and reading, and secretly pleased that I would not be expected to do the milking on Sunday evenings to help out the fishermen. I much preferred the indoor chores and the 4-H Club bookkeeping and would even do my brothers' accounts if they would muck out my stalls in exchange.

In Grade Eleven each girl at my school was taken aside for career planning. My peers called me "a brain" but the guidance teacher suggested that I go into nursing because "farm girls don't go to university." My aunt, after whom I had been named, was a nurse, and several of my peers were going into nursing, so I thought it would be the thing to do. I remember feeling that I didn't have any choice, but I wasn't terribly unhappy about it. I was caught up in the preparations, writing medical exams and ordering uniforms. The nursing school was a hundred miles away from the farm, so I would have to leave home. Before I left, the neighbourhood women held a party for me, and it felt as if I were being welcomed into the world of adult women.

The hospital in which the nursing school was located was typical of the 1950s, with sexism and classism thoroughly entrenched. Nurses stood when a doctor entered a room and doctors were never questioned, even when their decisions harmed a patient. A few of them were clearly uncomfortable with this god-like status, but most accepted it as their due. There were no female doctors or administrators, except for a matron.

During my training I began to see a lot of life that I hadn't known anything about previously. Abortion was illegal and I nursed women who died or would be left seriously disabled by self-induced or back-street abortions. The shame and intense frustrations of their partners and families were evident. I remember women sobbing that they had only had sex during menstruation and still got pregnant, trying everything to avoid a pregnancy. It was illegal to talk about family planning and there was an overwhelming conspiracy of silence from doctors and nurses.

Teens often got into "trouble," and shotgun marriages were common. The violence in these forced marriages was staggering. Tales of beatings, rape, and torture were told in secret to us as nurses, in the emergency department, on the maternity floor, and even more surprisingly to me, in pediatrics. I had not known about the cruelty and neglect of children before, and it often seemed to me to be a product of a parent who was too young and using alcohol to escape responsibility. I was amazed and then appalled, but most of all I remember the silence. No one did anything—no husband was called to account, no father was charged, no reports were made, and never was a woman counseled. In fact, we student nurses were constantly told not to talk, under the guise of patient confidentiality. Sometimes we were told that our careers would be terminated if we reported any of it. Women bore the brunt of that silence. I knew that I had been very lucky to be raised in a family of mutual regard. I vowed then that if I ever married and had children I would not let them grow up like that and, further, that their neighbourhood and community would be as safe and as nurturing as possible. I would not be silent.

One incident was particularly formative for my development as a feminist. The obstetrical floor where I worked was managed by an English-trained midwife who was considered quite progressive for the late 1950s. Usually fathers were sent home while their wives laboured, but this head nurse invited them into the delivery room after the birth. They were shown the newborn and then left alone with the new mother for a half-hour before the woman was moved to her room and the father was sent home. New parents loved this innovation and often talked about how marvelous that half-hour of privacy was.

One morning, a new father was seen hurrying out of the delivery room after only twenty minutes. The head nurse and I went in to move the woman. She was strangely silent, pale, and obviously in pain. We discovered that intercourse had taken place and all the episiotomy sutures were out. The head nurse's face was a mask of anger as she stared at the woman's vulva. She stalked out, saying that she'd have to call the doctor back to resuture her and how could she have allowed such a filthy thing to happen?

Only a year older than this patient, I was filled with pity and horror. I wanted to hold the now sobbing woman and assure her that she was not at fault and that all would be well, but I knew that the head nurse would not approve. It would not be seen as professional behaviour. Instead, I busied myself cleaning up the room. Then the obstetrician stormed in, shouting at the woman for allowing her husband to do this, for not calling out if she couldn't stop him. He then resutured her without freezing, to "teach her a lesson."

I was completely baffled by the head nurse's reaction, in particular because I'd expected more of a woman and especially because she'd seemed so progressive. Surely this was rape. Why was the woman at fault? I couldn't verbalize those questions then and I was warned never to tell anyone. Of course, everyone on staff knew because of the doctor's shouting and cursing. There was an aura of overwhelming shame around the incident. The staff gossiped about it for days afterwards, and in the cold, unsupportive care the woman was given, she was isolated in a single room and discharged to her mother and sister days earlier than was normal. I helped dress the baby and wanted to tell this woman not to be ashamed, but I said nothing.

It was years before I would understand my drive and passion to educate everyone about a different way of looking at power and sexuality, and to name my perspective as feminist.

Another nursing incident comes to mind. I was nursing a sixty-year-old man who was dying of kidney failure because of an enlarged prostate gland. He and I talked about the doctor's inability to save his life and I asked him why he had not come in earlier when the prostate problem could have been alleviated. He said, "Nurse, since I have been in hospital, I've learned that the proper word is penis, but all my life the only word I had was pecker and I knew that word was rude. How could I tell the doctor there was something wrong with my pecker?" He was losing his life not only because he lacked vocabulary, but also because he didn't know his own body. There was nothing wrong with his penis, and he didn't know he had a prostate gland.

As a feminist educator I believe that boys and men need as much education as girls and women to prevent such tragedies. Teaching patients and friends began to come easily to me as a professional in the medical community. But teaching my own children was much harder. My husband and I have one daughter and two sons. We model a safe, nourishing, and mutually supportive family life for them. But our own parents were not comfortable talking about sexual health and neither of us had school programs that were helpful. I had to force myself to teach my children about their bodies, to use scientific vocabulary and not baby-talk. Of course they shared their knowledge with their friends as children have done for generations. My neighbours, knowing I was a nurse, encouraged this education of the neighbourhood.

In 1969, Prime Minister Pierre Trudeau made his famous statement, "The government has no place in the bedrooms of the nation." Suddenly it was legal to talk about sexual health and contraception. I joined Planned Parenthood Vancouver as a volunteer and, in 1978, was hired as their education co-ordinator. I spent the first few years visiting preschools, sitting on tiny chairs at parent meetings in preschools and church basements, speaking about children's sexual development and how to begin teaching children about their bodies. The parents and staff were learning too, although at first the audience was made up exclusively by mothers, with no fathers and sometimes no staff. Everyone was nervous and I soon learned to use humour and the power of stories. I encouraged them to think about knowledge as power; about how powerless they were as children and teens when no one would talk; and about how vulnerable and disabled they were and sometimes still are. Then they'd want me to "get us started, talk to our kids first, then we can carry on from your example." So now we hold sessions where parents, children, and other family members often learn together.

I've learned to keep myself inspired and passionate by grabbing every new bit of research to share with my audiences. Schools now call for the staff to be educated as well as students and their parents. Professional groups—doctors, nurses, social workers, clergy, pharmacists, lawyers and others—began asking for education sessions. I stayed at Planned Parenthood until 1987 when I began to work as a private consultant, focussing on preschoolers, elementary students, their parents, and the professionals who worked with them.

In retrospect, it seems to me that I have been haunted by my patients from the late 1950s and early 1960s who were so badly hurt, disenfranchised from any power over their own lives or who died because they didn't have the knowledge they needed. Bernard of Chartres in the 12th century said that we are like dwarfs on the shoulders of giants; we cannot see better or further by ourselves but only by being raised up by others. I hope that I am making up for my dwarf-silence, especially for that young woman on the delivery room table.

As a parent I have maintained a feminist stance that seems at times to be at odds with my friends who are parents. I spent hours as a young and not-so-young mother in consciousness-raising groups and in gatherings of friends, listening to them talk about their hopes and dreams for their children and how much they wanted grandchildren. There were heated discussions about the wisdom of guiding children and teens firmly into professional training, marriage, and parenthood. I never wanted those things and sometimes felt physically ill listening to such driving ambitions. I felt passionately that my children were to decide for themselves, to be agents of their own lives and never to feel pressured to marry or to produce grandchildren for me.

Sometimes I wonder if my children fully understand and appreciate my physical and emotional distance, or whether my lack of involvement seems to them to be a kind of disinterest or even abandonment. They had a mother who spoke out in support of girls and boys on the same soccer teams, who sat on PTAs and constantly called for equality (such as boys in sewing and girls in woodworking) and that God be genderless in Sunday school. There were probably times when having a feminist mom was hard.

In some ways, my feminism began in the church. I was five years old when I first heard Eve condemned for eating the apple in the Genesis creation story. I was baffled. She had opened human eyes to knowledge. How could she not be the hero? My Sunday school teachers and my parents were amused and somewhat indulgent of my position, but I was considered to be odd. I often felt as if I were being merely tolerated, a fringe member of church life, even though I attended regularly. In the late 1970s I was introduced to Process Theology and began to feel that I was not so strange. Understanding God as creative energy and ourselves as part of that creation has given me a place in Christianity. Alice Walker writes in her novel *The Color Purple* that God gets really pissed off if we don't notice the purple colour of the crocus. This is feminist theology at its best. God wants nothing more of us than to join in creation, helping each other into full divinity. One path is feminism.

Criticism of my stance has sometimes been hurtful, sometimes puzzling, and almost always from men. One father began by praising my presentation but said he would not allow his wife and children to attend because it was clear to him that I was a feminist evolutionist. This was because I had said that breast cancer was an adult disease, not a childhood disease. He maintained that "God made men perfect and therefore only a feminist evolutionist would tell children that men could get breast cancer." Another man who attended an adult workshop didn't want my "feminist angle" in the schools. This was because I had joked that the clitoris didn't get erect spontaneously like the penis "because it doesn't need to practice, it is perfect."

In 1992 I was nominated for the YWCA Women of Distinction Award for Health and Education. I was overwhelmed by the letters of support to the nomination. Several letters for the YWCA award, and later for the Registered Nurses Association of B.C. (RNABC) Award of Excellence and the B.C. Council for the Family Award of Distinguished Service to Families, state that in my work I make the world safer for women and children by educating men, including male sexual offenders. I was proud to accept all three awards and humbled by the accolades. But most of all I want to accept that praise by acknowledging first the victims of silence and, second, those who share and support my feminist vision of equal sexual health for everyone. I don't do my work alone.

There are probably as many definitions of feminism as there are feminists. Some I like, some I do not. I especially like Robin Morgan's: "Women are not inherently anything but human." My impression is that too many men and some women define feminists as men-haters or male wanna-be's. Irish writer Rebecca West observed wryly, "I myself have never been able to find out precisely what feminism is. I only know that people call me a feminist whenever I express sentiment that differentiates me from a doormat."

It is disheartening when women misunderstand feminism. Phyllis Schlaffly said during the American campaign for the equal-rights amendment: "If these women's libbers were nice to their husbands they would let them do what they want to do. They just don't want to be nice. They want to be ugly." But actress Marlo Thomas said it best: "A feminist is a man or a woman who already knows for a fact that men and women are equal, and who wants society to wake up to that fact, so the world can stop operating at half strength. So that half the brain, half the inspiration, half the joy and beauty, half the human resources in the world will no longer be wasted."

Amen.

A Long, Strange Trip It's Been

Linda Uyehara Hoffman

Minidoka, Idaho. March 1943. A family council. The eldest brother, born in Japan, looks at his sons and his youngest brother, all born in the United States, and cannot understand why they want to join the army of a country that has taken all their possessions and put them into camps. Nor can he understand their explanation that they are Americans who want to prove their loyalty to their country. Looking at his youngest brother, he says, "And I guess we're supposed to take care of your wife and daughter." "Of course not," replies the wife. "I have a job in Chicago!" The next morning, my mother went to the camp office to start looking for jobs in Chicago.

My mother was born in Big Sandy, Montana in 1914, the eldest daughter in a family of five children. Her father worked on the railroad so they moved between different towns in Montana according to his placement. Her mother never adjusted to living in that isolated and foreign place. She would sometimes wander down to the train station and speak Japanese to the Natives getting on and off the train. She could not be counted on to do any of the housewifely chores on a regular basis, so everything fell on her husband's shoulders. In fact, the youngest child was fostered out to neighours because the family couldn't cope with an infant. My mother went to the University of Washington for a year but the burden of having two children away from home was too difficult, and she returned while her older brother continued. After her father was killed in a railway accident, the family moved to Los Angeles, where my mother met my father. They married in 1937 and I was born in 1940.

In the weeks following Pearl Harbor in 1941, we were catapulted into a time of uncertainty. My mother, not knowing what would happen to us, wanted me to be toilet-trained and well-behaved. If we ever got separated and I was sent somewhere else with strangers, she wanted me to cause as little trouble as possible. She taught me to read when I was three, and then in Chicago, enrolled me in a Catholic nursery, where I impressed the hell out of them by giving my name, address, phone number and my mother's work address and phone number. As with many of the jobs listed in the camps, the one in Chicago was not the position promised, nor the salary, so my mother, having figured out exactly how much we needed to live there, found a different job, working for a wholesale bookseller.

The worst rebuke my mother gave was, "You're being unreasonable," and I would feel terrible and vow not to be unreasonable. She also said, "The first person who raises their voice loses the argument," which I also took to heart. When I was older, about nine, she sent me out to buy milk. I went to the store across the street and they had no milk, so I returned home and told her. She said to me, "Linda, I sent you to buy milk. I didn't tell you to go across the street and buy milk. If you can't get milk at one place, I expect you to think where else you can go. Now go out and buy milk, please." So I went out and didn't come home until I'd bought the milk.

When we joined my father in Japan in 1946, I tried to be the son I thought he wanted. I don't know where the notion came from that Japanese fathers always wanted sons, but it was an idea I had even at the age of six. I knew from my reading what a tomboy was, so I climbed trees, played ball with him, rode horses. In retrospect, I don't really think he cared one way or the other; he loved children of any gender. But when my parents divorced because the Japanese woman he had been seeing gave birth to his child, I thought he finally had his son. And I carried that belief with me until I finally met Janey ten years later, though I never said a word to either of them. Yet I always felt safe and well-cared for, with my mother showing me, by her example, how to be a strong, independent, thinking person.

I skipped first grade at the American School in Tokyo, and then another half grade when my mother and I returned to Chicago from

Japan. When it was time for high school, I didn't want to go to the local public school, having been terrified with stories about the girl gangs who hung out in the washrooms. Figuring I couldn't make it through four years without going to the washroom, I decided to go to the city-wide girls' technical high school.

But my mother had researched private schools in the meantime, and asked me to write a scholarship exam at one called Francis Parker. I didn't want to go to any snobby private school but agreed that it couldn't hurt to take the exam since I might not get a scholarship anyway. When the scholarship was offered, I was persuaded to try private school for a year, with the idea that I could go back to the technical school if I hated Parker. As with all my mother's plans, though, I loved the new school, which offered acting, singing, and writing, and encouraged students to try every kind of performance. After graduating, I went to the only college that offered me a scholarship—Antioch College in Ohio—again at my mother's suggestion. Where Parker had been performing arts, Antioch was left-of-centre politics. Neither place, circa 1953 to 1962, had different expectations based on gender—everyone was expected to be as big, as smart, as strong as possible.

At Antioch I learned about political philosophies and ended up, of course, on the side of the oppressed. As a child, I had always rooted for the underdog, whether it was the Chicago Cubs or some kid being picked on in the playground. I guess I always felt it could just as easily be me. It was the heady era of civil rights, beatniks, and poetry, and "fair play" for Cuba. Kennedy was not the White Knight for many of us at Antioch—he was good on civil rights, bad on Cuba. We wept for Selma and the Bay of Pigs. I stayed out of the civil rights movement, not knowing my place as an Asian in this black-and-white confrontation.

And I envied my friends who became Freedom Riders. Some of my reticence probably came from my Japanese background, where you don't impose yourself on an ambiguous situation. However, I have a Japanese-Canadian male friend who became a photographer down south during the civil rights movement, and he had no identity problems in getting involved. So I think some of my holding back was also from being a Japanese-American woman who just couldn't push where she wasn't sure of her welcome—part of the good girl syndrome. I learned about the evacuation of Japanese-Americans reading *Prejudice* by Carey McWilliams and, going to my mother for a fuller story, heard for the first time about my family's and my own time in the internment camps.

Her interpretation was that it was economics—the Japanese were doing too well with their farms and their businesses, and the white folk wanted to take what they had built, using Pearl Harbor as an excuse. Knowing my father's enormous patriotism and his pride in being American, I was outraged by the story and furious that no one had ever taught me anything about this part of American history. At Parker we did discuss Pearl Harbor and whether it was a set-up by Roosevelt to get America into the war, but no one mentioned what happened to Japanese-Americans as a result. Yet it was just part and parcel of the America I knew at that time with the hatred on display in the south and the fearful hysteria towards Cuba. The evacuation joined civil rights and Cuba in my head as examples of American injustice.

My mother got her Bachelor of Arts degree from Roosevelt University half a year before I got mine from Antioch. As secretary to the Dean of Education at Roosevelt, she took free night school courses, eventually getting her Master's degree, and finally retiring as Dean of Continuing Education. I, on the other hand, realized in my last year at Antioch that I didn't really like studying and that I didn't have to go to grad school. I could just stop. So I did and went to New York.

I got a fifth floor walk-up on the lower east side (now it's all very fashionable, but then it was just cheap). I wanted to break into publishing, but realized when my counselor at the employment agency told me I should cut my hair or wear it back in a bun that perhaps I wasn't great material. I did get a job at a magazine called *Eros*, run by Ralph Ginzburg, a charismatic exile from *Esquire* magazine who immediately wanted to hire me when he heard I graduated from Antioch.

Eros, a hardcover, coffee table version of *Esquire*, had two "hot" issues—one with nude photographs of Marilyn Monroe taken by Richard Avedon and one with nude photographs of a white woman and a black man. The latter issue eventually put the magazine out of business when the U.S. Post Office got complaints about our direct-mail advertising, and Ralph was charged with distributing pornography through the mail. Nobody got upset about the Marilyn Monroe issue but there was a lot of screaming about the mixed race one, neither of which would raise an eyebrow today, since all the photographs were extremely tasteful and not all that revealing. Nonetheless, at the few parties I went to, I would say vaguely, "I work for a magazine," which was never enough, of course, and when people found out I worked for Ralph they wanted to know all about him. Ralph knew how to get press, and he certainly had his moment of fame in New York. And there I was—an "Oriental" woman working for a "pornographic" magazine, facing all the North American stereotypes connected to that kind of situation. *The World of Suzy Wong* and *Flower Drum Song* were casting at the time: the whore with the heart of gold and the good, submissive girl. I was a dream come true for a lot of white men.

And I felt ambivalent about working for *Eros*, though I did send all the issues that were published to my mother. In this time of sexual liberation I slept with a lot of men, but I could still get embarrassed by raunchy jokes. In fact, really raunchy jokes still embarrass me, whatever their sexual orientation, even while I'm laughing. And I'm still ambivalent about pornography—the blatant exploitation is easy to deal with, but there are instances where my civil libertarian views and my knowledge that what you read and see affects how you act come into conflict, and have yet to be resolved.

This was the burgeoning time of the women's liberation movement. *The Golden Notebook* by Doris Lessing was a revelation, especially the relationship between Anna and Molly. The scene where a conversation between the two women changes when a man enters opened up a world of insight into different ways of interacting which I had never before seen as gender-related. Suddenly I could see that the conflict I used to feel in college—wanting to be with my women friends and wanting to be with my boyfriend—was a qualitative conflict, because the time spent with a woman and the time spent with a man were different.

But I found the notion of "free women" odd. Through the experience of my mother's life, and through her presence in my life, I had always assumed that all women were free to choose what they wanted. So the anti-male rhetoric of women's liberation was a bit excessive for me, and I thought burning bras was pretty stupid. I must admit though that I did stop wearing bras and was grateful for the suggestion. I supported the movement in its theories and rejection of the stereotyping of women's roles. I didn't find the women's demands unreasonable, though I myself was pretty conventional in social situations. I had never questioned the fact that in the political groups, the men tended to dominate, the women tended to type and serve as "gofers." Once a woman took me to task for bringing everything down to the personal in a political discussion, and I didn't open my mouth for weeks afterwards. But I had never felt comfortable in groups. Although I had two very close friends, whenever I was with more than one person, I started performing whatever character seemed most appropriate. My life in New York was fairly isolated—I'd see a friend a couple times a week, see a guy I was having an affair with about the same number of times, go to a party maybe once every three months, and work all the rest of the time. But I read about the women's movement, and probably because of my upbringing was not shocked by unconventional behaviour.

Our unspoken family rule was that you try not to hurt anyone, and if no one's being hurt, what's the problem? So when a woman made a pass at me when I was a freshman working in New York, it was just a pass like any other, and I mostly didn't want to hurt her feelings. I was an inactive, silent supporter of what other women were working for and read the books—Simone de Beauvoir, Germaine Greer, Kate Millett. I got upset with Kate Millett when she came out, worrying that the respectability of the movement would be impaired. And I admired her courage for doing it.

After two years in New York I left because I was tired of being exotic and because *Eros* was not going to survive its lawsuit. I was tired of going to parties and being approached as a stereotype of the mysterious East. There was a limit to the number of personae I enjoyed creating for myself. I wanted to go to California where there were lots of Asians, and if I got noticed it would be for myself, not because nobody else in the room looked like me.

As it happened, San Francisco in 1964 was full of fading beatniks, emerging hippies, folk singing, and dope, and, in the arts circles I moved in, hardly any Asians. It was also the time of the Vietnam War. I lived in North Beach, then Haight-Ashbury; sang in folk clubs, worked at KPIX-TV, then the Sierra Club, and protested in Berkeley.

I met Avron at a party in the Berkeley hills, at the home of a man who manufactured acid. A woman at KPIX took me along, and while I was sitting outside on the patio, a guy walked up to me with a ladder and asked if I'd watch it for him, which, of course, I agreed to. When he returned from his stroll in the woods with a bunch of other people, he propped the ladder against a tree and climbed it. He knew the acid man, and I knew someone in his group, so I just got absorbed into that group. And then he called me, and eventually I moved from my unheated apartment in North Beach into his place on Clayton just off Haight. Avron was a poet working at the post office, and the first night we met we talked of going to Greece. Haight was very exciting, just starting up—coffeehouses opening, head shops, bookstores, all kinds of small businesses run by us. I was singing with a friend at the time, and we sang every week at the I and Thou, the first coffeehouse on Haight Street. There weren't many Asians around. I remember being struck by a couple that looked just like us—a small Asian woman with a white man with longish hair and a beard—walking down Haight Street on a Sunday afternoon. We acknowledged one another but didn't speak.

There were the politicos and the artsy types (soon to become known as hippies). I straddled the two but Avron was firmly planted in the poetry/dope scene, not seeing the point in demonstrations. Using the do-what-you-can and stand-up-for-what-you-believe-in-even-when-you-think-it'll-do-no-good arguments, I persuaded Avron to come to anti-Vietnam demonstrations with me. In certain respects, we're very much alike—our expectations of people are that they will operate from good will towards us; if they don't, fuck 'em. We have no burning desire to change them. Our attitudes toward life are also similar in that we consider all ideas without immediately rejecting them, unless people are being hurt by them. The political, for both of us, is personal, and vice versa.We left the country for three years, unhappy with the war in Vietnam and wanting to travel. In Paris, I realized I couldn't be an expatriate for the rest of my life and I certainly couldn't continue working for that immense bureaucracy known as Unesco. A bureaucratic cog I was not. So Avron applied to graduate schools in creative writing, and we went to the place that offered him money, the University of British Columbia.

On the bad advice of someone in the Canadian consulate in Chicago, we got married to make our entry into Canada easier. It turned out I'd have been better off applying as a landed immigrant on my own rather then entering as the dependent of a student. When I was given permission to work part-time, I got three part-time jobs.

We spent our first year in Vancouver bemoaning our cultural isolation. There was Pacific Cinémathèque and the Classical Joint, where I sang until I could find steady work. Then the following summer we went back to San Francisco. We saw the bars on the shop windows along Haight Street, and the dirt. We listened to the stories of our friends—about the glorious and dreadful years we'd missed, about the scariness of the neighbourhood and how we shouldn't go into Fillmore after dark. Finally we decided there were worse things than cultural isolation in Canada.

We became landed immigrants and I got a full-time job at the university library. When Avron got his MA, we sent out eighty letters applying for teaching jobs, but times had changed while we'd been away, and it wasn't so easy to get teaching jobs. So we continued as we had—I worked and Avron took care of the house and wrote poetry, and we were both perfectly happy. Until I got pregnant and, to my immense surprise, discovered that I wanted to have a baby.

Neither of us had really wanted to have children. I had not grown up babysitting as many of my friends had. And being an only child, I had no experience looking after siblings. The babies I had met cried a lot and thus had not endeared themselves to me. I was outraged that there was some kind of stupid biological clock that struck for me at the age of thirty-two. I burst into tears when I was told the pregnancy test was positive, because there was no way I could have a baby, being our sole support. I went home weeping and wailing to Avron with my terrible discovery, and he said, "Well, not now, but if that's what you want, we'll do it." So I had an abortion, and Avron got a job working at the library, and finally after a year and a half of trying, I became pregnant. Beautiful Miko arrived in June 1974, three weeks early, after five hours of hard labour with me singing "Long Black Veil." Avron fell madly in love with her and I thought she looked pretty good.

Being a mother, however, was everything I had originally feared. I had difficulty breast feeding because at her first feeding, Miko bit down so hard on my breast, it developed a sore; I became obsessed until I could feed her without pain. She was colicky and cried with incredible volume so that even other mothers were impressed with the power of her lungs. I was amazed at how hard it was to have a totally dependent creature on my hands. I had never been fond of needy people, and suddenly I was stuck with the ultimate needy person. Here was a situation that I could not walk away from when it became unbearable. Three decades of control were wiped out as I screamed and wept and became, against all my mother had instilled in me, unreasonable. Meanwhile Avron was incredibly supportive. He would come home after work and take Miko off my hands, leaving me to do things—like cook—that I felt competent doing.

I went to places where other mothers were, only to discover that their infants seemed much more independent than mine (and not as loud). I would surround her with toys, but all she ever wanted was me. I would feed her, burp her, change her, but as soon as I put her down she would howl. Infanthood was almost my undoing. It also helped me to be open about feelings that I hadn't expressed before, like anger and frustration. Not that I had a choice. I grew into my irrationality with Miko. And it wasn't the end of the world.

When I was at Antioch, I used to think that if I ever did have a child, I would not raise her the way I had been raised. I didn't think it was fair that I had had to make my own decisions about things so young, that there should have been more rules and things that I had to do whether I liked it or not. But we raised Miko just as I had been raised. We treated her like a rational human being, which, of course, she wasn't. But lo and behold, she became one.

Avron and I went to a non-sexist child-rearing workshop when Miko was an infant. One of the exercises was to imagine your child's life. Avron imagined everything he wanted—she'd go to school, university, get married; I imagined everything I feared—she would run away from home, she would drop out of school, she would get pregnant.

When Miko was fifteen months old, I decided I needed to get out as an adult in the world of adults. I volunteered one day a week at a press some poet friends were running, and when their typesetter left, I was asked to work three days a week. They agreed to cover my daycare costs and I found a wonderful family daycare where I left Miko. She cried for about forty-five minutes every day I left her then settled down to the inevitable.

Shortly after I began working, I was asked by a Japanese-Canadian acquaintance if I would be interested in working on a photographic history of the Japanese in Canada. I didn't know this man well; he was the partner of a white woman friend and, like me, he didn't know very many people of Japanese descent. This was the beginning of what would become for me a major involvement in the Japanese-Canadian community.

The group came together by word of mouth, and most of us didn't know one another. We were new immigrants from Japan and *sansei* (third generation)—a photographer, translators, a university lecturer, community organizers, a typesetter, a teacher—and many of us had never had any contact with the Japanese-Canadian community, nor had most of the *sansei* spent much time in the company of people who looked like ourselves. The immigrants were a revelation to me, coming as they did from a country where they were the majority. I was in awe of the women, who seemed so confident, so sure of themselves, so funny. The people who leave Japan are usually the ones who reject the rigidity of that society's structure, the rebels who don't or don't want to fit in. Those who joined the project (in fact, one of the women initiated it) were also committed to community development and history as a tool for bringing it about.

The exhibit group felt like family, since the only Japanese (or Asians for that matter) with whom I had spent any time was my family. I found myself acting with them as I did with my family. Gone was the extremely reasoned, always careful Linda. Building on the irrationality released by Miko, I started speaking spontaneously, not always thinking before I said anything, feeling free to explore thoughts out loud. I had always worried about hurting people's feelings and would run entire conversations in my head before saying anything. But with my new "family" I felt that I didn't always have to be right; they would like and accept me even if I were wrong or made a fool of myself. They'd know that I didn't mean to hurt them if I disagreed, that we were in this life together to help one another. I had been open in this way with my very close friends but never in a group.

"A Dream of Riches" was a great success. The photo exhibit used old photographs from people's family albums and interspersed text on the history of the Japanese in Canada. As part of the 1977 Japanese-Canadian centennial celebration, it found venues at the Vancouver Museum and the Museum of Civilization in Ottawa. But the main result of our work was the joy we felt working together and, for the sansei, the discussions we had about being of Japanese descent in a majority white culture—how none of us liked to look in the mirror because what we saw didn't reflect what was on the inside, and how to make the inside part of the outside. The long-term result was that most of the *sansei*, who had not before been part of the Japanese-Canadian community, became involved.

Another centennial project was a festival held on Powell Street, in the area that the Japanese had first settled in Vancouver. The festival was meant to be a one-off for the centennial year, but was so successful that the Powell Street Festival has become an annual event. In 1979, a *taiko* (Japanese drum) group from California was invited to the festival, and all of us volunteers thought it was the greatest thing we'd ever seen. The San Jose group encouraged us to start our own group, and Katari Taiko, the first *taiko* group in Canada, was born.

Most of the founding members were volunteers for the Powell Street

Festival and had known one another at the University of British Columbia; I was about ten years older. It was so exciting being part of this group of Asians, learning an Asian art form that was loud and aggressive, strong and graceful. Few in the group had ever studied music, and most had never gotten up in public before. For me it resembled the photo project with that sense of collective self-discovery, but with the added joy of performing.

Our first intention was to learn *taiko* so we could eventually play at the Powell Street Festival. But requests to perform began pouring in, and after two years of training, we began performing. The time commitment became serious. Operating as a collective took time; meetings and discussions seemed endless; drums had to be made and re-skinned; improving our basic skills was paramount for performing but so was learning new songs and new parts and arrangements. We also decided that we needed to set down some principles regarding ourselves as a group. I was stunned to discover, even in 1981, that most people in the group were not willing to describe themselves as feminists. The word still represented a threat to their families and to the Japanese-Canadian community, which was their main concern. I had always thought of "feminist" as an academic term, implying a great deal of cerebration around women's issues, but apparently that was not the mainstream view. Although I argued that we would be educating our families about the proper use of the term, because they would know we weren't wild-eyed radicals, the bottom line was that I didn't know the Vancouver Japanese-Canadian community like they did, and I had no family who would be offended. So we settled on "non-sexist" as a description.

If the composition of most *taiko* groups is anything to go by, Japanese drumming in North America has appealed primarily to Asian women. Katari Taiko has over the course of sixteen years had ten men in the group, never more than four simultaneously. The women who want to do *taiko* tend to be strong and feminist. So the men who have joined Katari Taiko have had to deal with being the minority in a collective dominated by outspoken women. We've often discussed why more men don't want to join the group, and think the most likely reason is that men don't look at us and say, I want to be up there with them doing that. Although we had all seen Kodo and Ryujin Daiko, two Japanese all-male groups, we never felt the urge to play *taiko* until we saw the mixed gender group of Japanese-Americans from San Jose. I think the men who do want to join are those who don't feel threatened by all the women and who are strongly attracted to the group energy.

Some of the women of Katari Taiko played the Michigan Womyn's Music Festival in 1989. We had been seen by Alix Dobkin at the Vancouver Folk Music Festival, and she asked if we would be interested in performing at Michigan. We said yes, and then discovered that the men (there were two at the time) could not come; in fact, boys over the age of three were not allowed in the festival area. After prolonged discussion, during which the men didn't say much, three women decided that they could not perform at an exclusive event; nine others wanted to go. During the festival, the partner of one of the men in the group had a son, and we wanted to announce the birth at the festival. It was, after all, our first *taiko* baby. So, with much trepidation, during our evening performance, we announced the birth to some scattered applause but otherwise not a very positive response. Afterwards, one of the black performers came up to me and said, "I'm proud of you for honouring your men."

Her support crystallized for me the difference between white women and women of colour in the women's movement. Members of a visible minority group share discrimination. The men are treated as badly as the women by the majority society, and that bond can't be denied. Whatever you deal with within the community, when it comes to facing the majority, you stand together as one group. As a woman you may have faced oppression within your group and you fight it within the group, but to the world at large you know there's a bottom line that puts you all together.

When we returned to Vancouver, we discovered that one of the men was very unhappy with our decision to go to Michigan. On reflection, we realized that if we had been asked to perform at a function that allowed only the Asians in the group to perform, we would have turned it down; we wouldn't have been able to justify excluding the white women. But because it was "just the men" who were excluded, we thought it was all right. We decided that Katari Taiko would not accept any performances that excluded any of its members, and that members who wanted to perform at exclusive venues would have to create a new group with a new repertoire of their own; they couldn't be Katari Taiko under another name. This resulted in the formation of Sawagi Taiko, made up only of women, playing their own material, mainly at Michigan.

I have performed four times at Michigan. The first time I was in a daze. It was very exciting being in a place of only women, where there was such a variety of sizes and shapes and ways of being, and where women did so much heavy work. That first year also, my mother and Miko came to the festival, along with an old friend of mine with her mother and daughter who was just Miko's age, fifteen. Somehow having two Asian families of three generations made me more sensitive to certain aspects of the festival—first and foremost, that the great majority of the women were white, and second, that the great majority of the women were lesbian. I worried a bit about Miko's reaction, but unnecessarily. She and Sara took it all in stride, only averting their eyes from the naked bodies, especially when they were very large. She remarked afterwards that it seemed weird back in Chicago to see women holding hands with men. I never worried about my mother; for her, Michigan and all it contained was just another wonderful aspect of life.

Michigan has provided me with much food for thought and many emotional releases. The year my father died, a gospel song made me burst into tears. The woman's depth of belief matched my father's belief in the United States of America, and I wanted to share those beliefs and couldn't. One year Kate Millett was at the festival, and she stopped to talk to us because she had lived some years in Japan. In the middle of our conversation, a young black woman sat next to me and started talking. After Kate left, she said to me, "I wanted to rescue you from that woman. She just goes on and on." I thought about all these young women who didn't know what Kate had done for them, how she had paved the way for their lives today, and I felt sad that history is lost so easily.

So here I am, in my mid-fifties, with a daughter aged twenty-one going through university. Miko is an interesting and wonderful person; I don't know how she got that way—she insists we never really raised her, and she's probably right. In high school she was part of a group of girls who called themselves the Rainbow Group. They were Chinese, mixed heritage, South Asian, and Jewish in a school that tended to form groups according to cultural background. And they all studied very hard. Now that she's in university, studying is an inconvenience, interfering with her work as program director at the campus radio station, the band in which she plays guitar, writes songs, and sings, her part-time job at a record store, and the rock concerts she wants to attend. She became a vegetarian at the age of sixteen, converting her father but not yet me. She has a social conscience, has worked hard to get more women involved at the station and to increase women's programming, and is very conscious of herself as half Jewish, half Japanese. I love and like her very much.

Avron continues to write poetry and work at the library, very active as a steward in the union. I have always been grateful that he has let me go my way, that I have been able to be so engaged outside the home because he has always been there. I try to remember when I am supposed to vacuum and sometimes he gets pissed off at me because I am still so undomesticated, though not unrepentantly. His tolerance has been not just for the time spent away but also for the time spent in the discoveries I've made on my own. My acceptance of myself as being of Japanese heritage was something that had to be done with other people, and he was very willing to let me do that.

My involvement with the Powell Street Festival and with the *taiko* group has resulted in my being much more comfortable in groups. I had been on the fringe of a women's group shortly after Miko was born, through a woman who shared our house. These were all bright, interesting, sensitive women who had been part of a consciousness-raising group for long enough to be very tight. I always did feel on the fringe, always did feel that I was playing some kind of role. Even after the photo project, I still felt that only part of myself was engaged with these women. Being involved with Asian community groups over the years has liberated me from the need to play "acceptable" roles in groups, and I believe that exclusion of the majority or those seen as powerful has a legitimate time and place.

When Katari Taiko gives its annual public workshops, most of the participants have been white (and female), so one year we offered an Asians-only workshop, and it was filled to capacity, male and female. Among groups who feel excluded by the mainstream, there are often times when you need to feel specifically invited to participate. Once you have discovered acceptance of that "other" part, you can then move on to the rest of the world. The acceptance I always felt among Asians, I now transfer to other groups assuming their good will and their willingness to accept all my parts. In general, most groups reward that trust, though I find it easier and more satisfying to work with women.

I grew from a child of model behaviour and immense obedience into a strong-willed woman. The trip has been exciting and rewarding; I can live with my mistakes, but I never want to look back and regret not having done something. I continue to play *taiko* in both Katari Taiko and Sawagi Taiko and am active in the Japanese-Canadian community mainly through the Powell Street Festival. In my view, a world that offers women and men equal opportunity is a feminist world. But women do not have equal chances and opportunity, and that means I must work to change that situation. I am on the board of the Women in View Festival, an organization committed to offering opportunities to all women, taking a pro-active stance regarding women of colour. My daughter, as the programming director at CITR, complains that whenever issues of race arise, she feels that everyone on the executive is waiting for her to say something; but she also understands that representing the absent is one of her functions. Having increased women's programming, she is now beginning to encourage representation by people of colour. I am not an academic, do not keep up with the reading around women's issues, but through my life and my interactions with people I continue learning. Thanks to a mother and partner who supported me in all my decisions, my entire family has grown into feminism.

The Sixth Sensory Organ

Larissa Lai

Photo by Brenda Miller

I have a sixth sensory organ, a way of knowing the world beyond what eyes, ears, nose, tongue or touch can tell me. It runs in the family. Maybe lots of people have them, I don't know. It's one of those embarassing things that you never think to discuss.

What are they? Two little holes, one above each ear. They tunnel into my head and are sensitive to the touch. Sometimes they itch. Sometimes a bit of pus comes out, like snot, I guess, or earwax. When I was small, I used to think that everyone had them, that they were a normal part of the human anatomy, like eyes, or elbows. My mother saw me cleaning one. "You have one of those too, eh?" she asked, raising an eyebrow. "One what?" "A little hole above your ear, like me." "What do you mean one? I have two! One on each side," I said. "Two? I've never heard of that before!" she responded. That's how I found out that it runs in the family, that some people have them on one side or the other. But I'm the only one I know of that has two.

I think they are for hearing and smelling sounds and odours from another world, one that co-exists with this one, one that only those with this strange organ can sense. I wonder if they are a remnant of a prehistoric past, of a time when humans were more closely related to fish, a time when our scales glittered hard and translucent, and we had thick tails that undulated in smooth curves and propelled us through water. They are like two tiny gills meant to draw oxygen from water. They have forgotten their original task as they have forgotten other

199

histories, although sometimes a little liquid comes out that smells of the sea.

One of them, the right one, tends to get infected. It gets blocked with dust and then all the fluid it can't expel builds up inside my head, like memories I can't articulate. A doctor suggested that she operate to have it closed over. My hand went up to my mouth in horror. Where would all the memories go?

Fistula, she called it, an unnecessary little hole. Fistula, as in little fissure. I think of water seeping through rock, wearing down its seeming solidity in a slow trickle.

There is a legend about the origin of fossils. It says that the clouds pick up eggs and seeds from the ocean. When it rains, the eggs and seeds fall into the fissures in rocks and grow into stone replicas of their true selves.

This is a memory before race. This is a memory before species, inscribed in my body, a memory of lost motion, another self buried in DNA calling faintly for its full manifestation. Deoxyribonucleic acid, such a scientific term, such a term of our age, a word to describe one of the smallest most primal things there is, material proof of our beginnings. Is that what I long for, to revert, retreat to my smallest possible form? Or is it a desire for the opposite, to swell into the full blown monster wailing softly through the holes above my ears?

What is this obsession with the prehistoric self, my fish and mineral self, rock hard, scaly and ever-so-much larger than life? I would like to slip through a fissure in the treacherous rock of history and drop right down into a warm moist place inside the earth where I can return to my reptilian past and slap my tail happily in the mud. Sing a little song for warmth and quiet and well-considered breathing.

There is a song from my childhood with a strange power to terrify me. A song about a fissure. I can't explain the terror, except to explain the nightmare that I had as a child in connection with the song. You may recognize the song:

There's a tree in a hole
And a hole in the ground
And the green grass grew all around
All around
And the green grass grew all around

There's a branch on the tree
And the tree in a hole
And the hole in the ground . . .

This is the nightmare that terrified me beyond reason. I start the dream small. My small, safe self. My heartbeat begins to grow louder. It grows louder and louder and I, or something, no longer the small enclosed self, expands. I am huge. I am the planet. I am the universe. One wrong move and I will destroy everyone I love, my mother, my father, an old friend of theirs who is staying in the front room. I scream and scream and scream.

I am terrified of the uncontrollable monster within me, her buzzing insistence, the way she makes my elbows twitch. I am terrified of the sheer bulk of her, all muscle and sinew. What terrifies me most about her, though, is her fragility. That she could burst any moment and trickle away like an embarrassing stream of urine, and I won't even be able to say what I've lost.

According to the evolutionary model, the monster woman turns out all right. Her monstrous characteristics are selected out; her offspring become increasingly respectable over time.

Whoever imagined our generation would carry the residual memory of her loss? To the extent that as social creatures we plan our own evolution. Surely our ancestors tried to transform for the better.

The Taoist universe also begins with the memory of a reptilian woman. Nu Wa had a woman's head and the body of a snake. She scooped up a clot of mud. She squeezed and pinched it into a human shape. She put it onto the ground and it began to laugh. Its hearty guffaws so delighted her that she picked up a vine, dipped it in wet mud, and waved it over the earth like a magic wand. The droplets formed into a myriad of people. Perhaps it is she who permeates my dreams—a racially accurate dream of origins?

Newspaper headline: Chinese woman tells Chinese story. All is right with the world.

But after five years of various kinds of activism—lesbian, feminist, anti-racist, and anti-imperialist—I am growing frightened of how thin we have become. We turned the terms used against us to agitate for rights and recognition. We identified ourselves by race, by gender, by sexuality, by class in order to make ourselves visible, in order to validate our histories, in order to work towards getting access to the equality we are guaranteed constitutionally although it is kept from us by hidden agendas, structural inequities, glass ceilings, chilly climates and the like. We did it in order to insist that all the things that we are not be swept under the carpet in any discussion—social, political, legal, constitutional or historical. Amid charges of essentialism, or, more damaging, political correctness, we forged strategies to insist upon our presence. We didn't suspect how those strategies might constrain us, prevent us from understanding the contradictions and ambiguities we are faced with daily. We didn't know how the beautiful monsters would get trapped inside us, unable to escape and express themselves as agents who might affect our lives.

The monsters *are* beautiful. They are unruly and frightened. They are a mess of contradictions. They cannot agree upon what they are because they are not the same thing from day to day. They have the power to transform themselves in times of danger or desire. They are sleek and strong and their translucent scales glitter in the sun, but they are also sad.

My monster woman howls through my ear holes. I'm hungry, she cries, feed me. If there's one thing I've been culturally conditioned to do, it's eat. I will eat whatever's laid before me, regardless of where it came from. Roast pork, salt fish, fried tofu, sweet gai lan and then snake soup, eel hot pot, stir-fried dog. . . . Wait! We don't eat those things any more. They've been conveniently forgotten in our eastward journey to the West. You must forget the parts of yourself that prove the bigots right after all, regardless of the cost.

The snake woman, with a great flip of her tail, turns her scaly back. Her hunger is not sated, but she doesn't like to upset people.

I am possibly one of very few Asian Canadian women of my generation who was raised as a feminist, one of very few for whom the notion of women's equality was articulated and encouraged as I grew up. Of course, the feminism I was raised with growing up in St. John's, Newfoundland was of the brand many now refer to disparagingly as "white women's feminism." Inasfar as I experienced it, it focussed on work: how the value of women's work is belittled and the value of men's exaggerated—the glass ceiling—and how difficult it is for women to break into the "nontraditional workforce." I decided at an early age that this nontraditional thing was a challenge I was most definitely up for. I was good at math, I was good at science, and I wasn't afraid of hard work. (These were all prized skills for a good feminist girl at the time. Looking back I consider how interesting it is that all these characteristics fit perfectly with the dreariest stereotype of the Chinese immigrant.) But I wasn't prepared for the engineering department at the University of British Columbia. I wasn't up for the Godiva ride, or my inability to bond with my male peers (who relied heavily upon one another to get assignments—collectively—completed), or the blatant sexism of the professors and TAs. In spite of good marks in high school, and a perfect score on my Physics 12 exam, my ability to cope with much of the material was patchy. My high school education had been divided between Newfoundland and British Columbia, and there was a lot of groundwork I didn't have, and nowhere I could turn to get it. Most of the women engineering students I knew who were succeeding were brilliant but solitary, working like dogs to keep up and with little time to help anyone else.

The meaning of "glass ceiling" and "double standard" became abundantly clear. However, a feminism focussed purely around the notion of work, at that time, was becoming increasingly hollow. I won't produce the litany of pain that white folks these days love so much to hear from folk of colour, partly because I think that that in itself is evolving into a rather perverse relationship with the oppressor, partly because I still cling to an oddly traditional requisite to "keep face," and partly because it would be a misrepresentation on my part to do so. I will say, however, that the concept of race was beginning to enter into and merge with my conception of women's equality. By the early nineties, books such as *Sister Outsider, This Bridge Called My Back,* and *Piece of My Heart* proliferated, dog-eared, on my shelves and those of my friends.

The recognition that women of colour, or non-white women, as we were more likely to refer to ourselves then, had been oppressed not only by men, but also by white women, and that it was okay to say so was a tremendous revelation at that time. Memories of exemplary incidents spouted furiously from our mouths and pens where before there had been only memories of unease and discomfort with no analysis to explain where these feelings came from. In retrospect I find myself realizing the debt we owe (in particular though not exclusively) to Black women activists and writers whose pioneering work echoed in varying degrees and for various reasons among all of us. We had a hard time, however, developing tools which would constructively help to articulate the differences among us, and that would point in a direction of constructive action. At the same time, the rightwing backlash with it's conflationary and destructive concept of "political correctness" was gaining ground like crazy.

Nu Wa created the first person because she was lonely. She created the rest because she liked the sound of the first person's laughter, echoing through the quiet hills. But the people she created were not like her. To begin with, instead of a sinuous, scaly tail, they had legs. They were hateful towards her because she was divine. They were hateful towards one another for much more petty reasons.

The word lesbian is an uncomfortable word. The discomfort goes in both directions, like the body of a snake. It is an ugly word connoting impropriety and sexual deviance. It is a beautiful word for exactly the same reasons. *Lesbian, a native or inhabitant of Lesbos,* an island in the East Aegean, off the northwest coast of Turkey, annexed to Greece in 1913.

The snake woman doesn't understand. She doesn't read Sappho, although she understands imperialism. *Lesbian, a female homosexual.* But does this identification come from a Western preoccupation with sex, where radicalism is defined by how it denies the primacy of the heterosexual couple? In the West, a woman is traditionally defined by her relationship to a man. In Asia, a woman is traditionally defined by her relationship to her family, or, more precisely, her lineage. A reductionist argument, perhaps, especially in this neo-imperial age when it is impossible to separate the West from the East, if it was ever possible in some historically perfect past.

But it works for the snake woman. The snake woman is a snake woman not because she has sex with other women, but because she makes family with them. Thinking in terms of radical conceptions of the family, rather than in terms of radical conceptions of sex, I am able to go to the history books and find reflections of myself.

I would like to consider the silk workers of South China as my foremothers. The logic of this choice is perhaps weak, and certainly romantic. The logic of identity always is, shaped as it is by desire.

Historically, the silk workers, much studied by Western anthropologists for their practice of resisting marriage, come from the same province and county as my forebears, a county in the Pearl River Delta know as Xunde. In the 1930s when the silk industry was booming, many women in this area were able to obtain economic independence. It was believed that only the fingers of women were dexterous enough for the job of boiling and unravelling cocoons and twisting the fibres into thread. In modified accordance with an old tradition of marriage resistance, some bought their way out of marriage and set up house together. They would buy concubines to replace them in their husbands' households. Others simply declared spinsterhood and underwent a hair-combing ceremony recognized as a viable alternative to marriage.

As they grew older, and the silk industry declined, many joined vegetarian halls or sought service work in Hong Kong, Singapore or Malaysia.

See the monster woman beaming with contentment? She is not as alone as she had originally thought.

An old lover, another Chinese-Canadian woman, told me that because of my middle-class background and my Western upbringing that it was appropriation to claim such a history as this. Is it possible to love without possessing? And who is the possessor and who is the possessed? I am haunted by the women who have come before me, as I am haunted by the women I have loved. I don't want to believe that our culture is so fragile it cannot withstand the forces of our own desire. But it is true that, for someone as transplanted as me, there can never be any truth about the silk workers. There can be, however, a strange kind of romance. A romance of smoke and mirrors. A seed planted in rock, swelling into a stone replica of its true self. Who is to say how useful the stone can be? Stones are heavy, have been used as anchors for generations.

I can avoid my ex-lover and I can avoid the silk workers, refuse the ghosts that nudge against my side at night. Must our lives become mere games of avoidance? I cannot ignore the howl of history, the snake woman raging through her tiny airholes.

I could say (August 1992)

How long
have women been pushing
each other out of the most desirable places
gently nudging at first
giving way to a violent shove
when manipulation doesn't work

I wanted to tell you
how much your efforts
to turn other women's hearts
against me
hurt

but I couldn't
The truth is
I saw red
blood gushing straight
into my eyes
Said to myself
She only likes girls
who are privileged enough
to take care of her
pay her bills
clean her room
scrub her toilet
and calls oppression
when they haven't got
the resources to meet her expectations

Was I angry or
was it half true?
I could say
as a woman of colour
as a lesbian
as middle-class and educated
as all those things
that describe me
and don't
I could say
we have some powerful tools
in our hands
Tools as in building utensils
Tools as in weapons
I could ask you
to remember the moment

You said the words
yourself so many times
when we were friends
and I would nod my head
as you spoke
"white patriarchy is the enemy"

It's still there
despite what has fallen between us
I could say
I was angry
that you have used
the tools of our empowerment
as weapons against me
not with understanding or even the desire to construct
but as weapons
to isolate, to hurt, to maim
drain resources like dirty bathwater
you no longer need
or blood

I could say I was angry
but I don't want
to press the groove deeper
don't want
to re-open the wound
that if nothing else
time will close

I could tell you it hurts
I could tell you it scares me
as much as nazis
as much as strange men
on the street after dark
or corrupt priests with shifty eyes
thinking to pass their hands
or worse
over our bodies

I could tell you
I have gone into mourning
for what we called community
foolishly assuming
a perfect place to return to
mourning for what is left
or what might be coming

the day when we clasp our positions
to our breasts
or stand on them like islands
and bomb each other

This is not an excuse
for anything I might have done
to hurt you
This is not an accusation
There has to be
a way to disagree
without disempowering
a way to address
the secrets we have been shamed
into keeping
without destroying
what we have already built
Sometimes one grows tired
of always addressing
the white patriarchal oppressor
as though he is the most important
person in our lives
Sometimes I want to cry out
just to hear my own voice
behind the ragged borders
of my own communities
I could say
they don't want us
to speak to one another
don't want us to get through
the difficult parts
don't want us to see
that we are healing

I could say a lot of things
but I haven't yet
So far it's all I can do
to turn my head
and walk away

I didn't dare to try to publish these words the year they were written. I knew there were all kinds of problems with them—my own complicity in the very practices I beg my sister not to use against me, the way in which these words could be interpreted as "blaming the victim." At the same time, I felt they were important to say, but was just too plain scared of losing this newfound community which I felt I needed as a matter of life and death. It's hard to explain to someone who has never or not yet felt it, the depth of that need. To be in the centre of a resurgence of women and men of colour's voices articulating all those angry things that were once taboo was incredibly liberating and resonated in the deepest, most silent chambers of my heart like thunder smashing through a sick, artificial and ugly city. Of course, we were not the first to find these voices. There were many who had gone before us, most notably writers like Audre Lorde, Joy Harjo, Leslie Marmon Silko, Gloria Anzaldua, Cherie Moraga, Makeda Silvera, Dionne Brand. . . . But it was a first for us, and it was exciting and freeing to hear certain truths echoing freely through our writing and our conversation. At the same time, this newfound politic made room for an abdication of responsibility in how we treated one another, and indeed, sometimes, how we treated strangers. It also made room for an abdication of responsibility in terms of how those who hold the real power in this country treated us.

History howls loudly. And surely the snake woman controls the weather. There are many old stories of snake people living in rivers who, if provoked, can sink boats in the hurricanes of their wrath. But suppose she doesn't want to sink the boat? If I can't get along with those I am supposed to love, how am I supposed to get along with anyone else? Such as the white feminist who wants to rescue me from the sexism of Asian men and goes on and on about how women should stick together. Or the reverend's new wife whom I've met at the breakfast table at a small bed and breakfast I've been going to for years, who would like to convince me that I can be saved from my sins if I leave my new lover. Or the innkeeper, who, assuming I'm First Nations, tells me we should all be Native so we can get everything paid for with white people's taxes. It's hard to say anything, especially given that I'm already sensitive she hasn't recognized me after eight years of patronizing her business, although she recognizes the reverend on only his second visit.

A writers' retreat in 1995: a group of women are lounging in the living room after dinner. We start to talk about appropriation. One of the writers, a white woman, asks me if I think that white people should never write about people of colour. (It's natural that she would direct the question to me—in that particular configuration of women, I had the reputation as the radical. This is not always the case.) "Well," I begin, cautiously, "it's complicated." "But we want to know," she says, "yes or no?" Tonight I have my wits about me. Tonight I'm feeling generous. I don't say, "That's such a white question" (although I think it). I tell her I wish we lived in a world where respect and integrity were the order of the day, instead of one where the freedom of the individual with "power-over," as Starhawk calls it, comes before everything else.

In 1994, I worked on the organizing committee of the much misunderstood and maligned conference Writing Thru Race. I remember being invited to one of the regional meetings, attended by then chair Myrna Kostash, early in the conference's planning stages. I and a few others were there to explain why we felt the need for a writers-of-colour-only space. We talked about how much more difficult it was to be honest about our experiences when those who represented the forces of race oppression were present. We talked about how often in mixed forums, whites entirely hijacked the discussion and ate up all the time with tales of their own good deeds in foreign places, or in a worst case scenario (which rapidly materialized in the national public media) turned it into a discussion of "reverse racism," followed by endless platitudes concerning the need for (white folks') equality and a firm denial of the historically constituted reality. A big turning point in the discussion occurred when some of the white women in the room who had been active in the feminist movement during the seventies and eighties drew a parallel between women's needs for occasional closed spaces and people of colours' needs for the same. The meeting ended very positively, with many murmurings of mutual support and understanding from all those present. On my way back to my car, one of the women from the meeting came up to me. "It's so wonderful what you're doing," she said. "By the way, are you a writer as well?"

If I were Nu Wa I'd flood the place and start again.

The old man shook his head. "That is the trickery of the witchcraft," he said. "They want us to believe that all evil resides with white people. Then we will look no further to see what is really happening. They want us to separate ourselves from white people, to be ignorant and helpless as we watch our own destruction. But white people are only tools that the witchery manipulates; and I tell you, we can deal with white people, with their machines and their beliefs. We can because we invented white people; it was Indian witchery that made white people in the first place."

—Leslie Marmon Silko, *Ceremony*, 1977

I am five years old and on my way to Hong Kong for the first time in my life. I am at the airport with my mother. Due to delays and bad weather, we have missed a connection and need to get booked on a later flight. The Chinese woman behind the Cathay Pacific counter is more than solicitous to the middle-aged Englishman ahead of us in line, in spite of the fact that he is disorganized, full of facile questions, and has an outrageous amount of luggage—way more than the official limit permits. She gets him on the plane without problem, and doesn't charge him a cent extra, all the while smiling as beguilingly as the billboards promise she will. My mother gets to the front of the line and the woman is furious with her for having missed the flight. How could she have been so stupid? Our plane arrived a full fifteen minutes before the connection left. All the other transferring passengers made it. What was wrong with us? She makes arrangements for us with very ill grace.

Twenty-three years later, at the annual Powell Street Festival, a festival which celebrates the history of Japanese-Canadians in that neighbourhood, I see another Asian woman. She's dressed in funky clothes. She looks cool. I think to myself that I would like to get to know her. She sees me too, and smiles. Then we recognize each other. We used to be close friends. We used to work together. Until I got a job that she had also applied for. She had been furious. I had been defensive. Both of us experienced an intense and overwhelming sense of betrayal, she for seeing me get the job she wanted, me for not getting her support and goodwill for what proved to be a very difficult job. We are smart enough to know it was not our choice to be pitted against each other as competitors. We are smart enough to know that the employer would have compared our c.v.s closely and talked about us in comparison to one another. We are not superhuman enough to get over it. She can barely look me in the eye, nor I, her.

It is my pain I see reflected in your eyes. Our angers ricochet between us like the bullets we fire in battles which are not our own nor with each other.

Joseph Beam, *Brother to Brother: Words from the Heart*, 1984

Nu Wa was the first woman. She rose out of the earth, or perhaps, the ocean, like the Greek goddess Aphrodite. Before she arrived there was a man who died, whose body became the earth, but otherwise, there were none around until she made them.

It is interesting to me to note how few men there are in my life these days, how little they figure. The few who are my friends are respectful and thoughtful, but there are none that I let in close enough to hurt me. For the most part, I am blind to them. At a political level, even at the level of passionate disagreement, it is women who most affect me. Is this an outcome of my early introduction to feminism? Or just the fact that in a sexist world, women are more approachable than men? I'm not sure.

Occasionally, however, I am jarred into a shocked and angry recognition of the extent and subtlety of their systemic and institutional power. They exercise it without malice and without awareness that they are exerting it. I recently gave a reading at a local suburban bookstore. It was an "on" night. Surrounded by a cozy circle of listeners, mostly women, I felt comfortable reading some of the more intimate parts of the book. Other shoppers hovered around the area, half-browsing, half-listening, and then would wander off. I noticed a man lurking at a distance, leafing through books, hanging around, barely within earshot for the entire duration of the reading. Although he made me slightly uncomfortable, I chose to ignore him. I read for an hour, the audience and I talked for perhaps another hour afterwards. I like to read, and I like to talk to audiences, but I do find it exhausting. By the end of the two hours I was quite drained. As I was packing my things, the lurking man came up to me and all but demanded to know how I had gotten published. (How dare I publish before he had?) Could I give him any advice—should he try for a New York agent first, or a Toronto one? I answered briefly but politely. He would not let me go. I would have had to make a scene in order to get away, and I was much too tired to make a scene. He quizzed and prodded until so much time had passed that he could really keep me no longer. Then he threw a few conciliatory words at me about how I had a "nice style—very exotic." He was writing about sexuality himself, he had spent much time in Japan and was interested in theories of yin and yang. Of course people gave him a hard time, surely I must understand, writing the kind of material that I do. I was hurt and furious that this stranger could drain me like this, and then insult me on top of it, after I had already given so much. I swore to myself I would not let this happen again, that I would be rude, that I would make a scene. No woman, even the most abrasive, would have done this. No man would have done this to another man. And yet this man could do it to me, because, after all, it's a free country and he was entirely within his rights.

I remember a quiet Asian woman at a reading in the States. She was the only woman of colour in the audience. She sat towards the back, listening thoughtfully. After the reading, other audience members came to speak to me. I could see her out of the corner of my eye, deliberating—should she approach or not? It had been a particularly nice audience, and I was enjoying my conversation with the few women who had come to talk to me. I couldn't leave my seat to talk to her without being rude to them. I saw her swallow her nervousness before she approached. (It was strange for me to recognize I represented a daunting figure.) She came up to me, spoke briefly, as though not wanting to use up too much of my time. Then she moved away. I thought "come back," but did not say it. When I think about her in comparison with this agressive man, my blood boils.

The dynamics of such situations are subtle. It is the continuous barrage of them and the everydayness of each situation that drags one down, stokes the fire of a woman's fury. The lack of self-consciousness with which men stare, speak and occupy space is astounding when you think about it, when you stop thinking about it as normal. A hiking friend—another woman of colour—and I have a fun game. As we walk through some of the more popular trails around the city of Vancouver, we consciously try, inasfar as possible, to stick to the middle of the path. It is interesting to see who steps aside and who is so certain we are invisible that if we don't step aside, they would walk right through us.

Men's sense of entitlement, especially white men's sense of entitlement, has everything to do with imperialism, neo-imperialism, corporate imperialism—in other words, the general exploitation of women and men who they think of as less than them.

I am occasionally pleasantly surprised. After a recent reading at the local women's bar, a young man, not more than twenty years old, perhaps gay, perhaps not, approached me shyly and said how much reading my novel had affected him. He had brought his mother, a lesbian, with him that night to see me. His energy and enthusiasm and gentleness were greatly uplifting to me because they gave me hope.

But I still fear, resent and cannot avoid men's collective, systemic and random power. I try to avoid walking alone at night because some unexpected man might be waiting in the dark. Although I have thirst for knowledge, I avoid universities because they repress the very kinds of knowledge that interest me. I don't like what the corporate agenda, which is, after all, a patriarchal agenda, is doing to the way we share our resources in the country, nor do I like the way it exploits Third World workers, particularly Third World women.

These days I find myself less certain as to where to direct my energies. I have a sense that the communities in which I discovered so much joy and power are collapsing partially under their own weight and partially under the weight of moderate conservativism supported by an un- or surreptitiously articulated fascist impulse supported by a very real, very active fascist minority. And then I think, no, these communities, however loosely defined, are not collapsing, they are evolving, they are adapting. I have two strategies of my own: 1. to speak, inasfar as possible, from the core first, to speak with my world at the centre (rather than the margins) and explain afterwards if necessary and desirable, 2. to remain open to change and challenge. In this way it becomes possible to imagine and create new worlds by beginning with the assumption of their existence and then leaving them open to modification. The ability to do both of these things requires the use of every sense available from the most verifiable to the most intuitive.

Many women I know have turned to therapy as it has become clear to them that the simple binaries of society—white/not white, male/female, straight/gay, working class/upper class, able-bodied/disabled—are not water-tight, and are interlinked in very complicated ways. Coming to our own power has also meant coming to our own responsibility in order to take control of our lives and live as full and complex human beings, rather than merely as victims and oppressors. Not that discussions of oppression and victimization have ceased to be useful; only that if we are to survive, we must widen them. As a tool for looking inward, and for analyzing personal history, therapy has provided a balance against all the group-oriented political work that many women have been doing, without rest, for years. But in spite of all this, I can't go for it. I can support and applaud friends who say it has worked wonders for them, but I won't go. Inasfar as I believe in the binary of West vs. East (and to a certain level, or at certain times I do, and must) I think of therapy and its emotional logic as a Western thing, not suited to the Asian concept of "face"—a cultural construct perhaps, but one that I can no more easily dispose of than I can of my eyes or heart or liver. To tell a stranger/professional the deepest darkest things about my childhood, and by association, my family would induce such shame that the benefits would not even remotely outbalance the scars produced. I would experience it as a violent disruption. A respected friend and fellow writer tells me she thinks of the imperative to keep face as oppressive, that it must be unravelled if we are to become truly ourselves. I am intrigued by what she says. The struggle continues.

Let a hundred flowers bloom, let a hundred schools of thought contend.
—Mao Tse-tung

Of course, history tells us that terrible acts of repression occurred very shortly after the implementation of Mao's edict. Could that history have been written differently?

There was a cohesiveness to the movements of the baby boomer generation that I feel to be lacking in my own. We live in a cynical age and find ourselves with little choice but to adopt the individualist mode of operating that global capitalism offers us. The borders and definitions of identity and identity politics are becoming too ragged—real people cannot be contained within them—and yet many of the ideas and practices provided by identity politics remain profoundly liberating. How does one live in the contradiction? Within the academy, some of what the post-structuralists and post-modernists say makes sense, but the inherent snobbery of the language makes it impossible to use at a popular level (unlike the language of hate, which requires no translation).

I have to ask myself what it is about identity politics that works for me and what I feel to be lacking. Are there other ways to understand the world and my place in it that would more accurately reflect the way I experience life? Must I replace one system of thought, one way of being with another, or can they co-exist? Do I have to name them? For instance, there are aspects of a Taoist conception of the universe that make great sense to me—an investment in the notions of perpetual change and transformation. And then sometimes I run screaming from Asian-influenced spiritual practices precisely because in the West they come so drenched in orientalism that I can't bear it. I know that I can't afford not to bear it. As a westernized woman, I have no choice but to go into that world in order to pull out the things which are useful, to transform or reconstruct them, make them into something useful and liberating. My own history, especially the written-and-available-in-English part, is soaked in orientalism, and I can't be afraid to get dirty if I am to retrieve those parts of myself.

So these are imperfect tools. Identity politics was and is also an imperfect tool, but nonetheless useful and liberatory. By what faculty does a woman know when to engage what strategy?

The snake woman rattles her tail softly. She has been listening all along.

I know of a room where the lights are sometimes on and sometimes off. I can never tell before going in which way it will be.

The narrow feminism of my childhood grew as I did, influenced by the things I read, the things I experienced, the things I talked about with my friends, teachers, allies and acquaintances. My introduction to identity politics in the late eighties and early nineties was another momentous shift. It was a shift in my own personal life; it was also a shift in the way I was perceived in feminist communities and in the world at large. This was a shift which afforded me the public voice I did not have before. But the change cannot stop there. The language of feminism, the language of anti-racism, like other useful tools, can be applied to reinforce or recreate power hierarchies in much the same way the language of democracy has. But they don't have to. The trick is to keep moving, to find other ways of talking, other ways of seeing the world, other ways of telling stories. The biggest barrier and the most difficult to overcome is fear.

We are not wrong to be frightened. The right-wing, with its accompanying me-first individualism, is gaining ground. Welfare is being cut to unlivable rates, women's shelters are losing funding, a head tax on immigrants has been re-introduced, progressive arts organizations are losing funding, health-care benefits are being threatened, women are still being battered, are still making seventy-one cents to every dollar men make. . . . There are all kinds of things to be frightened of. And in the U.S., black churches are burning, anti-queer ballot measures are introduced and in some cases voted in, the religious right has gained political respectability. . . .

I am often scared. So are most women I know. We are scared of one another because we have such a capacity to hurt each other. We are scared of the outside world. The sisterhood of feminism is a strange one because it offers the illusion of safe spaces when in reality there are none, though I still believe some spaces are safer than others. If we can understand that there is always danger, even in the most innocent looking places, perhaps we can still use the tools offered by various politics of identity. It is a time when it is easy to be scared, and at the same time I feel that I cannot afford to be frightened, now, especially now—because the fear opens the door to hatred, makes us unable to adapt to problems as they grow and change and intensify.

Speaking of speculative fiction writers William Gibson and Spider Robinson, a friend remarked to me that they are able to imagine the outlandish things they do because, as straight white men, they are that much more free than the rest of us. I believe that as women, and as women of colour, we too can imagine deeply and widely, and also that we can remember just as deeply. I believe that the act of doing so is profoundly liberating. The key to liberation is to recall what we were, the parts of ourselves that we want to bring into the future. If women can recall their histories and retain their memories, then men's histories and the systems of oppression they justify will no longer hold water.

I am increasingly conscious how historically situated we are. How life moves and changes, and that each change emerges out of the previous. In a Taoist universe, the closer a person approaches divinity, the greater her ability to transform herself from one form to the next, from swallow to flower to lizard to human to snake.

There is an old Chinese myth about how women loving women come to be. A pair of heterosexual lovers live a life of vampirish sexual excess, during which they make callous use of innocent men and women. They are reincarnated as women, and before they are born, that is, before their genders have been determined for the next life, their parents pledge them in marriage to one another. They are born, live a life of debauchery, and come to a tragic end. Of course this tale comes out of the Confucian patriarchal order of things, an order which obliterated all physical records that disputed it in around the year 600 by the Western calendar. Still, older memories seep up through the cracks. Books and scrolls can be destroyed, but we do have other ways of remembering. Memory flows in our blood, appears on the body as clues to another past. It is a past that cannot be remembered accurately, that cannot be recalled through anthropological study, or reconstructed through ancient texts. These things are imperfect clues fraught with nervous tension that of late we have been toning back with the term "problematic."

217

It takes thousands of years for moving water to corrode rock. But slowly the fissure stretches into a yawning cave. What will you find when you step into the moist darkness? No shimmering automobiles or cell phones to propel your voice into an ear neighbourhoods away. No perfect sisterhood where all women are equal. Romance will take your warm hand in her cool one and guide you into a mirror. Mirrors are made of glass. You will bleed.

Perhaps there are caves within the caves. In one of these dark places I will make room for my own metamorphosis. Nightly, the snake woman and I will come out through a hole in the surface. We will walk through the windy streets, listening to the world through our own strange ears as we turn corners in every city, just disappearing the moment you turn your head to look.

I would like to thank Monika Kin Gagnon and Shani Mootoo for their support and feedback on this piece.

Body of Knowledge

Helen Lenskyj

As a feminist whose major research and advocacy interest since 1982 has been woman and sport, I am often asked how I arrived at this issue: was I a competitive athlete? My family and friends find this enormously funny—apparently I don't look like anyone's idea of a sportswoman. This isn't too surprising, since we don't see many small, middle-aged female athletes on the sports pages of the newspaper. However, I am a recreational athlete, and I see this as an integral part of my identity as a woman and a feminist. At the same time, I see the physical and the intellectual as two key strands of my feminism.

While I was growing up in Sydney, Australia, I had the misfortune to be susceptible to bronchitis, and popular wisdom in those days was to keep children like me indoors during the winter even though winter in Australia is a laughable concept to most North Americans. And so, although the girls' school that I attended had sport and physical education four days per week, for several winters I was only allowed to participate in the indoor activities. My mother also insisted that I wear long stockings all through the winter term, when nearly everyone else wore socks.

I was soon considered a rather over-protected kid by my peers, and I missed out on learning many of the basic motor skills needed for sport. Initially, I hated the feeling of being pampered and tried hard to keep up, but was discouraged by the fact that my ability in almost every school sporting activity—basketball, tennis, softball, swimming, running—was so inferior. Sport in my school was a highly competitive venture, and the fact that I routinely came last in any race was eventually so demoralizing that I started viewing myself as a sport failure. In the last two years of high school, I was very relieved to find that students like myself, who took the higher level academic subjects, no longer had sport scheduled into their timetables.

Looking back on my childhood, I often think of this quiet little girl in her wrinkled grey stockings watching from the sidelines. At a recent lunch with "old girls" from my school, I met a physical education teacher whom I had not seen since I was about ten. She admitted that she was taken aback when I gave her a copy of my book *Out of Bounds: Women, Sport and Sexuality* and told her about my life today. The girl she remembered was, in her words, "a bit frightened of joining in sport." We laughed together as we shared this new-found common ground—as active women and as lesbians.

During the late 1970s, I slowly began taking steps to reclaim my body: cycling, yoga, running, and, most significantly, martial arts. My introduction to yoga at the age of thirty-six was illuminating, to say the least. I felt compelled to take up some structured physical activity after running to catch the bus one day, an effort that left me out of breath for about ten minutes. My first experiences with yoga confirmed that I was so out of touch with my body and physical capacities that I was virtually a physical illiterate. Inverted yoga positions like the plough, where the legs are raised over the body to touch the floor behind one's head, almost immobilized me. When the instructor directed us to move our hands from their outstretched position by our sides to touch our toes (now on the floor behind our heads) I found that my brain could not convey this relatively simple message to my hands. The only solution was to move my fingers inch by inch along the floor until they ended up in the vicinity of my feet. This did not bode well for my aspiration to train in martial arts.

The next year I began studying hapkido and continued training three times a week for four years, completing three belt levels. Hapkido is a Korean system of self-defence, with prescribed movements for defending oneself against a variety of holds, punches and knife attacks. Hapkido satisfied my need for a regular, structured physical activity, while at the same time fitted with feminists' growing concern that women need to be able to protect ourselves against attack. I shared that concern, since I often travelled alone on public transport late at night and, up to that point, had no faith in my physical capacity to protect myself or to escape from an attacker.

For most of my hapkido training, I was one of only two or three women in the club, and at times the only woman. I frequently grappled with the dilemma this posed. Training with men resembled "the real thing" because men are statistically more likely than women to perpe-trate an attack. And since the hapkido system stresses technique, not brute force, in theory I should have been able to hold my own against the men. But I often wished that some allowance could be made for my size, just in the interest of fairness.

I was never bothered by the one aspect of martial arts that some women find difficult—reluctance to defend oneself for fear of injuring one's attacker. Instructors in wen-do, a women's self-defence system, often report that women have difficulty even punching a pillow held by another woman, although there is no danger that the punch will injure her. I believe, and my experience confirmed, that good self-defence training gives a woman both the physical confidence and the mental attitude needed to use appropriate force to defend herself or others from attack. Rather than experiencing fear or anger as immobilizing, women can learn to channel this energy effectively to defend themselves.

Hapkido was literally a life-altering experience and I attribute several major turning points in my life to my newly discovered integration of body and mind. In the four years that I trained in hapkido, I left my marriage, completed my PH.D., and began questioning my heterosexual identity. Equally important, I realised that I could make women, sport and physical activity the primary focus of my research. By 1980, I had completed an M.A. on immigrant girls' and women's education in Canada from 1890 to 1930, and then switched to the topic of girls' and women's physical education and sport over the same period for my doctoral thesis, which was completed in 1983. A shortened version of my thesis later became the first section of *Out of Bounds*.

I found the prospect of doing research on women and sport very exciting—in fact, it sometimes seemed that a process that was so pleasurable and fascinating couldn't possibly count as real academic work. Although it is certainly not unusual for feminist researchers, like other politically active scholars, to be impassioned about their work, the topic of sport is still not popular among feminists.

Apart from the obvious explanation that many feminists view sport as incurably male-defined and male-dominated, I think there are other reasons for many women's reticence. Feelings of alienation, discomfort and guilt about our bodies, our physicality and sexuality lead many women to develop a mind-body split. Of course, there are powerful social forces pointing us in this direction; damaging childhood experiences in the family, school, and community will no doubt leave their mark on our sense of bodily integrity. Today, when I ask audiences of women if they have experienced the humiliation of being picked last for the team in physical education classes, there are always raised hands, including those of young women. It seems that some teachers still used these cruel methods of team selection in the last decade. What is most disturbing is the long-lasting sense of physical inadequacy imprinted on our psyches by these childhood experiences.

The general feminist antipathy to sport and sport research that I have encountered has other manifestations, too. Only four Canadian universities offer a separate course on women, sport, and physical activity in their physical education programs, and only about ten percent of women's studies programs have a full-time faculty member whose major research interest is sport and physical activity. Women's studies collections in university libraries tend to neglect sport as a subject area, and feminist anthologies have only recently begun to include chapters on sport.

On a more personal level, feminist scholars doing research on sport and leisure soon grow accustomed to hearing dismissive comments about their work (What leisure?), and these topics are often excluded from the list of important feminist issues. Sport is seen by many feminists as a domain that is ruled by men and dominated by masculinist values, and feminists' general lack of interest in the politics of sport results in the perpetuation of traditional sporting systems and practices. The small number of feminist activists working in the chilly climate of mainstream sport certainly need the support of women outside sport, and I believe that all feminists should understand the crucial links between sport and the broader equity issues facing women in society, including racism, classism, and homophobia.

Even if physical activity were seen only as important from a women's health perspective, this alone would justify its inclusion on the feminist agenda. Regular physical activity has significant health benefits, including maintenance of healthy body weight and composition, prevention of heart disease and high blood pressure, improved fat and carbohydrate metabolism, alleviation of anxiety and depression, increased self-esteem and positive body image. Premenstrual and menopausal symptoms are also relieved through regular exercise. Osteoporosis is a serious health issue for women, especially during and after menopause, and there is research evidence to show that exercise, in conjunction with dietary calcium, is effective in its prevention and treatment. For larger women, apart from the possibility of weight control which may be a choice for some, there is the potential for enhanced body image and acceptance through movement classes conducted by and for larger women.

Thinking further about the mind-body question and the integration of the intellectual and physical dimensions of my own feminist consciousness, I am aware of the limitations of conventional language. "Intellectual" is too narrow a term to cover the integration of social, emotional, and cognitive learning: understanding my own and other women's experiences, reading and discussing feminist books, and so on. In reference to physical learning, I need to go beyond the idea of being at ease in my body to the understanding that "my body *is* myself." The concepts of physical literacy and illiteracy are useful; my physical self constitutes the way I am literate in the world, the way I "read" and "write" my life. It is disturbing that many women, including feminists, are more likely to act as if "my head is myself, my body is . . . (something else)." For me, and no doubt for many women, that "something else" was for many years a separate, vulnerable entity, a burden and a liability, rather than a source of strength and pride. I don't think it was coincidental that the major changes in my life around 1980 involved the integration of my body and my mind.

My formal introduction to feminism occurred in 1979 when I became a card-carrying member of the Feminist Party of Canada. My feminist consciousness had been on hold for several years before this. I have a clear memory of borrowing a library copy of one of the early feminist classics in about 1970—it may have been Germaine Greer's *The Female Eunuch*. After reading a few chapters, I deliberately shut the book because at some unconscious level its contents were too dangerous and too disturbing for me to read. At that time, my survival as a wife and mother at home with two young children depended largely on denial, and any reflection on my condition was a luxury in which I could not indulge. I was not ready to pick up these books again for almost a decade.

The Feminist Party was a fledgling political party based in Ontario but with a national membership. One of its major long-term goals was to run candidates in provincial and federal elections. Internal conflict was largely responsible for its demise after about five years. For a few years, I co-ordinated the Feminist Party's study group, which met every few weeks to discuss a short reading—initially the essays in Vivian Gornick and Barbara Moran's anthology *Women in Sexist Society.* The group was very important to me as a source of intellectual stimulation and emotional support, and many of the women I met there are still friends today.

My research on women and sport has introduced me to some inspirational researchers, academics, and advocates, women (and some men) whom I am happy to consider colleagues and friends. Since my university teaching is in a graduate school of education and not a physical education department, sociology of sport conferences are one of the few occasions in my work life where colleagues acknowledge my contributions to this field and seriously engage my ideas. By contrast, sport still tends to be a neglected issue at women's studies conferences, and those of us who are in sport and leisure studies have grown accustomed to having our work dismissed as irrelevant—not to mention sitting through hours of presentations without the benefit of fitness or refreshment breaks.

Some of my feminist friends and colleagues share the joy of movement and the sense of fulfillment that comes from feeling fit and strong. Others seem to find more satisfaction in overwork and stress, which are worn, in some circles, as badges of honour. Apart from the mind/body split, I believe that socialization into conventional femininity promotes two feeling-states that are antithetical to physical literacy and body celebration: fear of movement ("Keep your legs together," "Don't hurt yourself") and lack of entitlement to self-care ("I don't have time for walking/fitness/swimming/vacations"). After a lifetime of internalizing messages about our bodies' physical and sexual vulnerability, we are reluctant to celebrate our physicality. And our continued position as second-class citizens erodes the sense that such celebration is in fact our birthright.

Our socialization as women around body and self-care issues is extremely powerful. In addition, the mission of feminists to change society has its own self-censoring agenda. "How could you bother with something as frivolous and self-indulgent as sport," they ask, "when the global problems confronting women are escalating every minute?" Yet, each time feminist colleagues suffer stress-related illnesses, the answer seems simple: a healthy activist is more effective than one who is burnt out.

My experiences in physical activity make me think that gaining physical literacy is an ongoing process for women. I began swimming again on my fiftieth birthday, after more than twenty-five years of virtually no swimming, and this experience confirmed many of my reflections on the body, and on the joys of movement. A relatively new fear of being underwater emerged, even though I had loved diving as a child. For months I simply told myself that I could enjoy swimming without ever being submerged, and that having this fear didn't make me a wimp. It was extremely difficult to be gentle with myself, rather than critical. Gradually I began to teach myself to do the crawl (which meant keeping my face in the water at least half of the time). It was a major victory to complete a length of the pool, although I always found myself panting at the end. Discussing this problem with an experienced swimmer, I learned that the major problems for adult swimmers are fear and inadequate exhaling. Such a simple answer.

This new insight—practical and attitudinal—marked a turning point. A simple trick like telling myself that it was interesting to be staring down at the bottom of the pool (and thus ensuring adequate time for exhaling) actually worked. Another breakthrough occurred the first time I tried out my new-found skill in salt water during a trip home to Australia. The added buoyancy, combined with a view that really was interesting—plants, rocks, and small fish at the bottom of the pool—produced an amazing feeling of lightness, speed, and fluidity. It also prompted me to experiment with diving underwater for a closer view—something I had avoided for years.

I believe that it is essential for feminists to work towards reclaiming our physical bodies through sport and recreation. These activities do not have to be cast in the masculinist mold; there are countless examples across the country of woman-centred, grass-roots sporting initiatives, ranging from women-only wilderness adventure trips to recreational softball leagues. Women engaged in these initiatives have literally changed the rules of the game. They challenge the idea that winning is everything; they stress the importance of fun, fitness and the achievement of personal goals; they provide child care, car pools, and subsidies; and they value co-operation and shared decision-making. Men's sport is no longer the only game in town. Let's get out and play!

My Evolution as a Lesbian Feminist Writer

Mary Meigs

Photo by Rollie McKenna

The following will be an attempt (at seventy-nine) to describe my not-yet-completed evolution as a lesbian feminist. My coming-out as a lesbian in an autobiographical book *Lily Briscoe: A Self-Portrait* was the first political action of my life that engaged my whole self. It freed me from old terrors; it was also a public declaration of my defiance of homophobia. Before coming out I was colluding with the forces that kept me fearful and silent. I seemed to be agreeing that I should keep silent because homosexuality was offensive to society. In fact, I was protecting myself from the disapproval of society, though I was already protected by class privileges and by the luxury of an inherited income. The material comfort prevented me from having a real understanding of what feminism is, that is, a knowledge of and opposition to all the forms of oppression of women in a society run by men. To come out as a lesbian was to protest against the only kind of oppression with which I was familiar—homophobia.

My inaction before I came out was, in essence, a declaration of neutrality, and neutrality is a protective device. I believe now that protective silences that cover up oppression or abuse should be broken and should stop masquerading as discretion or loyalty.

When I began writing *Lily Briscoe* in 1972 (I was fifty-five) I thought of myself as a feminist. But I see now how far I was from being one, for I'd hardly thought about the implications contained in the word—that it meant a re-examination of all one's ideas about the world and society, about politics and sex, that it meant asking questions about everything one read and saw and heard. I was in the halfway state in which one calls oneself a feminist but still argues with radical feminist interpretations. I didn't yet acknowledge the effects of patriarchal conditioning on me—as an artist, as a lesbian, as a member of a privileged class, separated from what I thought of even then as "the real world." The facts of "real" life are war, the Holocaust, the atom and hydrogen bombs, every form of genocide including starvation and the destruction of millions of acres of land by herbicides. "Real" life means massacres, assassinations, torture and terrorism, the forced flight of helpless human beings from their homes, cruelty to and the killing of millions of animals.

Although I had always read voraciously, as a painter I'd lived through my eyes, with a kind of impersonality that strained out connections. I could see human suffering but saw it more as subject matter for drawing and painting (the artists I admired most were Goya and Rembrandt) than as materials for thought and judgment. It is easy for painters in picturesque places to become alert tourists whose obligation is only to look; I'd been doing this for most of my adult life. But writing even one sentence forces you to think, and in the strangest way, enables you to know what you think. So it happened that the first sentence of my first book—"Does every life deserve an autobiography?"—began the thinking process that led to my gradual evolution as a feminist.

At that time I was living in Brittany, in a region where people lived and worked as they had for hundreds of years. The older women had hard, muscular bodies and iron wills; they were slightly contemptuous of unmarried women who thought they were working when they were painting pictures or writing books. Or reading books, for that matter, which I spent many hours doing: all of Racine's plays, books on the early Celts, which inspired a series of illustrations based on the legend of Cuchulain, a macho hero if there ever was one, and *Sexus, Nexus and Plexus* by Henry Miller. Clearly I was not a feminist if Henry Miller could make me laugh out loud even at his most sexist and if I could think of it as a kind of liberation to like him so much. This, in spite of the fact that I'd read both *Sexual Politics* and *The Second Sex*, which had obviously not broken up my intractable habits of thought.

When I moved to Montreal from France I began to have conversations with lesbian feminist friends. I remember arguing about mother-love and about Simone de Beauvoir's statement in *The Second Sex* that gender roles are entirely learned. I believed, and still believe, that human and animal mothers instinctively bond with their newborn babies (at least if they have been properly mothered themselves) and that this bonding has been essential to evolutionary progress. My friends said that bonding was imposed by patriarchy. As for gender roles, I believe that they are imposed but not necessarily learned. My twin sister accepted the prescribed female role and I rebelled against it, though we had an identical upbringing.

Part of my education as a feminist was to learn not to throw away all my old beliefs and cultural joys, particularly in the domain of literature, painting, and music. My feminist conscience was telling me that I should prefer women's creative work in all these domains. Reading *Sexual Politics* and *The Second Sex* should have made it easier for me to exclude Henry Miller, D.H. Lawrence, and other sexist writers from my canon. I knew that it had once been more comfortable for me to float along with the patriarchal tide than to go against the current as I was beginning to do now that *Lily Briscoe* was out. But I remembered the elation I felt when I read great male novelists and poets who helped shape my writing and when I looked at the work of painters who influenced my own painting. I still revere Blake, Whitman, and Henry James and am moved by Matisse, Cézanne, Manet and many other painters, and by the musicians who tower above history. I feel the same elation when I read Jane Austen, George Eliot, the Brontës, and Virginia Woolf, as well as the marvelous work of poets, novelists, and those who have built the structure of feminist theory.

I feel rage, too, at the invisibility and powerlessness of women. Rage is often unproductive and can be a waste of energy but it can also be converted into the energy to think, to speak out, to write. Women's amazing courage is the source of their growing power. They risk their lives by speaking openly about the horrors they have endured at the hands of men. They are up against an exponential increase in violence. Through barbarous brutality, and punishment, and through the tyranny of religious practices, men attempt to take away the power that women have gained. My reading now is almost entirely by women; I want to catch up (and never will) with the universe of women's experience.

If I had not been a lesbian, I would probably have made the compromises women made sixty years ago with the heterosexual world. I might, like my twin sister, have married and had children. I might have weakened in my determination to be a painter and might never even have begun my first book. In short, I wouldn't have lived the life I've lived, where every step has opened up a wider landscape. At nineteen I was only vaguely aware of the world, at forty-one I had only a glimmering of the meaning of feminism. My political education began when I began to write and came out as a lesbian. It took me years more to learn that in addition to all the injustice in the world that I knew about, there was much worse about which I was still ignorant. Learning and unlearning comprised my education as a feminist and made me feel miserable as well as enlightened.

I had to learn in what ways I was not yet a feminist. What questions hadn't I asked? What books hadn't I read? How much did I take for granted inside my sheltered life? I hadn't made the connection, for instance, between the minute percentage of women's art in museums and the domination of the world of art by men. I'd studied the work of great women painters and sculptors and read the books of great women writers, yet a sense of the ways in which women's art has been marginalized came to me from reading the work of lesbian feminists: Virginia Woolf, Mary Daly, Adrienne Rich, Andrea Dworkin, and many others. The unlearning had to do with the recognition of the clichés in my thinking, the ready answers—and the learning never ends.

There has always been a struggle in me between ideology and how I live it, between my own work and the political action that would take me away from it, between moral discomfort and physical comfort. It helps to think and write. With each book I write, I sense the changes in me that have come from reading women's books, and of my own slow evolution toward an understanding of what a lesbian feminist reading of life would be. For me it is a study of the kinds of oppression that are part of my own experience: suffocation by upper-class principles and squeamishness, the blindness of privilege, the oppression of enforced heterosexuality. One of my interests as a writer is in microcosms of warfare and cruelty, the damage that one lover can do to another, and in the make-up jobs, the falsification by our egos of reality. My writing is partly about ways in which those of us who are in relative safety protect ourselves against bearing witness, particularly through denial.

The friend who hammered tirelessly away at me, whom I always opposed at the beginning of one of her metamorphoses, then listened to, and finally believed, was Barbara Deming. Barbara lived her beliefs through non-violent action against nuclear testing and later, in the civil rights movement and the protest against the Vietnam War. During World War II, I had declared my allegiance to the apparatus of power

by leaving my job as a teacher to join the WAVES. All of us in the
services assented to monstrous crimes that we believed were "necessary."
As a pacifist, Barbara questioned the organization of society and the
power of the state. She asked questions about war, the means of making
war, and the use of genocidal weapons. She challenged a power that
every nation-state has always taken for granted—the right to compel its
young male citizens to kill men, women and children in another nation,
to ask them to be willing to die for a country (theirs), to expect them to
commit atrocities. The civil rights struggle against segregation and racism
challenged another deadly power—to hold a whole race in bondage.
Barbara was always in the vanguard during these pre-feminist years of
social protest while I continued my life as a painter. I listened to her
evolving thoughts and my own thinking changed, but instead of gaining
courage through action I felt fear—of physical violence against me and
of being put in jail. I stayed at home rather than joining the great civil
rights marches or the anti-Vietnam War demonstration at the Pentagon.
I stayed home when Barbara, not long before her death, joined the
women who made the 1983 march to Seneca Falls.

It took years even for Barbara to evolve into a radical lesbian feminist.
For many of her women friends feminism became the logical response to
sexism in both the anti-war and the civil rights movements. Feminism
for Barbara also grew out of her decision to come out as a lesbian. She
had argued in defence of her own sexual life with male friends who
thought her insistence on this freedom diverted her from more important issues. As it turned out, lesbian rights became a key issue in feminist
politics. Barbara declared her lesbian independence in *We Cannot Live
Without Our Lives* and from then on all her energies went into the
lesbian and feminist revolutions and into the building of her own lesbian
community at Sugarloaf Key in Florida.

As always, I was following along in Barbara's wake, arguing fiercely
and then being persuaded. If she could come out in a book, I thought,
perhaps I could too; I started writing and sending pages to Barbara, who
encouraged me to go on. *Lily Briscoe* is not the portrait of a feminist, but
rather of a painter who reluctantly admits that she is a lesbian and works
her way over the patriarchal obstacle course to relative freedom. This
was something I was able to do with my whole being, as an artist and
with a sense of exhilaration. I was committing myself in writing to a
position that I could hold without backsliding or regret.

There are still lesbian painters and writers in hiding who are proud of being accepted by men and of belonging to what they perceive as a sexless category: painters or writers. They are apt to think of "woman writer" as a pejorative and would angrily reject the term "lesbian painter" or "lesbian writer." Even now, to come out publicly as a lesbian is to be initiated into the sexual politics from which one has hidden. One has announced: I am one of those you (the heterosexual "you") fear, one of those you don't want your daughter to be, one who can be categorized as a man-hater, whose views are bound to be questionable because they have, it is said, a permanent bias. These feelings are often roiling in people's heads at the very moment that they are smiling kindly at you. It is not you, of course, that they fear, but, in my case, us. You think that we are dangerous. You think that if you give us an inch, we'll take a mile. We may try to steal your daughter from right under your nose.

More than once I have been puzzled by the puzzlement of a heterosexual friend who assumes because she or he is free of homophobia that homophobia is no longer a threat, and that perhaps we are making much ado about nothing. To a lesbian, or a gay man, homophobia is present everywhere: in the media, by the frequent linking of homosexuality with criminality or sickness; in the minds of religious fundamentalists who invoke Sodom and Gomorra; in the universal harping on the joys of heterosexual marriage; in the armed forces, in public and private schools, in the Catholic and other churches. Straight society believes that family consists of a man, a woman, and ideally, at least one child. Homosexuality is a crime in China and in Muslim countries and in some states in the U.S. No matter what gains we have made in visibility and power, homophobia is widespread. It is in the minds of Canadian lawmakers who are afraid to lose votes by approving spousal rights for lesbian and gay couples. It is alive even in lesbians and gay men, still in the closet, who turn their self-hate against openly gay people.

Many competent writers are engaged in the task of reclaiming lesbian writers for heterosexuality. A thoughtful writer like Lyndall Gordon, in *Virginia Woolf: A Writer's Life*, seems subtly to undermine Woolf's love for women. She speaks of "a scented adoration in Orlando which is not easy to share;" she says of Woolf, "To Vita she gushed and postured." She does not relate Gerald and George Duckworth's abuse of Virginia as a child and young girl to Woolf's life and writing. A feminist reading of Woolf's life such as Louise de Salvo's *Virginia Woolf: The Impact of*

Childhood Sexual Abuse on Her Life and Work, which has been so derided
by the Woolf establishment, insists on the effects of sexual abuse, on the
possibility of Woolf's madness as the result of it, or as an escape from it.
A feminist reading, lesbian or not, is uncompromising, sees new truths
and new meanings which make people uncomfortable. De Salvo says
with complete naturalness, "But she chose lesbian love with Violet
Dickinson and with Vita Sackville-West as a positive, adaptive response
to her abuse, as other women have as well."

The hard part for lesbians is to keep doggedly asserting our right to be
witnesses of life. I consider myself lucky to have a small voice in this
world, as a writer and as an old woman (I was seventy-one in 1988 when
The Company of Strangers was filmed) who came out as a lesbian in a film
that was shown all over the world. Every breaking of silence adds to our
power. I believe that we often have a gift for dispassionate vision and the
ability to see the Emperor's nakedness. Lyndall Gordon writes that Ethel
Smyth, that rarest of birds, a woman composer (and a lesbian), said to
Virginia Woolf, "You see, Virginia, I feel very passionately . . . that,
once women throw off their susceptibility to male notions, something
new in the way of light and heat will be diffused in the world."

To label is a knee-jerk reaction—easy, tempting, useful—that can
destroy rational discussion and force us to defend ourselves. Labels can
deny the truth by changing the subject. Unfortunately, the repetition of
words like patriarchy, sexism and oppression turns them into clichés,
which lose their power of precise definition and gain a power to anger
people. I myself am angry if someone says to me, "You hate men." This
is the most common and handiest accusation used against lesbians, for if
I hate men, it is because I am a lesbian feminist and everything I say
about men is believed to be one-sided and therefore invalid. The words
patriarchy, sexism, and oppression contain accusations against men, and
many women want to protect men from accusation, particularly if they
know men who are neither patriarchal nor sexist nor oppressive. But
there are times when a label speaks the truth and rings authentically like
pure metal. When Colonel Greta Cammermeyer said, "I am a lesbian,"
knowing that she risked dismissal from the army, she spoke her own
truth in the simplest possible way. The words patriarchal, sexist, and
oppressive accurately describe the evils of our society.

Today we are living in a time when the patriarchal tide is in full
flood. The crimes continue against women, against very young girls,
against female infants: beating, rape, torture, ostracism, genital mutilation

(performed by women to please men). Young women are being used as sex slaves and underpaid as industrial slaves all over the world. The crimes against women can no longer be hidden; they are being secretly filmed and are appearing on our TV screens. Via TV, I am a witness of women's witnessing. Feminism to me means resistance to and exposure of all these crimes against women, including that of using women to commit crimes against themselves and their daughters. It is to tell the news of every kind of abuse.

I deeply admire the courage of the women who have spoken out against the atrocities that women suffer at the hands of men. Many of the victims of these atrocities testified at the Cairo and Beijing conferences and then returned to abusive societies in their own countries. One of them, a radical feminist Bangladeshi, has had a *fatwah* issued against her for openly declaring her views about the abuse of women in Bangladesh.

Some women at the Beijing conference opposed lesbian rights, which should be part of the spectrum of human rights, as anti-Christian or anti-Muslim. The American religious right, comprised of both men and women, is a powerful reactionary force that would like to put lesbians back in the closet and wives in the home. The Catholic church forbids abortion and contraception. Children's minds are being contaminated by a barrage of hate messages against women on TV, in advertising, in every form of communication. Mainstream politics cuts and cancels programs designed to help women and alleviate women's poverty, while arms sales exceed foreign aid. And yet, thousands of women are aware of these threats and have the courage to resist.

A few years ago I had a dream about Barbara Deming. I was looking out the window of a house on a hill and saw Barbara climbing up the winding road below. She was wearing her old beret and the pleated plaid skirt that swung as she walked. I leaned out and called, "Wait for me!" and she looked up, waved, and went striding on. It was one of the wonderfully encouraging dreams I sometimes have. It said to me, each of us has to make her way alone, but we are helped by the great women we have known who are still alive in us, and the great women in the world who seem to bear the world on their shoulders.

Letters to My Sister

Joan Meister

November 1, 1994

Dear Meem:

The other day I actually said it out loud. To a friend on the phone. I said, "I don't think I want to do this any more." And "this," of course, is the disabled feminist stuff. It's been such hard and thankless (and unpaid) work for about ten years now. But I'd *never* said it out loud before. Saying it out loud makes it more real or valid or something. I'm feeling burned out.

We disabled women really do have a lot of extra shit to pack around. We face at least a triple level of oppression: first of all we are women; *and* we have a disability; *and then*, we might also be an older woman, a lesbian, a First Nations woman or any other kind of an oppressed woman, *and then* we might have any one of about nine distinctly different kinds of disabilities. *Or* . . . more than one disability at the same time in different combinations!

I bet you don't even know about all of them. We've got mental disabilities and physical disabilities. Under mental, we've got your consumers of mental health services and women who are labelled mentally handicapped. Some women with mental health issues call themselves psychiatric survivors. Women who are labelled mentally handicapped would really rather not be labelled at all—it would sort of be like people making a big deal about the fact that we have green eyes. It's just the way we came. And calling these women retarded is sort of like calling me a cripple. They still use retarded in the States but that's mostly the professionals and what do they know? Women make up the largest portion of people with mental health disabilities and together, both kinds of mental disabilities make up by far the largest proportion of the population of people with disabilities.

Then there are the women with physical disabilities. Five sub-groups here: blindness and low vision; deafness and hard of hearing; learning; hidden; and, mobility. Hidden refers to something like epilepsy, allergies, or even mild multiple sclerosis. I think it's stupid (and probably indicative of the "hierarchy of disability" that exists in the world—my disability is better/more important/more needy than yours) that the international symbol for disability is a stylized white wheelchair on a blue background. Those of us in wheelchairs are just a very small part of a small portion of the disabled population.

And then there are a couple of newly recognized kinds and they both sort of bridge the mental and physical groups. There are women with brain injuries which usually result from things like car accidents or strokes. The good thing about brain injuries is that it's possible to get a bit better over time, unlike a spinal chord injury, for instance. And that leaves us those with HIV/AIDS, who call themselves "positive women." As we've been learning lately, young women are the largest growing population here. *None* of this is good news. Furthermore, since the incidence and severity of disability increases with aging and the Baby Boomers are getting older, there soon will be more than the current sixteen per cent or so of Canadians who have a disability.

And so ends "Disability 101." We'll do "Vocational Rehabilitation" next class. Honestly, sometimes I'm amazed at how many ways there are of looking at life as a woman with a disability and even more amazed by all of those folks (non-disabled, by and large) who don't see me at all—literally or figuratively—or ever look at my life and its differences.

The bottom line, in case you were wondering if substance abuse or cancer or whatever is a disability, is that as far as I'm concerned, disability is an issue of self-identification and determination. If you believe your green eyes are disabling, that's for you and only you to say. We don't exactly run an exclusive club and, believe it or not, we do not have women beating down the doors trying to sign up!

No wonder I'm feeling burned out. This stuff is *conceptually* very hard, never mind getting to the very important doing-something-about-it phase. Money and power are partly what are required, of course. And women with disabilities are significantly deficient in these areas. Except for what we manage to eke out of government. Money, I mean, not power. Never power.

I wish you were here. I love you, Meem.

Joan xoxo

December 15, 1994

Dear Meem:

So you wanted more information about what I do, not just who I do it with and why? Well, here goes. . . .

It's a bit embarrassing to have to say it but mostly I schmooze politicians and bureaucrats and acquire money for various projects which I then supervise. Imagine, me a boss! But I'm really tired of dealing with the political and bureaucratic levels of government and what that does to a person. When you start out, you first have to learn the players, then which games to play with whom, and then you make darn sure you know how to play them—well. If the government changes, then you sort of have to do a lot of it all over again. And there aren't any "how to" books on this stuff.

Burned-out doesn't quite describe what I'm trying to tell you about. Ottawa kind of palpitates with petty intrigue and people being forced into positions where they must always know who is behind their backs. It's best not to think too hard about just what kinds of decision-making and implementation take place on behalf of all Canadians by people like these. But it's sort of catchy. Actually, it'd better be, or you wouldn't do too well if you happen to be the brand new chairperson of a brand new bunch of disabled feminists who are operating autonomously from the rest of the disability community (the "don't jeopardize your funding by rocking the boat" crowd). Bone-tired, cynical, and soiled are the words that come to mind to describe how dealing with Ottawa leaves me feeling.

And that's how "they" make you feel. To be honest, though, on some weird level or another, I kind of enjoy it. Believe it or not, I am capable of being very charming and I'm good at schmoozing and manipulating people. Maybe that comes from being the baby of the family whose mother died when she was very young. I'm good at strategy, too. I think everyone who has to deal with bosses or bureaucrats (or fathers) on an unequal footing should learn how to play backgammon. It's good practice. I have found that if you treat some of this stuff as a game, it's not as scary and you can win. Sometimes. They're not expecting any skills from a woman in a wheelchair, after all. And not only that but there are some truly wonderful women who work there and who do use their meager influence to help us out.

In addition to Ottawa, the cumulative effect of years of dealing with a bunch of mostly wonderful women, all of whom have disabilities of one sort or another, is just downright exhausting. Most women with disabilities do not have highly developed organizational or political skills. Isolation and poverty explain why many women, especially those disabled from birth, have never taken part in the same kind of politicizing and socializing processes that I went through as a non-disabled, feminist leftie. The rest can be blamed on the discriminatory attitudes of our society, especially those passed on by parents, professionals, and institutions. Most women with disabilities *do* know that they're getting jerked around, but don't quite know what to do about it.

This, of course, means that I feel that the onus is on me to do it—all. So that's what I've been doing for the last ten years. And that certainly doesn't mean to say that I've been doing it all alone. If I hadn't had Shirley and a few core women on our board to share this work with, I could never have done as much for as long. There's something to be said for being pig-headed and obnoxious just like Daddy! And we've got a mostly new board (just as well—we were dropping like flies) and a wonderful new Chair. And, as I said before, some of the women in Ottawa are pretty neat and actually understand what we're doing and why. Good feminists every one, bless their hearts!

So that's why I do it. I don't think we've ever really had this conversation, have we? You moved out of the house and left town—for good. I was only sixteen then. Lots of changes. It almost feels like a silly distinction to make—the time since you've been gone. You've been there longer than here, haven't you?

I'll try to be a little more up-beat next letter.

Love you, Joan

January 1, 1995

Dear Meem:

HAPPY NEW YEAR!

The beginning of a new year and a time to pause and reflect. . . .

Sometimes it feels as though it's possible to split my life into two very separate parts: before and after wheelchair. My pre-wheelchair days were kind of busy. I seemed to have been propelled into the personal process stuff on a fairly tight timeline. I thought I fell in love with Arnie (now I'm not sure if I believe in the concept, quite frankly) and I thought at the time that we'd get old and grey together. Over the course of eight years I became irreparably disenchanted with his practice compared with his principles and moved out. I got involved with my union and learned a few things that Daddy hadn't taught me yet about politics. I was on the negotiating committee and after eighteen months of negotiations, we had a six-week strike. One of the issues was equal pay for work of equal value—a concept that remains to be well understood or won. We had eighteen people arrested on our picket line. Learned way more about the connections between bosses and media and other bosses and the police and the judiciary than a person really wants to know.

I also got involved with the far left (considerably farther left than the NDP!). Became quite promiscuous (do we ever use that word to describe men?), had a wonderful time until I realized that it was kind of boring, that I couldn't remember the name of that last guy I'd slept with, decided that I was better than that and stopped with the promiscuous. Then I just kept busy going to political meetings. Mostly.

There are some things I don't do any more in my post-wheelchair days. I no longer make jam or pickles or walk on the beach with the dogs or help fix the cars or almost anything else unless it can be done sitting down. I can still cook but I can't cut an acorn squash in half to save my soul. No leverage.

One of the significant differences in the post-wheelchair period is that my constituency has changed as well as my abilities. I may not make pickles, walk on beaches or fix cars, but I can still chair a hell of a meeting. I feel that you can't really work for your union, when you no longer work with the rest of the bargaining unit, on the job site. I find it more relevant to my life to fight for access to public parks in a wheelchair, not the oppressed working class. Now I work, MS notwith-standing, around issues concerning women with disabilities.

I seem to be at a point in my life where more clarity would be a good thing. It must be part of this feeling that a big change is coming. Writing to you always helps me think things through more clearly, dear Meem. Love, Joan

P.S. Arnie is a labour lawyer now and drives a Jaguar(!). Imagine, this is the guy who taught me how to tune dual SU carbs, to always *listen* to what your car is trying to tell you, to take them apart, and put them back together again. I think he just might still be having a hard time reconciling his practice with his principles!

March 8, 1995

Dear Meem:

HAPPY INTERNATIONAL WOMEN'S DAY!

I am theoretically a free woman now. At any rate, I no longer need to act like the Chair of DAWN Canada: DisAbled Women's Network Canada and I can actually be the Past Chair. Although that happened in November, I'm still trying to extricate myself from the job of Chair. Fortunately, my successor is a wonderful woman who lives in Vancouver so we can talk pretty much every day without worrying about long distance phone bills. It sometimes amazes me that people ever manage to get in touch with DAWN Canada since we don't have enough money for an expensive business listing in the phone book. Like I said, there's no how-to manual for this stuff so I've got to unlock the knowledge in my brain and share it with the new Chair. This is *still* amazingly hard work, especially for her. It's getting better but I'm still too busy.

So why has it taken me so long to get back to you? Let's just blame feminism, shall we? Let me explain a most fundamental connection. . . . As women, as feminists, we must take on many issues like childcare, violence, employment equity, substance misuse, health. . . . Alas, there are never enough of us to do all the work and so there's never enough time to do it all anyway. If lack of time weren't a big enough problem, lack of energy is the final arbiter for me and many other women with other kinds of disabilities. So there you go. I can't think of any solutions other than better funding for more resources and greater awareness, but I thought I'd just share that with you! (As if any mother doesn't know exactly what I'm talking about.)

You know, when I think of feminism, *my* feminism, I can't help but think of Daddy's influence on me. I know that your perception of him is far different from mine. For me, he is the source of all of my politics, maybe especially the feminism. Which doesn't mean to say of course, that you and I didn't have some strong female models in our aunts. And I had you. Who did you have? Mummy, I guess.

Ever since Mummy died, I've been a bit suspicious of my romanticized picture of her. Death is a bit hard to figure out when you're six but later, as time went by, I began to wonder. According to everybody, she was pretty much a saint—the best cook, the best hostess, the best wife, and the best mother to ever have walked the earth. It sounds as though an angry thought never crossed her mind, never mind her lips. Who was this woman, my mother? I bet she picked her nose and hollered at her kids just like everyone else now and again.

My memories must be so different from yours, you being twelve and me being six when she died. I know that Mummy dying must have had an effect on my feminism but I'm not sure exactly what. Why do I have so few memories of her? Why have I never been interested in having children? Or getting married, for that matter. It still beats me why I'm not a lesbian. I'm just not. I hear it works like that the other way around, too (!).

But then when I listen to my women friends talk about their relationships with their mothers, I don't feel so bad about not really having had one. Sometimes. And then sometimes I wonder whether she would have made me stronger or weaker, more or less confident/loving/vulnerable/compassionate. . . . Guess I'll never know, will I? I think your extra years with her made you a better person than I am, though. Something did. You are more compassionate and loving than me. But then I think I'm more confident and assertive than you and these are skills that I value in my work. I try not to be mean and horrible (I get tired and crabby easily but I can blame MS for that) but you can't afford to be warm and fuzzy when you're running an under-resourced, national, non-profit, feminist organization. Did I mention that DAWN Canada is just a tad uppity, too?

Sometimes I think I'd like to be able to cry but if I ever started, I might never stop. Don't remember crying much when I was little, either. Different reasons, I suspect. My joy quotient was pretty high when I was a kid. Now I feel that crying would get in the way of being strong and effective in my work. Ack! What a thought. Am I really saying that in order to do effective political work I can't be loving and compassionate but must be hard and sharp? I think that is what I'm saying. Good god. But now I'm not the Chair of DAWN Canada anymore, am I? More changes coming.

And then there's Daddy. His influence certainly was both positive and negative. You can't expect anything else from an eastern European patriarch, after all? But he's where I learned—by example, mostly—that there is no reason for discrimination based on gender or race or class or anything else. No one is born any better than anybody else. Period.

He also taught me about how to put in a good garden. Compost is not complicated; gardens are life; take good care of the soil. How things work, how to keep them working, and how to fix them when something screws up. How to make things, save things, re-use things. We never called it recycling back then and nor did anyone else. How you don't shit in your own nest (politically or environmentally). We've known this stuff all our lives. One of my first memories is Daddy teaching me how to plant carrot seeds—they were so little but so were my three-year old hands. He knew what he was doing.

He also taught me how to can beans and peaches and cherries and how to make jams, pickles, and crepes without a recipe. Remember, he called them "flat pancakes"? It seems that they were a staple in the Yukon if you were a single man, logging and panning for gold for a living during the Depression, and you didn't have much more than flour and water and the odd egg. Crepes, indeed. More like chapatis. (Have I ever talked to you about that generic cookbook that I'm going to write one of these times?) You mix in the flour until it coats the spoon "like this" and you cook them until they get brown "like *that*." As we both very well know, there's a right way and a wrong way to do *everything*!

I know Daddy so much better than Mummy. After all, I was thirty-three when he died. He taught me many important things but he's also the reason I learned about just how much male bullshit I was willing to put up with as the chief cook and bottle washer to our dad and brother. While I was learning that women are just as smart as men, I couldn't help noticing that men have all the power. (How *did* they get all the power?) Daddy and Jimmy both assumed that my labour was so much less valuable than theirs that they never bothered to say thank you or provide any kind of positive feedback whatsoever. There's nothing like bad experiences to shape what kind of expectations to have and standards to set! I guess that's why I'm happily living alone (with Sherman, your canine nephew). I have unrealistic expectations and *very* high standards!

And you meet all of them! I love you, Meem.

Joan xoxo

P.S. I made some of that yummy black bean soup I was telling you about. I'll try and write it down for you and send it soon.

July 14, 1995

Dear Meem:

WARNING: I'm feeling sorry for myself so you may not want to read this if you're having a bad day!

The reason I sometimes feel like whining and sniveling is that working on the issues of women with disabilities is harder than any other political work I've ever done. Back in '85, or even earlier for some, it was clear that we needed a feminist, autonomous, pro-choice national organization for Canadian women with disabilities: the women's movement was somewhat receptive to our issues but not accessible; the disability community was accessible but male-dominated and not receptive to our ideas. Both groups have gotten much better but there's such a long way to go.

Even though disability is no longer the federal funding flavour of the month we are still making bits of progress. DAWN Canada and the National Action Committee on the Status of Women did put on a wonderful conference on New Reproductive and Genetic Technologies (NRGTs). It was very much a good mingling of feminist minds, both disabled and non-disabled, on these very complicated issues.

I think that the main outcome of the conference was that about seventy feminists who have a specific interest in the whole area of new reproductive and genetic technologies realized that it is primarily a human (women's) rights issue. These women represented many areas of expertise: lawyers, homemakers, geneticists, researchers, bureaucrats and filmmakers, to name just a few. We came from every area of this country, Québec, Germany, and the States. We were women with disabilities, women of colour, older and younger women, lesbians and straight women, aboriginal women, and mothers. The proceedings from the conference will be translated into French and will be distributed internationally as far as we can afford it.

We put this conference together to acknowledge the need to look at these technologies from both a disability rights and a feminist perspective. NRGTs are being sold as providing women with more choices. Some choice. The purveyors of NRGTs can limit a woman's right to have a child with a disability by presenting disability as "bad" and something to be avoided. Prenatal technologies, developed to detect (and eliminate) disabled fetuses, can also be used to eliminate female fetuses. In China, large billboards encourage parents to "Have fewer, better babies" and their eugenic laws require couples to test for hereditary mental illness before marrying. This is scary stuff. And I worked too hard on the logistics of the conference and got very bagged out.

Have I told you lately that I hate having MS? Stupid, arbitrary, fucking "progressive", incurable neurological disease. They don't know anything about it: where it comes from, how to fix it or even how to treat it very effectively. *Men have walked on the moon*, for heaven's sake! Where are the priorities? It is certainly better for the big pharmaceuticals to keep us gobbling their high-priced and often addictive pills and use their research and development money to create more drugs or more markets for them than it is to fund projects that might actually fix some of our health concerns for once and for all. There's a reason why I call myself a socialist and a feminist. The two concepts are inseparable in my mind. Did I ever tell you that one of my secret desires is that DAWN Canada will not *need* to exist?

I also hate dealing with the people who really just want to use you for statistical purposes or as a guinea pig for some new, experimental drug or another. And those ever-so-earnest, fluffy, young occupational therapists who've just graduated from school and know exactly how to make my life better. Sure they do. And having to take a nap every day and all of those people who say, "I'd *love* to be able take a nap every afternoon." It's obligatory for me and takes out about three hours of my functional time in the world *every day* and I don't have a choice. It's either nap now or pay for days. I always end up missing the closing plenaries at conferences, too. And those irritating forms that must be filled out to prove that I'm not pretending to have MS and use a wheelchair *just* to get all of that free money. And don't get me started about "snow tire/chains/spike" jokes when it occasionally does snow here.

Did you know that this month is the beginning of my fourteenth year sitting down? Good god. Who would have thought? No wonder I feel like whining and sniveling sometimes.

But then sometimes I also feel as though I've been preparing my whole life to do exactly what I'm doing now. The parallels feel a bit creepy. Living with Daddy and Jimmy as chief cook and bottle washer (just who is worth what around here, anyway?). Getting involved with the labour movement (motions to table don't need to be seconded and aren't debatable, eh?). Joining the far left (didn't we agree that there could be no socialist revolution without women's liberation and no women's liberation without the socialist revolution, comrades?). Getting more active in the women's movement (when I did *what* it made you feel *how*? and those endless "basis-of-unity" versus "action now" discussions). Now, finally and joining the circle in a way, the disability community (just who is worth what around here anyway?) and disabled women's issues. And I must say that the thought has occurred to me that maybe since I didn't get that maternal kind of care early on, I need to get the kind of care that MS demands now. What do you think about that? I think that's pretty creepy, too!

Thanks for listening to all this shit.

Joan xoxo

P.S. Sherman wanted me to thank you for his birthday card. He always feels like such a special dog when he gets mail! Imagine me thinking that a wheelchair and a puppy wouldn't work. It's been working for eight years now and so far, so good.

October 21, 1995

Dear Meem:

What do you mean, the leukemia has come back? I thought that the bone marrow transplant was supposed to be a cure. I guess Jimmy will just have to go and be a donor again. With any luck, this one will be as easy as that first one five years ago. Are you sure you don't want to try my bone marrow this time? I guess it's the same possible problem since they still don't know where MS comes from: "Well, we have good news and bad news. Your leukemia is gone but you seem to have acquired this neurological disease. . . ." Let me know if they change their minds.

Thanks very much for the gorgeous blue vase that you gave me for my birthday. At certain times, in the late afternoon, it seems to gather light into itself and it glows with an interior and powerful radiance.

Forty-five sounds worse than it feels. I quite like having the comfort with myself and the confidence in my beliefs and experience that age brings. It doesn't get any easier or less complicated. We just acquire more skills as we go. (That's my story and I'm sticking to it!) But we're going to need all the skills we can muster. Right now, right here in Lotusland, there *are* women who wear swastikas on purpose and beat up on other women. I know some women who are planning a women-only event (accessible) who have declared a dress code as the only way they can think of to try to keep the Fascist Ladies Auxiliary away. Now there's a sobering thought. And the media very occasionally tells us that the skinheads have been beating up on people with disabilities in Germany for quite a while now. This was confirmed by the speaker from Germany at the NRGT conference.

I get particularly depressed when I see the young ones repeating the same mistakes, perpetrating the bullshit. Doing it to each other and to us. Turf wars. Reinventing the wheel. Coming late to the concept that we, as women, are in this together and that very few other women are the enemy. Why do I get this feeling that older women have been saying that to and about younger women since the beginning of time? Sometimes I guess I do feel quite old.

But the young women give me hope, too. I was on my way to the Indy 500, being pushed by a friend's eighteen-year-old daughter who is a magnificent young woman. (Tall, strong, confident, athletic, going to be a medical researcher.) She said to me that she has probably never intentionally dressed in a particular way for any man. I thought to myself how I hadn't figured that one out for about another ten years! Imagine the possibilities! If good young women start figuring all of it out really early there's just no telling what might happen. (But then I used to think that the socialist revolution was going to happen in my lifetime, too. Silly me.)

I just got a call last night from her dad and he said that she's been the victim of acquaintance assault. Post-feminism, indeed. Like we still don't have a lot of work to do? I heard on the radio that women make fifty-four cents to the male dollar—and we don't need employment equity legislation or something? Did you know, by the way, that thirty-five percent of women with disabilities live on less than $5,000 per year? Our unemployment rate is seventy-four percent and climbing. Meanwhile, women and children with disabilities are at least twice as likely to be victims of violence as non-disabled women. And so it goes—on and on and on. . . . Like I said, post-feminism, indeed!

Sons like yours (Lucas and Simon, my nephews!) and a few male contemporaries make all the work seem worthwhile and give me hope and stamina, too. It *is* getting better. And, of course, it's because they have been raised by wonderful women like you and many of my other friends. Have I ever thanked you for doing all that hard work? Thanks.

It's almost enough to make me regret not ever wanting to have kids. Almost. I'd still rather have puppies. Whenever I think about how hard I find things, I think about how hard it would be to be a good mother. Imagine being a good mother with a disability! Think about not being able to see or hear the little rascals. There are ways of accommodating all of the needs of disabled mums but *that* certainly isn't where the research dollars are going. According to DAWN Canada research, in the eyes of the powers that be (mostly old, male judges), a drunken and/or abusive father is often considered to be a better parent than a mother with a disability.

I'll stop. I'm afraid I don't have any cheery news for you right now. Let me know if you'd rather I stopped writing! I went to see my psychic. She said that she checked all of her available sources (?) and that you were going to be fine. Not sure what "fine" means but it sounds good!

I love you and am rooting for you always. There is a national network of rainbows being sent your way to help fight the bad cells.
Joan xoxoxoxo

P.S. Are you sure all of this kidney/liver/ear/lung stuff is what is supposed to be happening?

P.P.S. Didn't I ever tell you that I was taking care of the "Major Disease" item on the family agenda? What's the big idea doing leukemia *twice*?

January 2, 1996

Dear Meem:

Thank goodness the hohoho is over again.

You might be interested to know that I've been entertaining the notion of getting a life lately. Don't even know if I'd recognize it if I rolled over it with my wheelchair but figure it feels like time to check it out. Get a hobby. Join a choir. Take another silver jewelry-making course.

My psychic said I should get back in touch with the earth. Do you realize that I've not been out of a city for fourteen years! Lots of cities—Toronto, Ottawa, Sydney, Washington, San Francisco, Ottawa, Aukland, Nassau, Toronto, St. John's, Ottawa, Toronto . . . but only cities. After a while every newish, built-to-code (accessible, more-or-less), expensive hotel looks and feels exactly like the other except some have windows that open.

Remember when we were in the Hilton in Sydney? (That trip to Australia was just before you got diagnosed the first time, wasn't it?) The manager probably still has nightmares. Well if there's no cut-out under the sink, I'd have to brush my teeth sideways and then I tend to drip toothpaste down my front. After flying for twenty-two hours, I was practically hysterical. *Of course* I had to get him to get a maintenance guy to fix it *immediately*! After all of these years I am still amazed at how rarely "accessible" translates into a practical, common sense interpretation of the concept. Partially accessible is sort of like partially pregnant, I figure.

I mean, it's nice to have been compelled to stay in good hotels since I've been doing all of this government-sponsored, disability-related (and unpaid—do you know how much they pay their other "experts"?) travel, but I've always kind of liked tents. I just wish that Motel Six (and every bathroom in the world, actually) had grab bars by the toilets since I certainly can't afford to pay to stay in Hiltons and Westins. But a person's got to pee.

Actually, I wish that I could still just throw the dogs and the sleeping bag in the back of the car like I used to and *go*. It's definitely time for me to get out of the city. You'd think I'd be a little better at pacing myself what with MS and fatigue and knowing that we're in this for the long haul. There's just so very much to do.

I've been talking with a friend about the idea of getting some recreational property where he can go fishing and I can just hang out on the porch that goes around four sides of the house and looks out over the water on one side and into the forest on the other side. He happens to be a carpenter and can do/build/fix anything.

I think I'm going to go to bed. (Can you call sleeping a hobby?) And you get well.

I love you, Meem.

Joan xoxo

March 10, 1996

Dear Meem:

I never did send you that black bean soup recipe and now I can't. You died. I guess this is going to be my last letter to you, too. There are some things that I seem to have to write down.

It wasn't supposed to happen this way, you know. You were supposed to get better just like last time and then come out here. We would have dyed your short new hair (and the white tip of Sherman's tail) fuchsia again and you would have stayed in my brand new spare bedroom downstairs. Everything happened far too quickly. I'm awfully glad that Jimmy and I were able to come to Toronto and say goodbye.

You were very brave. I'm beginning to understand how Mummy achieved sainthood. You have, too. I guess what the psychic must have meant by "fine" was how calm and peaceful and brave and ready you were.

I took "fine" to mean that you'd get over this transplant, too. I was pretty alarmed when your kidneys got attacked by the Graft Versus Host disease and you decided that you didn't want a new one. All of a sudden the whole idea of self-determined death (yours) got up close and personal and in-my-face. But then they rallied and the GVH moved on to your liver. And then your ear and then your lungs. And you kept sort of getting a bit better, I thought.

But you didn't let me know how bad it was when I called every morning, did you? I had the impression that everything that was happening was sort of part of the leukemia package deal and that it, too, would pass. I bet what you were really doing was keeping me from getting distracted from all of that frantic work that I was doing to pull off those three national DAWN events in January, weren't you? We are such pragmatists, you and I. For what it's worth, Meem, I and many disabled women in Canada thank you for the extra space that you made for me and my work.

You see, as far as I'm concerned, I was supposed to die first. I'm anticipating not having enough fun in the fairly near future. And that would be my cue to take a powder. I wish we'd had time to talk about dying. What with all of the current media about euthanasia and assisted suicide, the whole question of dying is political *and* personal. And there just aren't too many people who can speak about this one dispassionately but from a first-hand point of view.

I have some ideas which are based on theory, but eventually I really do figure that if I'm not having any fun any more, then I'll stop. I know that sounds a bit simplistic but I don't think it needs to be much more complicated than that. I don't think that you were having much fun for the last while when your lungs were making that dreadful gurgling noise. How could I have been so unaware? Lucas told me on the phone after your memorial service that you pretty much all knew when you went in to the hospital back in December that you weren't likely to come out. It was a conspiracy. You asked for "no heroic measures" and that was your choice to make. So they left you on fluid IV with no medication, just morphine. And then you died.

Was that a kind of suicide? I guess not really, but then no one can gauge these things very clearly from outside. For me, suicide is another case of self-determination and choice. Just like personal safety, work, education, abortion, or so many other areas of a woman's life over which she cannot exercise *her* informed decision-making abilities because of poverty, isolation, lack of education, decent housing, even nutrition or any one of a number of other reasons. I demand choice and I'm going to arrange to have it. Period. But it sure would have been nice to talk to you about this stuff.

I miss you so much and I have a feeling that it's not going to get any better. And I've started crying lately. It seems to happen mostly during my afternoon nap. And sometimes I wake up crying in the morning. I do seem to be able to stop and it seems to be getting less frequent. Now I'm not saying that I'm going to take it up as a hobby or anything but at least I know now that I can stop. Maybe it's like most other things, you get better at it as you go. Sometimes I'd just like to stop learning stuff for a while. It's exhausting.

I will always love you more than I can say, Meem.

Joan xoxo

P.S. Here's a thought: "The wish to leave life is profoundly different from the wish to destroy it" (Jo Roman, *Exit House: Choosing Suicide as an Alternative*)

Just thinking about the possibility of controlling my own death makes me feel as though I still have a say over this anarchic body of mine. And that's good enough for now.

Other Than Mother

Cynthia Minden

When we were teenagers, we said we would never become mothers. It seemed like an easy choice then, when we were enchanted by all of the other possibilities in life. We were going to play in a symphony, travel, save the world, write stories about elephants—where did motherhood fit into that grand scheme? It was easy then to push the motherhood topic aside until later. Well, here it is, later. Some of us are struggling with the dilemma, no longer able to postpone the decision to be mother or not. It isn't a black and white choice, either, not easy to balance the pros and cons.

For me the motherhood issue has been a road easily travelled. My early fantasies never really changed and the idea of children never took root. I can't recall any major factors that might have influenced my choice to remain childfree—no great story that points to this as an inevitable decision. One tends to look for negative influences—some extraordinary dysfunction in the family, such as an abusive parent or a terrible disease. You might not dare to have children in case those traits were genetic. Few people assume that the choice to be childfree springs from a healthy, creative person. Isn't it the loveless, selfish, or overly ambitious who would choose other than mother?

To be childfree today, although not as uncommon as it once was, is still to be nonconformist, even though the climate of feminism in North America has broken many social taboos. My mother, for instance, didn't feel she had the same choices as I did. For her to have chosen childlessness would have been inconceivable. Marriage and family were ideas that she, along with all of her family and friends, took for granted. She was a popular and attractive young woman. At age twenty-four, when she and my father decided to marry, she told him that she would never have an "only" child, that two children were not enough, but three was the right number. After three children, though, she worried about a· "middle-child complex" and they decided to have another—me. With two sons and a daughter already, she really wanted her fourth child to be another girl, so she hung calendars with pictures of little baby girls all around the house and she prayed.

When I talk with my mother about not wanting children of my own, she reminds me that if *she* had felt that way, *I* wouldn't have been born. And when you consider the wonderful person that I am, who knows how positively wonderful my child might be. I always chuckle at this attempted conspiracy, but it's the only prodding my mother has done around the subject. She remembers me at nine years old swearing that I'd never marry or have children, both promises I have kept.

My mother tells me now she wishes that the choice to not have children had been a genuine option, that she feels women of her generation were "kind of dumb" to have never considered a meaningful life without children. How many other women would have appreciated having that choice? How many women feel disappointed today by the paths their lives have taken? I imagine there are many, for I believe that motherhood is not, *should not* be an automatic response to being a woman. Children are not the issue, but the presumptuous mapping out of women's lives; the lack of agency inherent in the housewife trap.

For a mother to admit to her child that she might have opted for childlessness is a bold statement. I didn't take this confession personally, for I know that my mother is glad she has her four children, and I feel proud that she has the openness to admit her ambivalence. She could not have said this had it not been for the mood of candour that has developed during the past three decades. Maybe I glimpsed this covert inclination of my mother's, since from childhood on, I never assumed that I would become a wife and a mother. My parents were both in their early forties when I was born. I always felt loved and wanted, but by then, I imagine that the mother role had become rather tedious. At forty-three, I am just a year older than my mother was when she had me and, in a way this appalls me. The very idea of starting *now* with diapers and feedings and crying is enough to send shivers down my spine.

Born in 1953 into a traditional family, I was subject to all of the typical social influences prevalent in Canada at that time. Girls were supposed to be nice, get good grades at school, maybe work as a secretary or a cashier or something that would assist the boss, who was male, or the business owner who was, of course, male. Then we would get married, start our families, and support our husbands in their careers until death would us part, probably the hubby first. After that, well, maybe some volunteer work in the gift shop at the hospital and if we were really lucky a semi-private room in the Home For the Aged. Our children would visit us and make small talk. Bleak or what?

By a bizarre twist of fate, my earliest feminist values were given to me by my father who, ironically, was a true patriarch. My father was born in Russia in 1910 and maintained a strong family identity. He revered the role of motherhood, speaking about his own mother with adoration and impressing upon me a rule that children are *never* to utter a bad word, or even think a bad thought against their mothers. So it's odd that I can trace my feminist roots back to him. He was, however, a complex and emotional man, and he instilled in me a sense of self-worth at an early age.

When I was eleven, I arrived home from school one day and stood before my father in the living room. He was shaking his head, a look of incredulity on his face. "You want to learn what?" he asked again. "Typing," I said too loudly, impatient with his questioning. Finally, he looked as though my message had sunk in and he sighed impatiently and began to shuffle away. As he reached the doorway, he half-turned, pointed at me and said, "You, you have brains, do something creative with them." I was furious at my father for being stubborn. What was the big deal about typing, anyway? All of my friends were taking the after-school class.

Over thirty years later, my father's words still echo, only now his meaning is clear. He was offering me the opportunity to be an ambassador, while I had assumed the role of the ambassador's secretary. Although his belief in me and my potential to be whomever I chose gave me confidence, sadly, I didn't recognize this while he was alive. My father died soon after my thirteenth birthday, an event that changed my life in a strangely complicated way. Had he lived, we would have locked horns during my teens, as I didn't understand the magnitude of his vision for me. And with the second rise of feminism in the 1960s, which kindled my rebellious fires, my father's patriarchal attitudes would have set me in a fighting stance. I needed to find things out my own way, to explore my options, maybe *not* go to university straight from high school, maybe even learn to *type*. He would not easily have accepted my teenage rejection of his authority and dominance.

His early death was a huge blow to my family, as he was both our sail and our anchor. My family's connection to the arts, to philanthropy, to *big* ideas, dreams—those were seeds that he planted in us all. He was a spirited man, whose fondness for music filled our home with such a variety of sounds, like swooning opera arias, crashing symphonies, and crooning songsters. At three or four years old, with the music booming, I would stand on a little stool beside him, frenetically waving my arms about, as he would direct his conductor's baton toward a pretend orchestra in our den.

His love of painting filled the walls with canvasses that he would pluck from the back alley studios of painters whose careers he tried to foster. My father dabbled in painting himself, though he never took it seriously and didn't approve of the arts as a career choice for his four children, at least not for his sons. For me, though, he invented a game to teach me about the grand old master painters. He collected slides of the paintings that he loved. I would perch breathlessly upon a chair and try to guess the name of the person who had painted the glowing image that was projected on the big screen in front of me. Ballet dancers were always by Degas; people with long, angular faces were usually painted by Modigliani (whose name I loved to pronounce); and those voluptuous dreamy nude women were probably by Renoir.

My father's passionate nature was also reflected by his strict authority and dominant role as head of our family. He honoured debate but didn't particularly welcome challenge. After he died, it took me many years to understand my relationship with him and his affect on me. Though I felt pinned under his authority when I was approaching adolescence, I feel enormously sad that I never knew my father during my adult years.

When my father died, my struggle became directed solely towards my mother, who offered me then a role model that I was to profoundly reject. She had married a man with ambition and drive and his interests became hers. Running a household was her full-time occupation, but there's a haziness in my recollections, as I can't picture her engaged in the motherly tasks that were depicted by the popular TV sitcoms of the day. What is memorable is that I was a lonely child as my three siblings were quite a bit older and involved in their own activities. With my mother's attention directed toward the needs of her husband, both in health and then during his illness, I was looked after by kindly house-keepers who taught me how to crochet and took me skating. I loved each one of them before their lives took them elsewhere.

My mother is typical of the women of her generation and class. They were not expected to choose other than mother and most of them didn't, fulfilling their duties as wives and mothers ahead of ambitions or careers. But I could see that times had changed and my mother's story was not one that I was anxious to repeat. My father had left me with a nugget of self-confidence and the ambition to explore my potential. That was gold.

The year was 1966. I took my father's teachings and fled from the singular role model of the women in my family. By the age of thirteen, I had been indoctrinated with a sense of possibility and curiosity, a desire for independence and a rebellious spirit. Of course, I didn't realize all that at the time. My teenage years were spent hanging out with friends, wearing blue eyeshadow and trying to be popular; "struggling to achieve mediocrity," as my brother has teased. I also played the guitar badly and wrote mournful songs about make-believe lovers going off to fight in the Vietnam War, neither of which I knew much about.

My brother (the middle child that I came to relieve) has been my dearest and closest friend. From the day I was born, he took a keen interest in me. Sharing my father's passionate and challenging nature, but not his strict views, my brother has always had feminist values, envisioning life's possibilities in a new and creative way, and differently from mainstream recipes. As a young teenager and reeling from the death of my father, I was vulnerable and confused. My brother was then living in Berkeley. His friendship and an open invitation to visit him kept me sane and eventually helped to steer me back onto a productive path.

In the 1960s and '70s, when I was in high school and college, it was practically unthinkable for my friends to consider marriage or babies. We were all going to be somebody and we weren't going to let motherhood change our plans. The birth control pill was now easily available; with a youthful sense of hopefulness and possibility we were going to *decide* our futures. I went to college in Santa Cruz, California, then went on to study music in Toronto, practicing the flute, attending classes at the Conservatory and receiving a diploma in the obscure domain of Renaissance counterpoint. All the while, I was developing skills and economic independence, a sense of myself and my own possibilities. It was a time of questioning old values for us young adults. I wasn't particularly informed about feminism as an ideology, but it was in the air and I was breathing. I read poetry, books about Martin Luther King and the Black Panthers. (The old classics had always made me yawn, with their boring depiction of women.)

Motherhood was the last thing on my mind even though I had loving relationships with male friends. A rift had formed in what was once a given; that *womanhood* is synonymous with *maternalism*. To come of age with that gem of an idea was extraordinary. With this in mind, we set out to educate ourselves, to become skilled, to become professionals. I played flute in a chamber ensemble called Trio Con Brio. We performed at numerous receptions, openings, and weddings. Because I was always the one writing the promotional material and contracts, I started an arts administration company and, for ten years, booked entertainment for social and corporate functions, wrote promotional material, and did some artist management. Later, I co-founded an arts centre in Toronto that offered workshops, studios, gallery and performance space. The concept that we simply didn't *have* to be mothers gave me the gift of possibility.

Then, one by one, many of my friends chose motherhood after all, perhaps not until they had reached their late thirites, but bit by bit the tide turned from a rejection of the motherhood stereotype to an embrace of nurturance. Motherhood enters the picture again as a natural way for a woman to seek ultimate fulfillment. But I don't believe that—call me a conscientious objector. I *did* feel rather left out, though, when suddenly most of my friends were discussing home-births and breast-feeding and I didn't then have many other-than-mother friends. But I didn't feel motivated to have a child and haven't yet looked back with regret.

As a child, I never played with bake sets or little prams, never played at being a little mother. My favourite doll was a decrepit Raggedy Anne, who was my friend, not my baby. I told her all my secrets and that I wanted to be a fire chief, a singer, or a writer. However, when I was about thirty-six, I went through a brief period when I did feel little pangs of baby-longing; my eyes would fill with tears when I saw an adorable baby in the supermarket. This was bizarre, as I had never before wanted children and I don't believe that *all* women feel a biological urge to be mother. My partner of seven years was very open to the possibility of having a child together. The baby-longing lasted only a short time and now seems like a strange little tsunami on an otherwise calm sea.

But I became curious about those maternal sensations—whose voice is this: mine, society's, mother nature's? It's impossible to separate biology, socialisation, and acculturation, as we are not simply creatures of instinct. Wanting to examine these ideas, I looked for reading material. Walking into bookstores gave me my first clue. Have you ever noticed that there are *walls* of books on parenting, representing every possible variable? Books on how to deal with children with a multitude of characteristics, from eating disorders to mischief—gifted children, dyslexic children, hyper children, runaway children. Books about pre-natal care and post-natal care, birthing, feeding, exercising, thumb-sucking, and choosing schools. How to be a lesbian parent, a straight parent, a green parent, not a blue parent. Just try to find a book on choosing *not* to parent. You might have to look under "aberrant behaviour" in the psychology section.

Finally, after several computer checks under the word "childlessness," I was able to order three books from the regional library. The initial reading I did opened my eyes to the enormity of the topic. Voluntary childlessness is not simply a lifestyle choice after all. It needs to be regarded in a larger context—gender roles and expectations, religious and cultural values, reproductive motivation and options—a multitude of social factors. I recognised the need to look at childlessness within a socio-political framework that encompasses a larger arena than just my own life. The feminism that I had taken for granted now offered me a backdrop against which I could examine myself.

Women's reproductive choices continue to be hotly debated, as North America suffers attacks on abortion clinics and their doctors, as well as antagonistic dogma from both pro-lifers and pro-choicers. The tangled maze of new reproductive technologies throws fuel into an already raging fire. Funding pours into fertility clinics, while money for birth control research is comparatively negligible. I shudder every time I read about the mean-spirited attacks on abortion clinics. The media is full of such stories. What if I were to need an abortion? I picture myself threading my way through a jeering, snarling mob as I enter a clinic and I send another donation to the Canadian Abortion Rights Action League. It feels imperative to protect our option to terminate a pregnancy, if need be.

Each month we are reminded of our potential as child-bearers. While writing this piece, I suspected that I might be pregnant. There was an agonizing two weeks during which I thought that perhaps my choosing to write about voluntary childlessness had conspired to present me with the ultimate irony. Although I have always been comfortable about my decision to not have kids, I'm sensitive to the dilemmas attached to this choice. It's impossible to sail through your fertile years without at least a tiny pondering, a momentary musing about "what if." Societal messages are so pervasive that we seldom recognize the subtle ways in which we have been influenced and directed. When I turn on the TV, I'm often faced with babies whizzing along in Goodyear tires, selling insurance, or advertising breakfast cereal. These images reinforce the stereotype of what you and I are supposed to aspire to be. We are supposed to project the images of family and children into our visions for ourselves, so that when we imagine our lives unfolding, we automatically picture the Norman Rockwell version. The depictions of family life rarely vary and eventually even a single career woman like TV's Murphy Brown succumbs to the "inevitable." *Father Knows Best*, the ultimate in patriarchal synopsis, is everywhere.

There are prevailing attitudes among and about childfree people. Some childfree women feel the need to apologise for their choice with exclamations of, "I really do *like* kids," and, "I guess I'm just selfish." Some say that they are learning how to "parent" themselves or that they are "parenting the planet" as though accepting that a woman *must* parent. This apologist attitude must be purged if we have any hope of maintaining a cohesive feminist ideology and not dividing into camps of maternalism versus feminism.

Other people need to compare my childfree existence with other facts about my life in order to understand my decision. For example, I don't have children because I travel a lot, or have a career, or have cats or ducks or plants. It is thought that a childfree woman must compensate, must mother in other ways—care for animals, nurture the sick or elderly, work at a daycare.

I moved to the west coast in 1987 after untangling myself from arts administration and big city life. Now, living on one of the Gulf Islands, I feel like I've always been an "island person"—the rural community life really suits me. I've been weaving baskets for the past nine years and these have grown into fiber art sculptures that continually lead me in new directions. Recently I attended a pre-election "all-candidates" meeting. Each of the six hopefuls, introduced themselves by saying how many children they had—I'm a mother of three, a father of five, and so on. During the meeting, they spoke about their sense of responsibility and concern about education, health care, and environmental issues in terms of their role as parents. The reasons they care about these things, they insinuate, are *because* they have children. The appalling implication was that if you don't have children, you wouldn't be concerned with the future. I looked around the room and spotted many childfree women, all activists in the community. We have the time to do considerable community work while our friends who are mothers are doing other meaningful work raising the next generation.

Seen in this larger perspective, childfree women offset a growing global population. Does *everyone* really need to bring a child onto an already crowded planet? In P.D. James' novel *The Children of Men*, she describes a frightening world in which no child has been born during the past twenty-five years. The despair and sense of purposelessness that people felt was overwhelming; I realized then that perhaps my choice to remain childfree can only be made as a counterweight to the fact that so many other people do not make the same choice. My feminist values enable me to support voluntary childlessness as a positive, healthy choice. Thanks to the feminist struggle, some of us do have options, but dilemmas remain. If feminism gives us choices then we should all have these choices and all choices must be embraced. We must peel away the layers of cultural assumptions and expectations and attend to the bare bones of this pivotal issue.

And what about growing old, being a childless old woman? I've heard this often; "She'll regret it when she's older." I *am* apprehensive about the possibility of being the last survivor in my immediate family, the last limb on that branch of the tree. It really scares me; a deep loneliness wells up whenever I think about it. But I know that the present is fragile and the future unpredictable, and so it feels important to stay vigilant and creative and to invent a new way of growing older, with or without children. The reality of many families, the tight knots that harden around those relationships, rarely equals the cozy myth that we will all adore each other's company. Many a romanticized daydream about having children has turned into a nuclear family nightmare in reality. Our extended families must include friends, both young and old. I picture us replacing nursing homes with little cabins, surrounded by huge shared gardens, chicken coops and goat barns, and communal buildings with work rooms and fireplaces and care-givers living nearby.

It is discouraging that feminism has not yet invented a terminology for women without children. This lack helps to ensure that we continue to be marginalized in society.

Supporters of family values still think of us as barren, selfish old maids and pity us as unfulfilled women. These are disappointing and archaic attitudes. Feminism has been criticized for *not* challenging the "normalcy" and "universality" of motherhood. While this may be so, and an area which feminism needs to re-examine and critique, it is also evident that childfree women are no longer invisible. As more of us choose to be childfree, we will inevitably shift the focus.

Feminism manifests itself in many outward ways: tributaries flow into my work, my family and home life, my community involvement, my politics. But it is personal politics first of all: a cognisant emotional commitment to female equality, agency, and economic independence. My decision not to be a mother is one of the ways that I rope my feminist ideology into real choice, thanks to the openness, the questioning and the challenging times in which I grew up. Bolstered by the stimulation of those times, my decision not to be a mother feels right for me and acceptable.

I used to presume that since I have never wanted to be a mother, the issue of mothering doesn't concern me and is nothing I needed to think about. But when I began to think about myself as a childfree woman and a feminist, I realized that the idea of mothering is primary to the experience of all women, because whatever our choices, we make them with reference to given cultural expectations and assumptions. To be intentionally childfree is to defy the culture in which I was raised. I challenge the decree to "go forth and multiply." It is a contradiction to all of the programming, influences and expectations of my culture.

My former administrative work now translates into the winter performance series that I co-ordinate in the community hall and the several activist groups that I belong to. Studio work is my cornerstone, with opportunities for gallery shows now and then. I struggle to find time to pursue all my interests and I lead a full life with my partner Graham, our animals and an ever-expanding garden. If there are empty spaces yet to be filled, they will be filled with creative and personal challenges and not with our children.

I am a daughter, begat from generations of daughters. The youngest of my siblings, I have tied a knot in the family fiber. I am the golden goose with no egg.

Another Way to Live My Faith

Denise Nadeau

I am unravelling brightly coloured skeins of weaving cotton with Carmen, a Guatemalan refugee who, with her three young children, is staying with Maria in this two-bedroom apartment. We are working quietly so Maria can be interviewed for radio by my companera. Maria Suarez is with FIRE (Feminist International Radio Endeavour), an international feminist short-wave radio program based in Costa Rica. Originally from Puerto Rico, she worked in El Salvador and Nicaragua during the eighties as a popular educator. Her work with FIRE has made her focus more international; she is now involved in the international campaign for women's human rights. We are visiting her today in the suburb of San Pedro outside San Jose to find out more about how Latin American women's movements are linking with those in Asia, Africa, Europe, and North America.

My head is buzzing with an exchange I have just had with Maria. She was telling us about the 1994 UN Conference on Population and Development in Cairo, which she attended as a feminist journalist for FIRE. She told us about how the Vatican and OPUS DEI were at Cairo as part of their strategy to infiltrate the UN conferences and undermine the feminist agenda. (Translated as "The Work of God," OPUS DEI is a conservative elitist secular institute operating in eighty countries. Its members include about 75,000 middle-class professionals and about 1,300 priests. It relegates women to second-class status and sees itself as the defender of the true Church.) As she demonstrated more than a passing knowledge of Catholic Church politics I questioned her further. She admitted she was an ex-nun and her theological training had stood her in good stead at Cairo: when *the women's caucus was asked to pick someone to debate an American bishop with an anti-reproductive rights position she had volunteered.*

I said that I too was theologically trained, but that as a feminist I had disassociated myself with the Catholic Church, especially as it had grown increasingly right-wing in the past few years. In the women's movement in Canada I was a "closeted" Christian. She told me that she too had faced this dilemma but that religion is playing such a powerful role in international politics and in women's lives that we ignore it at our peril. Looking me in the eye she challenged me: "It is really important that voices like ours are heard; that women know there is another way to live their faith and that the homogeneity imposed by the Vatican and fundamentalist Christianity is false and a lie. There are alternatives."

For me feminism has been about a gradual process of accepting and claiming who I am. Maria's words were an invitation to move to another level of integration, another dimension of this process. Perhaps it was time for me to speak out of all the parts of my identity—I could claim my position on the margins of the Church as the basis for speaking out as a Christian.

For several years I have had trouble reconciling my multiple identities. I have been active in the women's movement since the early 1970s, yet this has not been the only sphere of my political and social activity. I have also worked for the past twenty years as a popular educator (a method of non-formal education with roots in Latin America, used with and by people, usually marginalized or excluded from decision-making, to organize to improve the conditions of their lives). This work is with women, community groups, ecumenical church groups, and labour; much of it has centred around work, free trade, and the economy, and this has situated me within the circles of coalition politics. I am also part of a network of radical Christians. As well I am a lesbian, a subterranean identity I carry in all the above but which also makes me part of another circle of friends and sub-cultures.

For many years I felt I hid parts of myself. In most of my political circles I hid my middle-class background. In feminist circles I was comfortable as a lesbian but downplayed my Christian identity, partly to respect the multi-faith and interracial nature of women's movements, and partly because I didn't want to be associated with Christian triumphalism or fundamentalism. In labour circles I could sometimes speak as a Christian and a feminist but my lesbian identity took a back seat. In

Christian circles those who knew I was a lesbian politely ignored it. And in lesbian circles—especially when I was dancing in a crowded women's club in a big city—I would just laugh to myself, wondering if the young woman dancing beside me with the nose ring and leather pants had as many invisible identities as I had and knowing this was the one place it didn't matter; we could just be lesbians here.

In any coming out—a bringing forward of one's truth—there is risk and danger as well as possibilities for more life and greater integrity. For me, those changes in awareness, and every step forward into greater wholeness, have meant shedding some safety and security that had made it easier for me to pass in the world of normalcy and respectability. This process has also involved me recognizing the extent of my privilege as a white middle-class woman and coming to terms with it. Much of my feminist education has occurred in those moments where I saw a clear choice of action or where something happened that caused me to shift how I saw myself, the world and feminism. These moments have usually been simultaneously personal, spiritual, and political. All were moments that, once a decision was made, meant there was no turning back.

I sit half-way down the hall stairs, trying hard to hear my parents' conversation in the living room. The day before I had been interviewed by the Montréal Star's *social reporter as one of the debutantes who had just come out at Le Bal des Petits Souliers. She asked me why I had chosen to take part. My heart froze. While it was true that I had chosen the only French "bal" over the English balls, I had little say in the matter. I hated the entire experience, feeling both awkward and embarrassed with the upper-class formalities, uncomfortable in my long stiff white ballgown, and, worst of all, invisible as who I really was in the elaborate pretension of being presented into Montréal high society.*

"My mother made me do it," I replied in a tense voice. Once I hung up, I knew I was in deep trouble. My mother would see this as a public shaming, a blot on our family. Yet I had finally claimed and named a piece of myself that was really me.

Today as I think of the independence of some young women in Canada, it's hard to believe that at the age of seventeen I felt I had no options. But it never occurred to me to rebel against the rigid expectations of my family and social class. I had a strict Catholic upbringing and, as a child and adolescent, little exposure to any world beyond that of my parents.

Growing up in Montréal, I went to a Catholic elementary school and later Sacred Heart Convent, a private English school for girls from well-connected Catholic families. My father was the first French Canadian manager of an English Canadian trust company. My mother's background was Irish Catholic and American Methodist and she was an active volunteer in organizations like the Canadian Cancer Society and the National Ballet. My parents circulated in the Anglo business and cultural circles of Montréal, a world of balls, cocktail parties, and golf clubs.

Every summer when we visited my father's family on the Gaspé coast I relaxed—there it didn't matter what you wore or who you knew. I ran wild with my poorer cousins, admiring the oldest girls who drank beer, didn't have curfews and, in my mind, weren't trying to impress anyone. In the fall when I returned to my sheltered Anglo society life I'd feel my spirit slowly shrivel.

Looking back there were moments when the narrow lens of my world-view opened just a crack. During my years at the convent the Second Vatican Council took place, proposing sweeping new changes in the Catholic Church. First my parents and then a progressive Sacred Heart nun herded us down to serve meals at Benedict Labré House, a soup kitchen in a poor section of Montréal. This nun, Margaret Power, talked about a different way of being Christian that involved being present with the poor. She would later leave her rich girls' school and move to live with the poor in Pointe St. Charles. Several of my schoolmates were Cuban, which only heightened the Cold War paranoia in our school; I can still remember practicing sheltering ourselves under our desks in the study hall as we anxiously awaited the resolution of the Cuban missile crisis. Québec's Quiet Revolution also touched my family as mailbox bombs went off in the vicinity of my father's business and social connections. Though I was too young to appreciate its significance, my father's promotion to Québec vice-president of his company occurred at a time when separatist militants were criticizing Anglo businesses for having no French Canadians on their executives.

University opened up a different world to me. I first went to McGill, living at home. I discovered Marxism and for the first time made friends with Jews and atheists. The turbulent relationship with my parents continued, the "debutante affair" being one in a string of conflicts. Finally after a year on valium—a psychiatrist's solution to my personal turmoil and conflict with my mother—my parents reluctantly agreed to my proposal that I switch to the University of British Columbia. I left Montréal in the summer of 1968.

If Vancouver at first seemed a bit provincial to this big-city girl, I soon discovered a world I had never seen in Montréal. I moved into a house that was part of the underground railway bringing up draft-dodgers from the U.S. who were escaping the Vietnam war, and discovered West Coast hippies on Vancouver's Fourth Avenue and the academic "left" at UBC. But I also placed myself in largely male-dominated circles and, rather than question the gender dynamics, did my best to fit in and compete with the boys.

In 1969 I read Kate Millet's *Sexual Politics* and was incredibly excited by her ideas. But my first taste of feminism came in 1970 in Montréal when I had returned home for the summer with my new boyfriend, also a Montréaler. One of his friends asked me to join her consciousness-raising group. I remember her cobalt blue kitchen where we met every week, but I can't remember what we talked about. Yet I can still recall that wonderful feeling of recognition that other women had experienced some of the same painful and difficult things I had. I realized that I wasn't crazy or neurotic and that my perception of reality might actually be accurate.

I step over the rotted grey wooden door sill into the dusty dimly-lit living room of a squat in east Oxford. A bald light bulb swings over the circle of about twenty women seated on benches and old chairs. It is January, 1972, and this is the Oxford women's group, known as Oxford Women's Liberation.

I sit on the outside, drawn into the discussion and the energy flying around the room. We are debating the Family Allowance Campaign and what role Wages for Housework should play in it. Some of the women call themselves socialist feminists, while others have broken with leftist groups; some are associated with autonomous groups like Big Flame while some are with Wages for Housework. There is a range of accents here—English working-class, middle and upper, a New Zealand twang, an Australian lilt, and my Canadian one. Some are students, some are unemployed and welfare claimants, some are middle-class dropouts.

They're talking revolution—how to change the economic structures of society, to restructure the way domestic labour, childcare, the family, paid work, and the welfare state are organized in order for there to be any real liberation for women. The debate is fierce: wouldn't fighting for the family allowance reinforce the institutionalization of women's unpaid labour in the home? Shouldn't we be working for equal access to paid work and equal pay? Don't we need to heighten recognition of the work women do at home and demand money paid directly to women, hence challenging and exposing how women's unpaid domestic labour holds up the base of the capitalist economy?

This is not just a theoretical debate. We are deciding whether to participate in the Family Allowance Campaign in Oxford. With no clear resolution a sheet is passed around to see who wants to work on the campaign. I sign up and move my chair forward.

That night was the beginning of my activism in the women's movement. Until then I had been an armchair feminist; I read books, went to consciousness-raising groups, and tried to get the men in my life to do the dishes and take up less space at meetings. As a graduate student I initially stayed within my safe little circle of students and expatriate Canadians. The Family Allowance Campaign changed all this.

In pairs we went door to door in East Oxford and Cowley, a working-class suburb of Oxford. We talked to women about the government's plan to cut the family allowance and replace it with a family tax credit (after much protest, a similar scheme was introduced in Canada in 1993). We were demanding that the family allowance be increased and paid directly to women in recognition of the work they did and so that they had money in their own right. For the first time I met women whose husbands drank away their pay-packet, who were afraid to talk to us because of their husbands, who were tired from night shift jobs with two and three kids around their knees as they answered the door—women for whom the family allowance meant they could feed their kids at the end of the month. I became painfully aware of the contrast between the grinding poverty of these low-income women and their families in rows of grey Council housing and the elegant and mannered wealth of the Oxford university community just two kilometres away.

In the next year and a half I became passionately involved in the British women's movement. We won the family allowance campaign, a sign of the vitality and growing vociferousness of women's liberation. I attended two national women's liberation conferences, one in London, the other in Bristol. With hundreds of women I debated theory and campaign strategies, attended workshops, passed resolutions, and danced through the night. On International Women's Day we marched through the streets of London, 50,000 women strong, chanting the Four Demands—Free Contraception and Abortion on Demand, Equal Pay, 24 Hour Nurseries, and Equal Education Opportunity. I went to meetings about the rights of women prisoners and demonstrations supporting welfare claimants and squatters, read Marxist feminist pamphlets and

Wages For Housework tracts. It was an exciting time—women were starting to create their own women's centres, bookstores, and health collectives, and vision, not reaction, fuelled our energy and our actions. The women's movement caught my imagination and my passion for justice, and it was at last a place where I felt I belonged.

It's midnight and I'm exhausted as I crawl into my sleeping bag on the floor between two other sleeping women. This is the organizers' shed. We hadn't had time to set up our tents before it began to rain. All night we have been driving over the mountain on the rough logging road, picking up truckloads of women who were too tired or too loaded down to hike the entire distance. This shed is now crowded with women and children, latecomers to the first Vancouver Island Women's Festival.

It is the summer of 1976 and a few of us had decided to organize this gathering after hearing about similar events in the U.S. Two hundred women from down-Island—Courtenay, Campbell River, Denman Island—and from Vancouver and Victoria, made their way over the overgrown logging road to this abandoned townsite called Port Khusam on the northeast side of Vancouver Island near Sayward. For three days, we camp, gather in circles and attend an amazing variety of workshops in the fields or on the rocky beach. The workshops include how to run a chainsaw, natural birth control, herbal medicine, self-defence, spirituality, midwifery, and fighting rape in your community. The organization of the festival is voluntary and co-operative—as you register you sign up for a shift on daycare, kitchen, first-aid or clean-up.

I am just falling to sleep when I hear a knock at the door. It's Susan, another of the organizers, who announces that Janet's truck is stuck in the mud on the other side of the mountain. Several women with children are in it and they need another vehicle to help get it out. I groan and roll out of my sleeping bag, pick up a flashlight, and head out into the rain.

The expression of feminism in rural British Columbia in the late seventies was certainly a far cry from what I had experienced in Britain. After returning in late 1973, and a year in Vancouver, I moved to Courtenay on Vancouver Island. I was hungrily searching to replicate the political fervour and clarity of analysis of the women's movement in Britain. Some of this analysis I found with my first women's group in Courtenay. Most members were recent mothers, some of whom were involved in the women's health movement and the politics of birthing. When I became pregnant I too became involved in the natural childbirth and midwifery movements, opting for a home birth when I had my son in 1977. For the next few years I cared for two young boys in an isolated homestead, feeling not only the delights of mothering but also depression as I watched my life evaporate into endless dirty diapers, sleepless nights, and hungry little mouths.

The six consecutive Vancouver Island Women's Festivals between 1976 and 1982 reflected very different dynamics. They were started by a group of us who were living with men, had young children, and were struggling to understand what feminism meant for us as women living in a rural area. Many who attended the festivals were urban feminists without children from Vancouver and Victoria; some were childless lesbians and some called themselves separatists. Some of these women moved to the country to set up women's land or to find a part-time refuge from the city. Such a large seasonal influx of lesbians made it easier for some of the rural women to come out as a lesbians. By the fourth year of the festival workshop topics included: Talking to One Another: Lesbians, Bisexuals and Straights; Building a Women's Land Trust; and Raising Sons. But many of the heterosexual rural women felt alienated by the separatist tone of a few and the festivals eventually ended as some of the old organizers dropped out.

In 1979 I entered a four-year working period that changed my perspective on rural feminism. From a pilot project educating women in six Vancouver Island communities about wife assault, we formed the Women's Self-Help Network which trained women to run self-help groups in four North Island communities. Most of the women we met in these single industry resource communities were wives of miners, loggers, and fishers who worked in the home as mothers; a few had managed to also find paid jobs as store clerks or waitresses. Most were unfamiliar with feminism and distrusted it. They came to the self-help groups for a wide variety of reasons: they were fed up with the isolation of living in a small trailer with children, and husbands always away on shift work; their husbands drank and were beating them and they were thinking of leaving; they had already left and were isolated single parents. We provided a mix of popular education, assertiveness training, peer counselling training, and community organizing skills.

Working with these women I began to realize just how middle-class my own feminism was. They had much fewer options than me. Leaving their husbands usually meant choosing to live on welfare and a life of poverty for themselves and their kids. I realized that it was no accident that most of the women who came to our country women's festivals were middle-class. Many of these women already knew how to run a chainsaw and cutting wood was an extra job they wanted to avoid. The spectre of a bare-breasted group of women chanting in the woods had little relevance to these women's lives as they tried to survive the vagaries of a resource-based economy with their families.

When I look back at those years between 1973 and 1983, I see now that much of my energy was involved in the personal feminist politics of taking control of your life. I flirted with non-traditional work such as commercial fishing, and built my own little cabin (with a lot of help from my friends). Having a homebirth was a refusal to have the medical establishment control my body. Organizing the women's festivals and self-help groups was an extension of the principle that women could support and grow together as women, on our own. In that climate claiming my lesbian identity was really not a big deal for me; it just seemed a logical progression in my development as an autonomous woman. But I stopped short at separatism or an anti-men ethic, which as a mother of sons seemed too short-sighted and more the self-indulgence of white middle-class women who had the money to opt out of the world rather than struggle to change it.

We arrive at the large crowded hall, loaded down with boxes of the kit. The kit is the training manual and modules we have produced in the final year of the Women's Self-Help Network. We are directed to a table which is between displays of a community water irrigation model from Botswana and the Urban-Rural Mission Project. I am suddenly aware that I am in the minority in this huge room with people from all over the world.

We are at the AGORA, the exhibition and display market of the sixth Assembly of the World Council of Churches, in Vancouver in June of 1983. When I had proposed to the Women's Self-Help collective that we try to sell our kit here most members had serious doubts. One woman objected to the fact it was Christian; another to the fact it was a mixed gathering of men and women. I persevered and here we are, talking to dozens of women from Africa, Australia, Asia, and the South Pacific, all interested in our kit.

During a break I walk over to the main tent. With 3,000 other people I listen to Lois Wilson, the first woman moderator of the United Church of Canada. She talks with passion about the need for justice for women working in free trade zones in Asia, and for those struggling against apartheid in South Africa. She is not

268

only a strong feminist but speaks with a global perspective that I have not heard in my own rural feminist circles.

Inspired, I walk to the photo display area and look at two exhibitions of black-and-white photos. One is the story of a Base Christian Community in El Salvador; the other that of the community work of a black South African women's group. I am struck by the depth of commitment to long-term struggle. And what strikes me most is that these people are struggling from a Christian faith perspective. A deep longing I've ignored for years surfaces in this room. I want that for my own work and life. I turn to leave, knowing something fundamental in me has shifted.

I returned to Courtenay from the World Council of Churches Assembly and immediately applied to the Vancouver School of Theology (VST) and was accepted for the fall of that year. Most of my feminist friends thought I was crazy. It was bad enough that I had reverted to Christianity and to Catholicism, but deciding to actually enter a Masters of Divinity program that prepares one for ordained ministry, especially when I couldn't get ordained as a Catholic woman, was impractical. Wasn't Christianity a hopelessly patriarchal religion that had not only kept women subordinate throughout the world but also played a central role in colonizing the South? How could I explain that it was not that clear-cut for me?

Born and raised a Catholic, I had stopped attending Church when I was eighteen. Christianity became irrelevant to my life at university when I discovered Marxism, a world-view with a much clearer vision of social change than what I had been exposed to in the Québec parish Catholicism of the 1960s. For fifteen years I felt no need for organized religion, though I had a religious or spiritual sensibility, and read feminist spirituality books, went to women's spirituality circles in the early eighties, and was fascinated by native spirituality.

Two factors brought me back to my Christian roots. One was my work. I was becoming increasingly interested in popular education, and discovered that liberation theology was playing a central role with popular education in the liberation struggles in Latin America. I also felt something was missing in our group work with women; we never talked about the spiritual dimension of our lives. In 1983 the Canadian Catholic Bishops Conference came out with a statement on Ethics and Economics which led me to believe that the Catholic Church was engaging with fundamental ethical principles around fighting poverty and for a just economy. I decided to join a prayer group with progressive Catholics to explore this further.

At the same time I was entering one of the most difficult periods of my personal life. My relationship with my son's father had been rapidly deteriorating and we eventually ended up in a custody battle where I feared I would lose my son because of the homophobia of the courts. The spiritual resources of my Catholic tradition were a lifeline for me in this "dark night of the soul." When we eventually chose mediation the result was a joint custody arrangement where I had my son half-time. I continued to draw on that spiritual tradition as I anguished with recurrent loss, self-doubt, anger, and grief.

Theological school proved a good choice for developing my work through exploring liberation and feminist theology. I began to learn Spanish and became involved with the Christian Task Force for Central America. In exchanges with Central American popular educators I discovered how base community groups had reclaimed the Bible for themselves. While studying and mothering I continued to work part-time as a popular educator, adding a church constituency to my work and a focus on Catholic social teachings on labour to my growing interest in women's struggles in the economy.

I met Christian feminists at theology school—women who didn't hang out with the women's movement but were fighting for the same things in their sphere. Some were lesbians. Some were concerned primarily with challenging the patriarchal structures of the church; others with rereading and reclaiming scripture and theology from a feminist perspective. Both groups were creating rituals and traditions to replace old ones that no longer worked for women.

The morning circle has started with the usual smudge and now a time of sharing. We are a circle of ten today: the eight students, the co-ordinator, and myself. It is almost the end of my term as the evaluator of the Native Family Violence Training Program in Vancouver. I had spent three years observing the trainees' work, visiting their communities and occasionally, like today, attending the training sessions and participating in their healing circles.

These circles were difficult for me. The women shared stories of losses of children, partners, and relations, in suicides, murders, illnesses, and accidental deaths and stories of recovering from childhood sexual abuse, violent relationships with husbands and boyfriends, and rapes by white men. The single male student had been abused in residential school and had survived several suicide attempts. During all this I had felt slightly ashamed of the orderliness of my childhood and my strict upbringing in a suburb of Montréal. My pain was nothing in comparison to that of the others in the group.

This day my self-definition shattered. One of the women in the group had just returned from a court appearance and had decided to share her story. She broke down in the middle, and in a voice shaking with sobs, voiced her fear that no one in this group would really love her now they knew she had witnessed a murder twenty years ago. A chord in me suddenly snapped. I found myself silently crying as I realized that deep down I believed the same thing—no one would love me if they found out what I was really like, who I really was, with all my failures and omissions.

When she was finished the group turned to me. As I sobbed, the gentle voice of one of the members of the circle said, "Denise, we wondered when you would finally get here."

I think every white middle-class feminist who is involved with women's movements in all their plurality and diversity has to come to terms with her race and class privilege. My turning point was deeply personal. I thought I had grasped the issue of privilege years earlier. In fact it was only an intellectual thing. I had not yet understood how my privilege affected my deepest behaviour.

When I graduated from VST in 1988 and was asked to apply for the job at the Native Education Centre, I hesitated at first. It was part-time; it wasn't a "church" position and didn't have much to do with my recent training at VST. At the same time I couldn't be ordained in the Catholic Church because I was a woman and I knew my chances of getting work in a church were minimal. I had worked in the Northwest Territories for three summers co-facilitating a cross-cultural exposure tour with the Dené with René Fumoleau, an Oblate priest, and I had learned how the healing movement sweeping First Nations communities involved spiritual and cultural renewal. So I decided to take the job, a decision I have never regretted.

During those three years I realized that theology school had little to do with spirituality; it trains you to think theologically and to be a religious functionary, but ignores the question of how you engage with the spirit in daily life. The Native Family Violence Program helped me understand that spirituality was integrally connected to personal healing and growth. But it took me a while to see how this applied to me.

What I learned was that my privilege had kept me from looking at my own pain and marginality. I figured I was fundamentally okay compared to the people in the training; somehow my background made me feel separate from them. For years I had unconsciously used the language of "us and them" in my work. That circle triggered the insight that deep down I was no different than the rest of the people in the room; in fact I was probably more removed from my basic humanity because of my privilege and in failing to see my own pain and the losses that I had denied for years. I realized that I too had experienced marginalization and loss as a lesbian—being labelled and discredited and vulnerable to losing my son because I didn't fit the norm. My privilege had prevented me from seeing our common humanity and how it was necessary to face my privilege, personal issues and pain before I could really begin to understand that of others.

This personal insight also translated at a political level. From the participants I learned about the complexity of finding solutions to violence against women in their communities. I had come into the program with strong opinions about all abusers needing to be removed from their communities and thrown in jail. As I watched the debates about what to do with abusers take place in the program and in the communities, I realized that sending Native men into the Canadian prison system only served to criminalize them further. As well I saw that First Nations women wanted to restore and rebuild their communities and they wanted to do it with First Nations men—most identified themselves as women who were part of a community, an identification lacking among most white feminists. Here I began the slow and ongoing process of educating myself to respect cultural differences, and to realizing just how narrow my white feminist perspective was.

It is time for the plenary and I join the stream of women crowding into the recreation hall at a government union holiday camp in Valle de Bravo, outside Mexico City. This is the First Tri-National Working Women's Conference on Economic Integration and Free Trade, in February 1992, and there are over two hundred of us, the majority Mexican. We are too many for this narrow room with no windows and insufficient chairs. I stand with a group crowded by the door, beside my new friend Viky, hoping she can help translate if I miss something.

The conference chair is going over the afternoon's agenda when a woman comes to the mike to make an announcement. I am chatting to a friend and don't hear what she says when a collective gasp moves through the room followed by a brief silence. I quickly turn to Viky and ask her what is going on. She tells me Bishop Mendez Arceo has just died of a heart attack; when I look blank she explains that he is known as the Red Bishop and his death means the loss of one of the few Church allies the popular movements have in Mexico.

Viky worked as an organizer with urban poor women including those from Base Christian Communities, but she was no fan of the Catholic Church. Two days earlier I had observed a group of urban poor women expressing great fear about how education cutbacks might mean the Catholic Church would take over the schools. Most of the Mexican women I met at the conference were strongly secular in their beliefs and analysis. So I was surprised at this undercurrent of religiosity, and that these women still identified openly with those who worked for The Church of the Poor.

I attended this conference as a delegate from a new group called Women To Women Global Strategies. Our mandate was to educate locally in B.C. and make links with women internationally about women, work, and the changing global economy. In Mexico I learned just how northern my understanding of feminism was. I also discovered how spirituality and religion were more part of women's daily life than in the North.

In a workshop on Women's Rights in Daily Life, I was the only North American in a group of fourteen from unions, the urban poor movement, and rural indigenous communities. Each woman spoke about the most urgent problems in their communities and especially how women were bearing the burden of cutbacks and structural adjustment programs in increasing workloads at home, in the community and in the multiple jobs they did in the informal economy for money to feed their hungry families. They drew up a list of corresponding women's human rights they felt were being violated—the right to housing, nutrition, food, education, health and health care services, and freedom from violence. To all these they added "the right to voluntary maternity."

A woman from Oaxaca explained how there had been a motion in the Chiapas state legislature to allow abortion as a way of limiting the indigenous population. While pressure from the Catholic Church had defeated the motion, these women were adamant in insisting that neither the state nor the Church had the right to interfere with women's reproductive rights. What was at stake was something greater than just the freedom to have abortions; women wanted the right to choose if and when to have children, depending on whether there were basic rights and necessities that would assure that their children would live. The right to voluntary maternity reframed the right to choice within a much broader perspective of reproductive rights, which included women's rights to bodily integrity and the protection of any collectivity of women from any type of population control program that violated women's right to choose for the integrity of themselves and their children.

From Mexican and Central American feminists I have learned what a gender analysis of the economy can mean and how important it is to defend women's rights as human rights. The fundamentalist attack on women's rights, and the lobbying at international UN conferences to replace the word *gender* with the word *sex* (thus returning to the notion that biology is destiny, rather than the notion that society constructs gendered roles and status for women) from the Women's Platform for Action at Beijing, suggests to me that women's movements are becoming real threats to the patriarchal powers that be. What I observed in Central America and through my work on women and the global economy is that feminism has become a global grassroots movement about radical social change—a movement which claims a redistribution of the world's wealth so that all children, all women, and all men can be fed and have "fullness" of life. And despite patriarchal institutions like the Vatican claiming to represent all Catholic women, I know that women of faith are also in the forefront fighting for dignity and full human rights for all women.

It is the fifth time this group of women have met. I look around the comfortable living room where we are meeting, waiting for someone to begin. We had spent the first part of the evening doing voice and movement exercises to get in touch with our own inner voices. Then we had gone off individually to different rooms in this large old house to reflect on a sacred text. For this group of women who come from a Christian heritage the text we have chosen is the "Magnificat," the alleged words of Mary, the mother of Jesus, found in the Christian Scriptures in the Book of Luke. We have come back to the circle to share our reclaiming, our revisioning of this text, using whatever creative form we choose.

The silence is broken when the first woman, an Anglo-Canadian, begins by reading aloud a dialogue with Mary she has written. She is disillusioned and frustrated with the promises of justice and social reversals in the text, promises that seem even more unrealizable now, 2,000 years later. Yet she is willing to continue hoping, while acknowledging her doubt that a poor woman embracing her worth is enough.

The next woman to speak is an Argentinian-Canadian who has an even more searing indictment of the text. Her piece is a deeply personal letter to Luke, the supposed author of the gospel. Moving between rage and tears she condemns this author who created the image of Mary as a passive and submissive virgin and mother, an image which has been used to portray the ideal of womanhood and to reinforce the colonization and oppression of women in Latin America. We sit in stunned silence at the emotional force of her presentation.

A Chinese-Canadian woman follows, sharing a drawing—vivid with slashes of red—of the rage she felt at a racist incident she had recently experienced. Her anger challenges the image of woman's "lowliness" in the text and is connected to her heart, the place where she uses her rage to fight for justice. A Filipino-Canadian woman reads a poem she has just written; in it she recreates the image of God and of woman different from the traditional Christian interpretation and affirms the possibilities of life we can create as women of justice. A Québecoise woman shares a lament—from this traditional image of Mary she has learned to care for others but never to care for herself. An Anglo-Canadian woman shares how she now reads the text as "bad news" for her as one of the privileged. I do a short movement piece; for me the text is about drawing the line, about trusting the spirit to give me the strength to take a stand in the present context of denial and despair as the rich get richer. The last woman to share is the "Baroness," a comic character who is the alter ego of one of our group members. In screeching haughty tones, dressed in a blonde wig, lycra tights and a miniskirt, she rereads the text as a rich woman hearing it addressed to her for the first time. As she ends her piece we collapse in laughter, releasing some of the emotion that has built through these powerful and very different testimonials of each woman's struggle.

This evening was part of a six-week course called "Spirit in Struggle" which I co-facilitated with Marilou Carillo in the spring of 1996. For me it was a both a breakthrough and a coming home. It was a breakthrough because we had finally brought together feminist liberation theology and healing work, and because we were affirming how each woman's different social identity and context shaped how she named the spirit. It was a coming home because it was a place where we could be fully ourselves as feminists, activists, and Christians.

Both Marilou and I are Catholic women who have been trained theologically. Marilou, as a feminist and woman of colour, and myself, as a feminist and lesbian, have found little space for our gifts in the institutional church. Here, with this very diverse group of women, we had found a place where we could offer "another way to live their faith"—that vision that Maria Suarez had challenged me with in Costa Rica.

My relationship with Christianity and Catholicism has been very uneven over the years. Catholicism was part of my upbringing and culture, especially as a young girl raised in Québec in the fifties and sixties. When I was in seminary I was not drawn, as some other Catholic women have been, to change denominations, choosing either the United or Anglican Church. I had little desire to do ordained parish ministry, which spared me the agony of fighting the dead-end battle for women's ordination in the Catholic Church. But I was left with another dilemma—how to claim my authority in a tradition where there was no recognition for women's unique contribution and gifts.

My journey as a Christian has been very much at the margins of the Church. Since the early 1980s I have been part of a loose national network of radical Catholics and progressive Protestants, women and men whom I have met through my interest in Central America and social justice issues. Many in these circles, especially the Catholics, do not regularly attend church and instead define practicing their faith as acting for justice in the world. Many have a contemplative spiritual practice, and attend annual silent retreats to renew their spirits for their continuing work in their communities. While these groups have been important sources of nourishment for me, many of the men in these circles have not seriously engaged feminism, nor is there much understanding of heterosexual privilege.

The first few years after I graduated from the Vancouver School of Theology I remained uncertain as to whether my "ministry" work was inside or outside the institutional church. In the early 1990s I did education work around Catholic social teachings on labour in the local Catholic diocese. This was a very frustrating experience as I received very little support from the parish priests; when I told the local priest in Courtenay about my job he had replied by asking me if I was married or single! I also participated in economic justice education with ecumenical social justice groups. By the mid-nineties social justice work had been cut from most Catholic dioceses throughout the country and the local church was growing increasingly conservative. It became clear to me that there was no longer space for me to do feminist education or social justice work inside the Catholic Church. I decided that I would no longer try to "fit into" the institutional church.

In one sense this decision was incredibly liberating because I no longer had to be "careful" about what I said; I no longer had to be cautious as a feminist and social justice activist. I no longer had to hide who I was. I had watched how self-destructive it had been for so many gay and lesbian ministers and priests who had been closeted in the Church. I now could discover that the more honest I was about who I was, as a lesbian, a feminist, and someone who believes the Christian scriptures are calling us to radical personal conversion and social change, the better I felt about myself.

Yet at the same time I felt spiritually homeless, cut off from my roots and with no clear community of faith to which I could relate. In moments of despair I would think I had wasted four years of my life getting this Masters of Divinity degree I would never use. Then, in the summer of 1995 I attended a retreat for women called "Scattered Fragments." The retreat used dance, drawing, claywork, and other means of creative expression and drew on many sacred traditions to help participants explore their spiritual journeys as women. Here I discovered that I was not alone in my journey and that in fact I had a community, one that was spread far and wide, and one that was deeply continuous with the Christian tradition of religious women.

Many moments marked that retreat for me. I was the youngest in a group of thirteen women, aged forty-five to eighty. More than half were Catholic religious; my biases against religious women—as staid, repressed, and subservient to the Fathers—were shattered as I watched these women dance, draw, and share their journeys, witnessing to the pervasive and persistent impact of feminism despite the efforts of the Vatican to crush it. Dorothy, the facilitator, who was a few years older than me, commented on how she was finally doing what she wanted and that what had held her back was herself. Despite its New Age tone, her statement rang true for me. Finally we blessed and broke bread together, a spiritual community of equals, needing no ritual priest yet at the same time acknowledging and affirming the priests amongst us. At the closing ritual, one of the elders, an American religious who had been active in the women's movement for thirty years, blessed me and affirmed that she would be with me in the mystery of my journey ahead.

I believe in timing, synchronicity, the right things happening when you are ready to move on. For me the retreat confirmed that my feminist spirituality was rooted in my own history and my heritage as a Christian woman. This history includes European religious women who were marriage resisters, the medieval Beguines—lay women who lived in community and worked with the poor, and religious women who came to North America alone, without men, to found orders and build schools and hospitals in the wilderness. If this is a history that also included colonialism and racism it is one I must come to terms with as my history. But it also includes the Sumerian and Mesopotamian goddess traditions that predate and underly the Jewish and Christian stories, as well as the traditions of feminine wisdom found in mysticism and earth-based spiritualities.

Feminist spiritualities that are now emerging are not based on an ethic of self-sacrifice and service to men but rather encourage us to be fully who we are, and to love ourselves first in order that we may love others. Many are based on an interfaith sensibility, a valuing and respect for the teachings of differing religious traditions. These are spiritualities shaped and transmitted by a community of women, including elders who pass on their wisdom and younger women who are experimenting with new forms.

It is this wide community of feminist women of faith which is the base from which I speak of an alternative vision of faith. I am slowly discovering ways I can bring questions of faith and meaning to the forums in which I work, usually outside churches, occasionally inside. I co-facilitate an interfaith group of women who meet regularly to reflect theologically on our struggles as activists. I am also exploring ways to integrate scripture, the body and healing work for groups of both women and men who are reflecting on how to act faithfully in these difficult socio-economic times. As religious fundamentalism is growing, world-wide groups of women, like the ones I am part of, are meeting throughout the world, reclaiming and redefining their faith as Jews, Muslims, Hindus, Christians, and Buddhists, linked in their common opposition to intolerance, exclusion, and injustice.

In reclaiming and renaming a feminist and inclusive version of my faith tradition, I feel I have something to offer from my place as an educated white woman who can pass in the belly of the beast, but who also can be thrown out and disregarded because of my sexuality and politics. I believe the Christian tradition can be radically subversive, with its vision of the "commonweal of God," which is a feminist rephrasing of the

Kingdom of God. Both the commonweal of God and its predecessor, the Jewish Jubilee tradition, call for an economic and social restructuring of society—the release of prisoners, the freeing of all slaves, the healing of the blind, the release of the oppressed, the redistribution of wealth and restitution of land to those who originally owned it, a year of fallow to restore the land, and the cancellation of debts. With a gender analysis that means the end of modern slavery for women, including migrant workers and all women working as domestics, sex trade workers, or workers in sweatshops and free trade zone factories. It means the end of and healing from women's imprisonment in violent and abusive situations; the end of gender discrimination at all levels and the eradication of women's poverty through the reclamation of land and resources and the cancellation of Third World debt.

More and more I see my role as a bridge, accessing and reframing this faith tradition for those who have left Christian churches in disgust but who desperately want and need a spiritual foundation for these changing and uncertain times. I think our differing faith traditions offer the moral imagination we need to reinforce our vision, and as well provide spiritual disciplines that can give us the inner strength for the "long haul" in our struggle to create feminist alternatives.

The journey of my feminist education has led me back to my cultural and spiritual roots. My encounter with other feminists has made me face myself and who I am. More rooted in what is liberating in my tradition, and critically rejecting what is oppressive, I want to continue to communicate with, be an ally of, and learn from other spiritually subversive women throughout the world.

The Academy of Motherhood

Patty Osborne

'm thirteen years old and ironing my brother's pyjamas. My two older brothers wear those long-sleeved cotton pyjamas with what my Home Ec teacher called flat-felled seams—double-stitched seams like the ones on blue jeans. Whatever they are called, they pucker relentlessly in the dryer. To get them to iron flat I have to press down hard on the iron at one end and pull the other end tight with my left hand. Then I push the iron along the seam, making sure to let go with my left hand at just the right moment to avoid the scorching steam that shoots out ahead of the iron. This is the beginning of my feminist education.

There are many other items of clothing in my ironing pile each week, and many of them are my brothers'. But those pyjamas are the most infuriating. I am affronted at having to iron something that is only going to be slept in. My brothers are not without solidarity; they have no objection to conspiring with me by putting their pyjamas away unironed. My mother need never know. But somehow she does know. Out come the offending pyjamas and back they go onto my pile of ironing, as my brothers slink away from the conflict.

One of the other jobs that I am assigned is to clean the boys' bathroom. This is where I learn that boys pee on the walls, and girls clean it up. There is no brotherly solidarity here, no attempt to clean up after themselves at all. Just a toothpaste-encrusted sink, a scum-covered bathtub, a toilet reeking of ammonia, and a young girl scrubbing through her rage.

I'm beginning to realize that there is something more going on here.

Why, just because I'm a girl, does my mother make me clean up after the boys?

For the Easter holidays, my parents have rented a motel unit at a nearby ski resort. My oldest brother has stayed at home, but my other brother, Tom, has brought along his girlfriend. The unit has a small bathroom, a tiny kitchen, a livingroom with a hide-a-bed, and a loft full of bunk beds. After skiing all day, we have just eaten dinner and we're having an argument about whose turn it is to wash the dishes—a job which, at home, is done by the automatic dishwasher. My mother and sisters think it is my turn, but I point out that I've done them once already and that Tom has not done them yet. I can see so clearly that it is Tom's turn. My mother insists that I should do them and the argument escalates around my silent brother. Finally, exasperated by all this pettiness, Tom says, "Everybody relax, I'll do the dishes." Despite his tone of voice, I feel like I have an ally. But his girlfriend astonishes me by jumping up and heading for the kitchen. "As long as I'm here, there is no reason why Tom should have to do the dishes," she says. She's nuts, I say to myself, but it feels like I've won the wrong battle.

It was becoming obvious to me that some things just weren't right. Like housework being a woman's responsibility. And as I read and heard more about something called "women's liberation," I could see that it wasn't right that men made more money than women or that women could not feel safe on the streets at night. But it was not until I started raising my children that I began to embrace feminism from the inside out. My growing children questioned everything, pushing me to examine the assumptions by which I lived. Through them I revisited the attitudes and rules that I had taken for granted as I grew up. In discussions ranging from simple questions like "Why don't boys wear skirts?" to the more complex issues of the distribution of wealth and power, I began to reorganize my beliefs, to construct my own value system. And feminism was at its core.

My family ran on traditional rules: my father, a doctor, was the most important person. He made the money and when the family went places, he drove the car. He also sat at the head of the table and carved the meat. My mother did everything else. She was the housekeeper, secretary, chauffeur, and disciplinarian. Of course, she made no money, and she got no respect. Not from me, and not from my father or my siblings. At the time I thought that all she cared about were trivial things like laundry and dusting.

My mother was in charge of getting us to do our chores. My three sisters and two brothers and I each took a turn at KP—setting and clearing the dinner table. While my sisters and I also emptied the dishwasher, cleaned the bathrooms, dusted, and did ironing, the only other job my brothers were responsible for was taking out the garbage—and they seldom did even this. Mom was an emotional, often angry person who seemed to me to be obsessed with a tidy house, ironed clothes, and properly folded towels. I felt that I was more like my father, who held himself above domestic detritus. When my parents fought, which happened more and more frequently, Mom would become embarrassingly emotional. Dad, of course, remained calm and calculated—a tactic which drove my mother crazy, and which I now see would have driven me crazy too. But at the time I admired my father for staying so superior and rational while my mother was losing control.

Schoolwork always came easily to me. With no particular effort on my part I did well and even skipped a grade. In high school I took math, chemistry and physics, although I put so little effort into studying that my grades slipped lower each year. My parents had high expectations for their children, both boys and girls. I knew I was just as smart as my brothers and sisters, and, in my arrogance, I knew I was definitely smarter than my mother.

But in the outside world, brains were not what counted. Brains don't show the way that legs and breasts do. Throughout my teens I longed to look like the girls on the pages of *Seventeen* magazine. Of course it was hopeless. They were tall and thin with perfect breasts and no hips to speak of. They had perfect hair on their heads, and no hair showing anywhere else. I was short, had small breasts and thick ankles, and was shaped like a pear. And I had lots of thick dark body hair.

But this didn't stop me from trying. I rinsed my hair in beer (lemon juice was for blondes), lay with cucumber slices on my eyelids, and made facial masks out of exotic ingredients. I tried the exercises that were guaranteed to "firm up those tummies" and "tighten up those thighs." I tried dieting but couldn't stick with it so I just skipped breakfast or lunch altogether. Nothing worked. I never got any taller and my ankles never got thin and bony. Remember, this was the age of the mini skirt. Legs mattered.

I also wanted clothes that were just like what the *Seventeen* models wore, but of course they were not made for my peculiar body type. Once I got into the brightly-lit change rooms in the department stores and struggled into another hipless little outfit, I would be filled with self-loathing and despair. I would quickly wriggle out of the ill-fitting garment, put my jeans and t-shirt back on, and slink out of the store. It didn't occur to me that clothes should be made to fit people, not the other way around.

Then along came the hippies and I finally had something to wear. While I never actually turned on and dropped out, those long Indian bedspread skirts and denim overalls did a great job of covering up my unacceptable body. Even body hair was allowed. I stopped reading fashion magazines and shopping at major department stores. And when I moved away from home I left behind the bathroom scales forever. I still didn't like my body, but at least I could ignore it more easily.

The only times I have truly liked the way I looked was when I was pregnant. My face took on a healthy glow and my big firm belly made my hips and thighs look smaller. Camouflage was not necessary—I finally looked the way I was supposed to. And I could even laugh at what was offered as "maternity clothes"—cute little puffy sleeved smocks that seemed aimed at turning us back into the innocent girls we were before we discovered sex.

I'm still working towards liking my imperfect body, and I think I'm getting the hang of it. I've taken to swimming countless lengths of the local pool, and have discovered that the rhythm of this eases my mind and brings forgotten muscles back to life. I've surprised myself by starting to like the body that I'm getting back in touch with. It also helps that I'm forty-three years old now. The female images that the media projects now look like babies to me. And even though I've met a lot of women, I don't know any that look or act like the smooth-skinned, perfectly-proportioned symbols of feminity that I see in movies, ads and TV shows. But teenage girls like my daughters often don't know that these "perfect" women don't exist—they think they just haven't met any yet.

During my second pregnancy David and I bought a small rural property and soon I was spending most of the summer camping there with my children. We put a little trailer up on blocks and supplemented that accommodation with a tent. Inside the trailer was a tiny dark closet and inside of that was a tiny mirror—our only mirror. If you got up really close you could check that your face was reasonably clean, that your hair didn't look too outrageous. Other than that the only reflection of myself I saw was in my children's uncritical eyes. As the weeks went by I started feeling better and better about myself. I stopped thinking about how I looked and started listening to how I felt. Back home we looked at the photos we had taken that summer and I squirmed to see that I was still short and pear-shaped, even though that was not how I had felt at the time. But inside me I hold onto the idea that the real problem is not my body—it's all those mirrors and plate glass windows out there.

Trying not to project my poor body image onto my children has helped me work on it for myself. Dieting was a common practice around our house when I was growing up, but I left that behind. I don't diet and so far my children don't either. We don't have a bathroom scale, and we don't comment on how much people weigh. Junk food is discouraged not because it will make us fat but because it is not healthy. And, at one of Meg Hickling's sex education talks at my children's school, I learned that many boys get quite pudgy just as they are entering puberty. Armed with this knowledge I have been able to make no comments as my eleven-year-old son bulks up in preparation for that growth spurt that will soon have him towering over his little round mother.

I'm twenty-six years old and living in a little old house with my partner, David, and our one-year-old daughter, Robin. Before we had Robin, David and I shared the housework and even went to the laundromat together. On the weekend we cleaned our apartment and shopped for food. David had a steady job and I was a potter so it was logical that after the baby came I should stay home to do childcare. And since I'm home anyway, it seems pretty selfish of me not to cook dinner, clean the house, and shop for groceries. David does help with domestic jobs, but when he gets home from work he's tired and I've been home all day . . . the pattern is so easy to fall into. I can spend whole days doing work that will just have to be done again the next day and the next. The futility of it is overwhelming. Despite the fact that I thought I was above all this, I am living my mother's life—a life for which I have no respect.

Like most of society, I could not see how important the job of parenting was. In fact, I didn't even consider it a job. It was something you did while you were doing something else—usually housework. The sign that you were doing a good "job" as a mother was that your house and your kids were clean and tidy. No one, including myself, ever looked at my happy, healthy daughter and told me what a good job I was doing. Like my mother before me, I was doing the unimportant, unskilled work (housework), and raising my daughter on the side, while my man was out in the world doing something meaningful—in other words, something that brought in money.

But unlike my mother, I had an inkling that there might be another way. In the late seventies there were new ideas floating around, and women were beginning to make other choices. It started to dawn on me that mothers should get time off too. That maybe a perfectly neat and tidy house wasn't a goal I wanted to pursue. That maybe I could find fulfillment elsewhere. One day when I was picking my daughter up from preschool I got to talking with another mom. "This preschool just gives me enough time to run home and get my vacuuming done," she told me. Just the way she said "my vacuuming" made a light go on. *She vacuumed her house every day.* This is how people kept their houses clean! A secret had been revealed to me; now I would be able to conquer those dust balls. But I never could keep it up. I just didn't care enough, and thanks to feminism, I was allowed not to.

But I was still torn between the demands of my child, the demands of my partner, and the demands I made on myself. And as our family grew, I was pulled in more and more different directions. Should I take the kids to the park (my mother says kids should get outside once a day), or should I get this house cleaned up (so it will look to David like I did something worthwhile today). I'm so tired, but will my daughter be illiterate if we put her to bed without a story tonight? There were so many things that I "should" be doing that my own needs were forgotten. I realized that I had to start listening to myself, to my own thoughts and feelings, and to raise my children my own way. I had to start taking charge of my life, and taking pride in my job as parent.

All this took me years to figure out. First, I struggled to separate raising children from housework—to look at raising children as my job (with any assistance willingly accepted), and at housework as everyone's job (with all hands on deck). When I started to do occasional work outside home, it got easier to leave things dirty and messy until someone else in the family noticed and did something about it. Pretty soon our bathroom got so disgusting that even David noticed. He didn't like cleaning it any more than I did. And when my sister told us that one of the upsides of being separated from her husband was that the bathroom was much cleaner since no one was splashing pee all around, David made the vital connection. Yes, urine all over the walls and floor had a lot to do with a tall man trying to pee into a short toilet bowl. He doesn't clean the bathroom any more often, but when they're at home, both he and our son now pee sitting down. Now if only I could get them to spread this idea around—we could see another bastion of male privilege fall.

These days when I get together with other women I feel the commonality of our experience. Now I belong. But until I was well into my twenties, I never felt any allegiance to other women. Comparing myself to them was the norm—they were usually thinner, taller, and better-dressed, although I was usually smarter. Not exactly a basis for deep friendships. I felt more comfortable with men friends. But all this changed when I became a mother. In our neighbourhood, during daylight hours, there just weren't any men. Waiting outside the pre-school room or the swimming pool, visiting the library for storytime, playing in the park—nothing but women everywhere. Approachable women. Women of all shapes and sizes who were no better or worse than I was. Often these were the only adults I would talk to all day. I had to let down my guard. We mostly talked about kids and housework, but occasionally I would meet someone who was willing to go deeper than that—to talk about her feelings, her frustrations, her struggles.

For the past few days the world has looked bleak. The house is a mess and I don't have the energy to clean it up. Did I really think that by not getting legally married I would escape the tedium of endless housework? And spending day after day with only a baby for company saps my energy. My head is muddled and there's no way out. I feel like I am just putting in time waiting for I don't know what. The only thing I can think to do is to plop Robin into her stroller and head up Fraser Street. My friend Donna lives about fifteen blocks away. Even if she isn't home the walk will do me good.

Donna is tall and thin and never still. When I first got to know her I would sit at her kitchen table sipping tea and waiting for her to sit down so we could talk. She never did. Occasionally she will sit across from me for a few minutes but most of the time she is moving about the kitchen and in and out of the other rooms of her little house, tidying, offering diversions to her two boys, preparing food, talking.

But today I find Donna in her living room curled up on her favourite white rattan chair with a crocheted afghan wrapped around her, sipping coffee and looking grumpy. Robin toddles off to play with the boys in the bedroom, and Donna starts to talk. "It's the first day of my period and I feel like shit—I hate everybody," she says. This cheers me up considerably—I've got my period too. I make myself a cup of tea and sit across from her. We trade stories of how unreasonable our lives are. She is taking a couple of correspondence courses and can never find the time to do her homework. I am trying to keep my pottery business going, which means long nights spent hunched over my wheel in our dingy little basement. Her partner never talks to her. Mine brings home all his troubles and dumps them in my lap. We're both fed up with our children's demands. Housework is definitely unfulfilling. Pretty soon we are laughing about the outrageous things we have to put up with. Donna thinks we might have PMS. We've only encountered the term a few times before, but from what she has gathered, this must be it.

I went on to have two more children and a lot more PMS. Donna and I helped each other through a lot of changes. In Donna's bathroom, I read my first *Ms.* magazine—there was a small stack of them on the back of the toilet. During my university years I had read Betty Friedan's *The Feminine Mystique*, and had tried to read Germaine Greer's *The Female Eunuch* and Simone de Beauvoir's *The Second Sex*, but they were too theoretical for me. *Ms.* talked about women's day-to-day struggles. Pretty soon I had my own subscription. As I read those magazines from cover to cover I pictured my daughter growing up with feminist magazines around the house instead of *Ladies Home Journal* and *McCall's*.

But for the most part, apart from *Ms.*, David and I and our children were living in an insulated, middle-class world. When our third child was born we moved to a suburban neighbourhood where the houses were a little bigger and the parks were much more numerous. David was involved in his union and in left-wing politics, but apart from that we looked just like any other family on our block. Every morning the fathers drove off to work and we mothers began another child-centred day.

Every year at Christmas my children's elementary school sends a notice home asking us for hamper donations for a "needy" family. This notice briefly and anonymously gives the age and gender of each child. My son or daughter will come in the door saying, Mom, we need to take some food to school for the poor people. This request always makes me uncomfortable, and it takes me a while to figure out why. It isn't only that I feel that society, through our government, should provide adequately for the basic needs of families. It is the labelling of a family as "needy"—somehow that makes them different from our family. They

are anonymous to protect them from the shame of others knowing they are "poor."
They live somewhere else, somewhere dark and dreary, and they will be
appropriately grateful for whatever we deign to give them. In my heart I know
there is something wrong with this picture, but I can't pinpoint what. No wonder
I get so grumpy when I reach into our cupboards to come up with a donation.

But then I reconnected with my friend Helen whom I had known
during my university years. When I first knew Helen she was single and
worked full-time in a bank. When I ran into her again so many years
later she was a single mother with two children, one of them a baby. Of
course she was on welfare since she did not receive adequate support
from her children's fathers. But she was still her energetic and funny self
and she worried about feeding her children nutritious food and not
letting them watch too much television, just like we did. She didn't like
being on welfare, but she wasn't ashamed of it. So when the Christmas
donation request came home from school that year, I told my kids that
Helen is one of those "needy" people and we asked her what she
thought of this hamper thing. Oh, they give us a choice of whether we
want a hamper or money, she said. I always choose the money because
there is usually so much junk food in the hamper.

Now that anonymous "needy" family has a face I recognize. And I
see the truth of the saying that many women are just one man away
from welfare. I often think of a poster from many years ago. A
middle-aged black woman is leaning on a fence. The caption says: Class
consciousness is knowing which side of the fence you're on. Class
analysis is figuring out who is there with you.

Even the hookers on Helmcken Street are from my side of the fence.
Walking from my office to the bus, I see them standing there in their
skin-tight pants, high heels, and low-cut blouses. They are the embodi-
ment of how a sexy woman is supposed to look. And often, if I look
hard enough, behind that heavy makeup I see the face of a girl who
could be my daughter.

When my children were very young I spent most of my time
immersed in cooking, cleaning, organizing, and loving, with very little
energy left to ponder life's bigger issues. Though I knew that I wanted
my children to be raised differently than I was, I had no definite plan.
But children are great teachers. They don't come equipped with a lot of
prejudices and assumptions. As my friend Donna once said, "Isn't it great
where our children lead us?"

I am sitting on the toilet changing my sanitary napkin. The bathroom door has no lock on it and I can hear my two-year-old daughter approaching. So far I have been able to hide this procedure from her but today my timing is off and she just walks on in and of course wants to know, What's that? She is neither embarrassed nor disgusted. She looks at the blood on the sanitary napkin with interest. She accepts my simple explanation that once a month blood comes out of my vagina and I have to wear the napkin to keep the blood off my underwear. After that she often asks, Have you got the blood again, Mommy?

Fourteen years later my nine-year-old son and I are in the grocery store. My thirteen-year-old daughter is sitting in the car reading. Travis and I are in the "Personal Hygiene" aisle, facing row on row of tampons and sanitary napkins. I try to remember out loud what kind my daughter likes. My enthusiastic son offers to run outside and ask her. I am skeptical but off he goes. I push the buggy on to the vegetable section to finish the shopping. A few minutes later my son comes running back into the store. "She told me the kind she likes—I'll go get them," he says in a loud voice. He comes back with a green and pink package of sanitary napkins which he tosses into the buggy. "These are the ones she likes. Can we get some nectarines now?" he asks.

Early on I lost my copy of Dr. Spock and I never replaced it. Periodically I would read the latest book on child raising, but mostly I winged it, relying on my own gut feelings—to trust that what I was feeling was true, and then to figure out how to deal with the situation. But there was one book that made a difference.

My middle child, Cassia, is in grade one. Each day she comes home from school and tells me how much she hates her teacher, or the kid who sits beside her, or the stupid song they had to sing in music class. I put on my best mother voice and try to reason with her. I say things like, I'm sure your teacher didn't mean that, and Maybe you should try harder to be friends. Instead of listening to my advice and seeing the other side of the story, Cassia gets angry. So I get angry too and she stomps off into her room. Even though I vow to do things differently tomorrow, the pattern repeats itself.

Then I get hold of a copy of the book, How To Talk So Your Kids Will Listen, How to Listen So Your Kids Will Talk. *I am skeptical of advice books by now, but in desperation I read it. The book advises me to shut up and listen (although it is put more delicately). The next time Cassia comes home from school I listen to her complaints without comment, except the odd "Hmmm" to indicate I'm listening. The results are amazing. Once she has unloaded all her complaints on me she goes off happily as if she hasn't a care in the world. It seems that all she needed was someone who would listen to her. Pretty soon I am using this technique all the time, and not only with children. My friend around the corner often tells me about her surly, abusive husband. I have never understood why she doesn't take my advice and leave him. But when I shut up and just listen to her, I realize that the time is not right for her to take this big step, and that she is the best judge of what she should do. I start treating my friends and children with more respect once I figure out that I am not expected to nor can I solve their problems for them.*

Part of my job as a parent was to protect my children from accidents and since accidents often happen when people make mistakes, I soon found myself desperately trying to prevent my children from making mistakes. After all, our society tells us that we should never make mistakes and if we do we should cover them up or blame someone else. I was running myself ragged trying to foresee any possible problem and soon decided that another strategy was needed. I started asking myself, What's the worst thing that could happen? If my daughter goes outside without her coat, what's the worst thing that can happen? She'll get cold and she might even figure it out for herself and come and get her coat on. If my son forgets to take his lunch to school, what's the worst thing that can happen? He'll be hungry and probably bum some lunch off the other kids. He may even figure out that he should remember his own lunch.

After a while I realized that making mistakes is how we learn. It is certainly the way I learned to raise my kids. I didn't want my kids to be ashamed of their mistakes or to try to hide them from me. I wanted to know what my kids were up to and for them to be the ones to tell me. So I let them make mistakes, and tried to be around to help them fix things. Pretty soon I saw that being able to admit that you made a mistake, that you tried something that didn't work, or that you just did something dumb, is tremendously liberating. It lets you get on with fixing the mistake rather than worrying about how you will cover it up. This was a freedom that I wanted too.

But then there are those situations in which the worst thing that can happen is unacceptable. It is fairly easy to teach children the dangers of crossing the street—it is harder to teach them how to handle all possible abuse scenarios. Part of being a woman is knowing that the world can be a dangerous place for us and our children. I don't want my children to be afraid, but I want them to be better equipped than I was.

I'm in my early twenties, living in a communal house and working as a housekeeper at Vancouver General Hospital. I've been hired to fill in for sick or vacationing workers, so I work wherever and whenever I'm needed. The work is boring but not unpleasant, especially if the patients are conscious and talkative. In each room I dust the furniture, clean the sink, and empty the garbage. Then I dry mop and wash the floor. In the afternoons, I team up with another housekeeper to wash and change any vacant beds. The workload is based on the speed and stamina of women twenty years older than me, so I pace myself carefully. I don't want to finish all the work too soon and make the older workers look bad.

I'm glad when I am called in to work in Heather Pavilion. During breaks, the women include me easily into their conversations. Many of them plan to stay in this job until retirement. It surprises me when one of them says that she only has ten more years to go. Ten years seems like such a long time to spend in this kind of a job. They urge me to get out and do something else. One woman tells me that for years her husband has worked night shift and she has worked days so that one of them can always be home for their children.

Our male counterparts are called cleaners. They sit on the other side of the cafeteria. They are responsible for keeping the halls clean. Each of them has a wide dry mop which they push up and down the halls to pick up dust and debris, and a large rag mop which they then use to wash the hallway floor. No bending over and cleaning under the beds for them. No turning and washing mattresses either. And they get a dollar more an hour than we do. The housekeepers joke that it must be because their mops are bigger.

One of the cleaners in Heather Pavilion is a short, balding, middle-aged man with a heavy Italian accent. He has a peculiar way of walking with no bounce at all—he seems to glide along the hallway behind his mop. I chat with him when we meet in the hall. He is interested and asks me questions. One day he asks if I would like to meet him after work. I tell him that I'm busy, and tell myself that he is probably a lonely immigrant living in a single room in a boarding house who thinks that all North American women are available. But soon he is everywhere. When I bend over to empty the garbage pail he is in the doorway looking at my bum. When I leave the locker room after work he is waiting in the hallway. When I come around the corner he is there, grinning widely at me. What does he see in me—in my ugly pink uniform and heavy brown shoes? What am I doing to attract his attention? I no longer meet his eyes or talk to him, but he will not be put off. It never occurs to me that I should report this guy, or that I should stand up for myself and make some sort of a scene—I'm much too polite for that. Instead my working hours are spent worrying about where he might accost me next and if he will follow me home. I'm glad that I don't live alone. When the phone rings I pray that I will not be called to work in Heather Pavilion. Soon after, I leave the job to go travelling.

Ten years later I am at an anniversary party in a rented hall. The guests of honour are a couple about my age, John and Kathy. David works with John and I've met Kathy a few times before. Kathy's parents are waltzing gracefully together. Something about the way her father moves tugs at my memory. As I study him, a picture of a man smoothly pushing a mop comes into my head. My stomach tightens. A feeling of dread washes over me. This is the "lonely immigrant" from the hospital. I see him again in his cleaner's uniform, leaning on his mop and leering. After a long day of washing floors and harrassing me, he enters his suburban home, and gives his daughter Kathy a hug.

I wish I had not been so naïve, that I had spoken up and complained about this man. That I hadn't allowed him to make me afraid, to make me feel powerless. But at the time all this remained vague and unarticulated. It was part of a bigger issue that I wasn't ready to face. I didn't want to think about how, as a woman, I was denied the right to feel safe at work and in my neighbourhood.

This unexamined outlook worked for me until my daughter Robin started kindergarten. The school was only three blocks from our house, so my neighbour and I arranged for our two girls to walk there and back together. For the first few weeks one or the other mother walked with them so they learned the route and felt confident. Then they were on their own. For several more weeks everything went along fine, but then Robin started phoning me from school asking me to come and get her. It turned out that the teacher had given them a talk about the danger of encountering strangers. Now Robin was afraid of every car or person that went by. I didn't know what to do. I wanted Robin to be careful out there, but I didn't want her to live in fear, and I didn't want to have to walk her to and from school for the rest of her life.

After thinking about it for a few days I realized that the teacher had not given her any tools for handling the situation. She had pointed out an important danger, but had left Robin feeling that at any moment anyone could grab her off the street. Avoidance was the only option offered, and I didn't see how my daughter could avoid walking down the street. She needed some tactics to use if the need arose, and she needed to feel she had some control. So I told her that usually when a child gets kidnapped someone tries to get that child to go somewhere with them, and if anyone asked her to go anywhere with them she should stand up tall and say, No, I have to go home now, in a loud voice. Then she should walk straight home or to the closest neighbour she knows. I showed her all the safe houses on her route between school and home. Almost at once, Robin regained her confidence and was able to walk to and from school without fear. It took me a lot longer to listen to my own advice.

At about the same time that Robin starts kindergarten, I get a job working evenings at an office downtown. My sister, who is the office manager there, got me the job. I enjoy the peace and solitude of the empty office and working independently with no interruptions, no emotional crises. Compared to raising children, this is a breeze.

When I get to the office about five p.m., people are just beginning to leave. By about seven even the last stragglers have gone, and I work alone except for the cleaning staff who come in around nine. Using a computer is still a novelty to me and I relish the chance to sharpen my skills.

At ten or eleven I decide I've had enough. I backup my work and shut down the machine. Locking the door behind me, I leave the office and take the elevator down to the main floor. From here things get a bit scary. I have only to cross the street to wait for my bus, and there are usually quite a few people out and about. But I still need to give myself a pep talk to avoid my fear. The bus takes me within a few blocks of my house which is in a residential neighbourhood on the east side of town. Getting off the bus, my stomach tightens, as I walk quickly, sometimes running, avoiding tall hedges by moving to the middle of the street. I turn into my own yard, hurry up the front steps and in the door. Safe. I don't tell David about my fear. I don't want to ask him to meet me at the bus stop because I am supposed to be a strong, independent woman. It will take me a long time to figure out that I don't have to feel afraid. That I can stand up tall and say No in a loud voice.

Ten years later, I am working the night shift again, teaching an evening computer course in a highrise office tower downtown. The adults in my class have little or no computer experience. I love the work, especially the feeling that I am in control of what happens in my classroom. I am responsible for making sure the atmosphere is helping my students to learn.

But when I leave the classroom to make my way home it's dark and there aren't a lot of people around. I must pay attention, stand tall and walk confidently through the streets to my car. I am alert, but not afraid. I have chosen an open, well-lit parking spot and after getting into the car I lock the door behind me. I must watch out for one particular thing, and this thing is a man, not a monster. And I know that I am much more likely to be assaulted by someone I know than by a stranger on the street. Being aware is better than feeling afraid and powerless.

It isn't fair that women and children are not safe, that we aren't free to walk or play in the streets at night. And it is true that men are usually the perpetrators of crimes against women and children. This is one of the reasons why parenting is such an important job. It is not only our girl children who need to be shown how to be confident and respectful of themselves and others—our boy children need this too. Lately I see that some men are starting to realize that violence against women and children is not a "women's" issue, it is a societal issue. Once we all start to deal with it, maybe things will change. But in the meantime I don't want to feel afraid and powerless, and I don't want my kids to either.

The first time one of my kids went on a week-long school trip it scared me to think of her all that distance away, staying with a family we didn't know—and I couldn't be there to check out the situation for her. I would have to rely on her to call us if anything went wrong. Then I realized that I had already been preparing her for this for a few years by encouraging her to listen to and trust her own feelings and to take responsibility for herself. If you don't like feeling cold, get your coat on. If you don't like being late for school, get up earlier. If you don't like the way someone is talking to you or touching you, tell them, and then tell someone else. If anything feels weird or uncomfortable about the family you are staying with, call home. Trust yourself and take responsibility.

Eighteen years have passed since I first took on this job as mother, and feminism has changed attitudes as well as laws. But there is much left to do. In my closet I keep a box of fifteen-year-old *Ms.* magazines and reading them is *not* like taking a trip back in time—the issues raised in 1980 are still issues today. While some of the obvious injustices have been righted, there is still a lot of subtle and not-so-subtle sexism around. It is tempting to expect my children to grow up to be activists, even though I never was. But I learned early on that you can't make children (or anyone) do anything. They will have to decide which battles they will fight. The most I can do is help them to see and analyze what's really going on.

My fourteen-year-old daughter has a wide circle of friends, all nice kids, from differing economic and ethnic backgrounds. One evening she comments on how mean many of her friends are to their mothers. This is new information to me, and we talk about why this might be, where they might have learned this behaviour. Perhaps, like me, they picked it up from their fathers. I remember how we treated my mother and I see how a pattern can repeat itself. Both my daughters babysit for the young family next door—a nice couple with four small children. But the father has *Playboy* pinups on the walls of his downstairs office and a *Playboy* screensaver greets me when I go over to borrow a computer manual. My daughters and I shake our heads and wonder how his ordinary, non-airbrushed wife fits into his thinking, and what message his young children are learning.

In school, classes are still sometimes divided along gender lines, pitting boys against girls. Male and female are called *opposite* sexes. Recently, a student teacher managed to change my daughter's co-ed gym class from the supportive and co-operative group it was under its regular teacher into a hostile place where the girls felt defeated before they even tried to learn a skill. Once I have overcome my anger toward this teacher, I may even be grateful to him for teaching my daughter the destructiveness of sexist attitudes. I know women are never going to change the world without the co-operation of men. So my kids and I talk about other, better ways to divide into groups. And about how the sexes are not opposite, just different in some ways. About how important group dynamics are to the comfort of its members. We try to decide if a certain teacher is singling out my daughter or if he treats all the girls badly.

And then of course there is the media. I don't believe in censorship, but when it's my money, I get to say what we watch. We have never had cable and in recent years we have put our television away in a closet, but my kids still see their share of corporate America's idea of reality. But at least TV has let women come out of the kitchen. Mainstream movies are much worse. My son and I spend a long time at the video store before he can come up with a movie that I will rent. Even eliminating the violent ones, it's hard to please me. I used to get angry, but sometimes you just have to laugh. Gee, this movie is just like real life—there are no women in it, or Oh goody, it's the old maiden in distress story. Even Roger Rabbit's cartoon girlfriend doesn't get to wear anything that fits her!

And *Seventeen* magazine is still around. My girls bring home an issue from time to time. It's good to see that these kinds of magazines are at least talking about anorexia and date rape, but their models still look like

295

underfed waifs and the focus is still on getting your man. And all those beauty makeovers and fancy ads are still telling us that the way to true happiness is through physical perfection—and disinfection. So we talk about these things, and we laugh about them too, reading the most ridiculous parts aloud to each other. And when we read or hear about famous men—artists, composers, writers, politicians—it is interesting to speculate about who was cleaning up after them and looking after their children, allowing them to have all the time they needed for their work.

I can see that my work as a parent is nearly done. Like most women I have gathered a lot of other jobs along the way, and now that my kids need me less and less, I am able to concentrate more on my own learning and growing.

My son is in Grade Four, and I have gone with his class on an overnight field trip to a Native longhouse. The class is divided into what are called family groups—five or six children and one adult. There are five small fires inside the longhouse and each family cooks their food over their own fire. At night we sleep in our sleeping bags on the wide shelf that stretches along each wall. During the day members of the local Indian band teach us about traditional food gathering: hunting and fishing, gathering wild food and medicines, weaving cedar bark. One of the elders from the band leads us in traditional ceremonies. On first sight she is a short, round woman wearing a faded turtleneck and an old pair of pants. But there is something about her that commands respect. She doesn't say much—she doesn't have to. When she walks into the longhouse we all quiet down and turn towards her. Just by clearing her throat she can get the attention of even the squirmiest child. I am fascinated by this woman who takes herself so seriously. She knows who she is and quietly takes up the space she is entitled to.

While I admired this elder from a distance, when I spoke with her, I turned into a bumbling schoolgirl. My self-confidence slipped as I automatically assumed the inferior role. Our trip to the longhouse lasted only two days, but I can still see that woman standing in the centre of the silent longhouse, taking all the time she needed before she began to speak. She was so centred on the task at hand, not distracted by all the peripheral things we women are trained to worry about. Does my hair look okay? Do these pants make me look fat? Is it okay to stand here? Can the people behind me see? Is it my turn to speak? Is what I'm saying important enough? Am I taking up too much time? And, of course, the big one: Does everybody like me?

These are things that didn't worry me much when my main job was raising children, but as I spend more time in the world of men and power I see how these distractions hold me back. When three of us, all mothers, meet with the school superintendent, a man who makes over $100,000 a year, wears well-tailored suits and sits at his expansive desk in his immaculate office, we explain our concerns at length. The superintendent listens but says little. Unsure of what his silence means, we explain things all over again from another angle, and in so doing we weaken our position. But by now our time is up, the meeting is over. He rises, thanks us for coming, and shakes hands with each of us. Another successful meeting: these women will feel they have had their say, and he has not had to commit himself to anything. A few days after the meeting the three of us talk about what happened and didn't happen, and about how to do it better next time. We chairmoms know that change will only come through perseverence.

The job of parent was the hardest work I'll ever do, and the pay was lousy too. I was often frustrated and exhausted, and sometimes the kids just drove me crazy. There was no sense of There, that's done, I can send that job out now. I was brought up to believe that the only useful, meaningful jobs were the ones that produced something tangible or that got results. But when I gave childraising the time and respect that I would give a "real" job, I realized that I'd been fooled. Childraising is important and meaningful—but we have to wait a long time to see the results of our efforts. In fact, childraising is always a work in progress. It is like creating art, like writing a book. Progress is not always straight ahead, and at a certain point the piece takes on a life of its own and takes the artist or writer to unexpected places.

When I started out on my crash course in motherhood I was naïve and unformed. Mine was an unexamined life and I was only beginning to see that it was up to me to make sense of things—that it wasn't enough to just follow instructions. In my day-to-day life with my kids I needed a philosophy that would keep me in touch with myself, that would bring some harmony to our home and help me raise responsible caring people. I never suspected that feminism would hold the key to a cohesive and harmonizing view of the world. I hope that this ever-evolving philosophy we call feminism will continue to guide my children and myself. And I'll be keeping one eye on my children as they follow their own paths because I want to see where they will lead me next.

Mindful Liberation

Val Paape

My feminist education began in the womb. According to family history, upon hearing that my mother was pregnant, my father proclaimed that he was going to have a baby and that it would be a red-headed girl named Valerie. Nine months later there I was—red-headed and female, a wanted baby, destined to be a well-loved child. My parents created an atmosphere that fostered my sense of being a worthwhile, competent person. My mother was generous with her love and good humour. My father encouraged me to do anything I wanted regardless of whether it was considered appropriate for girls. I believe his attitude—quite remarkable for the late forties and early fifties—came from his relative maturity (he was forty when I was born) and his sincere desire for a child. He also had tremendous respect for his own mother and sisters who had often, he maintained, saved their poor, immigrant family from hunger and cold while the father drank. From an early age, my father saw women as stronger-willed than men and better able to stand up to hardship and responsibility. His fervent desire for me was that I would be competent, responsible and above all, self-reliant. I can still hear him saying: "Valerie, you must be self-reliant."

From an early age, my life was partly constrained by the battle between the rigors of self-reliance and the demands of post-war femininity. Going to school in the fifties meant being subjected to the dress and behaviour codes and the attitudes that were being fostered to keep women in the home. This was the Marilyn Monroe era; Rosie the Riveter was dead. My first conscious experiences of being at odds with society's gender regulations concerned comfort and clothing, and my first feminist acts were rebellion in this sphere. If my comfort or freedom to move was constrained by clothing, I complained and often got a change. However, the truce was uneasy. At home, my preferences held sway but public appearance was a source of argument. My mother was more likely to bow to peer pressure and insist on my propriety while my father was more inclined to "let the kid wear what she wants." This split naturally created some doubt and, as I got older and peer pressure increased, I sacrificed more of my own comfort and desire to conform with social norms.

As a teenager, the problem escalated. I remember being sweaty and itchy in a crinoline one hot spring day and unable to concentrate on what was going on in class. It dawned on me how insane this was, how the boys did not have to subject themselves so, and I vowed never to wear anything so ridiculous again in my life. I did, of course, but rarely, and never again after age twenty-five; by that time the seventies were upon us and I had emerged from a progressive university with a post-graduate degree. Growing self-confidence merged with slightly more liberal times and I felt able, once again, to do as I chose.

As a girl, I often behaved as if there were a real choice about adopting feminine habits. I wasn't consciously aware of sexism but simply saw my own wishes and comforts as worthy. Years later I was indignant when I realized that there was a serious discrepancy between how I viewed myself and how society viewed me as a female. It never occurred to me that they were right and I was wrong. I never felt confused, just angry. I have done what I wanted, acting as though stereotypes and restrictions—which do indeed exist—do not apply to me.

The roots of my feminism thus lie in my revolt from gender stereotyping with its inequalities, abuses, and power imbalances between men and women. This aligns me more with the radical and liberal feminists of the early seventies than with today's "feminine feminism" which praises "women's ways of knowing" and "feminine values," and is accepting of biological determinism for desirable capabilities such as nurturing. I would also align myself with postmodern feminism to the extent that it critiques gender and the power imbalances it produces. The outer garment of my feminism comes from my life-long revolt against gender stereotyping. Underneath lie the interwoven threads of my philosophical and spiritual quest, spun from my continuous asking of the age-old questions, "Who am I?" and "What is the meaning of life?"

For a time, as a graduate student in the biological sciences, I devoted a couple of hours every Sunday morning to reading philosophy. From this grew a personal belief system based in existentialism which did not violate the rational, scientific view of the world I was adopting. I was not concerned with feminism. Although this was the late sixties, the department I was in was very egalitarian. The male-female ratio of students was about fifty-fifty and there was an atmosphere of camaraderie as we enthusiastically applied ourselves to ecological study and research, and rode the first wave of widespread environmentalism.

I was enthralled by nature. She was beautiful, good, perfect. Nature could do no wrong, not even in death. My love of her led me to spend increasing periods of time travelling into the wilderness, primarily by backpack and canoe. My various trips, taken almost exclusively with other women, would last up to two weeks and instilled a sense of physical strength and competence that I did not know I possessed. Wilderness canoeing, with the challenge of rough water and difficult portages in remote areas, is one of the most invigorating, self-affirming activities I have ever experienced. My own experience of strength enabled me to reject stereotypes of women as weak and fearful. I began to get a deeper sense of who I was: a strong person, capable of solving problems and coping with difficult circumstances. I also felt myself being lifted out of the rigidity and spiritual poverty of my highly rational view into a life with a mystical dimension. I began to have an abiding sense of being integral to the rhythms and mysteries of life; I experienced the power of my being to deal with nature's challenges and the ground of my being as inseparable from the source of her power. Wilderness travel, with its emphasis on getting from A to B, safely taught me to live in the present moment. Everything else is irrelevant once the universe shrinks to encompass only your exact position on the map and what is happening at the moment. Buddhists have a name for this quality of mind: mindfulness. They say that it is through mindfulness that we see the truth of existence and, thereby, come to know who we are.

Co-incident with my wilderness travel, in my early thirties, feminism was becoming an important lens for filtering and interpreting my experiences, and my attention was naturally drawn to feminists interested in spiritual matters. In my late thirties, I began practicing and teaching hatha yoga in the Iyengar method. Three distinct strands—yoga, feminism, and spirituality—became interwoven in my quest for identity and meaning. Through yoga I began to understand the body-mind connection and its importance for spiritual development. My readings in feminism and spirituality revealed two important schools—the feminist theologians and the spiritual feminists—and I began to incorporate many of their ideas into my philosophy for living and teaching.

The feminist theologians are primarily academic women, sometimes also clergy, who critique religious traditions for sexism and whose *raison d'etre* is reformation. Rosemary Radford Ruether is an excellent example. I was profoundly influenced by her insightful and devastating analysis of women in Judeo-Christian belief systems and came to understand from her and other feminist theologians how the religious and secular oppression of women converge in the denigration of the female body. I realized how incredibly fortunate I was to have developed such a positive relationship with my own strong and capable body, and to have experienced the immanence of spirit within my own flesh. By contrast, the spiritual feminists—women like Starhawk—seek to create an authentic female spirituality by weaving together various elements of feminism, paganism, and meditation practices adapted from the major religions. I attended a Starhawk workshop in 1987 and subsequently used some of her ritual elements to enrich and enliven my own workshops on yoga and feminist spirituality. I think there is tremendous value in the way paganism and Goddess worship celebrate female life and create a ritualized process for healing from the wounds of sexism. But I have not found that it is capable of taking me beyond conventional reality in the search for the ultimate nature of the self. In her book, *Diving Deep and Surfacing: Women Writers on Spiritual Quest*, Carol P. Christ provided an analysis of the spiritual journey that enabled me to integrate my experience, my own quest, and my teaching. Her conclusion—that a man's spiritual quest involves the giving over of power and embracing humility while a woman's quest involves coming to power and shedding false humility—gave me a western context for the spiritual significance of enabling women to feel grounded and empowered.

For a long time, the main way I expressed my feminism was to challenge negative stereotypes about women's bodies in order to prove them wrong. By developing my own physical strength, co-ordination, skill, and courage, I had learned that weakness, vulnerability, and fear were not defining attributes of women. As a yoga teacher, I encouraged other women to explore the source of their own courage and physical strength, and in this way—learning and teaching—I came to see the great importance of the mind and body working together. Yet I did not have the full story.

Two years ago, I found myself incapacitated with chronic knee, hip, and back pain resulting from an accumulation of old sports injuries and associated surgeries. Since I could not participate in the activities that had been central to my identity, my carefully constructed self-image began to disintegrate. I finally gave in to the pain and quit teaching, leaving myself without an income. Medical intervention made the pain worse. My therapeutic yoga practice reduced the discomfort but did not heal me. I had thought my "cure" was in my hands; that if I did all the "right" things the pain would go away and I would be able to carry on as before, proving that weakness, vulnerability, and fear had nothing to do with me. As it is turning out, this just isn't true.

After a year of chiropractic treatments and carefully moderated activity, I did begin to improve. Then, as I was having thoughts of returning to teaching on a part-time basis, I found a lump in my left breast. My greatest fear was confirmed—I had breast cancer. Over the course of two months, I moved through the various stages of diagnosis and surgery, with fear and vulnerability as my constant companions. This journey culminated with a mastectomy and the news that two of my lymph nodes bore the cancer. This was the worst news I've ever had in my life. While I had begun to accept and accommodate a body that was plagued by chronic muscular and skeletal problems, I was not—am not—prepared at the age of fifty-one to be entering the final few years of my life.

I am no longer self-reliant. I depend on my partner to support me financially, emotionally, and physically. I am learning to live with uncertainty, vulnerability, and a range of intense emotions such as anger, resentment, sadness, and fear. But when important decisions loom, like whether or not to undergo chemotherapy, I find that I am not helpless. In fact, I did extensive research and on the basis of that chose a course of unconventional therapies. I asked for support from my partner and my friends. I intensified my meditation practice and established an e-mail relationship with a meditation teacher far from my home. Whatever equanimity and balance I have experienced since the discovery of my cancer, I owe to these things. I believe that my experiences of physical strength and competence have contributed greatly to an inner strength that I am relying on now to meet the challenges that life is offering me. That strength also fosters an optimism and a belief in myself to heal.

My meditation practices are crucial to my well-being, my ability to cope with life's current challenges, and central to my spiritual quest. Through yoga, with its exploration of the mind-body relationship, I began to see how the mind generates inner chaos. So, a few years ago, I began a search for a meditation practice that would help me quiet my mind and further my search for meaning. Until recently, however, I hadn't realized that the ultimate purpose of meditation is to liberate us from our self-images and enable us to learn to love ourselves unconditionally. Self-esteem, insofar as it is built on abilities, accomplishments, and our roles in life, only gets in the way of self-love. When my physical abilities changed, my role as a teacher changed, and I was forced to withdraw from the world of accomplishment. I no longer knew who I was. Even worse, I hated the state I was in and longed for the impossible—my past. I was forced to confront who I was in the absence of all the things that had created my self-image. Without a meditation practice to guide me, I don't know how I would have gotten off the road of despair, frustration, fear, and self-judgment that I found myself on at that time.

I follow two specific meditation practices: Metta, or loving-kindness, and Vipassana, or Insight meditation, both from the Buddhist tradition. Buddhist philosophy is clear and relevant, and the practices, elegant in their simplicity, do not require taking on or understanding Asian cultural trappings. Loving-kindness meditation develops unconditional love for the self and others. Insight meditation is so named because its purpose is to gain insight into the nature of life and one's self and to develop wisdom from that insight. It is a meditation that uses the content of our current experience to develop mental control and self-knowledge, and to cultivate equanimity. The basic tool of Insight is mindfulness. When we are mindful, our awareness is focussed on the content of our experience as it is in the present moment without judgment or criticism. Once mindfulness is well established, we can see into the workings of the mind, the changeable nature of each passing moment, the dissatisfaction and suffering that we so often experience, and the fact that the essence of the self is not constructed from our thoughts, feelings, or sensory perceptions. The essence of the self is found in pure awareness which can be experienced through mindfulness.

In Buddhism I have found spiritual experience that goes beyond feminist concerns without negating those concerns or minimizing their importance. Buddhist practice enables a dialectic with feminism that is fruitful for both my spiritual development and my continually evolving feminism. This dialectic gives me two lenses through which to view reality. Though their origins are vastly different, feminism and Buddhism have two fundamental things in common: they both view conventional reality as concealing important truths and they both recognize that we are highly conditioned beings. Whereas feminism alerts us to the socially constructed nature of gender and its concealment of woman's potential, Buddhism unmasks our conditioned belief that there can be permanent satisfaction and happiness in materialistic endeavour. Both question the nature of the self. Unfortunately, feminism has never been able to articulate a satisfactory theory about the nature of the self. While feminism continues to serve me well as a tool for critiquing conventional reality, Buddhism has become the vehicle for me to explore the unconventional, unconditioned, ungendered nature of the self.

Nothing is permanent; the future is uncertain, and at some point in everyone's life, something comes to light to challenge the psychological and/or spiritual status quo. For many women, the challenge of a history of sexual abuse, the experience of motherhood, a drop in economic status or, like myself, confrontation with a life-threatening illness, may precipitate such a crisis. In all of these cases, the previously constructed self is besieged and one must either construct another one or investigate the possibilities of a more free-flowing, unconstructed nature of the self.

We can move into a more free-flowing way of being by relating directly to each moment as it is without judgment or the desire to have the conditions of that moment be any other way than they are. When we are in pain, physical or emotional, our typical response is to want not to be in that state. This can motivate us to do things that may improve our situation, but it can also increase our suffering. Not wanting to be in pain can turn into mental anguish that intensifies our fears and anxieties, especially when the situation is not likely to change in the immediate future.

I see clearly how I intensify my pain, fears, and anxieties every time I become angry about my situation and want it to be different. The desire to be able to do things as I used to do them and fantasies of a different future-self undermine my patience and commitment to the very things that have some chance of improving my situation. I have learned that self-love and compassion is impossible whenever we want to be experiencing something different from what is happening right now.

I do not find knowing this easy. It is not possible to say: "Okay, I'm not going to be angry, anxious, fearful or depressed." Feminists have long understood that repressing emotions doesn't work. But endlessly processing and feeding emotions by acting on them (many feminists believe that anger and rage are essential to action) doesn't work either. Buddhism offers another possibility—to let go. The emotions themselves are not the problem. The problem is allowing myself to be drawn into, and embellishing, my emotions, which removes me from my actual experience. Letting go of this stuff is a daily process. It is likely that I will never be rid of the disaster fantasies and blame scenarios, but I can learn to recognize them earlier, see them for what they are, and let go. Mindfulness helps.

In my experience, mindfulness brings quiet, calm, and contentment. It promotes a sense of being grounded in the process of living no matter how difficult the circumstances. This enables unconditional self-love and compassion to unfold and be nourished. Self-esteem that is dependent on specific skills and abilities pales in comparison. I no longer think of self-esteem as being limited by the constraints of conventional reality. Spiritual liberation allows for a self-reliance that transcends all other conditions. One could be totally dependent physically and economically and still be self-reliant in one's own mind and being. In this sense, self-reliance has brought me happiness and peace beyond my father's wildest imaginations.

It occurs to me that feminism's old handle—women's liberation—is a wonderful term. Liberation can occur on many different levels and different people are drawn to or have deeper needs for freedom in various aspects of their lives. Today's disputes about feminism may have something to do with our inability to recognize that different women need to be liberated in different ways. There are groups of feminists whose emphasis is on healing and groups whose emphasis is on equity, which represent alternative perspectives on personal liberation.

Two things are clear to me: liberation occurs in the mind, and is an evolutionary process—as we become free in one area of our lives, we become aware of the need for freedom in another. As my life continues to change and my spiritual practice deepens, my feminism continues to evolve. My greatest hope is that this is an evolution into wisdom, which comes from seeing reality without desire, judgment, criticism, or delusion. It is observation without the limiting constraints of attitude, belief or opinion. Just as we must lose the self to find the self, feminism—as a tool for investigating reality—must likewise be free even of itself.

To Be True
to a Warbler

Jerilynn Prior

I was too young to remember the little Washington towns and farms of Bow-Edison, Marysville, and Mt. Vernon where my father had worked during World War II. I learned later that we lived on those farms so Dad could milk cows because he refused to go to war. (Instead of receiving conscientious objector status, he was assigned to be a farm worker, which was considered an essential war service.) What I do remember is growing food, gathering berries, and never wasting anything. As Dad later moved from college to university to divinity school, where we didn't even have space for a garden, we continued to save and use everything. In Berkeley, I remember every Saturday having the task of mopping and waxing the stairs of our four-storey apartment building as we helped Dad with his janitorial job. To provide for us he cruised the Safeway bins to find cabbages with good insides, or bruised fruit; the school cafeteria cook saved the canned fruit juice and other leftovers for him (and us). Mom studied Greek on her own (to help Dad with his studies), got Greek characters for her typewriter, and typed students' theses to help out. Dad's learning was the most important thing in our family, and our daily chores were an important part of the family goal to get Dad through school so he could be a minister and work for God.

My parents created a secure world rich with imagination and respect. I knew of World War II and the Korean War only through what the other children said, or snatches of non-parental conversation. As a Grade

One student in Berkeley in 1950, I had no idea why the sirens screamed in my school, nor why we were made to hide under the desks—only that everyone was terrified. My folks didn't want me to know of, see, or feel the horrors of war. Instead they filled my brothers and me with positive stories (*Baba Yaga, Brighty of the Grand Canyon, Little Women*), and staged indoor picnics in front of the open fireplace in our two-room apartment. I have a vivid memory of standing around a wheezy portable organ, looking out on a chapel across the street with a luminous stained-glass Christ with upheld hands and singing the old hymn, *I feel the winds of God today, today my sail I lift.* Even though I knew we were poor, I always felt lucky and special and very much loved. I felt gifted because I could create a special occasion with only my imagination. I could tinker and make things work like my dad. I could study and read and excel with my mind like my mom. I was a special creature made by a loving God for some vague yet important purpose. And I always knew that there were others who had less.

How these threads gave me the drive to become a physician, I don't quite know, except that I have always felt some strong sense of stewardship to use what personal resources I had. I have known all my life that as a poor, rural woman I had to be *better*, my first task, no matter where I was, was always to be the best that I could be. What kept me going when I was very poor and hungry and alone was that I had a destiny to meet, a responsibility to be ready to perform some service that I would later understand. I would also have to guess that my feminism came first from identification with the poor and lonely and abused and later, from the perception that the world was constructed to give me fewer choices than the boys my age. These are certainly the sources of the confidence and determination that enabled me to apply nine times to medical school before being accepted (one of six women in a class of one hundred) to the University of Oregon in 1965, and to stubbornly work against the current and on the fringe of the medical establishment in the field of women's reproduction.

I didn't know at first I wanted to be a doctor. What I did know was that I wanted to help people. And I wanted to learn. The first people I had seen doing something I thought I'd like to do were the public health nurses who came to Larsen Bay. They were stout and straightforward and accepting. Some had been seasick for days on the medical ship, *Hygiene*, before they arrived.

At seventeen I won a National Health Foundation nursing scholarship and decided to start that programme at Linfield, the small Oregon liberal arts college from which my father had graduated when I was in kindergarten. It was a big change to go from a high school in a fishing town of 3,500 to this college, even though McMinnville, Oregon wasn't very big and Linfield had only about 1,200 students. Here were lots more people but I was alone in new ways; my roommate and I had nothing in common and I had to study in the furnace room to escape the incessant giggles and hallway escapades of the "California girls" who came to college to find husbands. The most difficult was feeling smothered by the dark oaks, without vistas or whipping winds, and being locked into the women's dormitory from ten at night until seven in the morning. I can still feel the anguish of a night that first fall when I couldn't find a window from which to see the full harvest moon. One day I ignored the threat of an alarmed dormitory door to sneak out into the fog for a long, dark walk in the wee hours of the morning.

Academic success was some consolation. I decided to try for medicine my first spring after scoring very high on a nursing entrance exam. I didn't want to give up on my liberal arts education but I thought I could set my sights higher. In those days, it was so rare for a woman to get into medicine that I felt I had to have a fallback plan. I began a second major in English (in addition to the pre-med requisite sciences) so I could go toward teaching if I didn't get into medical school.

In the spring after my third year, I got a job "manning" a lookout tower at the top of a mountain in the coast range. My knowledge of short-wave radio, weather, and being alone convinced them to let a "girl" do it. On the strength of that job reference, I was able to get a much better-paying job working for the U.S. Forest Service where I worked for two summers. Those lookout summers were times of renewal and peace, but it galled me that the Forest Service automatically gave a man a different title and twelve cents more an hour for doing the same job.

I thought that, once I got to medical school, I would be accepted. However, on my first day of medical school, standing over our cadaver, my lab partner, a man, turned to me brusquely to demand, "How did you get in? My buddy has a family to support and he didn't make it." I remember my heart racing and feeling that everything I had worked for hung in the balance. "I don't know," I said. "I guess I must have been *better*."

Although I had gotten into medical school, I wasn't at all sure I would get through. The lecture and memorization of facts required within a very hierarchical system was especially difficult for me. Every day I was faced with the reality that I viewed most "facts" differently than my male (and even most of my female) colleagues. For a long time I was puzzled, then vaguely peeved. But for a number of years now I have perceived my different way of thinking and my kind of stubborn commitment to this point of view as a gift rather than a disability.

I came to work on the science of women's reproduction not by some sober, single-sighted plan, but by a process that has felt meandering and unclear to me most of the way. I likewise evolved into a feminist early and in an equally instinctual way. Now, looking back, I can see that my quest to know the mysteries of how our reproductive bodies fit our lives, and my mission to enable us as women to become our best, are linked almost instinctually, and tied to who I am and how I have grown.

Let me start with how I got into studying women's reproduction. About the time I came to British Columbia in 1976, North America was in the midst of a fitness boom. Although I was by no means an expert in reproduction then, I was distressed by the proliferation of medical articles suggesting that women who were exercising heavily were destroying their reproductive potential. That message was not new. Women had been told for generations that their wombs would fall out and they would never bear children if they behaved in an "unwomanly" manner. Long before a language evolved to express it, women knew that their culture did not approve their learning their physical limits and achieving satisfaction for themselves in highly-tuned bodies. But this was the seventies. Women were taking up long-distance running and aerobics. A woman, Kay Switzer, had run, *and finished,* the twenty-six-mile Boston Marathon in 1969—a heroic achievement. She had finished the race not only because she had trained hard, but because her boyfriend had run interference with the marathon official who tried to remove her physically from the race. (She had used her initials to register for the famous marathon, not knowing that women weren't allowed to compete.) When I heard Switzer speak at a sports medicine conference in the early 1980s, I identified with her keenly, not simply because I had been in Boston at the time of her historic marathon, but because I too was pushing limits and threatened with eviction. Listening to Switzer almost fifteen years later, I had crested the age of forty with two children and a recent divorce to my account and was struggling to establish my credibility as a scientist in a medical establishment that remained decidedly sexist.

It's hard to describe what I feel when I perceive prejudice against women (or any disadvantaged people). Like Cadfael, the eleventh-century monk-detective-herbalist of the Ellis Peters mysteries, "my thumbs pricked" when I confronted the notion that exercise was bad for women. I was no athlete, but I liked to run and could pride myself on being physically strong. (It was part of my Alaska childhood that I had always tried, and often managed to hold my own with my older brother, whether carrying water, rowing boats, rolling oil barrels or climbing trees.) As both a scientist and a woman I sensed "foul play" in the way women were treated and discussed medically. It seemed that the cultural notion of how women *ought to be* was overriding the scientific biology. The way this limited women's potential made me angry and affronted my sense of legitimate science. I began to struggle to understand and to express the idea that a woman's hormonal system could adapt to exercise as easily as her muscles and heart, and that it was the same for men although less visible.

It wasn't easy to articulate what I knew intuitively—that there are two opposing views of women in relation to exercise. The traditional view—that physiological changes experienced by exercising women represent disease—dominates the medical world. By extension, this idea that women are betrayed by their bodies influences the way the larger world—including women themselves—view women. The alternative view—that women's bodies seek and adapt to achieve wellness within a complex social, cultural, and physical world—did not have even a vocabulary in 1980, let alone credibility. That lack of definition and credibility was paralleled by my personal situation. My first work on the adaptation model was accomplished when my part-time teaching position at University of British Columbia did not include an office, or even a desk of my own. My paper was tapped out at home on a portable Sears typewriter while I tried to get part-time daycare for my two-year-old. I wonder now at my audacity. It was driven by the strong instinct that women were being treated unjustly.

My new construct was a declaration of faith in the wonder of women's incredibly adaptive physiology and was the beginning of my attempt to separate cultural and social role-expectations from the so-called "truths" of science. It was also the onset of my feminist understanding that one can neither understand nor describe scientific data without context. Twenty years of fostering the precious intuition of "women's ways of knowing" and challenging dogmas have brought me to the firm conviction that what pass for scientific facts about women's reproduction are in reality cultural prejudices. It was once believed that hysteria in women was caused by the uterus flying up into the throat. Quaint as that may sound today, the view—unsubstantiated by science—that we are at the mercy of our reproductive organs has not much changed. What we "know" about women has been "proven" in cross-sectional studies. These inferior design studies divide subjects into two groups and contrast them at one point in time. By design, cross-sectional studies ignore the context and are strongly subject to bias in the choice of subjects. This type of study pretends that a single snapshot in time can explain a very complex physiology. This is the perfect way to (often unconsciously) confirm society's inferior view of women.

In contrast, participatory studies, which entail randomly selected women recording the dynamic social and situational ebb and flow of their lives and their reproductive changes over years, will eventually provide us with the kind of data that stands for scientific "truth." Although I naïvely expect women scientists to be different from the men who are most frequently involved in science, the disease model of women's health and physiology is adopted by women of science too and adhered to no less firmly.

In the mid-eighties, the letters PMS confronted us in virtually every magazine, each article relentlessly framing women's pre-menstrual symptoms as abnormal and thus, by extension, women as diseased. Again I felt offended. I wondered what part of the irritability associated with the days leading up to a woman's period reflected normal symptoms of hormonal changes, and to what extent our culture was granting women permission to be bitchy only before their flow.

At that point in my life, although I was trained in endocrinology, my schooling in women's reproduction was limited to a three-month gynaecology tutorial. I had been working out tools (such as a Menstrual Cycle Diary and a scientific way of using the old-fashioned basal temperature record) to study what was going on for women. Now I wanted to use them in a long-term, multi-layered "prospective" study, using non-invasive methods that would be tolerable for women, to prove that intensified exercise did not adversely effect the cycles of athletic women who had normal, ovulatory cycles. Almost immediately, I was faced with the situation of being a "no one from nowhere" woman researcher studying an uninteresting idea. At the same time, word quickly spread in the Vancouver running community that there was a woman doctor interested in studying women and exercise. Women were quite eager to learn about themselves, and hoped that they could continue to run and still remain healthy. They were curious, and surprisingly willing to keep records. When grant after grant was rejected, a friend volunteered to keep records for over a year as she trained for her first marathon. We finally managed to launch a poorly-funded pilot study, which ultimately showed, among other things, that the cheap, old-fashioned method of monitoring basal temperature was a valid scientific tool for documenting the ovulatory characteristics of women.

Many of us believe fundamentally that women are equal to men. Indeed, most of us who are successful in terms of the mainstream culture have been bolstered in our careers by this deeply-held belief. But the view that women and men are literally equal ignores the important factors of physiological difference and status within this culture. As a spill-over, perhaps, the equal-in-all-aspects view has led many of us as women to distance ourselves emotionally from our bodies, ignoring our menstrual cycles, controlling our fertility, and sometimes even requesting surgical removal of organs that trouble us, or interfere with our work. Maintaining this distance from our bodies takes considerable subconscious energy. After all, most of us do menstruate, may have emotional and physical symptoms before our periods, must live with breasts and the risk of getting pregnant, and eventually, through menopause.

It has been a reflex with me, as a woman and as scientist, to ask at every turn, "What does this mean?" What does it mean to say that what women experience is abnormal? What does it mean for science to say anything at all about what is *not* normal in women when science has not yet properly examined what *is* normal? How can we be in control of our own reproduction if we have no other authority than men (and women who have adopted the constructs of their male teachers) who know virtually nothing about these most female aspects of our lives?

I don't know exactly why I think this way, when so many others don't, but I like to relate the unconscious process that led me here to an experience I had the day my first period began.

I was then a rather headstrong, tomboyish girl of twelve living in Larsen Bay, a remote fishing village on Kodiak Island in Alaska. It was a world that was wilder than what we now call wilderness, and filled with big tides, long stormy winters, and gulls riding the updrafts over the bluff near our home. Until I was nine, my family had lived in rural north-western Washington, in western Oregon and then in Berkeley, California as my father finished school. By contrast, life in Larsen Bay, a predominantly Native village, was very difficult at first. It was a shocking transition for me to no longer be a poor kid in a rich kids' school at the bottom of the Berkeley hills. Now I was a different kind of outsider, thought well-off because I was white and struggling in a one-room school where there were few kids my age. We had traded a tiny city apartment for a low tarpaper shack with well-water down the bluff on the beach and a small generator for our rare electricity. I learned to play alone and watch my moves and quickly developed antennae to sense what others were feeling. I saw that there are many different kinds of people and many ways of getting on with life. I explored the brush behind the village, making secret hiding places under the big roots of fallen trees, and looking for Labrador tea in a bog. Sometimes we went berry picking or duck hunting or seal hunting with other villagers. I remember an elderly Aleut grandmother scolding me for picking sweet, soft tundra berries rather than the sour hard wild cranberry that was valued because it would keep (and, I now know, provide Vitamin C) during the isolated long winter. Anyone who had been successful in hunting or gathering always shared with the rest of the village.

The morning of my thirteenth birthday I had a peculiar, impending feeling. I went out and just sat in the outhouse. It was a lovely, unusually warm summer day and sun was streaming in over the top of the three-quarter door. At almost the same time as I realized I had started my period, a small yellow-green bird alighted on the door. I was so surprised at seeing this frail, brilliant migrating bird I felt like holding my breath so I wouldn't scare it away. In that barren and wild world of storms and gulls, it was a most beautiful and unexpected meeting. The little bird with which I communed on that important day, I later learned, was a Wilson's warbler. The bird came to mean to me the incredible beauty, resilience, and mystery of nature and was indelibly connected, for me, with my reproductive potential and being a woman.

The common theme through all of my education has been an internal necessity to integrate what I have analyzed and to put it into its social, ethnic, geographical or historical context. Where science is typically dedicated to dissecting things into smaller and smaller details, my instinct has always been to fit the small pieces into a congruent whole. Regardless of what I am taught, until I can put all the pieces together, I feel that

I know nothing. This integrative approach and need for context have given me courage to seek for truth that is congruent for me. I believe that this learning style, which was once so isolating, relates directly to my womanhood and feminism and that, long before I had words for it, or support in it, I was pursuing a pattern of thought and being that was feminist. This once subconscious, now very deliberate, feminism has been essential to the process of building my current work.

Despite that way of learning, and because life was so hard, I was oblivious to the women's rights movements of the sixties and seventies. It wasn't until 1986 that I began to want to understand what "feminist" meant historically and how it applied to me. I asked a woman sociologist colleague to give me a reading list so I could catch up on the history and personalities and ideas I had missed. If I had any doubts about my feminism, they vanished.

I had already clearly seen that facts don't stand alone, but are personal and important to someone. I also knew that very often facts about women are attached to agendas that are detrimental to women—not only to our sense of independence and achievement, but also to our health. I had come to accept (with very mixed feelings because it makes life hard for me) my different way of thinking as a gift that gave courage to see many things from a new perspective, including women's health. I had adopted a research style that aimed for scientifically valid designs that would be acceptable to the scientific world, but which were subversively women-centred and contained ideas and hypotheses never mentioned in funding applications.

All in all, I saw how my research could be called feminist because it is conducted *with*, rather than *on*, women. Each study since 1980 has been designed to focus on the individual woman, and structured to document subtle personal changes across time. It has also been conducted in an affirming way by teaching each woman volunteer to be a research assistant, providing her with social support and designating her a primary data-gatherer. When the study is over, both the individual and collective results are shared with the participants, without whom of course there would be no data.

My feminism, I could also see, was directly related to my religious beliefs. Although I was originally a Baptist (of the liberal stripe) like my parents, I came to be disillusioned with church bureaucracy and hypocrisy (which I saw related to the miniscule support for my parents, and as a national award winner and convention speaker when I was in high school). During the Vietnam War I was disgusted with the silence or complicity of the church. I married a man who, with my full support, turned in his draft card and was reclassified by his draft board as delinquent for military service. That was a dangerous time. FBI agents came to our walk-up fourth floor apartment on the edge of a black ghetto in Boston, our phones were tapped, and many who actively opposed the war were persecuted. Therefore, when we heard by word of mouth of a gathering in support of a deserter, we went. It turned out to be a silent Meeting for Worship at the Cambridge Friends Meeting-house (as Quaker church buildings are called). Very soon after we joined that Quaker group.

I realized that my sense of being unique and responsible was deeply congruent with the Quaker idea that each person contained "that of God" within. Within the Religious Society of Friends (as Quakers are properly known), silent worship allows each individual to commune with God within a community of spirit. The decision-making is collective, arising out of silent worship, and all people are valued for who they are and for being the best they can be. A number of aspects of the Society of Friends made me feel I had found a religious home. These include the Quaker peace testimony (which commonly leads Friends to largely unheralded sacrifice like imprisonment as conscientious objectors), their support for the disadvantaged, and the real as well as historical role for women as equals within the meeting.

In Boston as a medical student, I began my own witness against solving conflicts militarily. I refused to pay the ten percent telephone tax that was levied to support the Vietnam War. When I began to earn a salary I included a "war crimes deduction" on my tax form and donated that deducted amount (which initially was small as I earned only about $3,000 each year for my 120-hour work weeks) to charity. Only in the mid 1970s, as my income increased, did the IRS catch up with me. They pursued me into Canada, threatening to seize all my assets, but were unsuccessful because I had paid my Canadian taxes. However, after the Charter of Rights was enacted (and after divorcing my no-longer-driven-by-conscience husband) I began withholding the military portion of my Canadian taxes. Since then I have consistently witnessed against being forced to offend my conscience and pay for the military by putting the military portion of my Federal taxes into the Conscience Canada Peace Trust Account in Victoria, B.C. With their help and support from many others, Thomas Berger and I brought a Charter of Rights test case

through the courts beginning in 1986. We were never able to appropriately present our case because we were stuck with appealing a negative
tax court decision through the Federal Court and the Court of Appeal.
The Supreme Court twice refused to hear us. Our appeal to the United
Nations Human Rights Committee also ended unsuccessfully. Frustrated,
but clear about my conscience, I continue to withhold and have my
accounts seized, the only way I can be consistent with my beliefs.

I have had to use the same persistence in my academic goals. I was
able to obtain a full-time academic role at the University of British
Columbia only by writing a diplomatic and polite ultimatum—unless I
was given the recognition and a position that fit what I was doing, I
would stop. Since then, despite the difficulties of doing the clinical
research on women's reproduction that I believe I must do, I have been
able to work my way to a full professorship. What I am most known for
in the academic world is having shown that progesterone (the female
hormone that follows ovulation) and estrogen (the female hormone
made early in and throughout the menstrual cycle) are both necessary to
prevent bone loss in healthy young women. We subsequently have
shown that progesterone (given to mimic its place in the ovulatory
cycle) is good and acceptable bone therapy for young women with
mixed-up menstrual cycles or no flow. Because these are new ideas, and
medical science is very conservative, it will be many years before my
work is valued. But I am aware that, as financial resources for universities decrease and my younger colleagues do not even have an option for
academic positions, I am privileged to have this academic position from
which to work.

Which brings me back to what I feel I still need to do. It is easy to
believe that women-centred, physiologically accurate information about
what is "normal" in women exists in current medical literature, but is
ignored or not applied. But this is not true. We know very little about
the hormonal changes and variability of normal menstrual cycles, how
consistent ovulation is, and what changes occur during the transition
into the menopause. We also know very little from good randomized,
controlled studies, about the roles of estrogen and progesterone in
hormonal therapy of the menopause. The prospective studies that would
give us the needed information are difficult to structure and expensive to
fund; unlike molecular biology and studies of new drugs, they lack *science
appeal*. Ironically, there are lots of PMS studies by women experts who

clearly want to help women but which acknowledge neither physiological realities nor the inferior role of women in the culture. It is my firm belief that any accurate study of women's reproduction needs to document women's levels of outside stress, their mood, breast, and other experiences as well as their ovulation characteristics. Yet in my long search for feminist colleagues in the social sciences who are willing to work with me in understanding the complex integration of women's lives, I have so far been unsuccessful.

The bottom line is that it is not okay to think of womens' bodies as diseased because they are different from mens'. I continue to be guided by a relentless conviction that the key to empowering each of us, as women, lies in placing the authority and mystery of menstruation, pregnancy, and menopause with women. In order to do this, we need to start from the beginning and write and communicate to all women a new understanding of our reproduction that shows how intricate, adaptive, beautiful, and finely tuned to our lives it really is. When each of us as women is empowered with that knowledge—a blessing like that bestowed on me by the warbler—we will feel at home within our own bodies in a way that will give us strength to be our best in the rest of our lives.

North
to Feminism

Alison Reid

Feminism and northernness seeped into my bones together. They are inextricably entwined and together they shape my stance in the world.

I have lived in the Yukon since 1976. When I arrived at age twenty-three, I was ripe for a life different from the urban east. I couldn't have articulated what it was I wanted, but I knew it when I found it. North. Community. Sisterhood. Making changes inside and out. Solitude. Physical challenges. Darkness, light, darkness, in a steady dramatic rotation. Cold, colder, colder still, and then warm. Moon so bright on snow that I could ski and almost see clearly.

I grew up in an English suburb of Montréal and went to university in Waterloo, Ontario. My feminism then was immature, watery, largely unformulated, but founded on a deep-seated need to be independent and self-reliant, the origins of which I can only guess at. I was taking mathematics, and envisioned a future as an urban career woman.

One day, I spent a bus trip from Peterborough to Toronto beside someone who had just moved down from Yellowknife and who rhapsodized about living in the north. When I finished university, it seemed like a good time to find out for myself. I flipped a coin between Yellowknife and Whitehorse, and chance chose Whitehorse.

After six weeks of visiting friends on my way from Montréal to Vancouver, I had only four hours on a plane to make the riskiest leap of the trip, north to Whitehorse. I was alone and knew no one here. I expected it would be a tough year. This was both a self-test and freedom.

By foot, I wandered the downtown Whitehorse streets past funky little houses, strolled along the banks of the Yukon river, and gazed at the mountains all around. To my utter surprise, I immediately discovered that I liked this small town of 12,000. Avoiding half measures, I arrived in early November, straight into darkness and cold. Daylight diminished by an hour a week, and everyone I met was eager to share stories of forty-below-zero temperatures. The town seemed so accessible, and the people so accepting of me. By day four, I was thinking that I could stay here a long time. The feeling of belonging grew and grew, a perceptibly physical sensation.

A local department store hired me as a sales clerk. The stock we carried fascinated me: all kinds of bush equipment, from dog harness makings to kerosene lamps to traps, canvas and heavy duty camping equipment. An important part of my training was simply learning what all these things were. Later, some friends of mine recalled their introduction to me—I sold them a dog harness as lamp wick (or was it the other way around?—anyway, they swore it worked).

I worked with people who had lived a long time in the Yukon. They knew each others' parents and kids, and measured white people's credibility by how long they'd been here. There was tension between the old-time Yukoners and the lately-arrived "bush hippies." My sense then of the longtime non-native Yukoners was of conservative, somewhat racist and insulated people. In fact, they reminded me of the adults I grew up amongst in suburban Montréal, and whose lifestyle I had fled when I came north. My bush hippie friends, on the other hand, exuded a relaxed, accepting attitude to life, relationships and wage work that reminded me of my early days at university. Unlike my university friends, however, they were deeply involved in community organizations like Greenpeace Yukon, the Women's Centre, and local theatre groups. Many were building their own log cabins on squatter land, and lived without running water and electricity. It was a contrast to suburban Montréal that I found fascinating.

When I first arrived, it was a buoyant time for women activists in Whitehorse, because they had just recently started a successful Whitehorse municipal transit system. Years before they had identified transit as a need for women, had heard city council's indifference, and had gone about solving the problem themselves. Community and isolation seemed to breed a kind of dynamic problem-solving attitude which I found irresistible. Besides, anyone who hung around the Women's Centre quickly got swept into organizing activities, researching and writing briefs, laying out The OptiMSt (the Yukon women's quarterly newspaper), chairing meetings, and lobbying politicians.

The Women's Centre was full of women interested in other women, and who were canoeing rivers, building cabins, hauling water, making not much money, and organizing politically. They were strong Yukoners who expected to make changes. Many had a gut-level understanding of grass-roots feminism. There was a lot of rage and passion there, and often great safety for exploring personal stuff together. "The personal is political," we said to each other, and we believed it. I still believe it.

It was through the personal that I stepped into feminism. It was the era of consciousness-raising groups, when women were attempting to name our experiences and our feelings. In 1977, my first spring in the Yukon, I attended a women's retreat in a little town just south of Whitehorse. Women who began the weekend as strangers were able, even eager to talk about our sexuality; we moved from there into all elements of our lives. I'd never had such conversations with other women. I realized that friendships with women could have depth and breadth and potential, and that I needed them in my life. In the beginning, I hardly knew them. Well, I hardly knew myself either.

A group we came to call simply "the Thursday night group" formed, and continued for years. At the time, we all commented again and again about how deep we were going into ourselves, and how we'd never shared so much intimate detail of our lives with anyone before. The work I did in the group to peel away defences, to develop the words to name my feelings, and to value my growing knowledge of myself have all been of the utmost importance to me. And yet, for all of that, at least half of us left the group feeling hurt. The closest I can come to explaining why is to wonder if, in the end, we became too vulnerable to each other. The wounds and holes we opened up within the group were perhaps more than our skills and resources and wisdom could acknowledge, much less heal.

During this difficult time I never thought to reject feminism as a whole. I did withdraw from group work for a time (and have not been involved in a self-support group since), but in a sense I also took ownership of feminism. I recognized feminism as an evolving organic movement: dynamic, sometimes chaotic, explosive, and risky. My belief that I am part of the process that is feminism, that my insights and experiences feed it, as do those of all other women similarly involved began then. The way I plug into it ebbs and flows between organized activism and inward contemplation.

My sense of ownership of feminism is part-and-parcel of my sense of ownership of much of the political and social decision-making here in the north. The Yukon's population is so small (about 30,000 people), yet our territorial government and organizations have the authority and responsibilities parallel those of provinces one hundred times as populated. I have a strong sense of actually being able to make a difference here, and there are all kinds of opportunities to get involved should I choose to. A mundane example of the difference individuals can make is in the territorial elections—it is not uncommon for members of the legislative assembly to win by a handful of votes. I remember one election in which only five votes separated the top three candidates; it is more than just a cliché here that "every vote counts."

In 1986, I burned out on feminist organizing. Working for the new Yukon Human Rights Legislation became a nightmare. At public meetings, in the newspapers and on the radio, there were horrible things said about the proposed protection of gay Yukoners. It tainted my love for the Yukon and blew holes in my sense of safe community. I felt paralyzed in my role as coordinator of the Yukon Status of Women Council, and deeply ashamed of my lack of outspoken support for lesbian friends.

I retreated from active feminist politics for a while. My activism centred around my involvement with the collective that produces *The OptiMSt*. In 1994, it celebrated its twentieth year of continuous publication. We have always aimed to be a voice for Yukon women, and we struggle, with varying degrees of success, to be inclusive of all Yukon women. For me, it has its own very special sense of community, both within the group who produce it and within the greater Yukon community. With every issue my commitment to valuing women's voices and experiences is renewed. I don't agree with everything women write, and sometimes I wince at their views, but I learn from them. The grass-roots sense of feminism I first learned when I arrived here carries on.

Over the past few years, my contribution to the Yukon women's movement had been to provide volunteer bookkeeping services to a number of feminist organizations. However, I recently realized that I hate bookkeeping (like housework, it's never done) and there are others who can take it on. Now that I have passed on those responsibilities, I feel as if I have the space to do other, perhaps more creative things both within and outside of women's organizations.

One group that is new and still evolving is that of "the Crones" of the Women's Centre. Four of us who have long histories in the women's community here (we range in age from thirty-five to sixty years old) attend Women's Centre meetings as advisors. We have no ongoing responsibility, but we attempt to provide some history and support to the women who are currently active and to prevent a few wheels from being reinvented.

Land has a potent lure in the Yukon. In 1978, after I came back from three months in Hawaii, I was determined to own some, to establish roots that way. I took a plane to Vancouver, a ferry to Skagway, Alaska, then the last hundred miles on the White Pass Railway. What a great train trip home, over the snow-covered mountains on the first day of spring, spending the whole trip on the back "porch" of the train, feasting on the landscape, knowing home when I felt it. As it turned out my timing was excellent. The territorial government opened up a subdivision of two-acre lots, and my partner and I got our first choice.

My next challenge was housebuilding. I knew lots of women who'd built their own cabins, or who had actively worked on their own houses. And I knew how to start a chain saw and cut up firewood. Max had about the same amount of experience. As I write this, I'm sitting in the house we built, and am still amazed that we did it. We were twenty-six, poor (well, just rich enough for the $600 deposit on our lot), ignorant of virtually everything to do with house construction, and fortunately with plenty of experienced friends. Interest rates of ten percent at the time horrified us, as did being in debt, so we resolved to build cheaply and as we could afford. That meant no electricity for six years and no running water for five more after that. It was inconvenient, hard work, and cold going to the outhouse at forty below, but I treasured the evidence that I had truly escaped suburban Montréal.

Feminism at that time in my life meant fifty-fifty, that I could do everything Max could and as much. It meant mixing as much cement by hand, digging as much gravel from a nearby pit, cutting as many of the huge trees we needed for our corner posts, rolling as many of them through the woods to the logging road where our friend's wood truck awaited. It meant peeling the bark off as many logs, chainsaw shaping as many, and lifting my end of them all.

We spent two-thirds of our time figuring out the next step, and I felt chagrined every time Max had a better idea than I did. There was a certain defiant competitive edge fed by exhaustion, fear (of chain saws, falling trees, heights, failure, and being broke), personal pride, and exhilaration. I still really like this house and am proud of it, although I've never been tempted to build another one.

When I was twenty-eight and had lived in the Yukon for five years, I began to feel less and less enthusiastic about short-term jobs. I realized that to stay in the Yukon with a chance of decent work, I'd need more training. Accounting looked like it could offer a variety of potential opportunities, including self-employment, although I'd forgotten how much I loathed writing exams. I still work as an accountant, two days a week, for the first company that ever employed me as an accounting student. I find the fact that things have to balance soothing, and I like the solitary aspect of the work. And it pays well.

I had put off deciding whether I wanted a child until all my accounting courses were finished. When they were done in 1985, the issue came to the fore. I was thirty-two, and the clichéd biological clock was ticking. The decision-making process was mostly solitary. Arriving at my decision, all I could articulate even to myself was, "If I don't have a child, I'll miss learning things I could never learn elsewhere." In the end both Max and I decided that we would like to have one child. We agreed that we would both work part-time and share the child-rearing responsibilities. It's been a satisfying arrangement for all three of us, and it continues to this day.

Robin was born in 1989. I admit that I really wanted a girl. Labouring to birth her was an incredibly heroic act that was both my experience alone, and one I shared with billions of other women. Pure individual within community.

I was absolutely right—I am learning things with Robin that I would never have learned otherwise. She challenges me physically (the exhaustion from lack of sleep, the games of tag at any given moment), and she challenges my feminism in a way that no one else could, because for her I am trying to be a role model and live all kinds of aspects of my philosophy that I hadn't needed to before.

Robin has forced me to reconsider my emotions too. I have always believed theoretically that we need to support and encourage people to express their emotions and to take responsibility for them, beginning when they are children. I had never realized how poorly I did that myself, nor how uncomfortable I am with strongly-felt, loudly-expressed feelings. This discomfort occurs every day, because Robin is loud and articulate and can get into a snit in .005 seconds flat.

More mundanely perhaps, I have had to examine my disaffection with little girls looking cute in dresses. When she was five, Robin began her campaign to get a dress, and then proceeded to wear it every waking hour except the two hours a week that it was in the washer and dryer. She now owns three, the choosing of which we both had to agree on. Max stays out of these negotiations, probably because he has far less ego tied up in it. I have had ample opportunity to examine how my pride is affected by how Robin appears to others, and have had to sort through how that pride interacts with my respect for Robin as a human being with opinions, tastes, and desires different from mine. What is so unnerving about dresses anyway? Sorting through my reactions, I realize that while I would like Robin to be more androgynous than most kids are allowed to be, androgyny in practice seems to mean acting like a boy. I'm not comfortable with that either. I have to keep reminding myself that there are more variations in behaviour among girls or boys than between boys and girls. Robin makes this lesson easier because she is active, noisy, and physically strong. I would have been a poor mother for a quiet, shy, introspective girl.

I find this to be a confusing time to mother a girl. There is a lot of rhetoric out there to support equal opportunities for girls, but I see enough evidence of sexism and stereotyping to feel apprehensive and pessimistic. I hear the assumptions of friends and acquaintances that there are built-in differences between boys and girls. Their beliefs are often based on a sample of two—one girl and one boy. In one such conversation, I attempted to challenge the assumption that girls are less active than boys. I said that I found Robin to be physically energetic. The response was, "Oh, Robin is a bit of a tomboy." When I thought about this conversation later, I realized that this was one way that people hold on to their stereotypical views of girls—they call girls who don't fit their stereotypes "tomboys," i.e., not-girls. Insidious. Discouraging for a feminist mother of a girl.

Recently the Yukon government released a report entitled "Accapella North," a study of Yukon girls from about age eleven to about age seventeen. It described, often in the girls' own words, their experiences of school, home, and community, as well as their hopes for the future. I found it reassuring that although the self-esteem of so many girls drops in grades seven, eight, and nine, it seems to rebound again after that. However, the violence and sexual harrassment that many girls said they experienced in school (by their peers and by teachers), in their communities and at home is truly horrifying. As Robin enters the school system, where I have limited access, I wonder what it all holds for her.

Feminism is becoming gut-level for me—truly integral to who I am and how I perceive myself and the world. As I grow older and mature, so does my feminism. The pride I feel as a woman is now basic; old, entrenched beliefs that what men do are the important and interesting things are rapidly falling away. Feminism informs that pride, from awareness of what women have accomplished and are capable of now, to a physical pride in my own strength, self-reliance, and competence. Over the years I have put increasing value on what women have traditionally done, like child-caring, nurturing the family and others emotionally, listening attentively, and co-operating.

My attempts to integrate feminism into my own life have changed both my feminism and me. When some way of living equally seems to make sense, like sharing domestic work and finances fairly, I try to put it into practice. In doing so, other considerations come up: Max's back may be acting up so that I do most of the firewood chopping and stacking; I do so much accounting elsewhere that he does most of our personal bookkeeping. Such real-life considerations inform my view of "equally."

Lately I have been experiencing a need for solitude. I suspect that I have always had it, but since Robin was born it has been challenged both by her need for my time, and by Max and I becoming increasingly interdependent. There are informal hiking and ski trails just outside our door, and I spend hours on them alone. Recently I spent a couple of days by myself at a relatively isolated cabin owned by a friend. I noticed how my enjoyment of solitude in daylight hours turned to fear and anxiety when it became dark. The security I feel in my own home is based on years of safety there. Although I don't intend to live alone, it seems to me that fear of being alone is a big obstacle to being an independent woman. Somehow I want to work through this, but I am just at the beginning of that now.

Of course women's fears are not illusionary. Women are assaulted within and outside of our homes all the time. However, the experience of my retreat was that fear prevented me from planning my defences realistically, and it restricted me more than necessary. After it was dark I was afraid to tie my dog up two feet from the front door, which was beyond common woman-sense. I really want to be able to judge things more calmly and from an intuitive sense unblocked by fear. As with so many things, my motivation comes both from my own need, and from my need to help Robin grow up more freely. I look around me and realize that I know many women here who live alone, and that they will have much to teach me about living alone day after night after day. There is always more to learn in this community of women.

I take a break from writing this to put another log in the wood stove. There is more, always more to this feminist on-the-job education. After all these years, the Yukon still seems to provide what I need. North. Community. Sisterhood. Making changes inside and out. Solitude. Physical challenges. Darkness, light, darkness, in a steady dramatic rotation. Cold, colder, colder still, and then warm. Moon so bright on snow that I can ski and almost see clearly.

For All Our Children

Shirley Turcotte

I was born July 14, 1952 in St. Boniface, Manitoba and held hostage for the next fourteen years by my family, enduring child pornography, torture, and poverty, right before the glazed eyes of our average community. I was most likely conceived while my mother was being raped and I do not ever remember a day where someone in the house was not beaten, raped, or passed over to my father's friends for more of the same. I am neither white nor Aboriginal, but a half-breed: able to pass as white or Native, and at home in both cultures. I was also growing up in a time when women had enough energy once again to exercise and define their rights in a patriarchal society.

In my childhood there were no dolls, no TV, no light, no family dinners; just constant labour interrupted by twenty- to thirty-minute interludes of torture. There was no time to express feeling overwhelmed or incompetent at whatever task was presented to me, be it kill a chicken, fuck a dad or dog, or slave at some meaningless chore. Floundering meant possible death and certain emotional, physical and/or sexual torture. I just did or was done to and hoped the doing made the done-to less frequent for everyone, especially my siblings. I split my psyche into safe little compartments, raising my brothers in the dark smelly basements we were left to, stealing food and clothes, thinking up splendid plans for escape and scheming to avoid the next torture. It was like depositing feelings into a bank that I would later draw from in order to live fully.

All the hard labour instilled a work ethic I am grateful to have, and kept the hours of suffering to a minimum. If you have to live in hell, then I think mine was the best. It was easy to define who the bad guys were. I am always in awe of those survivors who had love mixed with the trauma. At least the abuse I experienced was not masked by love.

I first tried to kill myself at about age five, running naked in a Manitoba winter in an attempt to get "amonia," but it only made me sick and not dead. Not too long after, on a very bad day, I tried drinking rat poison and Javex. Barely touching my lips, I dropped the glass and it broke in the sink. I retreated to the wheat field and the sun poured into my heart, the grass and wind caressed my body, and I released a river of tears that washed myself out. The words on the wind told me to stay, that I had promise and purpose. I have met many adults, who as children were able to "be" in nature. This has kept them intact through the years of abuse. Wind, rocks, trees and water make wonderful listeners and replacement parents for so many of the world's traumatized children. I often think of nature as the universal parent.

When I came out of my "prison camp" at fourteen, I had no hymen, no pretty clothes, no sophisticated use of language, and no stories of family or normal experiences. I didn't know how much water to put in a bathtub, or what utensils to eat with. I was in awe of a bowl of fruit on a counter. It was as if I'd been raised in a cave by wolves. My short stay in a foster home was humiliating. Foster families were not trained in dealing with children traumatized by torture and abuse. My attempt to be normal and my constant failure to meet family expectations were unbearable to me. I did not fit in, and was on my own by grade eleven, holding down two jobs to pay my way.

Shortly after escaping my father's reach for good, I became seriously ill and landed in Winnipeg General Hospital. My father had left me riddled with infections. As a pedophile, he abused many children in a week with no regard for "safe sex." At the hospital, my genitals became a spectacle for the young male interns who gave me innumerable pelvic examinations, many even coming back for a second look. I would turn my head aside and weep silently during each examination, certain that I was a freak "down there." Eventually a very gruff, white-haired doctor rescued me. On seeing my tears, he stopped examining me in mid-procedure, then turned and screamed at the nurse that "this girl" was terrified and that no one was to touch me without his authority. She made nervous note of it.

I was so relieved that he had not spoken to me directly or said my name. I had never met such kindness before and did not know how to process the overwhelming feelings of gratitude for actually being "seen." I was not examined again during that hospital stay and was released when my normal temperature returned.

The pressure of being on my own without support was crushing. When I moved from Winnipeg to Toronto, I became trapped in a bureaucratic nightmare as Manitoba and Ontario children's aid societies and welfare agencies fought over who was responsible for me. Like so many children "in care," I found myself falling through cracks in the system. When it was discovered, for example, that I lived on my own without a legal guardian and wrote my own sick notes, I was kicked out of school in grade twelve. Without school to live for, I dissolved into temporary insanity and became suicidal.

One morning, after trying to kill myself with a drug overdose, I woke up in a mental institution feeling a warm, marvelous sensation on my left breast. I opened my eyes to see a strange wild woman with thick black hair laughing and stroking me. I had no idea where I was as I pushed her hand away and passed out again from the drugs they had given me. When I woke again to a commotion in the dining room, the wild woman was there with her bloated belly and shriveled body. She was sticking her fingers down her throat and regurgitating onto her plate. Nurses grabbed her and dragged her away. I would learn later about the tube feedings. Over the months I saw that whenever Helena started to talk, jump, or move, she was hauled away. My best friend while in lock-up, she was a miracle of a woman with hair and eyes that refused to die and a body that refused to live. She loved licorice and never uttered a full sentence. When they hauled her away for good, I was terrified that I could be her in another thirty years.

That half-year in the mental hospital at Whitby opened my heart, my feminism. Having escaped a life of torture, I was now in a world where shock treatment, drugs, and confinement were threatened, and used when we didn't conform, all in the name of mental health. By the time I was twenty, my home was a centre for people coming out of mental hospital. I never stopped remembering Helena or working for change in mental health perspectives.

In spite of my father's perversions, I am grateful to him for instilling in me the notion that I could do anything. There was no division between the genders. Being older I was expected to do more than my brothers. We were not given instruction and had to initiate and complete tasks based on our own ingenuity, be it slaughter an animal for food, cook, clean, or fix whatever was broken. Having known no limits in this way, I assumed that as an adult I could do anything.

In my early twenties I went to work for Bell Canada and became one of the first, if not *the* first, Canadian female telecommunications technicians since World War II. I loved technology. I loved the feel of a soldering iron in my hands. I loved how I looked in a tool belt and wore it at every opportunity. Children would stop and point as I walked down the street; I hoped the girls would remember when the day came to choose a career. I felt the glory of success and the agony of tokenism as press pictures were taken and industrial films were made. And for the first time in my life I felt proud. The mechanical age of step-by-step switching was converging with the transistor and then computer ages, and I was part of it. Bell's Adelaide Street office in Toronto was the pulse of the city; if the price of gold went up, I could hear it in the sound of the switches or the clacking of the cross-bar relays.

During my eight years in that office I never worked with another woman. Some of the men openly hated me without even knowing me. Some pasted *Playboy* centrefolds to my work station or sabotaged my work. One tried to rape me on midnight shift on New Year's Eve. Often I felt afraid, always I felt determined. Poverty was not an option for me. Some helped whenever they could, even giving me extra lessons in tool handling after work. One taught me how to tune up my car and do the body work in exchange for my good company and friendship, no more. When I left Bell Canada I felt I had helped pave the way for the many women who would follow.

I lived many lives in the seventies. At home I housed and counselled victims of childhood abuse and abuse at the hands of the many agencies set up to help them. During the day I was a technician extraordinaire, wage-earner and parent to some of my siblings. Once a week I was patient to psychiatrist Dr. Harvey Armstrong, and a part-time student at George Brown College. Intermittently, I lectured on either women and technophobia or child sexual abuse.

My life was full of compartments that had little in common. I kept each area secret from the other, although some even I didn't know about. My sessions with Harvey, for example, were a complete mystery to me. I would remember getting there, the waiting room, and the trip home. But I had virtually no memory of what we talked about, nor my childhood, other than a vision of canary yellow (the colour of my father's bathrobe) and the certainty that my father had sexually abused me. When I wasn't busy, I would dissociate, feeling nothing other than a desire to slash myself or jump off ledges.

I remember quite distinctly the day my worlds collided. I was in Harvey's office, re-enacting my life. My hands were in front of my face and I was trying to get away from the beating and rape. Harvey was the perpetrator, my father, and I was the little girl again. Somehow Harvey's words reached down into me—some sort of trust had been established—and I saw my *self* for the first time. "Then" had become part of "now" and I would have to stay in the room and consciously remember hell, or at least the more tolerable parts of it—the incest, physical abuse, and neglect.

Once my memories returned, I had a big decision to make: to be sane or not. I took one more trip to the mental hospital to see if that wouldn't be better than all the overwhelming feelings and horrible truths. I tried all the therapeutic wizardry—therapist gurus, truth serums, group therapies, basket weaving, medications, cognitive and behavioral reframing and so on . . . even sleeping with my "try this new approach" therapist. Most were a temporary diversion from my true feelings, some were a waste of time, and the last one was very damaging. Eventually, I found my way back to Harvey and felt my feelings and faced the truth after all.

It seems abusers are universally not very original: they rape, beat, brand, drive nails through hands, shave heads, electric shock, pee, shit, and involve animals for a little more variety. When my father wasn't being violent, he played his guitar and sang in his band. He rarely spoke to me and to this day I don't know what he did for a job or any of his thoughts other than those of a sexual predator. Occasionally, when he finished abusing me, he would fall to his knees and place his head on my lap, crying and begging me to forgive him. I would robotically stroke his hair in silence.

Today I rarely see my father. We have nothing in common. I am not afraid, angry, or interested in him. He is afraid, angry, and not interested in me. Never once has he asked how I am or what I might need. I don't know what he thinks of feminism.

Before beginning the work of integrating my psyche, I was so removed from my body that I had to collapse with a fever before I would attend to reality. Being back in my body meant being with the body on which Dad had left his marks. I had unattended venereal diseases as well as cervical cancer. Insanity seemed like a warm blanket compared to life, and I had to go on blind faith that I wouldn't hurt unbearably forever. The effects of malnutrition, structural damage, osteoarthritis in my hands and feet due to the physical trauma, would later be a piss-off. To this day I have not fully accepted the limitations of my hands—I want to play guitar again.

Reading Marilyn French's *The Women's Room* helped me to stay strong and was my first experience of "women's liberation." In general I viewed women as weak, powerless creatures who complained most of the time and left when the going got rough. Ashamed and embarrassed even to be a woman, I refused to have anything to do with them and saw myself more as a man. At that point *all* women were duplicates of my mother, who had escaped when I was seven. Dad fucked me, tortured me and passed my around, but he never left me. I mostly remember Mom being either overwhelmed and anxious or in a dazed dissociative state. I always worried she'd break. Like my father, never once did she ask me how I was or what I might need.

My mother crossed a line with me when her fear became bigger than her desire to save her children. I forgive her for passing the children to Dad. I forgive her terror and need to run. That sometimes happens to women held captive by monsters like Dad. But the line is crossed all the same when a woman leaves her children in danger. I can only barely forgive her for leaving me in such an impossible position where I was to fail so miserably. Who did she think would fill her shoes? Like her, I failed to protect my younger siblings. They were beaten and raped and I could do little to save them. Unlike her, when I finally could and did run I hauled my brothers out too, even though I feared for our lives. Maybe Mom was too tired; maybe my youth and ignorance gave me an edge?

For years I silently begged her to come and do her duty by me. Sometimes my knees would buckle and I'd find myself sprawled on the floor calling out for her. Years of birthdays and Christmases passed (and still pass) without a card, letter, or call. There are no pictures of me as a child. Today, more than thirty years after escaping from my dad, she cracks the odd joke and plants the odd iris. I initiate all contact and visit her once or twice a year for lunch. She is a woman I honour from afar. Yet I think of her as a feminist of sorts. She has lived without a man since my dad, doing only what she had energy for even if it isn't much more than TV and cigarettes. In spite of my pain, I respect my mother and the courage she showed in making her choices. Knowing that I only barely missed following in her footsteps, I count myself blessed to have stayed intact.

In the late seventies I was very attached to the essence of feminism and very detached from women and the women's movement. The essence of feminism to me was the equality and dignity of people. The idea that I, a woman, could have equal choices and walk where I wanted to walk in safety was essential to me, and I could easily see how patriarchy made doing so a struggle instead of a natural process.

However, part of the organized women's movement sometimes disappointed me. Its spokeswomen often seemed to use the worst elements of patriarchy to get their point across. To me, women shaming and ridiculing men, and making them look like imbeciles or monsters—instead of people with some inappropriate (and changeable) behaviours—seemed much the same as what so many men did to women. And it seemed at times that *all* women and *only* women were being portrayed as victims while all men and *only* men were being portrayed as perpetrators.

I liked it when I heard that women were capable of being strong, had a right to say "no" and "yes" and, sadly, that they too could be abusive. I wanted also to hear that not all men were bad, that they too were victims of patriarchy and violence. I worried that good people of both genders were being torn apart and alienated from one another, and that our resources for creating change were being eaten up in the process. Women were being told we could have and do it all and were getting thoroughly exhausted trying. Men were being told they were intolerable jerks and losing their confidence. I fervently believed that all of humanity was in this together, that men needed to help change the imbalance in order to live more fully, and that, for the health and growth of our children, we needed goodwill on all sides.

So I stayed more or less clear of the organized women's movement and focussed on children, their health and safety. It seemed to me we would all be much further ahead if the movement also focussed on the health and safety of children. Without safe, grounded, and respected children, nothing can change in the long term. Children who are too hungry and scared to speak, too tired or abused to feel, and too unstructured to be productive, grow up to be either victims or oppressors—the two main attributes of patriarchy.

I established my first real friendship with a woman during my late teens. Though Janny came from a wealthy and relatively healthy family, we became fast friends and created between us our own women's group as we began pioneering in male-dominated industries—she in aviation and sculpting, I in telecommunications and psychotherapy. It was an unusually serious time in our lives. We were two very strong young women who could not relate to other teens and were too independent and inflexible to fit into any existing group. We were very critical of both women and men and our relationship consisted of all-night arguing sessions about politics, women's rights, and our place as women in the world. Rarely did we discuss boyfriends, clothes, or fun; we had no idea how to play. Then, we wouldn't be caught dead in sexy dresses or army boots; now, in our forties, we wear both at the same time. As the memory of my mother faded I began to love and celebrate the friendship of women. It is through communion with women that I find my voice, learn what I think and know who I am.

I met John in my mid-twenties. I had never expected to marry, but I saw that a life with John might work, so we married quickly and invited no one. I knew if I waited or planned I would never follow through. The thought of living with a partner was terrifying and I kept my own apartment for six months after we married. Within the week we were married the law changed and I automatically retained my birthname. I was sure the goddess of feminism was with me.

At the time, I was still suffering from post trauma and the repressed memories of sexual abuse and I did not approach the sexual aspect of marriage in a healthy way. Thankfully, John had very few expectations; he took me as I was and taught me that not all men are cruel or even unkind. He also taught me about nature—his religion—and how to escape into it and move around safely. We spent many years camping, canoeing, bird-watching, and exploring Canada.

I kept my work and history separate from John and he never pried. If someone had to sleep at the foot of my bed because they were too frightened to stay in their room, or I had to drive someone to the hospital because they had slit their wrists, he never said a word. I kept myself secret partly out of shame, partly out of pain, and mainly out of fear. John was such a clean and gentle part of my life. I was afraid he'd be hurt by knowing where I came from and those who still lived there.

The best work we ever did was create our son Jeff, who was born just before my thirtieth birthday. I had never worried about birth control, assuming I could never have children, not because doctors had specifically said so but because their condescending tone and body language had indicated it. When I did become pregnant, I knew the baby was a miracle. I had not yet recovered all my memories, but I did remember being pregnant with my father's child, at about age eleven. My father's only precaution with me was to pull out early, so he watched my periods like a hawk. When I missed one, he aborted the fetus himself in a bathtub. I had also seen other children abused and believe that at least four children may have actually died. Somewhere deep inside me I felt responsible and a real sense of failure at not having rescued them. Pregnant, I was afraid my very touch could cause my child's demise. During the birth, I was in a state of post trauma, with flashbacks that made no sense to me or anyone else. I kept calling for John to "get the baby," sure that the doctors were going to kill him.

Jeff spent his first eleven months screaming. He had to be fed every two hours around the clock, refused my breast, and threw up everything over four ounces. He hated physical contact. Nannies, housekeepers, and sitters left within days, though I eventually found a wonderful woman who took pity on us. Much of my hair fell out and even my teeth were loose in my mouth. And just before having Jeff tested for autism, I took him off all milk and soya products and put him on mashed potatoes, tiny portions of meat, vegetables, fruit, and water. This turned him around almost overnight. With him feeling better after that first year, I was able to muster enough energy to repress the resurfacing memories. I simply loved being a mother.

As a feminist I was unclear about raising a boy. I wanted to ensure that my son would grow up sensitive to women's issues and following his own nature. I read him gender-equal stories and sang him gender-equal songs. Peter Alsop's music rang through my house for years. As a torture survivor I knew very little about how to raise Jeff and a great deal about how not to raise him. Now that he is a teenager, I look around the walls of his room and see two Aboriginal posters with prayers, one *Universal Soldier* poster, a rope of sweet grass with a sweet grass turtle, his own sacred medicine bag hanging over his pillow, and three *Forgotten Realms* and *Ravenloff Dungeons & Dragons* posters. His favourite stuffed toy still sits on his bed and I know he treasures his hand made Aboriginal star blanket, which was given to him by a medicine woman in Saskatchewan. Raising this kind, smart, charming, delightfully funny young man has allowed me to do many things that I missed as a child. I've laughed and loved more with Jeff than with anyone in my life.

When I think of the schedule I was keeping in the early eighties, I get dizzy. Raising Jeff with John, working in engineering at BC Tel and co-running SEPSA, a non-profit, feminist-based organization offering counselling and training in the area of child sexual abuse: it felt good, and kept the second phase of memories at bay. But unresolved memories are tricky things. The repressed parts of me were always working their way home to that present me who could put things right. The past was about to meet my future yet again.

When a filmmaker from the women's studio at the National Film Board of Canada approached me regarding a film she was making on women working in non-traditional fields, I asked her to read the manuscript I had written on child sexual abuse. While Canada was still in deep silence about the trauma of our children, SEPSA had statistics suggesting that one in four girls and one in six boys were victims of sexual abuse. I thought the studio should make a film and get the country talking about it. The resulting film, *To A Safer Place*, was based on part of my family's life and led to a very unsafe time for me.

What I thought was going to be a twenty-minute film to tote around to public forums turned out to be a catalyst for tackling the important issue of child sexual abuse worldwide. Many survivors everywhere were given permission to speak. Although I knew the statistics, nothing could have prepared me for the stories that would be placed into my heart so fiercely.

From My Diary, 1987

Ontario: *A woman literally dancing out of the theatre . . . skipping and laughing her story . . . "I can tell . . . I can speak!"*

New Brunswick: *An old Aboriginal woman, maybe seventy, allowing the crowd to disperse, waiting, finally arriving, moving right into me, her voice full of power and purpose: "Me too, I've never told before." She puts something inside of me that makes me bigger than I am.*

Newfoundland: *A woman frozen in her seat, first memories flashing like fast forward on a movie screen. I am honoured to help unglue her and over a cup of tea she tells me the relief of finally knowing what's wrong.*

Québec: *A lawyer man tells me the story of his body, wanting more from me . . . "Why don't you speak more for me? For other men like me who have been victims too?" He seems so big before me. He has money, power and he speaks so eloquently. I turn the question around back to him. He stands there quite stunned. Maybe he will.*

Québec: *She brings pictures, her daughter dead now, killed, murdered. She wants to know, "What about them—the ones that don't survive?" I have no answers.*

Ontario: *Hands flashing, such speed! Signer/interpreter telling me the stories of those all around me. Hands flashing stories of abuse, eyes telling everything I have heard in so many cities before and yet telling even more.*

Day after day, one radio station after another, one TV station after another, story on top of story. My own body giving way, overwhelmed.

Manitoba: *A person in the audience remembers me from school and brings a picture of me from a yearbook. I melt in her caring.*

Manitoba: *A survivor sits on one side of the theatre: such courage, such enormous courage. Her offender father sits on the other side, a psychologist there with his colleagues. Such an outrage, such an enormous outrage.*

Alberta: *Rose, shaman, the great powerful Aboriginal woman, came to the premiere. I have heard of her over the miles. She corners me. "Do you know someone came to the film instead of killing themselves tonight?" She removes her earrings and places them on my ears. So much dying in the Aboriginal world. I am so sad.*

Québec: *She decides to kill me. A woman so pained by her own life. "How dare you lie! The abuse never hurt me, so how could it hurt you?" For three cities she follows me and police protect me from her. She has different disguises and outsmarts the police. They cannot catch her. I am somehow relieved and scared at the same time.*

Ontario: *She braves the microphone, comes forward and tells of the people sharing her body.*

British Columbia: *Survivors light candles and sing a song of unifying support and love. So afraid to be naked here in my own city. A survivor who barely walked three years ago, struts across the stage to bring me flowers. A miracle? I don't think so. Just another sign of what can be.*

Ontario: *A man drives me to the house he grew up in, where hot semen burned down his throat, then to Niagara Falls, where his mother killed herself. He too finds an opening to speak for the first time.*

Prince Edward Island: *The workshop is not announced until after the fact . . . in case of . . . in case of what? The courage of these survivors to stay and live in the communities they were raised in. The courage to see their offenders on street corners, at Christmas gatherings, at other surprise encounters. I am in awe of all rural women.*

The stories unravel in waves of disclosures, one after the other. Letters, phone calls, people on the street. Lost childhoods, sometimes whole lives. I feel I am holding the nation's darkest secrets.

Back at work for BC Tel, employees stopped me in the women's room, in the halls, in the cafeteria. Each time there was a press release, another screening, a TV viewing, I was inundated with calls, one minute about circuit design, the next a call of distress. I could not switch hats fast enough. I left the company after many failed negotiations on how to solve what I considered to be *our* problem and they considered to be *my* problem. Seventeen years of a telecommunications career faded out of my life.

Along with the calls for help and the calls of support, came harrassment. Horrible calls and packages were sent my way. Men masturbated over my telephone answering machine. There was a barrage of death threats. My sister was also harrassed and her daughters were followed until she left the city she lived in. This was a very clear message to stop talking. With my sister's permission I continued. She had told me much about the group abuse we had endured in our very early years. I believed her, but had no memories from birth to age seven and had not personally felt the pain of what had taken place. We were afraid that if I stopped our voices would be limited forever. In the face of harrassment, I adopted an attitude of "I'm not afraid; I'll walk and talk wherever I want." By shutting down my fear I set myself up for a breakdown that unraveled the remaining chambers of memories I'd kept secret so long.

It seemed that what I had witnessed was more painful than what had happened to me. When nails were driven through my hands I could split and hide myself. Yet as a witness, I did not have the same control over my body and no control at all of what was happening to the bodies of others. In crisis as an adult, I experienced the horror of my own inability to stop or change what was happening. I felt I had failed miserably to be big enough, strong enough and smart enough to divert what was going on. Although today I forgive, I will forever regret not being what I needed to be to make things different.

For three years I waded through unspeakable memories. I was in enormous pain and shock as new ones surfaced. Hopelessness invaded my spirit and I was unable to find solace, even in nature. My marriage ended and I handed Jeff over half the time to his father. He was safest with John and both were safer a little away from me, though I felt devastated in his absence. For all of three years I was unable to cook or clean or ask anything from myself other than to parent Jeff the weeks I had him and do public work. I dismantled most of my major friendships and spent the next few years alone, pulling myself together and bringing the issues of child sexual abuse to remote Aboriginal communities in Canada.

Those years were so painful I barely thought about the women's movement, though I had a vague awareness that child sexual abuse had been entered on its official agenda. I continued my work, but changed how I did it. I became a recluse in Vancouver (except for seeing clients in private practice) and did all my lecturing and teaching outside B.C. I went back into therapy full-time and had a year-long relationship with a wonderful woman on the other side of the country. Unfortunately, I am not lesbian and could not continue with it over time. During that time, John and I had a "fairytale" divorce, where he lived (and still lives) just down the street from me, and Jeff's community, friends, and school remained as before.

I was very clear, in my next major relationship, to keep my partner aware of what was happening in my psyche, as well as in my work life. I no longer compartmentalize my two worlds and no longer protect the people I love from the truth about the world we live in. If people throw tomatoes or eggs at our house (this actually happens), I expect my partner to be out there cleaning the mess up with me. I no longer try to keep secrets to myself. And I no longer keep my work life separate from the wonderful community and friends that now surround me. My early experiences are not very central in my life any more, though once or twice a year the old feelings can be triggered. I try to include my friends minimally when the "beast" is up, but still keep the very depth of the pain private and express it alone.

I have found a much broader gender base in my work in Aboriginal communities, with often up to forty percent male participation. This has not been true in the "white" world, where child abuse seems to be treated as a women's issue rather than a community issue affecting us all. Men's empathy and imagination are equally necessary in the solving of our children's tragedies. Unfortunately, blaming and shaming seem to contribute to many men shying away from their responsibilities. At the same time, silence about female abusers has made life very difficult for many survivors.

The more I remembered and resolved in my own life, the more I was able to hear. There are horrible stories of atrocities not just in Canada but in every country in the world. Sexual addicts prey on children within families; child pornography rings and cults operate in many Canadian cities and towns, hiding within respectable organizations. Churches, children's organizations, community groups, and businesses are not immune.

Yet there seems to be nothing more resilient than the human spirit. Through my work I have seen the miracle of the spirit rising above impossible odds and thriving. I have worked with "outcasts" and "unfixables," only to see them grow to live full and exciting lives. If not for this fact, I don't know how I could have processed the knowing about what some people will do to prey on children.

Thirty-odd years of feminism has helped change the way we help others. Survivors now often get client-centred therapy that allows them to take back the control that was horribly stolen from them. We are learning more and more about how traumatic memory is stored in the brain and body, and the amazing ways in which people cope in order to go on. Survivors are starting to accept the fact that they often lack clear, concrete memories of the treacheries they were subjected to. Even with the outrageous backlash against the autonomy of women and the rights of children, including the false memory accusers, survivors insist now on being heard. I encourage every survivor, who can and wishes, to keep talking at whatever level feels comfortable. Knowledge of the existence of child sexual abuse and its impact has been locked back in the closet too many times for us to ever keep it secret again.

Life after trauma is very rich and kind to me. As I approach my second half-century, I see myself working less and caring more. I am no longer one of the few who carry the torch; there are more and more good, qualified people to help survivors heal. Over time, I have realized that the impacts of sexual, emotional, and physical abuse and starvation are more far-reaching than I could ever have known. The onset of early menopause, accompanied by osteoporosis, osteoarthritis and compromised adrenals are my personal legacy of trauma. And based on my experience counselling other survivors, I know I can expect other physical ramifications to emerge in the years to come. I pray that all women and men will value the essence of feminism by promoting the equality and dignity of people. I especially pray for the feminist movement to have the courage, the heart and the wisdom to adopt all the world's children, to love them, to nurture them and to protect them.

I have been both blessed and fulfilled by the privilege and honour of living my life in the wake of this prayer.

Biographies

FAY BLANEY, is a Homalco woman of the Coast Salish Nation. She is a mother of two, a graduate student, an educator, and a community activist. She was recently appointed a vice-president of the National Action Committee on the Status of Women, and is also involved with the Aboriginal Women's Action Network. She lives in Vancouver.

KATE BRAID has worked as a carpenter, carpentry instructor, and labour educator for the past twenty years. Last year she finally made a commitment to the other thing she loves by enrolling full-time in Creative Writing at the University of British Columbia. She has published two books of poetry, *Covering Rough Ground* and *To This Cedar Fountain*, both by Polestar Press. She is currently writing a novel about a woman carpenter.

BRENDA LEA BROWN lives and works in a downtown Vancouver co-op community with her husband and their son. She makes her living as a freelance writer of corporate communications. In 1976, she was awarded the BC ACTRA nomination of Best Dramatic Writer/Radio for *The Fellow Who Looks Like Me*. *Bringing It Home* is the second anthology she has edited. *British Columbia, Visions of the Promised Land*, essays by B.C. writers and artists, was published in 1986.

RAMINDER DOSANJH is a human rights activist who has lived in Vancouver since immigrating to Canada in 1970. She has taught ESL at Vancouver Community College since 1972 and is a founding member of the India Mahila Association. She hosts a weekly television program on current issues and resources on the multicultural channel and writes a regular column called "Women's Viewpoint" in *Voice Magazine.*

PAMELA DOS RAMOS grew up in Georgetown, Guyana and now lives in Calgary, Alberta. She has an MA in Counselling and teaches Multicultural Counselling as a part-time Adjunct Professor for Gonzaga University. Pamela is past president of the Canadian Congress for Learning Opportunities for Women, a national voice for women's educational training in Canada. Pamela is currently owner of *Pathways to Diversity*, a training, consulting and counselling company.

MARGARET DRAGU was born in Regina, Saskatchewan in 1953. She has enjoyed a long career as a performance artist and choreographer, and has presented her work internationally in many venues. She is also a writer, filmmaker, and video artist. Dragu has co-authored two book: *Revelations: Essays on Striptease and Sexuality* (Nightwood) and *Mothers Talk Back (Momz Radio)* (Coach House Press).

RACHEL FARAHBAKHSH moved to Toronto from Michigan as a four-year-old in 1968. She has a degree in International Development from Mount Allison University in New Brunswick, and also holds a nursing diploma. She was a founding member of Metro Youth for Global Unity, which established an international peace pavilion in Dartmouth Nova Scotia in 1995. She and her husband are followers of the Bahá'í faith. They have two children, Carmel and Isaiah.

URSULA MARTIUS FRANKLIN, University Professor Emerita, University of Toronto, holds a PH.D in experimental physics from the Technical University in Berlin, and taught in the Faculty of Applied Science and Engineering for more than two decades. She a companion of the Order of Canada and a Fellow of the Royal Society of Canada, and is also the author of *The Real World of Technology*. Dr. Franklin has written extensively on the impact of science and technology, particularly on women, peace, and justice.

LYNDSAY GREEN is a partner in The Training Technology Monitor, providing services on the applications of technology-assisted learning. Her career has focused on the use of communications technologies and the needs of women, Aboriginal people, and educators. Her volunteer positions include Chair, Professional Development for Women in Film and Television, Chair, Fund-Raising for the Legal Education Action Fund (LEAF) and member, Committee for '94. She is included in *Making A World of Difference: A Directory of Women in Canada Specializing in Global Issues*.

JOELLE HANN graduated from McGill University with honours in literature. In 1990 she received the Shapiro Award for Creative Writing from McGill's English department. Joelle is a member of the editorial board of *Geist* magazine. Her poetry has appeared in *The Fiddlehead, Antigonish Review, Sub-Terrain, CV2,* and the anthology *Breathing Fire.* She is currently enrolled at New York University.

DOROTHY TODD HÉNEAUT joined the National Film Board in 1968. She produced the film *Not a Love Story*, a documentary on pornography, and directed *Firewords*, a documentary on three Québecoise writers. In 1996 she completed *You won't need running shoes, darling*, a film about growing old. She lives in Montréal.

SUZANNE HÉNEAUT has been working in the film industry since 1975. She has produced or co-produced a number of feature films and television programs, many with her production company, Les Productions Zann. She has been working for TFO, the French television network of TVOntario. She lives in Toronto.

MEG HICKLING has touched the lives of thousands in her work as a sexual health educator. Her commitment to issues like violence against women and pornography is evident in her leadership of conferences (Ending Family Violence) and in her presentations to children on sexual health and sexual abuse prevention. Her awards include the 1992 YWCA Woman of Distinction Award for Health & Education, the 1994 RNABC Award of Excellence and the 1994 B.C. Council for the Family, Distinguished Service to Families Award. She lives in Vancouver.

LINDA UYEHARA HOFFMAN plays in two *taiko* groups, Katari Taiko and Sawagi Taiko, and is active in the Vancouver Japanese Canadian community as a volunteer for the Powell Street Festival Society. She serves on the Board of Directors for Women in View and the Vancouver Folk Music Festival, and works as a Communications Assistant for Vancouver New Music, a society that produces concerts.

LARISSA LAI was born in LaJolla, California and grew up in St. John's, Newfoundland. She currently lives in Vancouver where she works as a writer, curator, critic, and activist. In 1995 she received an Astraea Foundation Emerging Writer's Award. In 1996 her novel *When Fox Is a Thousand* (Press Gang) was nominated for the Chapters/*Books in Canada* First Novel Award.

HELEN JEFFERSON LENSKYJ is an associate professor at the University of Toronto where she teaches in the Graduate Department of Education and the School of Physical and Health Education. She has published extensively on the topic of women, sport and physical activity. In 1995 Helen was inducted into the National Girls and Women in Sport Hall of Fame, not for her swimming performance but for her research and advocacy work in sport. She is a late- blooming recreational athlete.

MARY MEIGS was born in 1917 in Philadelphia, and grew up in Washington, D.C. She graduated from Bryn Mawr College in 1939 and studied at the Arts Student League in New York after serving as a WAVE in World War II. She had one-woman shows in Boston, New York, Paris, and St. Sauveur, Quebec. Her first book, *Lily Briscoe: a Self-Portrait* was published in 1971, followed by *The Medusa Head* (1983), *The Box Closet* (1987) and *In the Company of Strangers (1990)*, all published by Talonbooks. She lives in Montréal and is at work on a new book, *The Time Being*.

JOAN MEISTER is a feminist and trade unionist who worked in the women's and labour movements until 1981 when she began to use a wheelchair due to the effects of multiple sclerosis. Since then, she has been active in the B.C. Coalition of People with Disabilities and DAWN: DisAbled Women's Network, British Columbia. She has also served as secretary of the National Action Committee on the Status of Women. She lives in Vancouver.

CYNTHIA MINDEN is a fibre artist, writer, community worker, and musician who lives on Denman Island, B.C. She earned a degree at the Royal Conservatory of Music in Toronto, then freelanced with chamber ensembles, eventually concentrating on her own group, Trio Con Brio. She moved to British Columbia in 1990, where she began experimenting with basketry techniques. She is currently writing a collection of essays about voluntary childlessness among women.

DENISE NADEAU works as a popular educator with women's organizations, labour, ecumenical justice and anti-poverty groups. She is also a writer and dancer. She has a MDIV from Vancouver School of Theology (VST) and has taught popular education as a sessional instructor at VST and the UBC School of Social Work. She is the author of *Counting Our Victories: Popular Education and Organizing* (Repeal the Deal, 1996).

PATTY OSBORNE is the mother of three children. She also runs the Vancouver Desktop Publishing Centre, and teaches desktop publishing. She is the central co-ordinator of B.C. Family French Camp, chair of North Vancouver Parents for French, and does other volunteer work in support of her children and her community. Patty is also a member of the editorial board of *Geist* magazine. She lives in North Vancouver.

VAL PAAPE moved from Wisconsin to Manitoba in the early seventies to work as a research biologist. After a career as a high school teacher and adult educator, she began teaching yoga, feminist spirituality and meditation. She writes a regular column for *Herizons* and has outfitted and guided wilderness canoe trips for women. While writing her piece for this book Val was diagnosed with breast cancer. She is drawing on her own spirituality and feminism to guide her healing journey. She lives with her loving partner, Amanda, and their orange cat Bounty.

JERILYNN PRIOR is a Professor of Medicine in the Division of Endocrinology at the University of British Columbia. She is director of the Vancouver Centre of the Canadian Multicentre Osteoporosis Study, a nine-centre, Canada-wide population-based study of osteoporosis in adult men and women. She is know for her work on progesterone and bone, for studies of ovulation disturbances within seemingly normal menstrual cycles, and for her stand against viewing menopause as a disease.

ALISON REID moved to Whitehorse for a year in 1976 and never left. She has variously worked with the women's quarterly newspaper *OptiMSt*, the Women's Centre, the Yukon Status of Women Council and is now a "Crone" for the Women's Centre. She has shared many projects with her partner Max, such as building a log house, living without electricity and running water for years, co-founding Lost Moose Publishing, and raising a daughter Robin, now 7. For wages she works as an accountant.

SHIRLEY TURCOTTE is a Registered Clinical Counsellor and a founding director and trainer for the Pacific Centre for Focusing, a Vancouver-based national education and counselling centre for counsellors' continuing education and survivors of childhood trauma. The NFB film "To a Safer Place" is based on part of her family's life story. For almost two decades she was simultaneously a pioneer telecommunications expert and a pioneer child sexual abuse expert and child activist. She is a member of the Manitoba Métis Federation.